GREAT MINDS

On Happiness

Edited and with an Introduction by
NIMA OMIDI

FIRST EDITION

PERENNIAL BOOKS

Published by Perennial Books
Vancouver

www.perennialbooks.com

Copyright © 2014 by Nima Omidi
All rights reserved

New translations of *The Bhagavad Gita*, *The Dhammapada*, *Meditations*, and *Nicomachean Ethics* first published 2014, copyright © 2014 by Nima Omidi
Revised translations of *Republic*, *Counsels and Maxims*, *Pensées*, *Moral Epistles*, *Principal Doctrines*, *That Men Are Not to Judge of Our Happiness Until After Death*, and *Of Managing the Will* first published in 2014, copyright © 2014 by Nima Omidi
Introduction and "Introduction to Plato's Discussion on Happiness" first published in 2013, copyright © 2014 by Nima Omidi
All rights reserved

Library and Archives Canada Cataloguing in Publication

On happiness / edited and with an introduction by Nima Omidi.

(Great minds)
Includes bibliographical references.
Issued in print and electronic formats.
ISBN 978-0-9920757-0-5 (pbk.).--ISBN 978-0-9920757-1-2 (pdf)

1. Happiness--Literary collections. 2. Happiness in literature.
I. Omidi, Nima, 1985-, writer of introduction, editor of compilation
II. Series: Great minds (Series)

PN6071.H2O55 2013   808.8'0353   C2013-905723-4
                                            C2013-905724-2

1

GREAT MINDS
On Happiness

a perennial book

Contents

Introduction   vii

On Happiness

Introduction to Plato's Discussion on Happiness	3
from REPUBLIC by Plato	9
from COUNSELS AND MAXIMS by Arthur Schopenhauer	31
from THE BHAGAVAD GITA	123
from THE KING JAMES BIBLE	151
from PENSÉES by Blaise Pascal	177
from MORAL EPISTLES by Seneca	195
from THE DHAMMAPADA	225
from MEDITATIONS by Marcus Aurelius	247
from NICOMACHEAN ETHICS by Aristotle	271
PRINCIPAL DOCTRINES by Epicurus	299
THE ENCHIRIDION by Epictetus	307
from TUSCULAN DISPUTATIONS by Cicero	331
TWO ESSAYS by Michel de Montaigne	379
Sources	411

Introduction

In matters of politics, ethics, and metaphysics, we encounter a great diversity of opposing views; but when it comes to the question of how the individual can attain *happiness* regardless of his or her circumstances, the message across all cultures, major philosophies, and world religions is nearly universal. Even philosophies which, on the surface, seem to oppose one another (e.g. Stoicism and Epicureanism), nonetheless agree on a fundamental level about what creates lasting happiness, and what leads to a life of perpetual suffering.

This consensus may surprise us. After all, if the path to happiness has been so firmly established for thousands of years—if the wisest thinkers from disparate cultures, throughout the ages, have essentially agreed on what it means to be truly happy, and how this is achieved—why do we still consider happiness so elusive, even chimerical? Why are most people so dissatisfied, so restless, so miserable? We must not look for drawn and melancholic faces as evidence of this general unhappiness in humankind: in most people it manifests as a weary, numb, and empty life of alienation—alienation from ourselves, from our work, and from others. The bitter irony and caustic wit that characterize so much of our modern social intercourse are the most obvious symptoms of this underlying, near-universal despair. So if the path to lasting happiness is so clearly laid out, why has it made no inroads into the human condition? Why are so few people truly happy?

The first reason is that the path is *difficult*. The road to happiness is, paradoxically, *unpleasant*, at least for the first many paces. The second reason is that, while the wisdom of happiness is universal among the *wise*, our societies, which are put together and sustained largely by the *unwise*, not only fail to teach and promote the virtues that lead to happiness, but even exalt the opposing vices—the very qualities that produce unhappiness: self-interest, greed, attachment to material things; and these, in turn, inflame the other qualities at the heart of unhappiness: dishonesty, hypocrisy, envy, lust, wrath, fear, hatred. Market economic theory takes as its foundation the narrowest and most base view of human nature, assumes the most ignoble and criminal traits to be predominant and intractable, raises these to the level of virtue, and thus establishes a society in which the people are compelled to prove its wretched principles correct. Self-interest, which causes harm to others as well as to the *self*, is venerated as the highest morality; greed is called the highest good; and man's "pursuit of happiness" involves the pursuit of its very opposite. *That* is why people are unhappy.

And when the mass of people hold the wrong view, it becomes even harder for someone in the pursuit of wisdom and true happiness to achieve his goal, or to even have the courage to start. Indeed, when the truth is the *opposite* of what society says it is, a person of wisdom can even be viewed as mad, and treated accordingly.

Yet in this information age, truth and wisdom have a louder voice than ever. Millions of people, rebelling against the emptiness and dissatisfaction that society's values have left them to stew in, are actively looking for a better way to live—which begins with a better way to *think*. And the world is full of great teachers (though also, it is true, many profit-seeking charlatans). We can have some reasonable hope, then, that happiness will one day become the human condition—that is, if we survive our own stupidity long enough to see such a time: for spiritual progress is slow, and technological progress, which threatens to destroy us in every way, moves at breakneck speed.

As free and widespread as true wisdom is today, however, there remain two major impediments to its promulgation: first, the more information that is out there, the more wisdom becomes obscured by stupidity and corruption, and the harder it becomes for the unguided seeker to find truth: we can only hope the cream always rises—but, unfortunately, hot air too has a tendency to seek elevation; second, most of us come to these teachings far too late in life, and we are not mentally equipped to absorb or even understand them. While it may be better late than never, if we really want to attain wisdom with a minimum of suffering along the way, the teaching of wisdom must begin at birth. Wisdom must be firmly established in our educational institutions, and that is a long way from happening (we are actually moving backward). At present, our schools are merely facilities for the indoctrination of society's corrupt values: children are firmly grounded in the virtues of self-interest, competitiveness, blind obedience, indolence, insincerity, and superficiality, along with some instruction in math, science, and rudimentary grammar. They are taught to *play the game* of school, which prepares them to play the game of work and society, but meanwhile all passion for learning is bored out of them, *grades* come to be more important than *knowledge*, technical skills more valuable than the wisdom of life, just as wealth and status later take precedence over character and even personality.

With respect to societies as a whole, it is difficult to imagine a reversal of the dehumanizing and morally corrupting forces driving the species toward decadence and extinction. Yet the human condition has always been wretched—at least since the beginning of "civilization"—and this has never kept gifted individuals from transcending the conditions of the world and achieving real and lasting happiness. In truth, this ultimate and abiding happiness is only available to the rare few, because it comes with *enlightenment*, something most of us never achieve. That said, many of us can certainly work toward becoming much happier than we currently are if we begin to understand the roots of human suffering, acknowledge our own individual weaknesses, and develop the strength of will to train our minds in self-restraint, discipline, equanimity, and the other virtues that lead to happiness.

So what are these virtues that wise men, throughout the

ages, have put forward as productive of happiness, and how can they be attained? Alternatively, what are the vices and weaknesses we must eradicate in ourselves in order to end our suffering and become truly happy? Before we answer these questions, it would be prudent to define *happiness* according to some of the authors in this collection.

Some Definitions of Happiness

"What is the happy life?" asks Seneca. "It is peace of mind, and lasting tranquillity." The happiness we are seeking must not be confused with *pleasure*, which is short-lived, provides diminishing returns, and more often than not is followed by *pain*. The happiness sought by the wise is true, deep, and *abiding*: "it is a characteristic of real joy that it never ceases, and never changes into its opposite."[1] This happiness is acquired only by the wise: "The wise man is joyful, happy and calm, unshaken—he lives on a plane with the gods."[2]

This is a high ideal that few of us ever achieve; and while some people enjoy more pleasure or less pain than others, even these lucky ones are nonetheless being constantly pulled between the pairs of opposites, are always at the mercy of Fortune, and are therefore always in the grips of desire and aversion, love and hate, greed and fear. Accordingly, the proportion of pleasure we enjoy over pain is almost irrelevant as long as we are still affected by either of these: "For one who sustains himself by any prop may fall."[3] As long as our happiness depends on receiving pleasure and securing ourselves against pain, our position in life is precarious and filled with apprehension.

"All men seek happiness," says Pascal. "This is without exception. Whatever different means they employ, they all tend to this end. The cause of some going to war, and of others

---

[1] Seneca.
[2] *Ibid.*
[3] *Ibid.*

avoiding it, is the same desire in both, attended with different views. The will never takes the least step but to this object. This is the motive of every action of every man, even of those who hang themselves." We are all pursuing happiness in one way or another, and the fact that so few people are happy suggests that it really is unattainable for most of us, or that we are looking for it in the wrong places. The unwise seek to satisfy their own self-interest—what they believe will make them happy—but their lack of self-knowledge inevitably leads them to error. The wise, on the other hand, begin with understanding their own nature, proceed to fulfil their fated duty in life, and limit their desires to those that are truly necessary. To test whether we are among the wise, and whether our happiness is true and abiding as opposed to merely a temporary respite from suffering, we may question ourselves as Seneca suggests: "if you are never downcast, if your mind is not harassed by apprehension through anticipation of what is to come, if day and night your soul keeps on its even and unswerving course, upright and content with itself, then you have attained the greatest good that mortals can possess. If, however, you seek pleasures of all kinds in all directions, you must know that you are as far short of wisdom as you are short of joy."

According to Schopenhauer, since the fundamental condition of our existence is *suffering*, "*to live happily* only means *to live less unhappily*—to live a tolerable life." The pursuit of happiness, then, is a quest to minimize and, if possible, eliminate our pain. And since evils will befall us with certainty, to attain abiding happiness we must somehow become impervious to these evils. Clearly, then, achieving happiness is an internal feat, and does not depend entirely upon ordering our lives in a particular way, surrounded by the things we love and protected from the things we wish to avoid: for ill fortune will eventually assail us in one way or another, and the greatest evils—sickness and death—are inevitable.

In addition to freedom from pain, Schopenhauer adds a single other necessity for happiness, the absence of *boredom* (though boredom, too, can be seen to be a form of pain). If we can live without suffering and without boredom, "the essential conditions of earthly happiness are attained; for all else is chimerical." This is the view of Pascal as well, who says that all our suffering arises from our essential *boredom*—our inability to stay in our room. It is this restlessness which impels us toward innumerable evils.

Aristotle's definition of happiness is the most concise. Happiness, he says, "is *a virtuous activity of the soul.*" The necessity of virtue for attaining happiness is indeed a universal theme. Therefore, in order to learn how we may become happy, we must know what is meant by *virtue*.

What Is Virtue?

We find that the principal virtues extolled in all great philosophical works are the same. In *The Bhagavad Gita*, Krishna enumerates some of the most crucial: "Fearlessness, purity of heart, steadfastness in knowledge, and yoga; alms-giving, self-restraint, worship, study of one's own scriptures, austerity, uprightness; Harmlessness, truth, absence of anger, renunciation, serenity, absence of calumny, compassion to creatures, uncovetousness, gentleness, modesty, absence of fickleness; Energy, forgiveness; fortitude, purity, absence of hatred, absence of pride." He adds that these are the qualities that "belong to one born for a divine lot," or the good life. Virtues are the traits that set the good and happy man apart from the evil and wretched one; Marcus Aurelius describes "that which is peculiar to the good man: to be pleased and content with what happens, and with the thread which is spun for him; and not to defile the divinity that is planted in his breast, nor disturb it with a crowd of images, but to keep it tranquil, following it obediently as a god, neither saying anything contrary to the truth, nor doing anything contrary to justice. And if all others refuse to believe that he lives a simple, modest, and contented life, he is neither angry with any of them, nor does he deviate from the way that leads to the end of life, to which a man ought to come pure, tranquil, ready to depart, and without any compulsion, perfectly reconciled to his lot."

Similarly, Seneca asks, "Now what is the chief thing in virtue?" His answer: "It is the quality of not needing a single day beyond the present, and of not reckoning up the days that are ours; in the slightest possible moment of time virtue completes an eternity of good." He adds, "No man is good by chance. Virtue is something which must be learned."

Aristotle separates virtue into two distinct but related types: "we say that some of the virtues are *intellectual* and others are *moral*: philosophic wisdom, intelligence, and practical wisdom are *intellectual virtues*, while liberality and perfected self-mastery are *moral virtues*. For in speaking about a man's character we do not say that he is wise or has understanding, but that he is good-tempered or one of perfected self-mastery; yet we praise the wise man with respect to his state of mind; and of states of mind, we call those which merit praise *virtues*." However, a person can hardly be good-tempered and possess perfected self-mastery unless he has a virtuous state of mind. Therefore, good actions arise from a good inner state, and a good inner state is reinforced by the outcome of our good actions. Conversely, when our condition is wretched, we inevitably produce wretched acts with evil consequences, which make our condition even worse.

Yet the life of virtue is characterized more by what we refrain from doing than by what we do, and the height of virtue is really to be rid of *vice*. Therefore, in order to understand virtue, we must understand what we mean by *vice*.

What Are the Vices?

According to Krishna, the following are some of the vices we must eradicate in ourselves: "Ostentation, arrogance and self-conceit, anger and insolence, cruelty and ignorance." These qualities "belong to one born for a demonic lot." Unwise and wretched people are "Self-important, stubborn, filled with pride and intoxicated by wealth." They perform sacrifices with "hypocrisy, without regard for their purpose," and are "[e]gotistical, arrogant, power-hungry, lustful, angry, and jealous of everyone." Christ explains "out of the heart of men, proceed evil thoughts, adulteries, fornications, murders, thefts, covetousness, wickedness, deceit, lasciviousness, an evil eye, blasphemy, pride, foolishness: all these evil things come from within, and defile the man."

The seven deadly sins of later Christianity list the worst vices: Lust, Envy, Gluttony, Sloth, Pride, Avarice, and Wrath; and similarly, the Bhagavad Gita explains that there are three gates to the "self-destructive hell" that is the life of the wicked: "Lust, Wrath, and Greed."

Why the Vice-Ridden Have Wretched Lives

In the *Republic*, Plato's Socrates considers who is happier, the good man or the evil man. He explains that "the real tyrant, whatever men may think, is the real slave, and is obliged to practice the greatest adulation and servility, and to be the flatterer of the vilest of mankind. He has desires which he is utterly unable to satisfy, and has more wants than anyone, and is truly poor, if you know how to inspect the whole soul of him: his whole life he is beset with fear and is full of convulsions and distractions." The evil man's mind "will be full of meanness and vulgarity, and burdened with servile constrictions. The best elements in him will be completely enslaved by the minority rule of his lowest and most deranged impulses." In his endless pursuit of power and the gratification of his base urges, he only becomes more dissatisfied and more enslaved: "he grows worse from having power: he becomes and is of necessity more jealous, more faithless, more unjust, more friendless, more impious, than he was at first. He is the purveyor and cherisher of every sort of vice, and the consequence is that he is supremely miserable, and that he makes everybody else as miserable as himself."

Krishna describes the nihilistic worldview of these wretches:

INTRODUCTION

> They say, "there is no God, no truth, no moral law, no spiritual order, only pleasure brought about by lust. What else?" Holding this view, these ruined souls of small intellect, of wicked deeds, rise as the enemies of the world for its destruction. Filled with insatiable desires, full of hypocrisy, pride, and arrogance, holding unwholesome views through delusion, they work with unholy persistence. Beset with immense cares ending only in death, sensual enjoyment their highest aim, they are assured that is the best life the universe has to offer. Bound by a hundred chains of hope, given over to lust and wrath, they strive to secure by unjust means hoards of wealth for sensual enjoyment. "I have gotten this today," they say, "tomorrow I will get that. This wealth is mine, and that wealth will be mine in future. I have destroyed this enemy, and I will destroy others too. I am like a God, I enjoy what I want, I am successful, I am powerful, and I am happy. I am rich and well-born. Who else is equal to me? I will sacrifice, I will give gifts, and I will rejoice in my own generosity." Thus they are deluded by ignorance. Bewildered by their many fancies, entangled in the snare of delusion, addicted to the gratification of lust, they fall into a foul hell.[1]

The pursuit of pleasure is the lowest life for a human being and also the one that produces the greatest suffering. The deceptive and destructive nature of pleasure is described by all the wise:

The Bhagavad Gita: "For those delights born of the world of the senses are only generators of pain, having a beginning and an end, O Arjuna; a wise man does not rejoice in them."

---

1 *The Bhagavad Gita.*

The Dhammapada: "He who lives looking for pleasures only, his senses uncontrolled, immoderate in his food, idle and weak—Mara the Tempter will certainly overthrow him, as the wind throws down a weak tree."

Seneca: "And do you rate, I will not say among heroes, but among men, the person whose Supreme Good is a matter of flavours and colours and sounds? Nay, let him withdraw from the ranks of this, the noblest class of living beings, second only to the gods; let him herd with the dumb brutes—an animal whose delight is in fodder!" "Pleasure is low, petty, to be deemed worthless, shared even by dumb animals—the tiniest and meanest of whom fly towards pleasure." For pleasure "is simply the good of cattle."

Schopenhauer: "pleasure is only the negation of pain, and pain is the positive element in life." Pleasure is something which temporarily checks or arrests the *will,* "freeing us from its action; and hence pleasure is a state which can never last long." Pleasure serves only "to entrap the victim in order that he might be delivered over to pain."

Pascal: "The consciousness of the falsity of present pleasures, and the ignorance of the vanity of absent pleasures, cause inconstancy."

Epicurus: "No pleasure is in itself evil, but the things which produce certain pleasures entail disturbances many times greater than the pleasures themselves." (And this from the philosopher of pleasure.)

What makes the life of vice so unhappy is the addiction and enslavement to pleasure, the fear this necessitates, and the endless dissatisfaction arising from insatiable desire.

Fear

When we are attached to things that lie outside our sphere of control, the fear of loss makes even the most blessed life unbearable. For anything that we call "ours" can be taken from us without notice, including our loved ones and our own lives. The more we burden ourselves with worldly treasures, the more we have to lose and the more we have to fear . . .

> . . . for whoever is apprehensive of any loss of these things cannot be happy: the happy man should be safe, well fenced, well fortified, out of the reach of all annoyance, not like a man under trifling apprehensions, but free from all such. As he is not called innocent who but slightly offends, but he who offends not at all, so it is he alone who is to be considered without fear who is free from all fear, not he who is but in little fear. For what else is courage but an affection of mind that is ready to undergo perils, and patient in the endurance of pain and labour without any alloy of fear? Now, this certainly could not be the case if there were anything else good but what depended on honesty alone. But how can anyone be in possession of that desirable and much-coveted security (for I now call a freedom from anxiety a security, on which freedom a happy life depends) who has, or may have, a multitude of evils attending him? How can he be brave and undaunted, and hold everything as trifles which can befall a man?—for so a wise man should do, unless he be one who thinks that everything depends on himself.[1]

Plato illustrates the apprehensive condition of the tyrant in an allegory:

> "You know that the slave-masters live securely and have nothing to fear from their servants?"
> "What should they fear?"
> "Nothing. But do you observe the reason for this?"

---

1 Cicero.

"Yes, because the individual has the support and protection of society as a whole."

"Very true," I said. "But imagine that one of these owners—the master say of some fifty slaves—is carried off by a god, with his family and property and slaves, into the wilderness, where there are no free men to help him. Will he not be in an agony of fear lest he and his wife and children should be put to death by his slaves?"

"Yes," he said, "he will be in the utmost fear."

"The time has arrived when he will be compelled to flatter some of these slaves, and make many promises to them of freedom and other things, much against his will. That is, he will have to cajole his own servants."

"Yes," he said, "that will be the only way of saving himself."

"And suppose the same god, who carried him away, surrounds him with neighbours who will not suffer one man to be the master of another, and who, if they could catch the offender, would take his life?"

"His case will be still worse, if you suppose him to be everywhere surrounded and watched by enemies."

"And is this not the sort of prison in which the tyrant will be bound? He whose nature is such as we have described, is full of all sorts of fears and lusts, is he not? His soul is dainty and greedy, and yet alone, of all men in the city, he is never allowed to go on a journey, or to see the things which other free men desire to see, but he lives in his hole like a woman hidden in the house, and is jealous of any other citizen who goes into foreign parts and sees anything of interest."

"Very true," he said.

"And amid evils such as these, will not he who is ill-governed in his own person—I mean the tyrannical man, whom you just now decided to be the unhappiest of all men—will he not be even more miserable when, instead of leading a private life, he is constrained by fortune to be a public tyrant? He has to be the master of others when he is not even master of himself: he is like a diseased or paralytic man who is compelled to pass his life, not in retirement, but fighting and combating with other men."

"Yes," he said, "the similitude is most exact."

"Is his case not utterly miserable? And doesn't the actual tyrant lead a worse life than he whose life you determined to be the worst?"

"Certainly."

Cicero provides the example of one such tyrant, Dionysus, who at least was aware of the wretchedness of his own condition: "when Damocles, one of his flatterers, was dilating in conversation on [Dionysus's] forces, his wealth, the greatness of his power, the plenty he enjoyed, the grandeur of his royal palaces, and maintaining that no one was ever happier, Dionysus said, 'Have you an inclination, Damocles, as this kind of life pleases you, to have a taste of it yourself, and to make a trial of the good fortune that attends me?' And when he said that he should like it extremely, Dionysius ordered him to be laid on a bed of gold with the most beautiful covering, embroidered and wrought with the most exquisite work, and he dressed out a great many sideboards with silver and embossed gold. He then ordered some youths, distinguished for their handsome persons, to wait at his table, and to observe his nod, in order to serve him with what he wanted. There were ointments and garlands; perfumes were burned; tables provided with the most exquisite meats. Damocles thought himself very happy. In the midst of this apparatus, Dionysius ordered a bright sword to be let down from the ceiling, suspended by a single horse-hair, so as to hang over the head of that happy man. After which he neither cast his eye on those handsome waiters, nor on the well-wrought plate; nor touched any of the provisions: presently the garlands fell to pieces. At last he entreated the tyrant to let him go, for now he had no desire to be happy. Does not Dionysius, then, seem to have declared there can be no happiness for one who is under constant apprehensions?"

But the problems of the vice-ridden do not end with apprehension, for when such a person is free of fear, it is usually because he is dissatisfied with his lot—he does not value what he has and still desires much, and so his fearlessness does not arise from transcending his weakness, but is another symptom of his unhappiness. "Now, the less our peace of mind is disturbed by fear," says Schopenhauer, "the more likely it is to be agitated by desire and expectation."

Wealth, Materialism, and Greed

There is no greater impediment to our spiritual growth and to the attainment of happiness than *greed*. All religions and philosophies denounce greed, and they have more than one reason for doing so: greed is a cause for attachment and thus fear, it indicates selfishness and self-love, it alienates us from our basic nature, it makes enemies of our fellow-men, and, in short, it brings endless suffering to ourselves and everyone around us. When we are preoccupied with accumulating worldly treasures, we neglect our spiritual condition. Jesus warns, "Lay not up for yourselves treasures upon earth, where moth and rust doth corrupt, and where thieves break through and steal: But lay up for yourselves treasures in heaven, where neither moth nor rust doth corrupt, and where thieves do not break through nor steal: For where your treasure is, there will your heart be also." Seneca echoes this: "The soul, I affirm, knows that riches are stored elsewhere than in men's heaped-up treasure-houses; that it is the soul, and not the strong-box, which should be filled." The pursuit of money is in most cases incompatible with the pursuit of virtue, for in order to build wealth we must generally neglect certain moral values: "No servant can serve two masters: for either he will hate the one, and love the other; or else he will hold to the one, and despise the other. Ye cannot serve God and mammon."[1] Even if we acquire money honestly, without exploiting others, and by doing work that is useful rather than harmful, the act of hoarding it or using it to indulge in pleasures beyond our need is in itself a vice. Every dollar we spend on superfluous pleasures could be used to help someone in need. The capitalist philosophy is good at producing sophistic arguments justifying greed, but morally it is indefensible, and spiritually we are not fooling ourselves. An exception may be those rare individuals who are exceptionally gifted at increasing wealth by making wise investments, and who hoard and invest their money their whole lives only to give it all away at the end, thus helping more people in the long run. Most of us, however, must admit that we are only indulging ourselves when we consume beyond our needs. We may argue that, in compiling a closet full of shoes, we are supporting the economy, but we could also support the economy by buying shoes for poor children who do not have any. And in truth, the decisions we make with our extra funds could not only fuel the economy, but could even guide economic activity in virtuous directions, rather than toward the wasteful production of unnecessary garbage. Without doubt, greed produces waste that is destructive not only to the individual, but also to the human species and the planet as a whole. It is for good reason, then, that all wise thinkers condemn it.

"If thou wilt be perfect," says Christ, "go and sell that thou hast, and give to the poor, and thou shalt have treasure in heaven: and come and follow me." He adds, unambiguously, "Verily I say unto you, That a rich man shall hardly enter into

[1] Luke 16:13.

the kingdom of heaven. And again I say unto you, It is easier for a camel to go through the eye of a needle, than for a rich man to enter into the kingdom of God." (That some people in America can exalt Jesus and Mammon at the same time is mind-boggling—the height of hypocrisy and ignorance.) The Dhammapada says, "I do not call a man a Brahmin because of his origin or his mother: he is arrogant, and he is wealthy: but the poor, who is free from all attachments, him I call indeed a Brahmin." And again in the New Testament: "Blessed are the poor in spirit: for theirs is the kingdom of heaven."

Beyond the moral danger of greed, it is also quite often unavailing, and wasteful of our lives. Even those who succeed in becoming wealthy often do not live to enjoy it: "How often it happens that a man is unable to enjoy the wealth which he acquired at so much trouble and risk, and that the fruits of his labour are reserved for others."[1] We also often observe that those who seek wealth the most ardently acquire it the least; for "avarice has no greater impediment than itself; the more strained and vigorous it is, the less it produces, and generally grows rich more readily when disguised in a mask of liberality."[2] Further, the pursuit of wealth can be destructive because it arouses jealousy, in others as well as ourselves. Says Seneca, not one among the wealthy "rejoices as much in his own wealth as he resents the wealth of another." The great Stoic advises, "we must spurn wealth: wealth is the diploma of slavery. Abandon gold and silver, and whatever else is a burden upon our richly-furnished homes; liberty cannot be gained for nothing. If you set a high value on liberty, you must set a low value on everything else."

Those of us on the path to wisdom lose our greed quite naturally, with little or no struggle, for we are too preoccupied with higher things. When the soul begins to reach toward the divine, it "casts no backward glance at wealth; gold and silver—things which are fully worthy of the gloom in which they once lay—it values not by the sheen which smites the

---

[1] Schopenhauer.
[2] Montaigne.

eyes of the ignorant, but by the mire of ancient days, whence our greed first detached and dug them out."[1]

Yet if wealth should accrue to us as a result of our authentic and selfless action, we need not scorn it or renounce it, as long as we use it virtuously and selflessly. As Pascal says, "I love poverty because He loved it. I love riches because they afford me the means of helping the very poor."

Lust and Preoccupation with the Body

> He will have many masters who makes his body his master, who is over-fearful on its behalf, who judges everything according to the body.[2]

If we look closely, we see that greed is usually a *secondary* vice, and is really an offshoot of that most primitive and ineradicable vice, *lust*. Aristotle explains that the life of money-making "is one of constraint, undertaken under compulsion, and *wealth* is evidently not the Good we are seeking, because it is merely useful and for the sake of something else." That "something else" is *sensual pleasure*. Though it is true that we seek a minimum of wealth in order to house and feed ourselves, when our pursuit of wealth goes beyond necessity and verges on *greed*, then the motive can usually be traced to the desire to satisfy our lusts. (Indeed, if we believe Freud, almost all our actions can be explained by the sex drive.) Plato concurs with his student with regard to the connection between greed and lust: "the third [element], having many forms, has no special name, but is denoted by the general term *appetite*, due to the extraordinary strength and vehemence of the desires of eating and drinking and the other sensual pleasures that are the main elements of it; we also call it *acquisitiveness* or *money-lust*, because money is the means of

---

[1] Seneca.
[2] Seneca, *Epistles* XIV. Not included in this collection, but can be found in the Great Minds book *On Solitude*.

satisfying desires of this kind."

The Dhammapada teaches, "he is wise who knows that lusts have a short taste and bring much pain in their wake." Lust must be eradicated completely, says the Buddha, or we will always be enslaved by it; there is no moderation when it comes to this insatiable vice: "Cut down the whole forest of lust, not just one tree! Great danger comes out of this forest. When you have cut down both the forest and its undergrowth, then you will be liberated! As long as a man's love of women is not destroyed—without a trace!—his mind remains in bondage, as the calf that drinks milk is in bondage to its mother." Seneca echoes this: "For no man is free who is a slave to his body." Later in *The Dhammapada*, a reminder of lust's stubborn and endless recurrence: "As a tree, even though it has been cut down, is firm as long as its root is safe, and grows again, so, unless the feeders of thirst are destroyed, the pain of life will return again and again."

We must realize that it is not *acting upon* lust that causes our suffering, but the lust itself, the distraction and mental anguish that come with endless craving. Christ explains, "whosoever looketh on a woman to lust after her hath committed adultery with her already in his heart. And if thy right eye offend thee, pluck it out, and cast it from thee: for it is profitable for thee that one of thy members should perish, and not that thy whole body should be cast into hell. And if thy right hand offend thee, cut it off, and cast it from thee: for it is profitable for thee that one of thy members should perish, and not that thy whole body should be cast into hell." It is not enough to resist temptation, because the temptation itself brings suffering and turns life into endless torment. That is why the eye itself must be restrained, so that we do not even see the object of temptation. Montaigne explains the meaning of "Lead us not unto temptation"[1] as follows: "We do not pray that our reason may not be combated and overcome by concupiscence, but that it may not even be put to the test, that we may not be brought into a state in which we may even

---

[1] Matthew 6:13.

have to suffer the approaches, solicitations, and temptations of sin: and we beg of Almighty God to keep our conscience quiet, fully and perfectly delivered from all association with evil." Similarly, "Socrates does not say, 'Do not surrender to the charms of beauty, stand your ground, and do your utmost to oppose it.' 'Fly from it,' says he, 'run from the sight and encounter of it as from a powerful poison that darts and wounds at a distance.'"[1]

Any preoccupation with the body leads to craving and attachment, and therefore suffering. We must regard the body "as a burden which must be borne: not as a thing to love, but as a thing to oversee."[2] We ought to take care of ourselves and remain healthy, but we must not allow ourselves to become obsessive on this point either. For much of our concern for the body actually does it more harm than good, for instance excessive exercise, too much sex (which can drain us of energy and bring disease), and anything else that places a higher value on the body's appearance and pleasure than on its health. "It is a mark of low intellect," says Epictetus, "to spend much time in things relating to the body—to be immoderate in exercises, in eating and drinking, and in the discharge of other animal functions. These things should be done *incidentally*, and our main strength should be applied to our reason."

When we think of pleasure, the bodily pleasures are the first that spring to mind, and they are indeed the ones that most of us are eager to satisfy. Aristotle explains why, despite the fact that the intellectual and spiritual pleasures are superior to the bodily ones, the majority of people pursue the former and neglect the latter: "the bodily pleasures, by the very fact of their being so intense, are pursued by those who cannot enjoy other pleasures. Such men in fact create violent thirsts for themselves . . . because they have no other things to take pleasure in."

---

[1] Montaigne.
[2] Seneca.

Envy

Greed inevitably leads us to envy, when our dissatisfaction with what we have makes us covet our neighbour's goods. Or rather, comparing our own fortune with those of others makes us dissatisfied with what we have, even if all our needs are being met. "*Envy* is natural to man," says Schopenhauer, "and still, it is at once a vice and a source of misery. We should treat it as the enemy of our happiness, and stifle it like an evil thought. This is the advice given by Seneca; as he well puts it, we shall be pleased with what we have, if we avoid the self-torture of comparing our own lot with some other and happier one." Indeed, we can measure our unhappiness by our degree of envy: "Envy shows how unhappy people are; and their constant attention to what others do and leave undone, how much they are bored." Those who are constantly striving to enrich themselves become envious of those who have more, and at the same time incur the envy of those who have less. "Victory breeds hatred," *The Dhammapada* teaches, "for the defeated are unhappy. He who has given up both victory and defeat lives in peace and happiness."

Humility and simplicity curb our own vices and protect us from the enmity of others. For "no form of hatred is so implacable as the hatred that comes from envy; and therefore we should always carefully refrain from doing anything to rouse it."[1]

Hatred

"To speak angrily to a person, to show your hatred by what you say or by the way you look, is an unnecessary proceeding—dangerous, foolish, ridiculous, and vulgar."[2] "For hatred will never cease by hatred: hatred ceases by love—this is a

---

1 Schopenhauer.
2 Schopenhauer.

timeless law."[1] Hatred can arise from envy, enmity, and, perhaps most commonly, contempt—the sense of being intellectually or morally superior to another. "But I say unto you, That whosoever is angry with his brother without a cause shall be in danger of the judgment: and whosoever shall say to his brother, Raca, shall be in danger of the council: but whosoever shall say, Thou fool, shall be in danger of hell fire."[2] The wise understand the ultimate equality and unity of all of creation, and that hatred directed at any part is finally directed at the whole: "Verily I say unto you, Inasmuch as ye have done it unto one of the least of these my brethren, ye have done it unto me."[3] Therefore to hate anyone or anything is to rebel against Nature, and there is no surer path to unhappiness than that.

Self-Interest

Pleasure-seeking, greed, lust, hatred, and wrath all arise from the pursuit of our "self-interest," or rather, of what we believe is our self-interest. The paradox of selfishness is that it is utterly destructive to the self, while *selflessness* is the best thing for *ourselves*. "The selfish man suffers in this world, and he suffers in the next," *The Dhammapada* teaches. "He suffers when he thinks of the evil he has done, and he suffers more in continuing on the evil path in this life and the next." When we go beyond our needs, the pursuit of our own interest generally comes at the expense of others: "He who, by causing pain to others, wishes to obtain pleasure for himself, he, entangled in the bonds of hatred, will never be free from hatred. What ought to be done is neglected, what ought not to be done is done; the desires of unruly, thoughtless people are always increasing. But they whose whole watchfulness is always directed to their body, who do not follow wrong

---

[1] The Dhammapada.
[2] Matthew 5:22.
[3] Matthew 25:40.

actions, and who steadfastly do what ought to be done—the desires of such watchful and wise people will come to an end."

Indeed, even as we pursue the necessities of life, we must not allow ourselves to become unduly anxious or distressed. Epictetus urges us to "lay aside such reasonings as these: 'If I neglect my affairs, I will not be able to support myself; if I do not punish my servant, he will be good for nothing.' For it is better to die of hunger, exempt from grief and fear, than to live in affluence with perturbation; and it is better that your servant should be bad than you unhappy.'" Christ, too, instructs us that we must have faith that nature will supply all our needs, just as it does for all creatures, without our having to trouble ourselves or pursue our wants at the expense of our own good or the good of others:

> Therefore I say unto you, Take no thought for your life, what ye shall eat, or what ye shall drink; nor yet for your body, what ye shall put on. Is not the life more than meat, and the body than raiment?
>
> Behold the fowls of the air: for they sow not, neither do they reap, nor gather into barns; yet your heavenly Father feedeth them. Are ye not much better than they?
>
> Which of you by taking thought can add one cubit unto his stature?
>
> And why take ye thought for raiment? Consider the lilies of the field, how they grow; they toil not, neither do they spin:
>
> And yet I say unto you, That even Solomon in all his glory was not arrayed like one of these.
>
> Wherefore, if God so clothe the grass of the field, which to day is, and to morrow is cast into the oven, shall he not much more clothe you, O ye of little faith?
>
> Therefore take no thought, saying, What shall we eat? or, What shall we drink? or, Wherewithal shall we be clothed?
>
> For after all these things do the Gentiles

> seek: for your heavenly Father knoweth
> that ye have need of all these things.
>
> But seek ye first the kingdom of God,
> and his righteousness; and all these things
> shall be added unto you.

If we follow our own nature and perform those actions that are required of us, in the spirit of service, without selfish motives, we will receive all that we desire (since we will be desiring nothing superfluous). That is the teaching of *The Bhagavad Gita:* "Nourished by your selfless service, the Gods shall indeed bestow on you the enjoyments you desire. But he who enjoys—without offering to Them Their gifts—he is verily a thief." The wise, therefore, will do as *The Dhammapada* instructs: "Cut out the love of self with your own hand, as you would an autumn lotus." And Christ similarly teaches, "If any man will come after me, let him deny himself, and take up his cross, and follow me. For whosoever will save his life shall lose it: and whosoever will lose his life for my sake shall find it. For what is a man profited, if he shall gain the whole world, and lose his own soul? or what shall a man give in exchange for his soul?"

Self-Interest Requires Self-Knowledge and Wisdom

Besides the wretchedness that arises from selfish living, the pursuit of self-interest is generally misguided because the unwise do not even understand themselves well enough to know what is really in their own interest. Like rats who believe they are pursuing their self-interest when they bite the cheese on the trap, the unwise are lacking crucial information, and so are unknowingly chasing their own doom. The unwise act mindlessly and rashly, led by their impulses, and even when they reason, they do so poorly and go in the wrong direction. For observe how often we regret our most important decisions, and how many of us believe we have misspent our whole lives. Cicero:

> And it is said that when he was disposed to play at ball—for he delighted much in it—and had pulled off his clothes, he used to give his sword into the keeping of a young man whom he was very fond of. On this, one of his intimates said pleasantly, "You certainly trust your life with him;" and as the young man happened to smile at this, he ordered them both to be slain, the one for showing how he might be taken off, the other for approving of what had been said by smiling. But he was so concerned at what he had done that nothing affected him more during his whole life; for he had slain one to whom he was extremely partial. Thus do weak men's desires pull them different ways, and while they indulge one, they act counter to another.

Indeed, even the wisest of men cannot help but fall into error when they pursue desire, because our desires contradict one another. Aristotle explains, "The reason why no one thing is always pleasant is that our nature is not simple, but complex, involving something different from itself; so that if one part of this nature does something, this is unnatural to the other part, and when the two natures are evenly balanced, what is done seems neither painful nor pleasant." This is why the height of wisdom is to renounce desire altogether, since even if we pursue the best of all options available to us, we are still likely to run into trouble. Even the pursuit of wisdom is met with rebellion from that other aspect of our nature, the one which strives to satisfy its base urges as often as it can and by any means. As Aristotle argues, however, it is the rational capacity that distinguishes man from the animals, and it is the fulfilment of this element that leads to happiness, while feeding the other element reduces us to animals. And animals, says the philosopher, are not happy; at best they are ignorant—though this is a condition many of us mistake for happiness.

The "Bliss" of Ignorance

For the majority, happiness means mindlessness—forgetting one's worries, fears, and desires out of careless numbness as opposed to transcendence and awareness. This is the life of mindless work and mindless play—self-denial in a dehumanizing job during the day, and self-denial in television, sex, or drunken revelry at night. As Pascal tells us, the only path to happiness for the majority is *diversion*:

> When I set myself to considering the different distractions of man, the pains and perils to which he exposes himself at court or in war, whence arise so many quarrels, passions, bold and often bad ventures, etc., I discover that all the unhappiness of man arises from one single fact: that he cannot stay quietly in his room. A man who has enough wealth to live on, if he knew how to stay with pleasure at home, would not leave it to go to sea or to besiege a town. A commission in the army would not be so attractive were it not insufferable to stay in the same town; and men only seek conversation and the diversion of gambling because they cannot remain with pleasure at home.

Pascal explains why diversion, the source of "happiness" for most people, is also the cause of our greatest despair (which Kierkegaard calls the despair that is unconscious of being despair): "The only thing which consoles us for our miseries is diversion, and yet this is the greatest of our miseries. For it is this which principally hinders us from reflecting upon ourselves, and which makes us insensibly ruin ourselves. Without this we should be in a state of weariness, and this weariness would spur us to seek a more solid means of escaping from it. But diversion amuses us, and leads us unconsciously to death." Seneca would agree with Pascal, and he disagrees "with those who strike out into the midst of the billows and, welcoming a stormy existence, wrestle daily in hardihood of soul with life's problems. The wise man will endure all that, but will not choose it; he will prefer to be at peace rather than at war." But the ability to live without diversion, and to instead enjoy a quiet life of contemplation and awareness, requires a nature like Seneca's, one that is at variance with the natures of common men.

Today, our whole lives are an endless stream of diversion, and so pathetic is our condition that we cannot even remain amused with the same diversion for long: we require a constant bombardment of distractions to keep us from thinking of ourselves and confronting the wretchedness of our situation. In this sense, technology is the great saviour and destroyer of mankind, providing the means for ultimate self-forgetfulness as well as complete alienation from ourselves. Even travel, which many claim to pursue for cultural or spiritual reasons, for "experience," is more often an escape from ourselves and from the surroundings we associate with our unhappiness. Philistines who never read classic literature or cultivate an appreciation for great music and art, who are insensible to the natural beauties of their own home towns, suddenly become cultured and curious when the subject turns to travel. And because their minds have not been properly cultivated, the true benefits of travel are lost on them: "they seeing see not; and hearing they hear not, neither do they understand."[1] How many young people travel from North America to Europe just so they can party in a new venue! They go to the birthplace of Western civilization and treat it like Las Vegas; indeed, they would prefer the fake pyramids to the real ones, for the latter are too remote from nightclubs, casinos, and prostitutes.

---

[1] Matthew 13:13.

Seneca criticizes those who travel for the sake of attaining wisdom:

> Are you surprised, as if it were a novelty, that after such long travel and so many changes of scene you have not been able to shake off the gloom and heaviness of your mind? You need a change of soul rather than a change of climate. Though you may cross vast spaces of sea, and though, as our Virgil remarks, *Lands and cities are left astern*, your faults will follow you wherever you travel. Socrates made the same remark to one who complained; he said: "Why do you wonder that globe-trotting does not help you, seeing that you always take yourself with you? The reason which set you wandering is ever at your heels."

"Can wisdom," Seneca asks, "the greatest of all the arts, be picked up on a journey? I assure you, travel as far as you like, you can never establish yourself beyond the reach of desire, beyond the reach of bad temper, or beyond the reach of fear; had it been so, the human race would long ago have banded together and made a pilgrimage to the spot." The person we are matters more than where we go, and "for that reason we should not make the mind a bondsman to any one place. Live in this belief: 'I am not born for any one corner of the universe; this whole world is my country.' If you saw this fact clearly, you would not be surprised at getting no benefit from the fresh scenes to which you roam each time through weariness of the old scenes." Marcus Aurelius advises us to escape *into* ourselves, rather than away from ourselves and our current surroundings:

> Men seek seclusion in the country, seashores, and mountains; and you too are accustomed to desire such things very much. But this is altogether a mark of the

> most common sort of men, since it is in your power whenever you choose to retire into yourself. Nowhere can a man find a more quiet retreat, and more freedom from trouble, than in his own soul, particularly when he has within him such thoughts that, being contemplated, immediately bring on perfect tranquillity; and I affirm that tranquillity is nothing else than the good ordering of the mind.

Similarly in *The Dhammapada*: "Men, driven by fear, go to many a refuge, to mountains and forests, to groves and sacred trees. But none of these is a safe refuge, because it cannot deliver a man from fear."

Why are we always seeking to divert and escape from ourselves? What exactly is it that drives us away from ourselves and makes it impossible for us to be happy at rest? Pascal explains, "As men are not able to fight against death, misery, ignorance, they have taken it into their heads, in order to be happy, not to think of them at all." This results from "the natural poverty of our feeble and mortal condition, so wretched that nothing can comfort us when we think about it." Like Schopenhauer, who says that life is given to us "not to be enjoyed, but to be overcome—to be got over," Pascal believes the basic condition of our existence is suffering: "If our condition were truly happy, we would not need diversion from thinking of it in order to make ourselves happy." He adds,

> If man were happy, he would be the more so, the less he was diverted, like the Saints and God. "Yes," you say, "but is it not to be happy to have a faculty of being amused by diversion?"—No, for that comes from elsewhere and from without, and thus is dependent, and therefore subject to be disturbed by a thousand accidents, which bring inevitable griefs.

This happiness of the masses is not the one we are seeking, for ours depends on *awareness* as opposed to ignorance. The ignorantly happy may have easier lives, but their experience of life lacks the depth and dimension of one who attains happiness after passing through the full extent of human suffering. Montaigne explains:

> Souls that, through their own stupidity, only discern things by halves, have this happiness, that they smart less with hurtful things: it is a spiritual leprosy that has some show of health, and such a health as philosophy does not altogether scorn; but yet it is not right to call it wisdom, as we often do. And in this manner someone in antiquity mocked Diogenes, who, in the depth of winter and quite naked, went embracing a snow figure to test his endurance: the other seeing him in this position, said, "Are you very cold now?" "Not at all," replied Diogenes. "Why, then," pursued the other, "what difficult and exemplary thing do you think you're doing in embracing that snow?" To take a true measure of constancy, one must necessarily know what the suffering is.

The Superiority of Intellectual Pleasures

Those of us who choose not to seek our happiness in the mindless pursuit of pleasure must look for it in the pleasures of the mind. For those who have the capacity to enjoy them, these are the superior pleasures, because they are not tainted by desire and pain, and because they lead us toward the self-knowledge required for true happiness. Cicero tells us of Critolaus, "who having put the goods of the mind into one scale, and the goods of the body and other external advantages into the other, thought the goods of the mind outweighed the others so far that they would require the whole earth and sea to equalize the scale." And Schopenhauer asserts that "purely intellectual occupation, for the mind that is capable of it, will, as a rule, do much more in the way of happiness than any form of practical life, with its constant alternations of success and failure, and all the shocks and torments it produces. But it must be confessed that for such occupation a preeminent amount of intellectual capacity is necessary."

Contemplation of higher things—the nature of existence, consciousness, our place in creation, etc.—is indispensible if we are to acquire transcendence. Even if we come to no conceptual answers, the act of contemplation itself enlarges the mind, expands the soul, and in time helps us attain an intuitive, ineffable understanding of life and the nature of the Self. "A mind employed on such subjects," says Cicero, "and which night and day contemplates them, contains in itself that precept of the Delphic God, so as to 'know itself,' and to perceive its connection with the divine reason, from whence it is filled with an insatiable joy. For reflections on the power and nature of the Gods raise in us a desire of imitating their eternity. Nor does the mind, that sees the necessary dependences and connections that one cause has with another, think it possible that it should be itself confined to the shortness of this life." And Epicurus, perhaps the most misunderstood of the ancient philosophers, makes this case for the importance of intellectual contemplation: "It is impossible for someone to banish his fear about the most important matters if he does not know the nature of the whole universe, and lives in dread because of myths and superstitions. Hence without the study of nature there can be no enjoyment of pure pleasure."

Such study can generally occur only in solitude, free from the distractions and corrupting influences of society. Indeed, some degree of solitude is itself necessary to our happiness.[1] Schopenhauer argues,

> No man can be in *perfect accord* with

---

[1] See the book *On Solitude* in the Great Minds series.

anyone but himself—not even with a friend or the partner of his life; differences of individuality and temperament are always bringing in some degree of discord, though it may be a very slight one. That genuine, profound peace of mind, that perfect tranquillity of soul, which, next to health, is the highest blessing the earth can give, is to be attained only in solitude, and, as a permanent mood, only in complete retirement; and then, if there is anything great and rich in the man's own self, his way of life is the happiest that may be found in this wretched world.

How to Attain Happiness

The following sections describe what we must learn and what we must do in order to overcome our natural frailties and arrive at true happiness. The primary change that must occur in our minds is the destruction of delusions which give us false expectations of life and lead us toward wrong action. Next, we must learn to restrain the mind, which is wont to veer in all directions toward endless desires and fears that make life a perpetual torment. Understanding what needs to be done is the easy part, and it is likely that much of this information is widely known on an intellectual level. What the great minds offer us, however, are the persuasive rationales behind the wisdom, and this will hopefully inspire the reader to finally believe in the truth of their teachings. Yet even conviction is not enough when it comes to achieving happiness, and the process of training the mind involves more than stuffing it with wise sayings. Once we know what we hope to achieve, and how we must be if we wish to be truly happy, we must incorporate the teachings into our lives, and practice meditation with great discipline until we begin to see improvements in our nature. The practice of meditation is not discussed in much detail in this volume, but the committed reader should seek to learn this art through books and qualified instructors. Mindfulness meditation trains us to become aware of our thoughts and bodily states, giving us the most essential tool for achieving the self-awareness that leads to happiness.

Self-Knowledge and Self-Control

What does Socrates mean when he says, "The unexamined life is not worth living"? He means that we must know ourselves, and we must scrutinize our lives to ensure that we are living authentically and with purpose, fulfilling our human potential. We must also seek to understand others, the nature of our species, and the nature of existence itself, so that we may live *consciously*, knowing our place within the whole. If we go through life without reflection, without understanding *why* we do what we do, we end up living like the beasts, in constant fear, at the mercy of our impulses, without a deep sense of our own existence; we float through our days, dragged and tossed by social and natural forces, with only a superficial grasp of life, completely unaffected by its profound and inspiring mystery.

For man "is obviously made to think," says Pascal. "It is his whole dignity and his whole merit; and his whole duty is to think as he ought. Now, the order of thought is to begin with self, and with its Author and its end.

"Now, of what does the world think? Never of this, but of dancing, playing the lute, singing, making verses, running at the ring, etc., fighting, making oneself king, without thinking what it is to be a king and what it is to be a man."

The capacity for this sort of self-reflection does not depend on intellect alone—it requires a particular nature—for many of the most powerful rational minds never pursue self-knowledge, squandering their energies on learning "the way of the world" as opposed to the wisdom of life. Such people, with their intellectual and spiritless worldviews, often proclaim that life is meaningless—they dismiss the *thing-in-itself* and simply take it for granted. "So what?" their faces seem to say.

"Who cares?" Such lives are not worth living because they are wasted, wretched, and akin to the lives of animals, minus the dignity of innocence.

"One must know oneself," Pascal urges. "If this does not help us discover truth, it at least serves as a guide to living our life, and there is nothing better." Marcus Aurelius puts it more decisively: "By being indifferent to the workings of another's soul, seldom is a man made unhappy; but a man who does not observe the movements of his own soul will certainly be unhappy." Even in the most basic sense, self-analysis is essential to our growth, for without it we are doomed to repeat the same mistakes. And yet some of the most gifted logical thinkers are particularly adept at rationalizing their errors, as well as justifying any abiding weaknesses in character that compromise their potential for happiness. "If we have made obvious mistakes," says Schopenhauer, "we should not try, as we generally do, to gloss them over, or to find something to excuse or extenuate them; we should admit to ourselves that we have committed faults, and open our eyes wide to all their enormity, in order that we may firmly resolve to avoid them in time to come. To be sure, that means a great deal of self-inflicted pain, in the shape of discontent, but it should be remembered that to spare the rod is to spoil the child."

Many of us, rather than gaining self-awareness over the course of our lives, only become more and more alienated from ourselves as we put on all sorts of social masks while playing the game of life. It may be permissible to adopt temporary roles—like the doctor who puts on a white coat and a grave expression to produce the impression of medical authority—as long as we do not inwardly identify with this fiction. Montaigne advises:

> We must play our part properly, but as a part of a borrowed character; we must not make a real essence of the mask and outward appearance, nor make of something foreign something that is our own; we cannot distinguish the skin from

> the shirt: it is enough to make up the face without making up the heart. I see some who transform and transubstantiate themselves into as many new shapes and new beings as they undertake new employments; and who strut and fume even to the heart and liver, and carry their state along with them even to the toilet room: I cannot make them distinguish the salutations made to themselves from those made to their office, their retinue, or their mule.

Yet many, who are always either working or socializing mindlessly, forever exchanging one mask for another, spend so much time away from themselves that they eventually have no selves left to speak of. Such people, if they ever get a moment to commune with themselves in retirement, experience the horror of one who is buried alive in a casket. Indeed, for someone who lacks a *self*, there is nothing worse than solitude, for it is like keeping company with *nothingness*; such people cannot remain alone for long without succumbing to dreadful panic.[1]

It is critical, then, that we not lose ourselves in this way. To that end, we must avoid excessive identification with our roles, and at no time should we produce an altogether false persona for the sake of impressing others or currying some social favour. Such behaviour is not only spiritually destructive and detrimental to our happiness, but it is also contemptible from a social standpoint. Schopenhauer describes why this is the case:

> . . . let me utter a word of protest against any and every form of *affectation*. It always arouses contempt; in the first place, because it argues deception, and the deception is cowardly, for it is based on fear; and, secondly, it argues self-

---

1 See the book *On Solitude* in the Great Minds series.

condemnation, because it means that a man is trying to appear what he is not, and therefore something which he thinks better than he actually is. To affect a quality, and to plume yourself upon it, is just to confess that you have not got it. Whether it is courage, or learning, or intellect, or wit, or success with women, or riches, or social position, or whatever else it may be that a man boasts of, you may conclude by his boasting about it that that is precisely the direction in which he is rather weak; for if a man really possesses any faculty to the full, it will not occur to him to make a great show of affecting it; he is quite content to know that he has it. That is the application of the Spanish proverb: *herradura que chacolotea clavo le falta*—a clattering hoof means a nail gone. To be sure, as I said at first, no man ought to let the reins go quite loose, and show himself just as he is; for there are many evil and bestial sides to our nature which require to be hidden away out of sight; and this justifies the negative attitude of dissimulation, but it does not justify a positive feigning of qualities which are not there. It should also be remembered that affectation is recognized at once, even before it is clear what it is that is being affected. And, finally, affectation cannot last very long, and one day the mask will fall off. *Nemo potest personam diu ferre fictam*, says Seneca; *ficta cito in naturam suam recidunt*—no one can persevere long in a fictitious character; for nature will soon reassert itself.

It is futile to try to escape ourselves or to become something we are not. Sooner or later, one way or another, we pay a heavy price for this self-deception. Honesty with others is a virtue, but honesty with ourselves is absolutely essential to our happiness. Cicero explains the connection between honesty and happiness as follows:

> ... every good is pleasant; whatever is pleasant may be boasted and talked of; whatever may be boasted of is glorious; but whatever is glorious is certainly laudable, and whatever is laudable doubtless, also, honourable: whatever, then, is good is honourable; therefore what is honourable alone is good. Hence it follows that a happy life is comprised in honesty alone.

"Take away honesty," he says, "and how can you imagine anything happy?" Remaining honest with ourselves also protects us from that most grave self-delusion, hypocrisy. For it is all too easy to believe we are one thing when we are truly another: "He who wishes to put on the saffron robe without having cleansed himself from sin, who lacks self-control and truth—he is unworthy of the saffron robe."[1]

Even if we know ourselves well, however, it is not so easy to subvert those natural drives which cause us so much suffering, and some of us may even question whether we should. After all, if we are recommending that we stay true to our nature, should we not give our natural inclinations free rein?

From a strictly theoretical standpoint, we may argue in favour of such freedom; but wisdom, which depends as much on experience as it does on reason, teaches us that this animal part of our nature stands in fierce opposition to the rational part and is the source of all our suffering. Our two natures are incompatible, and if we are to be happy, we must either reduce ourselves entirely to beasts (as many attempt to do), or strive toward what we call the "divine"—that is, enlightenment. The first way, however, cannot lead to happiness because, try as we might, we cannot be animals, for our more developed minds and our *imaginations* have robbed us of the animal's innate sense of moderation: the beasts rarely venture beyond

---

1 *The Dhammapada*.

necessity in satisfying their needs—not because they are wise, but because they cannot even conceive of wants beyond their needs; further, they possess an instinct to conserve their energy—an instinct which, if possessed by men, might keep them from saying and doing so many pointless and stupid things.

It is too late for us to return to our animal ignorance; and the high ideal of the human life is to move toward transcendence, not to regress toward the beasts. Our knowledge has brought with it suffering—that is, of course, the meaning of the story of Adam and Eve—and the only way to end our suffering is to cultivate the wisdom to overcome our frailties. This means attaining self-knowledge and developing self-control. Our suffering is a stepping-stone toward self-realization—the birth-pain of the universe coming to know itself. Transcending it is not merely a matter of relieving ourselves and living in peace, but of clearing the clouds from our consciousness so that we may see the truth of existence itself. "Therefore, O Arjuna, restrain the senses first, so that you can cast off this wretched destroyer of knowledge and wisdom."[1]

Meditation is an essential tool for cultivating this self-control. In *The Bhagavad Gita*, Krishna provides the following instructions for meditation: "Once seated, make the mind one-pointed, with the actions of the body and the senses controlled, and practice yoga for the purification of the self . . . When his well-restrained thought is established in the Self only, without longing for any of the objects of desire, then he is said to be a Saint . . . By whatever cause the wavering and unsteady mind wanders away, from that let him restrain it and bring it back directly under the control of the Self."

Achieving self-control is a difficult but possible task: many have achieved it throughout history and up to the present day. Think of the self-immolating monks who do not even utter a sound as they burn themselves to death: whatever other wisdom they lack, they certainly do not lack self-control. Yet as with all human capabilities, in order for us to develop self-

---

[1] *The Bhagavad Gita*.

control, it must be present in our nature to some extent—and not all of us will be able to achieve it. Fortunately, those who truly seek self-control indicate, by that very commitment, that they likely possess the required nature to achieve it. The unwise, on the other hand, rarely even consider restraining those impulses that, they believe, give them so much pleasure, but that ultimately cause them so much pain.

"Doubtless," says Krishna, "the mind is restless and hard to restrain; but by practice, and by detachment, it can be conquered. Yoga is hard to attain for a man of uncontrolled self; but by him who strives by the proper means and is self-controlled, it can be acquired." Similarly in *The Dhammapada:* "It is good to tame the mind, which is difficult to restrain and rushes wherever it likes: a tamed mind brings happiness. Let the wise man guard his thoughts, for they are difficult to perceive, very artful, and they rush wherever they like: thoughts well guarded bring happiness."

It is easier to achieve restraint in our actions than in our thoughts—and it is in *our minds* that we suffer. Indeed, the constraints of living in society keep our actions mostly under control, while our minds are generally free to entertain all sorts of tormenting fancies. It is *desire* that causes suffering, not so much the action we take to satisfy the desire. It is the *will* itself that is always craving more and more, ensuring our lifelong dissatisfaction—though it is true that it teases us with occasional short-lived rewards for our suffering. It is better to submit the *will* to the tyranny of our *reason* than to allow both will and reason to become enslaved to outside forces. Schopenhauer explains:

> And self-control may not appear so very difficult, if we consider that every man has to submit to a great deal of very severe control on the part of his surroundings, and that without it no form of existence is possible. Further, a little self-control at the right moment may prevent much subsequent compulsion at the hands of

others; just as a very small section of a circle close to the centre may correspond to a part near the circumference a hundred times as large. Nothing will protect us from external compulsion so much as the control of ourselves; and, as Seneca says, to submit yourself to reason is the way to make everything else submit to you.

Self-restraint is necessary in all our activities, including our work. Though it is true that, on close inspection, most "workaholics" are motivated by the hope of ultimately satisfying some primitive desire, many others are compelled by an authentic creative drive, or some other higher principle, and if they were asked to explain why they work so fervently, often for very little reward, they can provide no rational response. Such noble types would nonetheless be wise to exercise moderation in their work, if only for the sake of the work itself. Most artists know how easy it is to fall into an obsessive craze, and while such monomaniacal excursions are sometimes necessary to the act of creation, they are also often pathological and destructive: the work suffers from a loss of perspective and restraint, and the artist burns out, leaving him incapable of further work. It is also common to throw everything we have into producing one outstanding creation while draining ourselves of the physical and spiritual energy we need to sustain a long artistic career; and some artists accelerate their efforts with the use of drugs, but pay for it in the long run with a broken mind or a premature death: "It is possible, for instance, to make a tree burst forth into leaf, blossom, or even bear fruit within a few days, by the application of unslaked lime and artificial heat; but after that the tree will wither away."[1] Such are those artists who write one great novel or produce a single musical masterpiece, and thereafter produce nothing of any worth. Our whole lives long, output must be balanced with input, work with learning, reaping with sowing, if we are to maximize both the quality

[1] Schopenhauer.

and quantity of our creation. The same applies to the spiritual path: it is better to meditate a little every day in our own homes, to read and study, all while living in the world and facing the challenges of social existence, than to spend ten days in a spiritual retreat and then never give our practice another thought, as if wisdom comes with a certificate of completion from an authorized place of worship.

Dharma

> You must always bear this in mind: what is the nature of the Whole, and what is my nature, and how are the two related, and what is my part in the Whole? And ensure that no one hinders you from always doing and saying the things that are in accordance with that Nature of which you are a part.[1]

Self-knowledge gives us awareness of our *dharma*, or duty—the part we are to play in the whole. Once we know and accept our dharma, we must not rebel against it, even if the part allotted to us by Nature is not what we—that is, our imagination—would have chosen for ourselves. Surely, most of us would like to have been fated for glamorous, fulfilling, and financially rewarding work, but the reality is that most of us are called to more humble roles. Our society tells people that they can be whatever they want and achieve anything as long as they work hard, stay focused, make sacrifices, etc. But we know that is all nonsense. Just as one who reaches an adult of height of five feet, has poor hand-eye coordination, and suffers from asthma, will never be able to play professional basketball no matter how hard he works, so too are the rest of us limited by our natures and precluded from certain kinds of work. We may strive to improve upon our weaknesses in order to pursue higher-paying work, but we often do

---

[1] Marcus Aurelius.

so at our own peril, sacrificing our happiness for the sake of money and status; further, we will always be at a competitive disadvantage to those who are naturally suited to such work. For both practical and spiritual reasons, then, we would be well-advised to accept our dharma and rejoice in proper work in accordance with our nature. Marcus Aurelius advises, "Love the trade that you have learned, poor as it may be, and be content with it; and pass through the rest of life like one who has wholly entrusted everything to the gods, thus making himself neither the tyrant nor the slave of any man." Similarly, in *The Bhagavad Gita*, Krishna says, "The duty born with oneself, O Arjuna, though faulty, one ought not to abandon; for all undertakings are surrounded with faults, as fire is surrounded with smoke."

Unfortunately, in an economy in which most jobs are unnatural and completely divorced from our humanity, the greater proportion of us will have to do work that is opposed to our dharma. "Men let themselves out to hire; their faculties are not for themselves, but for those to whom they have enslaved themselves; it is their tenants who occupy them, not themselves."[1] Our minds and souls have changed but little since our tribal days, when all social duties had a direct relation to life; yet our work today is increasingly inhuman, asocial, and ill-suited to our minds, bodies, and souls. The more specialized an economy becomes, and the more technology advances, the worse this problem becomes. The best we can do under such circumstances is align our dharma with work that is a close approximation of our nature, and not deviate too much from our innate capabilities. However, the fact that most people are miserable in their jobs suggests that there is a shortage of these *approximately human* duties, and also that many people are drawn away from their dharma out of greed and lust. Therefore, Montaigne's recommendation, quoted above, that we play our role somewhat superficially, without absorbing it into ourselves, is more critical today than ever. In our society, the best most of us can do with our work is bear

---

[1] Montaigne.

it with patience and use it for practice in enduring suffering, just as some monks lie on burning coals or starve themselves.

Krishna says, "Better to struggle in one's own *dharma*, though devoid of merit, than to flourish in the *dharma* of another, though praised. Better is death in one's own *dharma* than life in another's, for such a life invites fear and danger." If we know ourselves, and if we rid ourselves of greed, lust, vanity, and any other weakness that might drive us toward unsuitable work, then we will be free to live in harmony with our dharma. Those who do not gain an awareness of their own dharma pass their lives in aimless occupation, always busy, with nothing to show for all their toil. Marcus Aurelius warns against such a life devoid of dharma or purpose: "Watch that you do not fall into another kind of error: the folly of triflers who busy themselves in life with much activity, but who have no object toward which they direct their whole effort, and no aim upon which they focus their whole thought." Knowledge of our dharma keeps us from wrong action and allows us to fulfil our nature by engaging in proper work. For as we shall see, selfless action in accordance with our dharma is the best way to achieve happiness.

Selfless Action, without Attachment

The way of renunciation and seclusion practiced by monks is not suitable for most of us; while there may be some whose true dharma is to live a monastic life, many who do so are actually going against their dharma and attempting to escape themselves. It is easy to see why some believe that a happy life requires renouncing all action, since any activity of the *will* is attended by suffering. But as Krishna rightly says, "No one, verily, even for an instant, ever remains doing no action; for everyone is helplessly driven to action by his own nature." Action is the fundamental characteristic of Nature, it is the essence of existence, and none of us can escape action until he is dead. "Our nature consists in motion," says Pascal; "complete rest is death." And Krishna tells us, "These worlds would be ruined if I stopped performing action; I would be the cause of chaos and confusion, and of the destruction of these creatures." Of course, even the monks are acting, though their activity is relatively subdued. Some sort of action is essential to our happiness, for "[n]othing is so insufferable to man as to be completely at rest, without passions, without business, without diversion, without study. He then feels his nothingness, his forlornness, his insufficiency, his dependence, his weakness, his emptiness. There will immediately arise from the depth of his heart weariness, gloom, sadness, fretfulness, vexation, despair."[1] Schopenhauer concurs:

> To have no regular work, no set sphere of activity—what a miserable thing it is! How often long travels undertaken for pleasure make a man downright unhappy; because the absence of anything that can be called occupation forces him, as it were, out of his right element. Effort, struggles with difficulties! that is as natural to a man as grubbing in the ground is to a mole. To have all his wants satisfied is something intolerable—the feeling of stagnation which comes from pleasures that last too long. To overcome difficulties is to experience the full delight of existence, no matter where the obstacles are encountered; whether in the affairs of life, in commerce or business; or in mental effort—the spirit of inquiry that tries to master its subject. There is always something pleasurable in the struggle and the victory. And if a man has no opportunity to excite himself, he will do what he can to create one, and according to his individual bent, he will hunt or play Cup and Ball: or led on by this unsuspected element in his nature, he will pick a quarrel with someone, or hatch

---

[1] Pascal.

> a plot or intrigue, or take to swindling and rascally courses generally—all to put an end to a state of repose which is intolerable. As I have remarked, *difficilis in otio quies*—it is difficult to keep quiet if you have nothing to do.

If we cannot avoid action, then, the questions become what is right action, what is wrong action, and in what frame of mind should our action be approached?

Krishna succinctly explains the difference between right and wrong action: "Ignorant men work for their own gain, and are attached, Arjuna; but wise men work for the welfare of the world, and are unattached." Marcus Aurelius similarly says, "Labour not unwillingly, nor without regard to the common interest." And of course the idea of selfless service reaches its spiritual height in Christianity: "but whosoever will be great among you, shall be your minister: And whosoever of you will be the chiefest, shall be servant of all. For even the Son of man came not to be ministered unto, but to minister, and to give his life a ransom for many."

When we act with selfish desire, the *will* comes into play, and any act of will causes suffering. The actions of "ambitious men, avaricious men, and so many others who run blindly ahead and whose course always carries them before themselves, such actions, I say, are erroneous and sickly."[1] Selfless action, however, in accordance with our dharma, comes so naturally and effortlessly that it incurs no suffering; and because we perform this action under the principle of *duty*, without personal motives, we remain detached from the results, and thus we are free from the anxiety that accompanies any action we do for personal gain. "He who has renounced selfish attachment to actions, whose doubts have been cloven asunder by wisdom, who is self-possessed—he is not enslaved by actions."[2] With the mindset of selfless action in accordance with dharma, even something as common and

---

1 Montaigne.
2 *The Bhagavad Gita.*

mundane as feeling nervous before an exam would no longer apply to us; for if we probe into the cause of such nervousness, we find it can be traced to the fear of being denied future pleasures: we think, "If I don't do well on this test, I won't get a good grade, I won't get a summer internship, I won't get a good job when I graduate, I'll never make good money, I won't be able to attract a good-looking wife, I'll be lonely my whole life, my life will be ruined." Even if such thoughts do not occur consciously, they are nonetheless at the root of our anxiety. Indeed, all anxiety can be traced to the fear of losing something personal, whether that be something as significant as a family member, or something as meaningless as our reputation in the eyes of the rabble. If, on the other hand, we write the test from a standpoint of necessity, seeing it as a step that is required of us for the performance of our selfless duty, then we become free from egoic attachment, we lose our anxiety, and more likely than not, we perform better on the test than we would have done in a selfish frame of mind. Montaigne describes how the selfless mind is "always in repose and in health, not without action, but without vexation, without passion. To be simply acting costs him so little that he acts even when sleeping." Similarly, *The Bhagavad Gita* says, "The man whose attachment is gone, who is liberated, whose mind is established in knowledge, who acts for the sake of sacrifice—the burden of his action melts away." Yet just because we view our action as a required duty, and have nothing to gain from its outcome ourselves, does not mean we put in a mediocre effort, for it is part of our duty to perform it to the best of our ability. Marcus Aurelius exhorts us,

> Every moment resolve firmly, as a Roman and as a man, to do what comes to hand with perfect and natural dignity, with compassion, freedom, and justice. Relieve your mind from all other cares. This you can do if you perform every action as if it were your last, dismissing the wayward thought, the passions that divert you from

> the commands of Reason, the desire to make an impression, the admiration of self, the dissatisfaction with your lot. See how little a man needs in order to live a life that flows in quiet, like the existence of the gods. And the gods, for their part, will require nothing more from him who observes these counsels.

The action we take in accordance with our dharma is what is necessary and good; any other action is unnecessary, and unnecessary acts, just like unnecessary desires or pleasures, lead to suffering.

> Do what is necessary, in accordance with the Reason of a social animal, and as Reason demands. For this brings not only the tranquillity that comes from doing well, but also that which comes from doing few things. For the greatest part of what we say and do is unnecessary, and if a man puts this away, he will have more leisure and less uneasiness. Accordingly, on every occasion a man should ask himself, "Is this one of the unnecessary things?" Now a man should put away not only unnecessary acts, but also unnecessary thoughts, for then superfluous acts will not follow either.[1]

One who has self-awareness and a sense of what he requires in order to live authentically, "knowing exactly what he owes to himself, will on his part find that he ought to apply to himself the practices of the world and of other men, and, in order to do this, ought to contribute to public society the duties and offices that pertain to him. He who does not in some way live for others, does not live much for himself."[2]

---

1 Marcus Aurelius.
2 Montaigne.

We find that even among artists and entrepreneurs, those who act out of genuine passion, indifferent to any personal reward, produce the best results.

Conversely, "[i]n the man who is drunk with that violent and tyrannical drive, we discover, of necessity, much imprudence and injustice; the impetuosity of his desire carries him away. His movements are reckless, and, unless Fortune assists a great deal, of very little fruit."[1]

Consider the star athlete who is so focused and disciplined that he is free from anxiety about the result of the match: he is performing his duty to the best of his ability, and that is all he can do; the rest is up to fate. Now compare him to the fan sitting at home, pulling his hair out over something that doesn't concern him in the least. The first exhibits action free from attachment, while the second exhibits idleness with attachment. Montaigne explains,

> Men perform like things with different degrees of effort and different exertions of will; the one does well enough without the other;[2] for how many people hazard themselves every day in war without any concern for which way it goes, and thrust themselves into the dangers of battles, the loss of which will not trouble their next night's sleep? Another man is at home, out of the danger which he would not have dared to face, and is more passionately concerned about the outcome of this war—his soul is more anxious than the soldier who stakes his blood and his life. I have been able to engage myself in public employments without quitting my own matters a nail's breadth, and have given myself to others without abandoning myself.

---

[1] Montaigne.
[2] Action without passion: compare this with the teaching of *The Bhagavad Gita*: action without attachment to its fruits.

There is nothing more absurd than being attached to the fruits of another's actions, and though the example of the attached spectator may seem beneath us, most of us are in some way similarly attached to things that are completely out of our control.

Acceptance

Epictetus instructs us to recognize the difference between those things that are in our own power, and those that are not; we must relinquish attachment to the latter and accept all that Fortune brings:

> There are things that are within our power, and there are things that are beyond our power. Within our power are opinion, aim, desire, aversion, and, in a word, whatever affairs are our own. Beyond our power are body, property, reputation, office, and, in one word, whatever are not properly our own affairs.
>
> Now the things within our power are by nature free, unrestricted, unhindered; but those beyond our power are weak, dependent, restricted, alien. Remember then, that, if you attribute freedom to things by nature dependent, and take what belongs to others for your own, you will be hindered, you will lament, you will be disturbed, you will find fault both with Gods and men. But if you take for your own only that which is your own, and view what belongs to others just as it really is, then no one will ever compel you, no one will restrict you, you will find fault with no one, you will accuse no one, you will do nothing against your will; no one will hurt you, you will not have an enemy, nor will you suffer any harm. . . .

> If, then, you shun only those undesirable things which you can control, you will never incur anything which you shun. But if you shun sickness, or death, or poverty, you will run the risk of wretchedness. Remove aversion, then, from all things that are not within our power, and transfer it to things undesirable which are within our power. But for the present altogether restrain desire; for if you desire any of the things not within our own power, you must necessarily be disappointed; and you are not yet secure of those which are within our power, and so are legitimate objects of desire. Where it is practically necessary for you to pursue or avoid anything, do even this with discretion, and gentleness, and moderation.

How can we train ourselves to accept the "slings and arrows of outrageous Fortune"? The great stoic suggests we practice by learning to accept the small inconveniences and annoyances of life:

> Begin therefore with little things. Is a little oil spilt or a little wine stolen? Say to yourself, "This is the price paid for peace and tranquillity; and nothing is to be had for nothing." And when you call your servant, consider that it is possible he may not come at your call; or, if he does, that he may not do what you wish. But it is not at all desirable for him, and very undesirable for you, that it should be in his power to cause you any disturbance.[1]

Similarly, Marcus Aurelius instructs us to begin every morning by saying to ourselves, "Today I will meet with the

---

[1] Epictetus.

meddlesome, the ungrateful, the arrogant, the deceitful, the envious, and the selfish." He adds, "All these people are such because they are ignorant of what is good and evil. But I have long known the nature of good and its beauty, and the nature of evil and its ugliness, and I know the nature of the evildoer, for he is my brother." It is all too easy to become irritated by the stupidity of others, but as Christ says, "why beholdest thou the mote that is in thy brother's eye, but considerest not the beam that is in thine own eye?" Acceptance, patience, and non-judgment are essential to our happiness, for when we judge others, we are criticizing all of Nature, and in doing so we prove ourselves to be deluded, rebellious against the Whole, and therefore worthy of harsh judgment ourselves: "Judge not, that ye be not judged. For with what judgment ye judge, ye shall be judged: and with what measure ye mete, it shall be measured to you again."[1] As Marcus Aurelius teaches, there is nothing more absurd, wretched, and conducive to suffering, than to struggle against the reality of existence, for everything happens out of *necessity*: "A man's soul does violence to itself first of all when it becomes an abscess or tumour on the Universe, so far as it can. For to be vexed at anything that happens is a separation of ourselves from Nature, which contains within it the nature of all its parts." We must realize that "Providence is the source from which all things flow; and beside it there is Necessity, and all that is for the welfare of the whole Universe, of which you are a part. And what the nature of the Whole brings about is good for every part of the whole, and sustains it. The Universe is preserved by the changes of the elements, and so also by the changes of things composed of the elements. Let these principles be enough for you; let them always be fixed in your mind." Likewise, Schopenhauer assures us that "[t]here is nothing that better fits us to endure the misfortunes of life with composure, than to know for certain that *everything that happens—from the smallest up to the greatest facts of existence—happens of necessity.*"

Indeed, where do we even get the notion of criticizing

---

1 Matthew 7:1-2.

Nature? Can there be anything more ludicrous than to question the very basis of our own existence—the universe which, were it any different than it is, could not have created the very minds that now sit and complain about it? The fallacy arises from our imagination, which can picture, rightly or wrongly, a better state of affairs for the human species than the one which currently prevails. Why can't the species be a little more wise, a little less arrogant and stupid? Why is there so much injustice and inequality? Why can't we stop killing one another over competing delusions, or allowing millions of children to starve to death? Why must such an evil and indolent man have so much wealth, and such a good and hard-working family be in poverty? In our idealistic minds, we can certainly imagine things being *better*.

Yet the truth is that we cannot know what is better or worse, and indeed *better* and *worse* are false concepts created by the mind, useful for the most practical concerns—e.g., "this tastes better than that, so I shall eat this"—but completely inapplicable to examining life itself and the nature of existence. Schopenhauer advises, "Whatever fate befalls you, do not give way to great rejoicings or great lamentations; partly because all things are full of change, and your fortune may turn at any moment; partly because men are so apt to be deceived in their judgment as to what is good or bad for them." And *The Bhagavad Gita* teaches that the wise man is "above the pairs of opposites, free from envy, equanimous in success and failure, though he acts, he is not bound."

The wise, therefore, in cultivating acceptance, also develop *equanimity*, reacting the same way to "good" and "bad" events alike. For as it stands we do not even know what is truly in our own best interest, let alone the best interest of others and the Whole. We may certainly lament the death of a loved one, for instance, but we cannot say that the death is an evil or an injustice, particularly if we understand that life is *suffering*, and that to live in this world is not necessarily, from a higher standpoint, a "good" thing; this indeed is the Hindu and Buddhist view, where the goal of Enlightenment is to put an end to the cycle of rebirth into the wretched world of forms.

Krishna tells us that one who possesses equanimity "can neither rejoice on obtaining the pleasant, nor grieve on obtaining the unpleasant—he is steady-minded, undeluded, resting in Brahman." Further, he is "of the same mind to friends and foes, relatives and strangers, the good-hearted, the indifferent, the neutral, the hateful, the righteous, and the unrighteous." When his student, Arjuna, complains of the difficulty of attaining equanimity, "due to the restlessness of the mind," a complaint we can all certainly relate to, Krishna replies, "Doubtless, O Arjuna, the mind is restless and hard to restrain; but by practice, and by detachment, it can be conquered." Hence, equanimity requires not only acceptance, which is the intellectual component, but also restraint of the mind, which requires training, practice, and constant vigilance.

Equanimity means viewing all things as alike, going beyond such distinctions as love and hate, good and bad, friend and foe. "*Give way neither to love nor to hate*, is one-half of worldly wisdom," says Schopenhauer. And as Krishna teaches, "He should be known as a perpetual renouncer who neither hates nor desires: for, free from the pairs of opposites, he is easily set free from bondage." Likewise in *The Dhammapada*: "One must go beyond pleasure and pain: for the absence of what is pleasant brings pain, and the presence of what is painful is unpleasant." Thus, the virtue of equanimity helps free us from attachments; as the instruction continues, "avoid selfish attachment to anything, for its loss will bring pain. They are free who are attached to nothing and averse to nothing." We begin to see the interconnectedness of all the virtues, and how cultivating one will help us develop another; the same, however, applies to vice, and a single weakness in our character threatens to throw our whole being into corruption, just as one who falls into drug addiction might end up becoming a thief and a prostitute as well.

The best way to develop equanimity is to stop viewing things as separate and disconnected. If we can do this, then we can also stop making qualitative distinctions. Judgment and non-acceptance arise from the perspective of separateness, but wisdom teaches us the principle of *dependent arising*, that no part can exist without all the other parts, and that even those things we view as opposed to ourselves are really necessary for our own existence. Thus all judgment and hatred amount to self-judgment and self-hatred.

> He whose self has been made steadfast by yoga, who sees the same thing everywhere, sees the Self abiding in all beings, and all beings abiding in the Self.
> He who sees Me everywhere and sees everything in Me, to him I do not vanish, nor to Me does he vanish.
> Whoever, intent on unity, worships Me who abides in all beings, that yogi dwells in Me, whatever his mode of life.
> Whoever, by comparison with himself, sees the same everywhere, O Arjuna, be it pleasure or pain, he is deemed the highest yogi.[1]

When we properly understand the interconnectedness of all things, we can no longer make value judgments, and so we begin to lose our prejudices as well as our feelings of superiority or inferiority to others. "The marks of a wise man are that he censures no one, praises no one, blames no one, accuses no one; says nothing concerning himself as being anybody, or knowing anything; when he is in any instance hindered or restrained, he accuses himself; and if he is praised, he smiles to himself at the person who praises him; and if he is censured, he makes no defence."[2]

It is certainly true that many of us, particularly those endowed with virtue, are bound to look upon this vicious and unjust world as poorly designed, to say the least, and we may even agree with Schopenhauer when he says that "our whole existence is something which had better not have been." But

---

[1] *The Bhagavad Gita.*
[2] Epictetus.

in the end we simply cannot know *why* things are the way they are, and to put our own paltry minds against the Infinite Wisdom is absurd and even insane. We must have faith in the order and ultimate goodness—or at least correctness—of the universe, and resign ourselves to never knowing the fundamental *why* behind it all. (This *why* can never be known intellectually, though an enlightened person may come to understand the truth by intuition.) To achieve happiness, then, it is essential that we rid ourselves of deluded expectations—or any expectations at all; otherwise our lives are sure to be an endless series of shocks and disappointments. "Demand not that events should happen as you wish," Epictetus says; "but wish them to happen as they do happen, and you will go on well."

Ridding Ourselves of Expectations

Our expectations that life should be a certain way, that we are entitled to certain pleasures and enjoyments, is the illusion behind what we call our *disillusionment*. Most of us recognize this gradual awareness that creeps into our lives as we progress deeper into society, the awareness that life is not at all what we thought it would be. Hollywood films, TV shows, even our education systems, reinforce our romantic delusions and make us believe we are entitled to lives of glamour and excitement, or at least fulfilling careers and interesting social lives, and that even the tragedies we experience ought to be profound and meaningful. If our reality is not living up to our imagined ideal, we feel we must be doing something wrong, that there must be something defective in ourselves, and this belief only makes our situation worse. Another problem is that many of us fail to see through the feigned happiness of others—an illusion that is easy to produce in the age of social media—and so we falsely believe that everyone around us is happy except ourselves. Since, in a way, we are all competing for happiness, most of us are unwilling to admit we are not happy, and we go out of our way to make our lives appear much more interesting and exciting than we believe they are: we compile pictures of joyful nights on the town, exotic travels, and happy moments with family and friends (many of whom we often cannot stand in real life), and naturally we leave undocumented our many hours of confusion, boredom, and despair. We know we are creating this illusion, and we suspect others are doing the same, yet we cannot shake the fear that others might *really* be happy and that we are missing out on something essential in life. We are not.

Schopenhauer describes this almost universal phenomenon of disillusionment:

> A careless youth may think that the world is meant to be enjoyed, as though it were the abode of some real or positive happiness, which only those fail to attain who are not clever enough to overcome the difficulties that lie in the way. This false notion takes a stronger hold on him when he comes to read poetry and romance, and to be deceived by outward show—the hypocrisy that characterizes the world from beginning to end; on which I shall have something to say presently. The result is that his life is the more or less deliberate pursuit of positive happiness; and happiness he takes to be equivalent to a series of definite pleasures. In seeking for these pleasures he encounters danger—a fact which should not be forgotten. He hunts for game that does not exist; and so he ends by suffering some very real and positive misfortune—pain, distress, sickness, loss, care, poverty, shame, and all the thousand ills of life. Too late he discovers the trick that has been played upon him. . . .
>
> So it is that the young man is generally dissatisfied with the position in which he finds himself, whatever it may be; he ascribes his disappointment solely to the

state of things that meets him on his first introduction to life, when he had expected something very different; whereas it is only the vanity and wretchedness of human life everywhere that he is now for the first time experiencing.

It would be a great advantage to a young man if his early training could eradicate the idea that the world has a great deal to offer him. But the usual result of education is to strengthen this delusion; and our first ideas of life are generally taken from fiction rather than from fact.

In the bright dawn of our youthful days, the poetry of life spreads out a gorgeous vision before us, and we torture ourselves by longing to see it realized. We might as well wish to grasp the rainbow! The youth expects his career to be like an interesting romance; and there lies the germ of that disappointment which I have been describing. What lends a charm to all these visions is just the fact that they are visionary and not real, and that in contemplating them we are in the sphere of pure knowledge, which is sufficient in itself and free from the noise and struggle of life. To try and realize those visions is to make them an object of *will*—a process which always involves pain.

Nothing but life itself can prepare us for the mundane reality of life, the banality and absurdity that characterize our careers and our social existence. Yet by the time we come to accept this reality, we have probably made many irreversible mistakes as a result of our deluded beliefs. The sooner we break these delusions the better. Rather than inflicting lies on our children in the form of vacuous and unrealistic films and stories, rather than instilling in them an ineradicable longing for magic and adventure that can never be fulfilled in real life, we ought to expose them to materials that awaken their self-knowledge and their understanding of the world. As for ourselves, we must accept the truth once and for all: the human condition is suffering; pain is the default state, and pleasure is, for the most part, only the temporary alleviating of pain: "after some little time, we learn by experience that happiness and pleasure are a *fata morgana*, which, visible from afar, vanish as we approach; that, on the other hand, suffering and pain are a reality, which makes its presence felt without any intermediary, and for its effect, stands in no need of illusion or the play of false hope."[1] As such, the pursuit of happiness entails not the pursuit of a steady and uninterrupted stream of pleasures, but the avoidance of unnecessary pain. We should "direct our aim, not toward securing what is pleasurable and agreeable in life, but toward avoiding, as far as possible, its innumerable evils."[2] If we adopt a plan of life "which proceeds by avoiding pain—in other words, by taking measures of precaution against want, sickness, and distress in all its forms—the aim is a real one, and something may be achieved which will be great in proportion as the plan is not disturbed by striving after the chimera of positive happiness."[3]

In ridding ourselves of false expectations about the world, we stop expecting people to act a certain way, and we come to accept them as they are. One of the dangers of developing virtue is that we unconsciously begin to expect goodness and virtue from others; and the wiser we become, the more the ignorance and wickedness of others becomes unfathomable to us. Yet with acceptance, equanimity, an understanding of the unity of all things, and freedom from false expectations, we lay the groundwork for that most necessary of virtues, *forgiveness*.

---

1 Schopenhauer.
2 *Ibid.*
3 *Ibid.*

INTRODUCTION

Forgiveness and Doing No Harm

When we truly accept the Whole and all its parts as they are, we come to develop *forgiveness*; and when we deny our self-interest and put our faith in Nature, we cultivate the ethic of *doing no harm*. These two virtues are embodied by all the great spiritual leaders, and especially Christ. Paradoxically, when we are prepared to submit ourselves to any suffering at the hands of Nature and our fellow-men, while refraining from inflicting any harm ourselves, we actually suffer less than those who seek to avoid suffering and aggressively defend their "rights." For suffering is entirely in the mind, and when we resign to it, knowing that one way or another, sooner or later, it will befall us, then we cease to struggle against it, and we commit no action against our own principles merely for the sake of protecting ourselves from harm. Surely we must avoid harm when we can, but must not do so by inflicting it ourselves. For "it is better to receive an injury than to do one," says Cicero. Epicurus asserts that a "happy and eternal being has no trouble himself and brings no trouble upon any other being; and so he is free from anger and partiality, for these imply weakness." The Dhammapada instructs, "No one should attack a Brahmin, but no Brahmin, if attacked, should let himself fly at his aggressor! Woe to him who strikes a Brahmin, but more woe to him who flies at his aggressor!" And of course this is one of the essential teachings of Christianity (as well as one of the most ignored: see Tolstoy's essay *The Kingdom of God is Within You* for a powerful argument against the hypocrisy of the Church in this regard):

> Ye have heard that it hath been said, An
>   eye for an eye, and a tooth for a tooth:
> But I say unto you, That ye resist not evil:
>   but whosoever shall smite thee on thy
>   right cheek, turn to him the other also.
> And if any man will sue thee at the law,
>   and take away thy coat, let him have
>   thy cloak also.

> And whosoever shall compel thee to go a
> mile, go with him twain.
> Give to him that asketh thee, and from
> him that would borrow of thee turn not
> thou away.
> Ye have heard that it hath been said, Thou
> shalt love thy neighbour, and hate thine
> enemy.
> But I say unto you, Love your enemies,
> bless them that curse you, do good
> to them that hate you, and pray for
> them which despitefully use you, and
> persecute you;
> That ye may be the children of your
> Father which is in heaven: for he
> maketh his sun to rise on the evil and
> on the good, and sendeth rain on the
> just and on the unjust.
> For if ye love them which love you, what
> reward have ye? do not even the
> publicans the same?
> And if ye salute your brethren only, what
> do ye more than others? do not even
> the publicans so?
> Be ye therefore perfect, even as your
> Father which is in heaven is perfect.[1]

We are going to die anyway, and for the wise, the length of life is less important than the manner in which it is lived.

In truth, the ultimate virtue is not really forgiveness, because we should not be feeling injured in the first place, and so there should be nothing to forgive. The best way to free ourselves from blame, judgment, and enmity is to lose the belief that we have been wronged. Marcus Aurelius advises, "Put away your opinion, and then is taken away the complaint, 'I have been harmed.' Take away the complaint, 'I have been harmed,' and the harm is taken away." Likewise in *The Dhammapada*, "'He abused me, he beat me, he defeated me, he robbed me.'

---

[1] Matthew 5:38-48.

In those who harbour such thoughts hatred will never cease. 'He abused me, he beat me, he defeated me, he robbed me.' In those who do not harbour such thoughts hatred will cease." Let us remember that men and nature cannot live up to our ideals, which in the end are meaningless fancies; indeed, we can rarely live up to them ourselves. Forgiveness rids us of the bias and hypocrisy of our subjective view and reminds us that we are all One under God, or if we prefer, we are all parts of the same Whole. For often, what we hate in others is what we hate in ourselves. "For if ye forgive men their trespasses, your heavenly Father will also forgive you: But if ye forgive not men their trespasses, neither will your Father forgive your trespasses."[1] Such is the nature of *karma:* when we judge, we are judged; when we hate, we are hated; when we inspire fear in others, we live in fear ourselves; and all our evil thoughts and acts come back to us sooner or later in some way.

Karma

The Dhammapada instructs us about the nature of *karma*: "All that we are is the result of what we have thought: it is founded on our thoughts, it is made up of our thoughts. If a man speaks or acts with an evil thought, pain follows him, as the wheel follows the foot of the ox that draws the carriage." So says Socrates: "For thus that author of philosophy argued: that as the disposition of a man's mind is, so is the man; such as the man is, such will be his discourse; his actions will correspond with his discourse, and his life with his actions. But the disposition of a good man's mind is laudable; the life, therefore, of a good man is laudable; it is honourable, therefore, because laudable; the unavoidable conclusion from which is that the life of good men is happy."[2] Indeed, although we generally associate *karma* with Hinduism and Buddhism, the principle can also be found in almost all the great wisdom

---

[1] Matthew 6:14-15.
[2] Cicero.

of the West. Christ teaches that "every good tree bringeth forth good fruit; but a corrupt tree bringeth forth evil fruit. A good tree cannot bring forth evil fruit, neither can a corrupt tree bring forth good fruit." And, of course, the Golden Rule, which appears in some form in all major religions, states: "Therefore all things whatsoever ye would that men should do to you, do ye even so to them: for this is the law and the prophets."[1]

Epicurus explains why we necessarily suffer when we commit unjust acts, as we are immediately assailed by the pangs of fear and conscience, which cause us great suffering (sociopaths, however, have no conscience or empathy, and therefore suffer in another, much more severe way, in that they are deprived of any genuine human connection): "It is impossible for a man who secretly violates any article of the social agreement to feel confident that he will remain undiscovered, even if he has already escaped ten thousand times; for right on to the end of his life he is never sure that he will not be detected." Hence our evil acts engender evil thoughts of fear and self-loathing that lead to suffering (assuming we have a conscience); and, of course, these evil thoughts lead to more evil actions, causing a vicious cycle that can only be broken by self-awareness and striving for virtue.

As we learned, evil acts are those that are unnecessary, selfish, or against our true nature. By simply following right action in accordance with our dharma, and devoting ourselves to selfless service, we can begin to free ourselves from the karmic cycle of suffering. Of course, this is easier said than done. For there is one human weakness that is perhaps the most ingrained in our constitution, the most amenable to exaggeration and excess, and the most responsible for leading us into evil. This single vice is at the root of most of the others; and as a drug addict who wants to become healthy must first and foremost be cured of his addiction, so must we first eradicate, or at least severely restrict, our *desire*.

---

[1] Matthew 7:12.

INTRODUCTION

Limiting Our Desires and Aversions

> *Arjuna:*
> But what is the force, O Krishna, that drags a man, though reluctant, to commit sin?
> *Krishna:*
> It is desire, it is wrath, born of the energy of *rajas*—all-devouring, all sinful; that, Arjuna, is the foe here.[1]

If we allow our desires to go unchecked, if we let them stretch out far beyond necessity and into the endless region of fancy, perpetual dissatisfaction will be our lot. "You may be sure," says Seneca, "there is a succession in our desires; for one begins where its predecessor ends. You have been thrust into an existence which will never of itself put an end to your wretchedness and slavery. Withdraw your chafed neck from the yoke; it is better that it should be cut off once for all, than galled forever."[2] While the "wealth required by nature is at once limited and easy to procure," Epicurus says, "the wealth demanded by vain fancies extends an infinite distance." We must therefore set some limit on our desires and our *will*; but where we put this limit depends upon our knowing what is necessary and what is not.

Epicurus explains this difference between necessary and unnecessary desires: "Of our desires some are natural and necessary; others are natural, but not necessary; and others are neither natural nor necessary, but are due to illusory opinion. Those natural desires which entail no pain when not gratified, though their objects are vehemently pursued, are also due to illusory opinion; and when they are not gotten rid of, it is not because of their own nature, but because of the person's illusory opinion." Also, "[a]ll desires that lead to no pain when they remain ungratified are unnecessary, and the longing is

---

[1] The Bhagavad Gita.
[2] Seneca, *Epistles* XIX. Not included in this collection, but available in the Great Minds book *On Solitude*.

easily got rid of, when the thing desired is difficult to procure or when the desires seem likely to produce harm." Wisdom teaches us that our necessary desires are easy to attain, and that most of our suffering arises from our greed for excess: "He who understands the limits of life knows how easy it is to procure enough to remove the pain of want and make the whole of life complete and perfect. Hence he no longer has any need of things that can only be won by struggle and conflict." Similarly, Montaigne says, "The laws of Nature teach us exactly what we need. After the sages have told us that no one is indigent according to Nature, and that everyone is so according to opinion, they very subtly distinguish between the desires that come from her and those that come from the disorder of our own fancy: those of which we can see the end are hers; those that fly before us, and of which we can see no end, are our own. Poverty of material goods is easily cured; poverty of the soul is irreparable."

Aristotle draws a distinction between the pleasures that are only *incidentally pleasant*—those that relieve pain or satisfy our appetite, and that cease to be pleasant when we are in our settled state—and the pleasures that are *pleasant without qualification*—those that involve no pain or appetite, e.g. the pleasure of contemplation." Schopenhauer argues that we must impose limits even on these higher pleasures:

> But even in the affairs of the intellect, limitation is necessary if we are to be happy. For the less the will is excited, the less we suffer. We have seen that suffering is something positive, and that happiness is only a negative condition. To limit the sphere of outward activity is to relieve the will of external stimulus: to limit the sphere of our intellectual efforts is to relieve the will of internal sources of excitement. This latter kind of limitation is attended by the disadvantage that it opens the door to boredom, which is a direct source of countless sufferings; for to

> banish boredom, a man will have recourse
> to any means that may be handy—dissipa-
> tion, society, extravagance, gaming, and
> drinking, and the like, which in their turn
> bring mischief, ruin, and misery in their
> train.

Aristotle explains that this same need for moderation applies to our willingness to endure pain, and that we are greedy if we want to avoid pain altogether: "Now, *there can be too much of bodily goods, and the low and evil man is so by virtue of pursuing the excess, not by virtue of pursuing the necessary pleasures* (for all men enjoy in some way or other good foods, wines, and sexual intercourse, but not all men do so in the right manner or degree). But his relation to Pain is exactly the contrary: it is not excessive Pain, but *Pain at all*, that he avoids (which makes him to be in this way too a low and evil man)."

We must note that it is not only material goods or sensual pleasure that can be pursued to excess; our desire for honours, experiences, diversion, and even friendship can be equally insatiable: "it is advisable to put very moderate limits upon our expectations of pleasure, possessions, rank, honour and so on; because it is just this striving and struggling to be happy, to dazzle the world, to lead a life full of pleasure, which entail great misfortune."[1] Expecting too much from life, a habit arising from delusion and fantasy, is a major cause of our suffering. A materialistic society is bad enough, but one that extols the virtues of status and fame drives many of us toward an endless pursuit of ideals that we can never attain and that may not even exist. As Hamlet's friends advise him, if the world is a prison to us, it is our ambition that makes it one; our dreams cause our dissatisfaction, "[w]hich dreams indeed are ambition, for the very substance of the ambitious is merely the shadow of a dream."[2] And since a "dream itself is but a shadow," ambition is "so airy and light a quality that

---

1 Schopenhauer.
2 Hamlet, II, ii.

it is but a shadow's shadow." Those of us who are dazzled and entertained by these shadows yearn to be up there on the wall of the cave, part of the show. But the show is nothing, a mere illusion, and the more we strive for it, the more we become alienated from our real selves and from the light of truth. It is not merely that we expect too much from life, but that we expect the wrong things, or things that do not really exist, and only those who reach the mirage ever learn that there was nothing there in the first place. This would be a tolerable condition, were it not that the disappearance of one mirage coincides with the appearance of a new one in the distance; so we continue our hopeless and lifelong path toward *nothing*, always longing, always dissatisfied. "Limitations," on the other hand, "always make for happiness. We are happy in proportion as our range of vision, our sphere of work, our points of contact with the world, are restricted and circumscribed. We are more likely to feel worried and anxious if these limits are wide; for it means that our cares, desires and terrors are increased and intensified."[1] Marcus Aurelius says the same: "Occupy yourself with few things . . . if you wish to be happy."

The appeal to renounce desire may confuse us, since if we are not living to satisfy our desires, then what are we living for? "To what then should we devote our serious pains?" asks Marcus Aurelius. "Only this: just thoughts, unselfish acts, words that never lie, and a disposition that gladly accepts all that happens as something necessary, expected, and flowing from the One origin and source." We need not worry that if we give up our desires, we will have no reason to act. *The Bhagavad Gita* teaches us that "action comes from Brahman, and that Brahman comes from the Imperishable. Therefore, the all-pervading Brahman is ever-present in *selfless action*."

---

[1] Schopenhauer.

INTRODUCTION

Being in the Present

One way to free ourselves from desire is to be *present*. "For as folly, even when possessed of what it desires, never thinks it has acquired enough, so wisdom is always satisfied with the present, and never repents on her own account."[1] Our dissatisfaction with the present moment arises in part from our hopes for a "better" future, and this habit causes life to feel like an endless burden that must be overcome for the sake of that distant mirage.

> We do not rest satisfied with the present. We anticipate the future as too slow in coming, as if in order to hasten its course; or we recall the past, to stop its too rapid flight. So imprudent are we that we wander in the times which are not ours, and do not think of the only one which belongs to us; and so idle are we that we dream of those times which are no more, and thoughtlessly overlook that which alone exists. For the present is generally painful to us. We conceal it from our sight, because it troubles us; and if it be delightful to us, we regret to see it pass away. We try to sustain it by the future, and think of arranging matters which are not in our power, for a time which we have no certainty of reaching.
>
> Let each one examine his thoughts, and he will find them all occupied with the past and the future. We scarcely ever think of the present; and if we think of it, it is only to take light from it to arrange the future. The present is never our end. The past and the present are our means; the future alone is our end. So we never live, but we hope to live; and, as we are always preparing to

---

[1] Cicero.

be happy, it is inevitable we should never be so.¹

Schopenhauer as usual says the same thing in a more dramatic and humorous way:

> Those who strive and hope and live only in the future, always looking ahead and impatiently anticipating what is coming, as something which will make them happy when they get it, are, in spite of their very clever airs, exactly like those donkeys one sees in Italy, whose pace may be hurried by fixing a stick on their heads with a wisp of hay at the end of it; this is always just in front of them, and they keep on trying to get it. Such people are in a constant state of illusion as to their whole existence; they go on living *ad interim*, until at last they die."

The importance of being present, and freeing ourselves from concern for the future or the past, is widely known, and yet it is an idea that is broadly misunderstood. The unwise use it as a license for mindless debauchery, and employ such catch-phrases as "you only live once" to justify all manner of self-destructive behaviour and to neglect any thought for the future consequences of their actions. "Pleasure-lovers spend every night amid false-glittering joys, and just as if it were their last."² Confusion also arises between the spiritual and practical meanings of "living in the present." Being present does not mean we do not contemplate the future or make plans, nor does it mean we forget our past, ignore our memories, or avoid gleaning lessons from our previous actions: it means that we do all these things while being *present*, without *losing ourselves* in the past and future, and making them more real than they are. Naturally, all our contemplations, whether fixed on the past, the future, the nature of man, the universe,

1 Pascal.
2 Seneca.

or our creative work, are occurring in the *present*—where else could they occur? But we can contemplate these things *mindfully*, without attachment, in which case we are being present; or we can contemplate them *mindlessly*, with attachment, in which case we fall into delusion. The author of a work of fiction may at times lose himself in his work, yet still be present, because he is present in his work: but if he were to become truly anxious about the affairs of his fictional characters—if, for instance, the death of a character he created caused him to mourn and sink into depression, then he would be verging on madness. Similarly, the less we believe the voices and images in our head as being anything *real*, besides being real as voices and images in our head, the more we become present; conversely, the more we believe these voices and images as being something other than our own creations, with an external reality of their own, the more we become deluded, and in extreme cases, psychotic. To be present does not mean to be imprudent. And when we are mindful in the present, we consider the potential consequences of our actions, we remember the consequences of similar actions in the past, and we act according to a lifetime of accumulated wisdom.

In short, we can know we are in the present if we are free from suffering even as we consider the future and the past. Being present frees us from unnecessary desire, aversion, hatred, and all the other vices that produce suffering. Even our most significant fears, of sickness and death, vanish in the eternity of the present moment, when we realize there is no such thing as a "length" or "duration" of life, but only this moment. "Throwing away then all things, hold to these few truths. Remember that man lives only in the present, which is an indivisible point, and that all the rest of his life is either past or is uncertain. Short then is the time which every man lives, and small the nook of the earth where he lives."[1]

---

[1] Marcus Aurelius.

INTRODUCTION

Why People Cannot Find Happiness

As harsh as it may sound, the reason why the vast majority of human beings cannot attain true happiness is because of their ignorance and delusion. Not everyone can be happy. The tyrant will almost always remain a tyrant, for not only is he incapable of change, but he generally does not *want* to change, does not believe he *should* change, and does not even understand what the happiness we are discussing really *is*: he understands only pleasure, and in his arrogance, he denies there is any happiness other than the gratification of his base urges. Indeed, the most wretched people will not even realize they are wretched—a condition Kierkegaard calls the despair that does not know it is despair. As Seneca explains, "he who does not know that he has sinned does not desire correction; you must discover yourself in the wrong before you can reform yourself. Some boast of their faults. Do you think that the man has any thought of mending his ways who counts over his vices as if they were virtues?"

We can seek to fulfil our nature, but we cannot change our nature itself. "Hence a man's intellectual as well as his moral qualities proceed from the depths of his own nature," says Schopenhauer, "and are not the result of external influences; and no educational scheme . . . can turn a born simpleton into a man of sense. The thing is impossible! He was born a simpleton, and a simpleton he will die." And Cicero assures us that virtue, the prerequisite of happiness, "is not easily connected with dull minds." Hence "the mass of mankind are plainly quite slavish in their tastes, choosing a life like that of brute animals," says Aristotle.

Our ignorance is compounded by our arrogance and pride, which prevent us from profiting from the wisdom of those who have gone before us. "Every generation, no matter how paltry its character, thinks itself much wiser than the one immediately preceding it, let alone those that are more remote. It is just the same with the different periods in a man's life; and yet often, in the one case no less than in the other, it is a mistaken opinion."[1] And most of us believe our own view is right: "if you examine the three classes of men, and ask of them in turn which of their lives is pleasantest, each will be found praising his own and depreciating that of others: the money-maker will contrast the vanity of honour or of learning, if they bring no money, with the solid advantages of gold and silver."[2] Plato's Socrates rightly concludes, however, that only the wise are qualified to judge which life is the best, because only they have experienced all three pleasures (honour, sensual pleasure, and intellectual pleasure) and are in a position to compare them. The others do not know the happiness of the wise, and can think of happiness only in terms of their own modulating pleasures:

> Those, then, who do not know wisdom and virtue, and are always busy with gluttony and sensuality, go down and up again as far as the mean; and in this region they move at random throughout their life, but they never pass into the true upper world. They neither look upward, nor do they ever find their way—they are neither filled with true being, nor do they taste pure and abiding pleasure. Like cattle, with their eyes always looking down and their heads stooping to the earth—that is, to the dining-table—they fatten and feed and breed, and, in their excessive love of these delights, they kick and butt one another with horns and hoofs made of iron; and they kill one another by reason of their insatiable lust. For they fill themselves with that which is not substantial, and the part of themselves which they fill is also insubstantial and incontinent.[3]

---

1 Schopenhauer.
2 Plato.
3 Plato.

Seneca describes such types in similar terms:

> All men of this stamp, I maintain, are pressing on in pursuit of joy, but they do not know where they may obtain a joy that is both great and enduring. One person seeks it in feasting and self-indulgence; another, in canvassing for honours and in being surrounded by a throng of clients; another, in his mistress; another, in idle display of culture and in literature that has no power to heal; all these men are led astray by delights which are deceptive and short-lived—like drunkenness for example, which pays for a single hour of hilarious madness by a sickness of many days, or like applause and the popularity of enthusiastic approval which are gained, and atoned for, at the cost of great mental disquietude.

Those on the path to wisdom may ask, along with Seneca, "why is it that folly holds us with such an insistent grasp?"

> It is, primarily, because we do not combat it strongly enough, because we do not struggle towards salvation with all our might; secondly, because we do not put sufficient trust in the discoveries of the wise, and do not drink in their words with open hearts; we approach this great problem in too trifling a spirit. But how can a man learn, in the struggle against his vices, an amount that is enough, if the time which he gives to learning is only the amount left over from his vices?
>
> None of us goes deep below the surface. We skim the top only, and we regard the smattering of time spent in the search for wisdom as enough and to spare for a busy man. What hinders us most of all is that

> we are too readily satisfied with ourselves; if we meet with someone who calls us good men, or sensible men, or holy men, we see ourselves in his description, not content with praise in moderation, we accept everything that shameless flattery heaps upon us, as if it were our due. We agree with those who declare us to be the best and wisest of men, although we know that they are given to much lying. And we are so self-complacent that we desire praise for certain actions when we are especially addicted to the very opposite. Yonder person hears himself called "most gentle" when he is inflicting tortures, or "most generous" when he is engaged in looting, or "most temperate" when he is in the midst of drunkenness and lust. Thus it follows that we are unwilling to be reformed, just because we believe ourselves to be the best of men."[1]

Aristotle describes the common man's immaturity and inability to attain wisdom:

> Hence a young man is not a fit student of Moral Philosophy, for he is inexperienced in the actions that occur in life, though the discussions of Moral Philosophy start from these and are about these; and, further, since he tends to follow his passions, he will hear as though he heard not, and his study will be vain and unprofitable, because the end aimed at is not knowledge but *action*.[2] And it makes no difference whether he is young in years or young in temper and disposition; the

---

1 Seneca.

2 Yet, according to the Gita, the end of all action is wisdom; so the problem is not that the immature man pursues action, but *wrong action*.

> defect does not depend on time, but on his living at the beck and call of passion, and following each object as it arises. For to such persons, as to those who lack self-control, knowledge brings no profit; but, to those who form their desires and act in accordance with reason, knowledge of such matters will be of great benefit.

Similarly, Christ says, "By hearing ye shall hear, and shall not understand; and seeing ye shall see, and shall not perceive: For this people's heart is waxed gross, and their ears are dull of hearing, and their eyes they have closed." And further, "He also that received seed among the thorns is he that heareth the word; and the care of this world, and the deceitfulness of riches, choke the word, and he becometh unfruitful. But he that received seed into the good ground is he that heareth the word, and understandeth it; which also beareth fruit, and bringeth forth, some an hundredfold, some sixty, some thirty." He asks, "Why do ye not understand my speech?" It is because of our wilful denial and dishonesty with ourselves: "Ye are of your father the devil, and the lusts of your father ye will do. He was a murderer from the beginning, and abode not in the truth, because there is no truth in him. When he speaketh a lie, he speaketh of his own: for he is a liar, and the father of it. And because I tell you the truth, ye believe me not." Similarly, *The Dhammapada* warns, "The deluded, who see truth in untruth, and see untruth in truth, never arrive at truth, but follow vain desires." And *The Bhagavad Gita:*

> As fire is surrounded by smoke, as a mirror by rust, as the foetus is enclosed in the womb, so is knowledge covered by passion.
>
> Wisdom is covered, O Arjuna, by this constant enemy of the wise—*desire*—which is greedy and insatiable.
>
> The senses, mind, and reason are said to be its seat; veiling wisdom through these,

desire deludes the understanding.

Those of us who have it in our nature to seek wisdom and happiness, who are compelled by that inner drive toward virtue, must be careful not to allow ourselves to be ruined by the influence of the wretched majority. Seneca advises,

> You should avoid conversation with all such persons: they are the sort that communicate and engraft their bad habits from one to another. We used to think that the very worst variety of these men were those who vaunted their words; but there are certain men who vaunt their wickedness. Their talk is very harmful; for even though it is not at once convincing, yet they leave the seeds of trouble in the soul, and the evil which is sure to spring into new strength follows us about even when we have parted from them. Just as those who have attended a concert carry about in their heads the melodies and the charm of the songs they have heard—a proceeding which interferes with their thinking and does not allow them to concentrate upon serious subjects—even so the speech of flatterers and enthusiasts over that which is depraved sticks in our minds long after we have heard them talk. It is not easy to rid the memory of a catching tune; it stays with us, lasts on, and comes back from time to time. Accordingly, you should close your ears against evil talk, and right at the outset, too; for when such talk has gained an entrance and the words are admitted and are in our minds, they become more shameless. And then we begin to speak as follows: "Virtue, Philosophy, Justice—this is a jargon of empty words. The only way to be happy is to do yourself well. To eat, drink, and spend your money is the only

real life, the only way to remind yourself that you are mortal."

Likewise, *The Dhammapada* says, "if a man does not see fools, he will be truly happy. He who walks in the company of fools suffers a long way; company with fools, as with an enemy, is always painful; company with the wise is a pleasure, like meeting with one's true family." We should also avoid looking to the common people for guidance on how to live: just because the majority hold certain values and live a certain way does not mean they are right, and still less does it mean the such a way is right for us. "There are things which, if done by the few, we should refuse to imitate; yet when the majority have begun to do them, we follow along—as if anything were more honourable just because it is more frequent! Furthermore, wrong views, when they have become prevalent, reach, in our eyes, the standard of righteousness."[1] Marcus Aurelius concurs: "He avoids much trouble who does not look to see what his neighbour says or does or thinks, but only to what he does himself, that it may be pure and just; or, as Agathon says, look not around at the depraved morals of others, but run straight along the line without deviating from it." The bad influence of cultural diversions can be particularly dangerous:

> All great diversions are dangerous to the Christian life; but among all those which the world has invented there is none more to be feared than the theatre. It is a representation of the passions so natural and so delicate that it excites them and gives birth to them in our hearts, and, above all, to that of love, principally when it is represented as very chaste and virtuous. For the more innocent it appears to innocent souls, the more they are likely to be touched by it. Its violence pleases our self-love, which immediately forms a desire to produce

[1] Seneca.

> the same effects which are seen so well represented; and, at the same time, we make ourselves a conscience founded on the propriety of the feelings which we see there, by which the fear of pure souls is removed, since they imagine that it cannot hurt their purity to love with a love which seems to them so reasonable.
>
> So we depart from the theatre with our heart so filled with all the beauty and tenderness of love, the soul and the mind so persuaded of its innocence, that we are quite ready to receive its first impressions, or rather to seek an opportunity of awakening them in the heart of another, in order that we may receive the same pleasures and the same sacrifices which we have seen so well represented in the theatre.

Finally, those of us who seek true happiness through virtue and wisdom must be prepared to meet with much opposition from those around us, even our family and friends, who may misunderstand our actions and even be threatened by them. For there is nothing more dangerous than to attack another's worldview, whether explicitly through our words, or implicitly in the way we live. Much of the "advice" we will receive along the way will be the advice-giver's attempt to justify his own life, and if we are wise enough to see that he is deceiving us, we must be still wiser and forgive his attempt to lead us astray, for above all he is deceiving himself.

> If you have an earnest desire towards philosophy, prepare yourself from the very first to have the multitude laugh and sneer, and say, "He is returned to us a philosopher all at once," and "Where does he get this supercilious look?" Now for your part, do not have a supercilious look indeed; but keep steadily to those things which appear best to you, as one appointed by God to

> this particular station. For remember that,
> if you are persistent, those very persons
> who at first ridiculed, will afterwards
> admire you. But if you are conquered by
> them, you will incur a double ridicule.

We must not allow such ridicule and opposition to stand in our way. However, since we face a real danger of incurring enmity or being negatively influenced by the zealously unwise, it is best that we keep our pursuit of wisdom and happiness strictly to ourselves.

Keeping Our Wisdom, Virtue, and Happiness to Ourselves

"Never proclaim yourself a philosopher," says Epictetus; "nor make much talk among the ignorant about your principles, but show them by actions. Thus, at an entertainment, do not talk about how people ought to eat; but eat as you ought. For remember that in this way Socrates too avoided all ostentation. And when persons came to him, and desired to be introduced by him to other philosophers, he took them and introduced them: so well did he bear being overlooked. So if ever there should be among the ignorant any discussion of principles, be for the most part silent. For there is great danger in hastily throwing out what is undigested. And if anyone tells you that you know nothing, and you are not nettled at it, then you may be sure that you have really entered on your work."

Seneca advises, "There is no need to fasten a placard upon yourself with the words: 'Philosopher and Quietist.' Give your purpose some other name."[1] He adds, your "philosophy must never be vaunted by you; for philosophy when employed with insolence and arrogance has been perilous to many. Let [philosophy] strip off your faults, rather than assist you to decry the faults of others." Christ, too, warns us not to flaunt

---

1 Seneca, *Epistles* LXVIII. Not included in this collection, but available in the Great Minds book *On Solitude*.

our virtue in public:

> Take heed that ye do not your alms before men, to be seen of them: otherwise ye have no reward of your Father which is in heaven. Therefore when thou doest thine alms, do not sound a trumpet before thee, as the hypocrites do in the synagogues and in the streets, that they may have glory of men. Verily I say unto you, They have their reward. But when thou doest alms, let not thy left hand know what thy right hand doeth:
>
> That thine alms may be in secret: and thy Father which seeth in secret himself shall reward thee openly.
>
> And when thou prayest, thou shalt not be as the hypocrites are: for they love to pray standing in the synagogues and in the corners of the streets, that they may be seen of men. Verily I say unto you, They have their reward.

Further, "Give not that which is holy unto the dogs, neither cast ye your pearls before swine, lest they trample them under their feet, and turn again and rend you." *The Bhagavad Gita* likewise says, "He who knows the All should not unsettle the unwise who know not the All," and, "This which has been taught to you is never to be taught to one who is devoid of self-control, nor to one who is not devoted, nor to one who does not do service, nor to one who speaks ill of Me." And Schopenhauer goes on at some length about the treatment that intellect and wisdom receive in society, and the importance of protecting ourselves from envy and hostility:

> To show your intelligence and discernment is only an indirect way of reproaching other people for being dull and incapable. And besides, it is natural for a vulgar man to be violently agitated by the

sight of opposition in any form; and in this case envy comes in as the secret cause of his hostility. For it is a matter of daily observation that people take the greatest pleasure in that which satisfies their vanity; and vanity cannot be satisfied without comparison with others. Now, there is nothing of which a man is prouder than of intellectual ability, for it is this that gives him his commanding place in the animal world. It is an exceedingly rash thing to let anyone see that you are decidedly superior to him in this respect, and to let other people see it too; because he will then thirst for vengeance, and generally look about for an opportunity of taking it by means of insult, because this is to pass from the sphere of *intellect* to that of *will*—and there, all are on an equal footing as regards the feeling of hostility. Hence, while rank and riches may always reckon upon deferential treatment in society, that is something which intellectual ability can never expect; to be ignored is the greatest favour shown to it; and if people notice it at all, it is because they regard it as a piece of impertinence, or else as something to which its possessor has no legitimate right, and upon which he dares to pride himself; and in retaliation and revenge for his conduct, people secretly try and humiliate him in some other way; and if they wait to do this, it is only for a fitting opportunity. A man may be as humble as possible in his demeanour, and yet hardly ever get people to overlook his crime in standing intellectually above them. In the *Garden of Roses*, Sadi makes the remark, "You should know that foolish people are a hundredfold more averse to meeting the wise than the wise are indisposed to the company of the foolish."

"Intellectual superiority offends by its very existence," says Schopenhauer, "without any desire to do so." We must keep in mind, however, that it is just as important to protect ourselves from our own pride as the pride of others; and that even if one is intellectually superior in some respects (for there are many kinds of intelligence), this does not imply an overall, objective superiority, for there is no such thing. Epictetus reminds us, "These reasonings have no logical connection: 'I am richer than you, therefore I am your superior;' 'I am more eloquent than you, therefore I am your superior.' The true logical connection is rather this: 'I am richer than you, therefore my possessions exceed yours;' 'I am more eloquent than you, therefore my style surpasses yours.' But you, after all, consist neither in property nor in style." We must recall our equanimity: as *The Bhagavad Gita* says, "One endued with wisdom and humility sees the same Self in the wise and the ignorant, in a cow, in an elephant, as also in a dog and in a dog-eater."

In general, it is wise to keep one's affairs to oneself as much as possible, and to never meddle in the disputes of others. Schopenhauer advises,

> You should regard all your private affairs as secrets, and, in respect of them, treat your acquaintances, even though you are on good terms with them, as perfect strangers, letting them know nothing more than they can see for themselves. For in course of time, and under altered circumstances, you may find it a disadvantage that they know even the most harmless things about you.
>
> And, as a general rule, it is more advisable to show your intelligence by saying nothing than by speaking out; for silence is a matter of prudence, while speech has something in it of vanity. The opportuni-

> ties for displaying the one or the other quality occur equally often; but the fleeting satisfaction afforded by speech is often preferred to the permanent advantage secured by silence.

Nor should we offer our opinions unless they are solicited from us, and even then, we must proceed carefully. It is enough to want to change ourselves without wanting to change the minds and characters of others.

> Never combat any man's opinion; for though you reached the age of Methuselah, you would never have done setting him right upon all the absurd things that he believes.
>
> It is also well to avoid correcting people's mistakes in conversation, however good your intentions may be; for it is easy to offend people, and difficult, if not impossible, to mend them.
>
> If you feel irritated by the absurd remarks of two people whose conversation you happen to overhear, you should imagine that you are listening to a dialogue of two fools in a comedy. *Probatum est.*[1]
>
> The man who comes into the world with the notion that he is really going to instruct in matters of the highest importance, may thank his stars if he escapes with a whole skin.

The truly wise are content to be considered foolish, and the truly happy do not care if others look at them with pity, falsely believing them to be miserable. Vanity is incompatible with wisdom and happiness.

---

1 "It is tested and proved."

Conclusion

The attainment of happiness is the highest human ideal, the ultimate fulfilment of human life, but this does not mean it is available to all of us, that we are somehow entitled to it. A small fraction of us are born to become true seekers, a much smaller fraction achieve enlightenment, while the great majority live in delusion from birth to death. This may seem unjust, but from a higher view, there is really no *better* way to be: the universe is full of beings of all levels of awareness, from the simplest cellular organisms to the enlightened human being and perhaps beyond, none of whom are better or worse off than another. And when we speak of happiness, we mean the end of *suffering*, the attainment of peace and tranquillity in life: but the happy life is not necessarily *better* for being more peaceful, or *worse* for being less dramatic and eventful than the life of delusion. These distinctions of value all arise from human subjectivity, while the ultimately objective view says there is no better or worse, higher or lower, more fortunate or less fortunate: there is only *diversity*. Even happiness is not *better* than suffering: it is only happier. For suffering has its benefits too, just as happiness has its drawbacks.

We seek happiness because it is the fulfilment of human life, but in the pursuit, we will suffer more than those who float through life without a care for their own growth and advancement. Suffering is the gateway to bliss. Like Dante's pilgrim, we must first pass through Hell, then Purgatory, before finally reaching Paradise. There are countless more people currently living in Hell than in Paradise. For happiness may be the goal of human life, but suffering is the abiding condition.

On Happiness

Introduction to Plato's Discussion on Happiness

In the passage that follows, Plato considers the essential question of whether it is the good life or the evil life that leads to the most happiness. His concern is not merely with which lifestyle is morally superior, but primarily with which is most pleasurable and painless.

Most of us, it would seem, have little choice with regard to which way we live, for that is ultimately decided by our character type. Although philosophical education can improve our character, after a certain point this becomes unlikely, since the very desire to improve is absent in one who is entrenched in an evil or deluded way of life.

Earlier, Plato discusses five types of political states and examines which of these is the happiest as a whole. These fives states are: the republic ruled by philosopher kings, the timarchy, the oligarchy, the democracy, and the tyranny. He goes on to show that the state ruled by philosopher kings is the happiest and the tyranny is the unhappiest.

In the section that follows, Plato draws a parallel between the five types of states and five corresponding characters types—the philosophical character, the timarchic character, the oligarchic character, the democratic character, and the tyrannical character—again with the aim of deciding which type of person leads the happiest life. The natures of these character types are as follows:

THE PHILOSOPHICAL CHARACTER

A lover of wisdom and knowledge, whose primary concern is seeing the *truth*. His knowledge is broad and deep, and he does not acquire it in the pursuit of honour or power, but for its own sake—to rid himself of delusion and to live an authentic life. He is temperate and resolute, unshaken by pleasure or pain, and is neither acquisitive nor vain. The philosopher has the capacity to grasp the eternal and immutable in Nature, and is not dazzled by appearances and the endless show of multiplicity and change. His ability to contemplate all of reality and all of time makes him impervious to greed and fear, since these depend on attachment to the superficial objects of existence as opposed to the *thing-in-itself*. Because of his contemplative nature, others may see him as passive, disinterested, and unaccomplished in the world.

THE TIMARCHIC CHARACTER

Ambitious, competitive, athletic, gregarious, but susceptible to insecurity and inner conflict. His mind is simple and sincere, he is hostile to intelligent people because of their potential cunning, and he is war-loving and patriotic. He is obedient to authority, can listen well but is incapable of forming or expressing opinions of his own. He enjoys sports and other diversions. He has a secret love of money which increases as he gets older, though he tries to hide it, and is inconspicuous about his enjoyment of pleasures. His education has been purely practical, with an overemphasis on physical as opposed to intellectual training, and so his knowledge lacks depth and good reason. Due to his poor rational capacity and his weak imagination, he has many character flaws, including avarice, pettiness, and sensitivity to the opinions of others. In short, he takes the middle road in life, submits to society's competitive spirit, and as such becomes an arrogant and ambitious man.

THE OLIGARCHIC CHARACTER

All he cares about is making money. The more he accumulates wealth, the more he values it, and the less he values goodness. For wealth and goodness are like two objects on opposite sides of a scale: as one rises, the other must fall. All his reason is devoted to figuring out how to make more money, and all his ambition is directed toward acquiring wealth. He is the money-loving businessman, or the politician who has acquired his seat through his wealth. Though he may belong to the ruling class, he does not rule in the proper sense of the word, does not truly serve society, but only serves himself. He is a consumer of goods. His type is commonly much admired, despite his narrow education, which again has been directed at the sole aim of making money, with no regard for acquiring wisdom. Like a pauper or criminal, he has base and destructive desires, but his carefulness generally keeps them in check. That is, he must maintain a reputation for honesty and restrain his evil impulses, otherwise it would have a negative impact on his business life. But there is no true moral conviction in him, no taming of desire by reason, only fear and compulsion. If he has the opportunity to spend other people's money, he can be careless and wasteful, but with his own money he is frugal. This man is never at peace with himself, and he has a sort of split personality in which the better desires in him generally master the worse. Therefore he has a certain degree of respectability, but this is mostly outward show, and on the inside he comes nowhere near true goodness.

THE DEMOCRATIC CHARACTER

Free-spirited, mercurial, multi-faceted, but full of unnecessary desires of an endless variety. His freedom causes him to lack self-discipline and self-control, and so he compulsively pursues those pleasures that are most fleeting and insatiable. The democratic character is hedonistic and fun-loving, yet fundamentally bored. He desires a varied and luxurious lifestyle, and if these ambitions are frustrated he becomes depressed; if he succeeds he falls into empty debauchery. In all, he consumes far beyond his needs, is wasteful and careless. His mind is devoid of sound principles and true knowledge, and so he has no firm foundation. He lacks moral sense and restraint, and believes his defects are virtues: he is shameless, and calls this courage; he is extravagant, and calls this generosity; he has no self-control, and calls this liberty; he is insolent, and calls this confidence; and he alternates between an exaggeratedly high opinion of himself and an utter lack of self esteem. He is stubborn, inflexible, and generally hostile or indifferent to the truth, particularly if it is inconvenient. He lives day to day and seeks the pleasure of the moment—one day it is drinking, dancing, and women, the next it is water and healthy food; one day it is intense physical training, the next it is laziness and ease; one day it is theatre and useless diversion, the next it is quiet philosophical study. He goes from one thing to another like a true dilettante, not because he is broadly curious—for he soon forgets one thing entirely before going to the next—but because he has no fixed self, no true skill or aptitude, no passion. There is no order or moderation in his life, he is utterly aimless, and yet he considers his way of living to be the best, and believes himself free and capable of anything.

THE TYRANNICAL CHARACTER

The tyrannical character is much like the democratic man, except more extreme, reckless, careless, and vicious. His desire for freedom makes him intolerant of the slightest constraint, thus making him insubordinate and difficult to work with. Even the dictates of Nature become unacceptable, and so he strives to look and behave younger than he is, desires immortality, is intolerant of others, is annoyed and even affronted by such unavoidable things as the weather, and in general believes he stands outside of Nature, and is therefore hostile to it. He has no sense of his own nature, and believes he should be able to do whatever he wants; therefore he does not acknowledge his own weaknesses or limitations; for instance, a tyrannical man believes he can to do anything a woman does, and a tyrannical woman believes she can do anything a man does; the adult believes he can act like a child, and the child acts like an adult in all the worst ways. As such, the tyrant is deluded, incompetent, ridiculous, and grotestque. All this arises from his irrational craving for so-called freedom. That is, his mind is so sensitive that he becomes resentful toward the slightest restriction, and so he flouts not only the laws of his society, but the laws of Nature itself. He is extremely individualistic, suspicious, and combative. With his friends he is superficial, artificial, and secretly vindictive. He is threatened by anyone who might be superior or even equivalent to him in any way, and so he surrounds himself with weak sycophants. The moment a friend opposes him in the slightest manner or exhibits his independence, he becomes an enemy. His pride is excessive, and anyone who wounds it may find himself in true danger. He may be successful in the world and even believe himself feared and respected, but all decent people detest him. His behaviour borders on criminality and may be downright criminal. He may be violent, treacherous, and parasitic. Morally he is even more indifferent than the democratic character: he is utterly faithless and nihilistic. His immorality, too, largely arises from his arrogance and pride—his contempt for all nature, including his own. His life is an orgy of pleasures—food, drink, sex—but every day new and strange desires crop up, all demanding satisfaction. The more he indulges himself, the more ravenous he becomes. As a result, he often spends more money than he makes, lives in debt, and may even exploit his own parents and plunder their life savings. When he does not get what he wants, he resorts to fraud, deceit, and manipulation. He will put on an act of friendship to achieve his ends, and then he will drop the act as well as the friend. As such he is always either a master or a slave with respect to others, and has no true friendships. He does not care about honour or dishonour, and overall is the epitome of injustice.

CONCLUSION

Plato explains how and why the philosophical character is by far the happiest of these five types. The tyrannical character is the unhappiest, followed by the democratic, the oligarchic, and the timarchic. Finally, Plato boldly and humorously puts an actual figure on the relative degrees of happiness, and shows mathematically that the tyrant is 729 times unhappier than the philosopher king.

from
REPUBLIC

by

PLATO

ON THE TYPES OF CHARACTER AND THEIR DEGREES OF HAPPINESS

"Now is it not clear," I asked, "that he who has been shown to be the wickedest, will also be the unhappiest of men? And he who has tyrannized the most and for the longest time will experience the greatest and most lasting unhappiness—although this may not be the opinion of men in general?"

"Yes," he said, "inevitably."

"And must not the tyrannical man be like the tyrannical State, and the democratic man like the democratic State, and so on?"

"Certainly."

"And as State is to State in virtue and happiness, so is man in relation to man?"

"To be sure."

"Then our original city governed by philosopher kings, and the city which is under a tyrant, how do they compare as to virtue?"

"They are the opposite extremes," he said, "for one is the very best and the other is the very worst."

"There can be no mistake," I said, "as to which is which, and therefore I will at once inquire whether you would arrive at a similar decision about their relative happiness and misery. And here we must not allow ourselves to be over-awed at the apparition of the tyrant and his retinue, but let us examine every corner of the city and look all around, and then we will give our opinion."

"A fair invitation," he replied, "and I see, as everyone must, that a tyranny is the most wretched form of government, and the rule of a philosopher king the happiest."

"And in estimating the men too, may I not fairly make a like request, that I should have a judge whose mind can enter into and see through human nature? He must not be like a child who looks at the outside and is dazzled at the pompous aspect that the tyrannical nature assumes, but must be one who has a clear insight into the character. May I suppose then that he will be a competent judge, and has also lived with a tyrant and seen how he behaves in his own home and with his own family, where he may best see the tyrant stripped of his dramatic attire—and has also seen him in crises of public life: such a judge shall tell us about the happiness and unhappiness of the tyrant compared with other men?"

"That again," he said, "is a very fair proposal."

"Shall I assume that we ourselves are able and experienced judges and have before now met with such a person? We shall then have someone who will answer our enquiries."

"By all means."

"Let me ask you not to forget the parallel of the individual and the State; bearing this in mind, and glancing in turn from one to the other, will you tell me their respective conditions?"

"What do you mean?" he asked.

"Beginning with the State," I replied, "would you say that a city which is governed by a tyrant is free or enslaved?"

"No city," he said, "can be more completely enslaved."

"And yet, as you see, there are free men as well as masters in such a State?"

"Yes," he said, "I see that there are . . . a few. But in general the people and the best among them are miserably degraded and enslaved."

"Then if the man is like the State," I said, "must not the same rule prevail? His mind will be full of meanness and vulgarity, and burdened with servile constrictions. The best elements in him will be completely enslaved by the minority rule of his lowest and most deranged impulses."

"Inevitably."

"And would you say that the soul of such a one is the soul of a free man, or of a slave?"

"He has the soul of a slave, in my opinion."

"And the State that is enslaved under a tyrant is the least able to do as it wishes?"

"Yes."

"And also the mind which, as a whole, is under a tyrant is least capable of doing what it desires, because it is under the compulsion of madness, and is full of confusion and remorse?"

"Certainly."

"And is the city which is under a tyrant rich or poor?"

"Poor."

"And the tyrannical soul must be always poor and insatiable?"

"True."

"And must not such a State and such a man be always full of fear?"

"Yes, indeed."

"Is there any State in which you will find more of lamentation and sorrow and groaning and pain?"

"Certainly not."

"And is there any man in whom you will find more of this sort of misery than in the tyrannical man, who is in a fury of passions and desires?"

"Impossible."

"Reflecting upon these and similar evils, you held the tyrannical State to be the unhappiest of States?"

"And I was right," he said.

"Certainly," I said. "And when you see the same evils in the tyrannical man, what do you say of him?"

"I say that he is by far the unhappiest of all men."

"There," I said, "I think that you are beginning to go wrong."

"What do you mean?"

"I do not think that he has yet reached the utmost extreme of misery."

"Then who is more miserable?"

"One of whom I am about to speak."

"Who is that?"

"He who is of a tyrannical nature, and instead of leading a private life has been cursed with the further misfortune of being a public tyrant."

"From what has been said, I gather that you are right."

"Yes," I replied, "but in an argument of this importance you should be a little more certain, and should not merely guess; for this choice between a good and an evil life is the most critical of all questions."

"Very true," he said.

"Let me then offer you an illustration, which may, I think, shed light on this subject."

"What is your illustration?"

"The case of rich individuals in cities who possess many slaves: from them you may form an idea of the tyrant's condition, for they both have slaves; the only difference is that the tyrant has more slaves."

"Yes, that is the difference."

"You know that the slave-masters live securely and have nothing to fear from their servants?"

"What should they fear?"

"Nothing. But do you observe the reason for this?"

"Yes, because the individual has the support and protection of society as a whole."

"Very true," I said. "But imagine that one of these owners—the master say of some fifty slaves—is carried off by a god, with his family and property and slaves, into the wilderness, where there are no free men to help him. Will he not be in an agony of fear lest he and his wife and children should be put to death by his slaves?"

"Yes," he said, "he will be in the utmost fear."

"The time has arrived when he will be compelled to flatter some of these slaves, and make many promises to them of freedom and other things, much against his will. That is, he will have to cajole his own servants."

"Yes," he said, "that will be the only way of saving himself."

"And suppose the same god, who carried him away, surrounds him with neighbours who will not suffer one man to be the master of another, and who, if they could catch the offender, would take his life?"

"His case will be still worse, if you suppose him to be everywhere surrounded and watched by enemies."

"And is this not the sort of prison in which the tyrant will be bound? He whose nature is such as we have described, is full of all sorts of fears and lusts, is he not? His soul is dainty and greedy, and yet alone, of all men in the city, he is never allowed to go on a journey, or to see the things which other free men desire to see, but he lives in his hole like a woman hidden in the house, and is jealous of any other citizen who goes into foreign parts and sees anything of interest."

"Very true," he said.

"And amid evils such as these, will not he who is ill-governed in his own person—I mean the tyrannical man, whom you just now decided to be the unhappiest of all men—will he not be even more miserable when, instead of leading a private life, he is constrained by fortune to be a public tyrant? He has to be the master of others when he is not even master of himself: he is like a diseased or paralytic man who is compelled to pass his life, not in retirement, but fighting and combating with other men."

"Yes," he said, "the similitude is most exact."

"Is his case not utterly miserable? And doesn't the actual tyrant lead a worse life than he whose life you determined to be the worst?"

"Certainly."

"He who is the real tyrant, whatever men may think, is the real slave, and is obliged to practice the greatest adulation and servility, and to be the flatterer of the vilest of mankind. He has desires which he is utterly unable to satisfy, and has more wants than anyone, and is truly poor, if you know how to inspect the whole soul of him: his whole life he is beset with fear and is full of convulsions and distractions, exactly like the State which he resembles. And surely the resemblance holds?"

"It does," he said.

"Moreover, as we were saying before, he grows worse from

having power: he becomes and is of necessity more jealous, more faithless, more unjust, more friendless, more impious, than he was at first. He is the purveyor and cherisher of every sort of vice, and the consequence is that he is supremely miserable, and that he makes everybody else as miserable as himself."

"No man of any sense will dispute your words."

"Come then," I said, "and as the general umpire in theatrical contests proclaims the result, you too decide who in your opinion is first in the scale of happiness, and who second, and in what order the others follow. There are five of them in all: the philosopher king, the timocratic man, the oligarchic man, the democratic man, and the tyrannical man."

"The decision will be easily given," he replied. "They shall be choruses coming on the stage, and I must judge them in the order in which they enter, by the criterion of virtue and vice, happiness and misery."

"Need we hire a herald, or shall I announce myself that the son of Ariston has decided: the best and justest man is also the happiest, and this is the most royal man, he who is sovereign over himself—that is, the philosopher king. And the worst and most unjust man is also the unhappiest, and this is he who, being the greatest tyrant of himself, is also the greatest tyrant of his State."

"Make the proclamation yourself," he said.

"And may I add, 'the the judgment remains true whether or not their true characters are known to men or gods.'"

"Let the words be added."

"Then this," I said, "will be our first proof; and there is another, which may also have some weight."

"What is that?"

"The second proof is derived from the nature of the soul: seeing that the individual soul, like the State, has been divided by us into three elements, the division may, I think, furnish a new demonstration."

"Of what nature?"

"It seems to me that three pleasures correspond to these three elements, and also three desires and governing powers."

"How do you mean?" he said.

"There is one element in a man that gives him *understanding*, another gives him *spirit*; and the third, having many forms, has no special name, but is denoted by the general term *appetite*, due to the extraordinary strength and vehemence of the desires of eating and drinking and the other sensual pleasures that are the main elements of it; we also call it *acquisitiveness* or *money-lust*, because money is the means of satisfying desires of this kind."

"That is true," he said.

"If we were to say that the loves and pleasures of this third part were concerned with gain, we should then be able to fall back on a single notion, and might truly and intelligibly describe this part of the soul as loving gain or money."

"I agree with you."

"And the passionate element, which we call *spirit*, is it not wholly set on ruling and conquering and getting fame?"

"True."

"Suppose we call it the contentious, or *ambitious*—would the term be suitable?"

"Extremely suitable."

"On the other hand, everyone sees that the element of *understanding* is wholly directed toward the truth, and cares less for gain and fame than either of the other two elements."

"Far less."

"'Lover of wisdom,' 'lover of knowledge,' are titles we may fitly apply to that part of the soul?"

"Certainly."

"And one element dominates in the souls of one class of men, another in others, and so on?"

"Yes."

"Then we may begin by assuming that there are three classes of men—lovers of wisdom, lovers of honour, and lovers of gain?"

"Exactly."

"And there are three kinds of pleasure, which are their objects?"

"Very true."

"Now, if you examine the three classes of men, and ask of them in turn which of their lives is pleasantest, each will be found praising his own and depreciating that of others: the money-maker will contrast the vanity of honour or of learning, if they bring no money, with the solid advantages of gold and silver?"

"True," he said.

"And the lover of honour—what will be his opinion? Will he not think that the pleasure of riches is vulgar, while the pleasure of learning, if it brings no distinction, is all smoke and nonsense to him?"

"Very true."

"And are we to suppose," I said, "that the philosopher sets any value on other pleasures in comparison with the pleasure of knowing the truth, and in remaining engaged in that pursuit, and always learning? Will he not rank honour and gain far lower? Does he not call the other pleasures merely necessary, in that if they were not necessary for life, he would rather not have them?"

"There can be no doubt of that," he replied.

"Since, then, the pleasures of each class and the life of each are in dispute, and the question is not which life is more or less honourable, or right or wrong, but which is the more pleasant or painless—how shall we know who speaks truly?"

"I cannot myself tell," he said.

"Well, but what should be the criteria? Are any better than experience and wisdom and reason?"

"There cannot be a better," he said.

"Then," I said, "reflect. Of the three individuals, which has the greatest experience of all the pleasures which we enumerated? Has the lover of gain, in endeavouring to learn the nature of essential truth, greater experience of the pleasure of knowledge than the philosopher has of the pleasure of gain?"

"The philosopher," he replied, "has greatly the advantage; for he has of necessity always known the taste of the other pleasures from his childhood upwards: but the lover of gain in all his experience has not necessarily tasted—or, I should rather say, even had he desired it, could hardly have tasted—

the sweetness of learning and knowing truth."

"Then the lover of wisdom has a great advantage over the lover of gain, for he has a double experience?"

"Yes, very great."

"Again, has the lover of wisdom greater experience of the pleasures of honour, or the lover of honour of the pleasures of wisdom?"

"Nay," he said, "all three are honoured to the extent that they attain their object; for the rich man and the brave man and the wise man alike have their crowd of admirers, and as they all receive honour they all have experience of the pleasures of honour; but the delight which is to be found in the knowledge of true being is known to the philosopher only."

"His experience, then, will enable him to judge better than anyone?"

"Far better."

"And he is the only one who has wisdom as well as experience?"

"Certainly."

"Further, the very faculty that is the instrument of judgment is not possessed by the covetous or ambitious man, but only by the philosopher?"

"What faculty?"

"Reason, with which, as we were saying, our judgment ought to rest."

"Yes."

"And reasoning is peculiarly his instrument?"

"Certainly."

"If wealth and gain were the criterion, then the praise or blame of the lover of gain would surely be the most trustworthy?"

"Assuredly."

"Or if honour or victory or courage, in that case the judgment of the ambitious or pugnacious would be the truest?"

"Clearly."

"But since experience and wisdom and reason are the judges—"

"The only inference possible," he replied, "is that pleasures which are approved by the lover of wisdom and reason are the truest."

"And so we arrive at the result, that the pleasure of the intelligent part of the soul is the pleasantest of the three, and that he in whom this is the ruling principle has the pleasantest life."

"Unquestionably," he said, "the wise man speaks with authority when he approves of his own life."

"And what does the judge affirm to be the life that is next best, and the pleasure that is next best?"

"Clearly that of the soldier and lover of honour; who is nearer to himself than the money-maker."

"And last comes the lover of gain?"

"Very true," he said.

"Twice in succession, then, has the just man overthrown the unjust in this conflict. And now comes the third trial, which is dedicated to Olympian Zeus the saviour: a sage whispers in my ear that no pleasure except that of the wise is quite true and pure—all others are only shadows; and surely a third victory in this matter would settle the question once and for all?"

"It should, but explain yourself?"

"I will work out the subject and you shall answer my questions."

"Proceed."

"Say, then, is not pleasure opposed to pain?"

"True."

"And there is a neutral state which is neither pleasure nor pain?"

"There is."

"A state which is intermediate, and a sort of repose of the soul from either—that is what you mean?"

"Yes."

"You remember what people say when they are sick?"

"What do they say?"

"That after all nothing is more pleasant than health. But then they never knew this to be the greatest of pleasures until they were ill."

"Yes, I know," he said.

"And when persons are suffering from acute pain, you must

have heard them say that there is nothing pleasanter than to get rid of their pain?"

"I have."

"And there are many other cases of suffering in which the mere rest and cessation of pain, and not any positive enjoyment, is extolled by them as the greatest pleasure?"

"Yes," he said, "at the time they are pleased and well content to be at rest."

"Again, when pleasure ceases, that sort of rest or cessation will be painful?"

"Doubtless," he said.

"Then the intermediate state of rest will be pleasure and will also be pain?"

"So it would seem."

"But can that which is neither become both?"

"I should say not."

"And both pleasure and pain are motions of the soul, are they not?"

"Yes."

"But that which is neither was just now shown to be rest and not motion, and in a mean between them?"

"Yes."

"How, then, can we be right in supposing that the absence of pain is pleasure, or that the absence of pleasure is pain?"

"Impossible."

"This then is an appearance only and not a reality; that is to say, the state of rest is pleasure at the moment and in comparison to what is painful, and painful in comparison to what is pleasant; but all these representations, when judged by the standard of true pleasure, are not real, but a sort of illusion or trick?"

"That is the inference."

"Look at the other class of pleasures, which have no antecedent pains, and you will no longer suppose, as you perhaps may at present, that pleasure is only the cessation of pain, or pain of pleasure."

"What are they," he said, "and where shall I find them?"

"There are many of them: take as an example the pleasures

of smell, which are very great and have no antecedent pains; they come in a moment, and when they depart leave no pain behind them."

"Most true," he said.

"Let us not, then, be induced to believe that pure pleasure is the cessation of pain, or pain of pleasure."

"No."

"Still, the more numerous and violent pleasures which reach the soul through the body are generally of this sort—they are reliefs of pain."

"That is true."

"And the anticipations of future pleasures and pains are of a like nature?"

"Yes."

"Shall I give you an illustration of them?"

"Let me hear."

"You would allow," I said, "that there is in nature an upper and lower and middle region?"

"I should."

"And if a person were to go from the lower to the middle region, would he not imagine that he is going up; and he who is standing in the middle and sees whence he has come, would imagine that he is already in the upper region, if he has never seen the true upper world?"

"To be sure," he said. "How can he think otherwise?"

"But if he were taken back again he would imagine, and truly imagine, that he was descending?"

"No doubt."

"All that would arise out of his ignorance of the true upper and middle and lower regions?"

"Yes."

"Then can you wonder that persons who are inexperienced in the truth, as they have wrong ideas about many other things, should also have wrong ideas about pleasure and pain and the intermediate state; so that when they are only being drawn towards the painful they feel pain and think the pain that they experience is real, and in like manner, when drawn away from pain to the neutral or intermediate state, they firmly believe that they have reached the goal of satiety and pleasure; they, not knowing pleasure, err in contrasting pain with the absence of pain, which is like contrasting black with grey instead of white—can you be surprised by this?"

"No, indeed. I would be surprised if it was otherwise."

"Look at the matter thus: hunger, thirst, and the like, are deprivations of the bodily state?"

"Yes."

"And ignorance and folly are deprivations of the soul?"

"True."

"And food and wisdom are the corresponding satisfactions of either?"

"Certainly."

"And is the satisfaction derived from that which has less or from that which has more existence the truer?"

"Clearly, from that which has more."

"What classes of things have a greater share of pure existence in your judgment—those of which food and drink and condiments and all kinds of sustenance are examples, or the class which contains true opinion and knowledge and mind and all the different kinds of virtue? Put the question in this way: which has a more pure being—that which is concerned with the unchanging, the immortal, and the true, and is of such a nature, and is found in such natures; or that which is concerned with and found in the changing and mortal, and is itself changing and mortal?"

"Far purer," he replied, "is that which is concerned with the unchanging."

"And is the essence of the unchanging as real as it is knowable?"

"Yes, it is knowable in the same degree."

"And true in the same degree?"

"Yes."

"And, conversely, that which has less truth will also have less essence?"

"Necessarily."

"Then, in general, those things that are in the service of the body have less truth and essence than those which are in the service of the soul?"

"Far less."

"And has not the body itself less truth and essence than soul?"

"Yes."

"That which is filled with more real existence, and actually has a more real existence, is more *truly filled* than that which is filled with less real existence and is itself less real?"

"Of course."

"And if there is a pleasure in being filled with that which is according to nature, that which is more truly filled with more real being will more really and truly enjoy genuine pleasure; whereas that which is less real will be less truly and surely satisfied, and will participate in an illusory and less real pleasure?"

"Unquestionably."

"Those, then, who do not know wisdom and virtue, and are always busy with gluttony and sensuality, go down and up again as far as the mean; and in this region they move at random throughout their life, but they never pass into the true upper world. They neither look upward, nor do they ever find their way—they are neither filled with true being, nor do they taste pure and abiding pleasure. Like cattle, with their eyes always looking down and their heads stooping to the earth—that is, to the dining-table—they fatten and feed and breed, and, in their excessive love of these delights, they kick and butt one another with horns and hoofs made of iron; and they kill one another by reason of their insatiable lust. For they fill themselves with that which is not substantial, and the part of themselves which they fill is also insubstantial and incontinent."

"Verily, Socrates," said Glaucon, "you describe the life of the many like an oracle."

"Their pleasures are mixed with pains—how can they be otherwise? For they are mere shadows and pictures of the true pleasure, and are coloured by contrast, which exaggerates both light and shade, and implants mad desires in the minds of fools. And then they fight over these pleasures—as

Stesichorus says the Greeks fought over the shadow of Helen at Troy—in ignorance of the truth."

"Something of that sort must inevitably happen."

"Then what about the spirited or passionate element of the soul? Is it not the same story again, when a man seeks his share of honour or success, and does so out of ambition, envy, rage, dissatisfaction, and without reason or sense?"

"Yes," he said, "the same will happen with the spirited element also."

"Then the lovers of money and honour, if they instead direct their ambition and desire for gain to the pleasures of wisdom, under the guidance of reason and knowledge—will they not experience the truest pleasures in the highest degree attainable to them, as long as truth is their guide? And will they not enjoy the pleasures that are most natural to them—if that which is best for each of us is also what is most natural?"

"Yes, certainly, the best is the most natural."

"And when the whole soul follows the philosophical element, and there is no internal division, each element will be just, and each will perform its own function and enjoy its own particular pleasures, which are the best and truest pleasures available to it?

"Exactly."

"But when either of the other two elements dominates, it not only fails to attain its own pleasure, but it even compels the other two to pursue false pleasures that are not their own."

"True."

"And the greater the distance that separates them from philosophy and reason, the more strange and illusive the resulting pleasure?"

"Yes."

"And is not what is furthest removed from reason also the furthest removed from law and order?

"Clearly."

"And the lustful and tyrannical desires are, as we saw, at the greatest distance from law and order?"

"Yes."

"And the royal and orderly desires are nearest?"

"Yes."

"Then the tyrant will live at the greatest distance from true or natural pleasure, and the philosopher king will be nearest to it?"

"Certainly."

"But if so, the tyrant will live most unpleasantly, and the king most pleasantly?"

"Inevitably."

THAT THE TYRANT IS 729 TIMES UNHAPPIER THAN THE PHILOSOPHER KING

"Do you know," I asked, "the degree to which the tyrant is unhappier than the philosopher king?"

"No, tell me."

"There appear to be three pleasures, one genuine and two spurious. Now, the transgression of the tyrant reaches a point beyond the spurious: he has run away from the region of law and reason, and has surrounded himself with certain slavish pleasures and made an army out of them. As a result, the full measure of his inferiority is not easy to describe, but we will try to express it in a figure."

"How do you mean?"

"I assume," I said, "that the tyrant is in the third place from the oligarch; the democrat was in the middle?"

"Yes."

"And if there is truth in what has preceded, he will be wedded to an image of pleasure that is thrice removed from truth compared to the pleasure of the oligarch?"

"He will."

"And the oligarch is third from the philosopher king, who we consider the best ruler?"

"Yes, he is third."

"Then the tyrant is removed from true pleasure by the space of a number that is three times three?"

"Manifestly."

"The shadow, then, of tyrannical pleasure in spatial terms will be a plane figure."

"Certainly."

"And if you square this and then cube it, you make the plane a solid, and there is no difficulty in seeing the vastness of the interval by which the tyrant is parted from the king."

"Yes, the arithmetician will easily do the sum."

"Or if someone begins at the other end and measures the interval by which the king is separated from the tyrant in truth of pleasure, he will find that the philosopher king lives 729 times more pleasantly than the tyrant, and the tyrant lives the same amount more painfully than the philosopher king."

"What a wonderful calculation! And how enormous is the distance which separates the just from the unjust with regard to pleasure and pain!"

"Yet a true calculation," I said, "and a number which nearly concerns human life, if human beings are concerned with days and nights and months and years. For 729 *nearly* equals the number of days and nights in a year."

"Yes," he said, "human life is certainly concerned with them."

"Then if the good and just man is thus superior in pleasure to the evil and unjust, his superiority will be infinitely greater in propriety of life and in beauty and virtue?"

"Immeasurably greater."

THAT WRONGDOING AND INJUSTICE DO NOT PAY

"Well," I said, "and now having arrived at this stage of the argument, we may revert to the words which brought us here: wasn't someone saying that injustice brings a gain to the perfectly unjust man who has a reputation for justice?"

"Yes, that was said."

"Now then, having determined the power and quality of justice and injustice, let us have a little conversation with him."

"What shall we say to him?"

"Let us make an image of the soul, so that he may have his own words presented before his eyes."

"Of what sort?"

"An ideal image of the soul, like the composite creations of ancient mythology, such as the Chimera or Scylla or Cerberus, and there are many others in which two or more different natures are said to grow into one."

"There are said of have been such unions."

"Then imagine now a multitudinous, many-headed monster, having a ring of heads of all kinds of beasts, tame and wild, which he is able to generate and metamorphose at will."

"You suppose marvellous powers in the artist. But, as language is more pliable than wax or any similar substance, let there be such a model as you propose."

"Suppose now that you make a second form as of a lion, and a third of a man, the second smaller than the first, and the third smaller than the second."

"That," he said, "is an easier task, and I have made them as you say."

"And now join them, and let the three grow into one."

"That has been accomplished."

"Next fashion the outside of them into a single image, as of a man, so that he who is not able to look within, and sees only the outer hull, may believe the beast to be a single human creature."

"I have done so," he said.

"And now, to him who maintains that it is profitable for the human creature to be unjust, and unprofitable to be just, let us reply that, if he is right, it is profitable for this creature to feast the multitudinous monster and strengthen the lion and the lion-like qualities, but to starve and weaken the man, who is consequently liable to be dragged about at the mercy of either of the other two; and he is not to attempt to familiarize or harmonize them with one another. Instead, he should allow them to fight and bite and devour one another."

"Certainly," he said. "That is what the approver of injustice says."

"The supporter of justice, however, answers that we ought to say and do all we can to give complete mastery of the entire creature to the man within us, so that he can watch over the many-headed monster like a good farmer, fostering and cultivating the gentle qualities and preventing the wild ones from growing, while he tames the lion-heart, makes it his ally, and finally takes care of the common interests of them all by reconciling the several parts with one another and with himself."

"Yes," he said, "that is quite what the maintainer of justice would say."

"And so from every point of view, whether of pleasure, honour, or advantage, the approver of justice is right and speaks the truth, and the disapprover is wrong and false and ignorant?"

"Yes, from every point of view."

"Come, now, and let us gently reason with the unjust, who is not intentionally in error. 'Sweet Sir,' we will say to him, 'what do you think of the noble and ignoble? Is not the noble that which subjects the beast to the man, or rather to the god in man; and the ignoble that which subjects the man to the beast?' He can hardly avoid saying 'Yes'—can he now?"

"Not if he has any regard for my opinion."

"But, if he agrees so far, we may ask him to answer another question: 'Then how would a man profit if he received gold and silver on the condition that he was to enslave the noblest part of himself to the worst? Who can imagine that a man who sold his son or daughter into slavery for money, especially if he sold them into the hands of fierce and evil men, would be the gainer, however large the sum he received? And will anyone say that he is not a miserable coward and wretch who remorselessly sells his own divine being to that which is most godless and detestable? Is this not a miserable bribe, with results far more ruinous than Eriphyle's sale of her husband's life for a necklace?'"

"If I may answer for him," said Glaucon, "it is certainly far more ruinous."

"Has not the intemperate been censured of old, because in him the huge multiform monster is allowed too much freedom?"

"Clearly."

"And men are blamed for their pride and bad temper when the lion and serpent elements in them grow out of proportion and gain strength?"

"Yes."

"And luxury and softness are blamed, because they relax and weaken this same creature, and make a coward of him?"

"Very true."

"And is not a man reproached for flattery and meanness when he subordinates the spirited animal to the unruly monster, and when, for the sake of money and greed, he teaches the lion in himself to allow itself to be insulted and trampled in the mire until it becomes a monkey?"

"True," he said.

"And why are mean employments and manual labour seen as vulgar? Only because they imply a natural weakness of the higher nature. The individual is unable to control the creatures within him, but has to court them and learn how to pander to them."

"Such appears to be the reason."

"And therefore, wishing to place people of this type under the same authority that we place the highest among us, we say that he ought to be the servant of the highest type, who is ruled by the Divine. But this authority is not, as Thrasymachus supposed, exercised to the detriment of the subject, but because everyone is better off being ruled by divine wisdom. If that wisdom and control cannot come from within, as would be ideal, then it must be imposed by an external authority, so that we may be all, as far as possible, under the same government, as friends and equals."

"True," he said.

"And this is clearly seen to be the intention of the law, which is the ally of the whole city. And we also see it in the authority we exercise over our children: we refuse to let them be free until we have established in them principles analogous to the constitution of a state; we cultivate this higher element until we have established in their hearts a guardian and ruler like our own; and when this is done we let them go their own way."

"Yes," he said, "the purpose of the law is manifest."

"From what point of view, then, and on what grounds, can we say that a man profits by injustice or intemperance or other baseness, which will make him a worse man, even if he acquires money or power by his wickedness?"

"From no point of view at all."

"What shall he profit, if his injustice is undetected and unpunished? He who is undetected only gets worse, whereas he who is detected and punished has the brutal part of his nature silenced and humanized, and the gentler element in him is liberated. Therefore, does he not then gain a true advantage by developing a character that is ennobled by self-control, justice, and wisdom, and is this not worth much more than physical strength and health and good looks, just as the soul is worth more than the body?"

"Certainly," he said.

"To this nobler purpose the man of understanding will devote the energies of his life. And in the first place, he will honour studies that impress these qualities on his soul and will disregard others, yes?"

"Clearly," he said.

"In the next place, he will regulate his bodily habits and training, and so far will he be from yielding to brutal and irrational pleasures, that he will regard even health as quite a secondary matter; his first object will be not that he may be good looking or healthy or strong, unless these help improve his self-control, but he will always desire to tune his body to match the harmony of his mind and soul."

"Certainly he will, if he is to be a true musician."

"And in the acquisition of wealth there is a principle of order and harmony which he will also observe; he will not allow himself to be dazzled by the foolish applause of the world, and heap up riches to his own infinite harm?"

"Certainly not," he said.

"He will look at the city that is within him, and ensure that no disorder occurs in it, such as might arise either from excess or from deprivation; and upon this principle he will regulate his property and gain or spend according to his means."

"Very true."

"And, for the same reason, he will gladly accept and enjoy those honours that are likely to make him a better man; but those, whether private or public, that are likely to disorder his life, he will avoid."

"Then, if that is his motive, he will not enter politics."

"By the dog of Egypt, he will! In the city he lives in he certainly will, though in the land of his birth perhaps not, unless he has a divine calling."

"I understand. You mean that he will be a ruler in the hypothetical city we are describing, which exists only as an idea. But I do not believe such a place will ever exist on earth."

"Perhaps," I replied, "it is laid up as a pattern in heaven, where he who wishes can see it, and seeing it in his mind's eye, he may establish it in his own soul. But whether such a place exists, or ever will exist in fact, is no matter. For he will live after the manner of that city, and will have nothing to do with any other."

"I expect so," he said.

from
COUNSELS AND MAXIMS

by

ARTHUR SCHOPENHAUER

Chapter One: General Rules

I

The first and foremost rule for the wise conduct of life seems to me to be contained in a view to which Aristotle parenthetically refers in the *Nicomachean Ethics:* "not pleasure, but freedom from pain, is what the wise man will aim at."[1]

The truth of this remark turns upon the negative character of happiness—the fact that pleasure is only the negation of pain, and that pain is the positive element in life. Though I have given a detailed proof of this proposition in my chief work,[2] I may supply one more illustration of it here, drawn from a circumstance of daily occurrence. Suppose that, with the exception of some sore or painful spot, we are physically in a sound and healthy condition: the sore of this one spot, will completely absorb our attention, causing us to lose the sense of general well-being, and destroying all our comfort in life. In the same way, when all our affairs but one turn out as we wish, the single instance in which our aims are frustrated is a constant trouble to us, even though it be something quite trivial. We think a great deal about it, and very little

---

[1] Book VII, 12. In the translation in this volume, this phrase is expressed as follows: "it is the absence of the pain arising from [the bodily pleasures] that the Man of Practical Wisdom aims at."
[2] *The World as Will and Representation.*

about those other and more important matters in which we have been successful. In both these cases what has met with resistance is *the will*; in the one case, as it is objectified in the organism, in the other, as it presents itself in the struggle of life; and in both, it is plain that the satisfaction of the will consists in nothing else than that it meets with no resistance. It is, therefore, a satisfaction which is not directly felt; at most, we can become conscious of it only when we reflect upon our condition. But that which checks or arrests the will is something positive; it proclaims its own presence. All pleasure consists in merely removing this check—in other words, in freeing us from its action; and hence pleasure is a state which can never last very long.

This is the true basis of the above excellent rule quoted from Aristotle, which bids us direct our aim, not toward securing what is pleasurable and agreeable in life, but toward avoiding, as far as possible, its innumerable evils. If this were not the right course to take, that saying of Voltaire's, "Happiness is but a dream and sorrow is real," would be as false as it is, in fact, true. A man who desires to make up the book of his life and determine where the balance of happiness lies, must put down in his accounts, not the pleasures which he has enjoyed, but the evils which he has escaped. That is the true method of eudemonology[1]; for all eudemonology must begin by recognizing that its very name is a euphemism, and that *to live happily* only means *to live less unhappily*—to live a tolerable life. There is no doubt that life is given us, not to be enjoyed, but to be overcome—to be got over. There are numerous expressions illustrating this—such as *degere vitam, vita defungi;*[2] or in Italian, *si scampa cosi;*[3] or in German, *man muss suchen durchzukommen;*[4] *er wird schon durch die Welt kommen,*[5] and so on. In old age it is indeed a consolation to think that the work of life is over and done with. The hap-

---

[1] The study of happiness.
[2] "To get through life, to overcome life."
[3] "If only we get over it!"
[4] "We must try to get along as well as we can."
[5] "He will get through the world."

piest lot is not to have experienced the keenest delights or the greatest pleasures, but to have brought life to a close without any very great pain, bodily or mental. To measure the happiness of a life by its delights or pleasures, is to apply a false standard. For pleasures are and remain something negative; that they produce happiness is a delusion, cherished by envy to its own punishment. Pain is felt to be something positive, and hence its absence is the true standard of happiness. And if, over and above freedom from pain, there is also an absence of boredom, the essential conditions of earthly happiness are attained; for all else is chimerical.

It follows from this that a man should never try to purchase pleasure at the cost of pain, or even at the risk of incurring it; to do so is to pay what is positive and real, for what is negative and illusory; while there is a net profit in sacrificing pleasure for the sake of avoiding pain. In either case it is a matter of indifference whether the pain follows the pleasure or precedes it. While it is a complete inversion of the natural order to try and turn this scene of misery into a garden of pleasure, to aim at joy and pleasure rather than at the greatest possible freedom from pain—and yet how many do it!—there is some wisdom in taking a gloomy view, in looking upon the world as a kind of Hell, and in confining one's efforts to securing a little room that shall not be exposed to the fire. The fool rushes after the pleasures of life and finds himself their dupe; the wise man avoids its evils; and even if, notwithstanding his precautions, he falls into misfortunes, that is the fault of fate, not of his own folly. As far as he is successful in his endeavours, he cannot be said to have lived a life of illusion; for the evils which he shuns are very real. Even if he goes too far out of his way to avoid evils, and makes an unnecessary sacrifice of pleasure, he is, in reality, not the worse off for that; for all pleasures are chimerical, and to mourn for having lost any of them is a frivolous, and even ridiculous proceeding.

The failure to recognize this truth—a failure promoted by optimistic ideas—is the source of much unhappiness. In moments free from pain, our restless wishes present, as it were in a mirror, the image of a happiness that has no counterpart in reality, seducing us to follow it; in doing so we bring pain upon ourselves, and that is something undeniably real. Afterwards, we come to look with regret upon that lost state of painlessness; it is a paradise which we have gambled away; it is no longer with us, and we long in vain to undo what has been done.

One might well fancy that these visions of wishes fulfilled were the work of some evil spirit, conjured up in order to entice us away from that painless state which forms our highest happiness.

A careless youth may think that the world is meant to be enjoyed, as though it were the abode of some real or positive happiness, which only those fail to attain who are not clever enough to overcome the difficulties that lie in the way. This false notion takes a stronger hold on him when he comes to read poetry and romance, and to be deceived by outward show—the hypocrisy that characterizes the world from beginning to end; on which I shall have something to say presently. The result is that his life is the more or less deliberate pursuit of positive happiness; and happiness he takes to be equivalent to a series of definite pleasures. In seeking for these pleasures he encounters danger—a fact which should not be forgotten. He hunts for game that does not exist; and so he ends by suffering some very real and positive misfortune—pain, distress, sickness, loss, care, poverty, shame, and all the thousand ills of life. Too late he discovers the trick that has been played upon him.

But if the rule I have mentioned is observed, and a plan of life is adopted which proceeds by avoiding pain—in other words, by taking measures of precaution against want, sickness, and distress in all its forms—the aim is a real one, and something may be achieved which will be great in proportion as the plan is not disturbed by striving after the chimera of positive happiness. This agrees with the opinion expressed by Goethe in the *Elective Affinities*, and there put into the mouth of Mittler—the man who is always trying to make other people happy: "To desire to get rid of an evil is a definite object, but to desire a better fortune than one has is blind folly." The same truth is contained in that fine French proverb: *le mieux est l'ennemi du bien*[1]—leave well enough alone. And, as I have remarked in my chief work, this is the leading thought underlying the philosophical system of the Cynics. For what was it led the Cynics to repudiate pleasure in every form, if it was not the fact that pain is, in a greater or less degree, always bound up with pleasure? To go out of the way of pain seemed to them so much easier than to secure pleasure. Deeply impressed as they were by the negative nature of pleasure and the positive nature of pain, they consistently devoted all their efforts to the avoidance of pain. The first step to that end was, in their opinion, a complete and deliberate repudiation of pleasure, as something which served only to entrap the victim in order that he might be delivered over to pain.

We are all born, as Schiller says, in Arcadia. In other words, we come into the world full of claims to happiness and pleasure, and we cherish the fond hope of making them good. But, as a rule, Fate soon teaches us, in a rough and ready way that we really possess nothing at all, but that everything in the world is at its command, in virtue of an unassailable right, not only to all we have or acquire, to wife or child, but even to our very limbs, our arms, legs, eyes, and ears, nay, even to the nose in the middle of our face. And in any case, after some little time, we learn by experience that happiness and pleasure are a *fata morgana*, which, visible from afar, vanish as we approach; that, on the other hand, suffering and pain are a reality, which makes its presence felt without any intermediary, and for its effect, stands in no need of illusion or the play of false hope.

If the teaching of experience bears fruit in us, we soon give up the pursuit of pleasure and happiness, and think much more about making ourselves secure against the attacks of pain and suffering. We see that the best the world has to offer is an existence free from pain—a quiet, tolerable life; and we confine our claims to this, as to something we can more

---

[1] "*Better* is the enemy of *good*."

surely hope to achieve. For the safest way of not being very miserable is not to expect to be very happy. Merck, the friend of Goethe's youth, was conscious of this truth when he wrote: "It is the wretched way people have of setting up a claim to happiness—and, that too, in a measure corresponding with their desires—that ruins everything in this world. A man will make progress if he can get rid of this claim, and desire nothing but what he sees before him." Accordingly it is advisable to put very moderate limits upon our expectations of pleasure, possessions, rank, honour and so on; because it is just this striving and struggling to be happy, to dazzle the world, to lead a life full of pleasure, which entail great misfortune. It is prudent and wise, I say, to reduce one's claims, if only for the reason that it is extremely easy to be very unhappy; while to be very happy is not indeed difficult, but quite impossible. With justice sings the poet of life's wisdom:

> Auream quisquis mediocritatem
>   Diligit, tutus caret obsolete
>   Sordibus tecti, caret invidenda
>   Sobrius aula.
> Savius ventis agitatur ingens
>   Pinus: et celsae graviori casu
>   Decidunt turres; feriuntque summos
>   Fulgura monies.[1]

—the golden mean is best—to live free from the squalor of a mean abode, and yet not be a mark for envy. It is the tall pine which is cruelly shaken by the wind, the highest summits that are struck in the storm, and the lofty towers that fall so heavily.

He who has taken to heart the teaching of my philosophy—who knows, therefore, that our whole existence is something

---

[1] Horace *Odes*, II, 10. "The chooser of the golden mean is certainly far removed from the squalor of the broken hovel and far enough from the envied splendours of the prince's palace. Caught by the storm, the crown of the mighty pine sways in the wind, the tallest towers crash heavily down, and the mountain tops are struck by thunderbolts."

which had better not have been, and that to disown and disclaim it is the highest wisdom—he will have no great expectations from anything or any condition in life: he will spend passion upon nothing in the world, nor lament over-much if he fails in any of his undertakings. He will feel the deep truth of what Plato[1] says, "nothing in human affairs is worth any great anxiety." Or, as the Persian poet has it,

> Though from thy grasp all worldly things
>   should flee,
> Grieve not for them, for they are nothing
>   worth:
> And though a world in thy possession be,
> Joy not, for worthless are the things of
>   earth.
> Since to that better world 'tis given to
>   thee
> To pass, speed on, for this is nothing
>   worth.[2]

The chief obstacle to our arriving at these salutary views is that hypocrisy of the world to which I have already alluded—an hypocrisy which should be early revealed to the young. Most of the glories of the world are mere outward show, like the scenes on a stage: there is nothing real about them. Ships festooned and hung with pennants, firing of cannon, illuminations, beating of drums and blowing of trumpets, shouting and applauding—these are all the outward sign, the pretence and suggestion—as it were the hieroglyphic—of *joy*: but just there, joy is, as a rule, not to be found; it is the only guest who has declined to be present at the festival. Where this guest may really be found, he comes generally without invitation; he is not formerly announced, but slips in quietly by himself *sans façon*;[3] often making his appearance under

---

[1] *Republic*, X, 604.
[2] From the *Anvar-I Suhaili (The Lights of Canopus)I*, translated by E.B. Eastwick, III, 6.
[3] "Unceremoniously."

the most unimportant and trivial circumstances, and in the commonest company—anywhere, in short, but where the society is brilliant and distinguished. Joy is like the gold in the Australian mines—found only now and then, as it were, by the caprice of chance, and according to no rule or law; oftenest in very little grains, and very seldom in heaps. All that outward show which I have described, is only an attempt to make people believe that it is really joy which has come to the festival; and to produce this impression upon the spectators is, in fact, the whole object of it.

With *mourning* it is just the same. That long funeral procession, moving up so slowly; how melancholy it looks! what an endless row of carriages! But look into them—they are all empty; the coachmen of the whole town are the sole escort the dead man has to his grave. Eloquent picture of the friendship and esteem of the world! This is the falsehood, the hollowness, the hypocrisy of human affairs!

Take another example—a roomful of guests in full dress, being received with great ceremony. You could almost believe that this is a noble and distinguished company; but, as a matter of fact, it is compulsion, pain, and boredom who are the real guests. For where many are invited, it is a rabble—even if they all wear stars. Really good society is everywhere of necessity very small. In brilliant festivals and noisy entertainments, there is always, at bottom, a sense of emptiness prevalent. A false tone is there: such gatherings are in strange contrast with the misery and barrenness of our existence. The contrast brings the true condition into greater relief. Still, these gatherings are effective from the outside; and that is just their purpose. Chamfort makes the excellent remark that *society—les cercles, les salons, ce qu'on appelle le monde*[1]—is like a miserable play, or a bad opera, without any interest in itself, but supported for a time by mechanical aid, costumes and scenery.

And so, too, with academies and chairs of philosophy. You have a kind of sign-board hung out to show the apparent

---

[1] "The circles, salons, what is called high society . . . "

abode of *wisdom*: but wisdom is another guest who declines the invitation; she is to be found elsewhere. The chiming of bells, ecclesiastical millinery, attitudes of devotion, insane antics—these are the pretence, the false show of *piety*. And so on. Everything in the world is like a hollow nut; there is little kernel anywhere, and when it does exist, it is still more rare to find it in the shell. You may look for it elsewhere, and find it, as a rule, only by chance.

II

To estimate a man's condition in regard to happiness, it is necessary to ask, not what things please him, but what things trouble him; and the more trivial these things are in themselves, the happier the man will be. To be irritated by trifles, a man must be well off; for in misfortunes trifles are unfelt.

III

Care should be taken not to build the happiness of life upon a *broad foundation*—not to require a great many things in order to be happy. For happiness on such a foundation is the most easily undermined; it offers many more opportunities for accidents; and accidents are always happening. The architecture of happiness follows a plan in this respect just the opposite of that adopted in every other case, where the broadest foundation offers the greatest security. Accordingly, to reduce your claims to the lowest possible degree, in comparison with your means—of whatever kind these may be—is the surest way of avoiding extreme misfortune.

To make extensive preparations for life—no matter what form they may take—is one of the greatest and commonest of follies. Such preparations presuppose, in the first place, a long life, the full and complete term of years appointed to man—and how few reach it! And even if it be reached, it is still too short for all the plans that have been made; for to carry them out requires more time than was thought necessary at the beginning. And then how many mischances and obstacles stand in the way! How seldom the goal is ever reached in human affairs!

And lastly, even though the goal should be reached, the changes which Time works in us have been left out of the reckoning: we forget that the capacity whether for achievement or for enjoyment does not last a whole lifetime. So we often toil for things which are no longer suited to us when we attain them; and again, the years we spend in preparing for some work, unconsciously rob us of the power for carrying it out.

How often it happens that a man is unable to enjoy the wealth which he acquired at so much trouble and risk, and that the fruits of his labour are reserved for others; or that he is incapable of filling the position which he has won after so many years of toil and struggle. Fortune has come too late for him; or, contrarily, he has come too late for fortune—when, for instance, he wants to achieve great things, say, in art or literature: the popular taste has changed, it may be; a new generation has grown up, which takes no interest in his work; others have gone a shorter way and got the start of him. These are the facts of life which Horace must have had in view, when he lamented the uselessness of all advice:

> quid eternis minorem
> Consiliis animum fatigas?[1]

The cause of this commonest of all follies is that optical illusion of the mind from which everyone suffers, making life, at its beginning, seem of long duration; and at its end, when one looks back over the course of it, how short a time it seems! There is some advantage in the illusion; but for it, no great work would ever be done.

Our life is like a journey on which, as we advance, the landscape takes a different view from that which it presented at first, and changes again, as we come nearer. This is just

---

[1] Odes II, 11. "Why do you wear out your soul that is too weak for eternal plans?"

what happens—especially with our wishes. We often find something else, nay, something better than what we are looking for; and what we look for, we often find on a very different path from that on which we began a vain search. Instead of finding, as we expected, pleasure, happiness, joy, we get experience, insight, knowledge—a real and permanent blessing, instead of a fleeting and illusory one.

This is the thought that runs through *Wilhelm Meister*, like the bass in a piece of music. In this work of Goethe's, we have a novel of the *intellectual* kind, and, therefore, superior to all others, even to Sir Walter Scott's, which are, one and all, *ethical*; in other words, they treat of human nature only from the side of the will. So, too, in the *Zauberflöte*[1]—that grotesque, but still significant and ambiguous hieroglyphic—the same thought is symbolized, but in great, coarse lines, much in the way in which scenery is painted. Here the symbol would be complete if Tamino were in the end to be cured of his desire to possess Tainina, and received, in her stead, initiation into the mysteries of the Temple of Wisdom. It is quite right for Papageno, his necessary contrast, to succeed in getting his Papagena.

Men of any worth or value soon come to see that they are in the hands of Fate, and gratefully submit to be moulded by its teachings. They recognize that the fruit of life is experience, and not happiness; they become accustomed and content to exchange hope for insight; and, in the end, they can say, with Petrarch, that all they care for is to learn:—*Altro diletto che 'mparar, non provo.*[2]

It may even be that they to some extent still follow their old wishes and aims, trifling with them, as it were, for the sake of appearances; all the while really and seriously looking for nothing but instruction; a process which lends them an air of genius, a trait of something contemplative and sublime.

In their search for gold, the alchemists discovered other things—gunpowder, china, medicines, the laws of nature.

---

[1] *The Magic Flute*
[2] *Trionfo d'Amore*, 1.21. "No other happiness than learning do I feel."

There is a sense in which we are all alchemists.

Chapter Two: Our Relation to Ourselves

IV

The mason employed on the building of a house may be quite ignorant of its general design; or at any rate, he may not keep it constantly in mind. So it is with man: in working through the days and hours of his life, he takes little thought of its character as a whole.

If there is any merit or importance attaching to a man's career, if he lays himself out carefully for some special work, it is all the more necessary and advisable for him to turn his attention now and then to its *plan*, that is to say, the miniature sketch of its general outlines. Of course, to do that, he must have applied the maxim *Gnothi seauton*;[1] he must have made some little progress in the art of understanding himself. He must know what is his real, chief, and foremost object in life—what it is that he most wants in order to be happy; and then, after that, what occupies the second and third place in his thoughts; he must find out what, on the whole, his vocation really is—the part he has to play, his general relation to the world. If he maps out important work for himself on great lines, a glance at this miniature plan of his life will, more than anything else stimulate, rouse and ennoble him, urge him on to action and keep him from false paths.

Again, just as the traveller, on reaching a height, gets a connected view over the road he has taken, with its many turns and windings; so it is only when we have completed a period in our life, or approach the end of it altogether, that we recognize the true connection between all our actions—what it is we have achieved, what work we have done. It is only then that we see the precise chain of cause and effect, and the

---

[1] "Know thyself."

exact value of all our efforts. For as long as we are actually engaged in the work of life, we always act in accordance with the nature of our character, under the influence of motive, and within the limits of our capacity—in a word, from beginning to end, under a law of *necessity*; at every moment we do just what appears to us right and proper. It is only afterwards, when we come to look back at the whole course of our life and its general result, that we see the why and wherefore of it all.

When we are actually doing some great deed, or creating some immortal work, we are not conscious of it as such; we think only of satisfying present aims, of fulfilling the intentions we happen to have at the time, of doing the right thing at the moment. It is only when we come to view our life as a connected whole that our character and capacities show themselves in their true light; that we see how, in particular instances, some happy inspiration, as it were, led us to choose the only true path out of a thousand which might have brought us to ruin. It was our genius that guided us, a force felt in the affairs of the intellectual as in those of the world; and working by its defect just in the same way in regard to evil and disaster.

V

Another important element in the wise conduct of life is to preserve a proper proportion between our thought for the present and our thought for the future; in order not to spoil the one by paying over-great attention to the other. Many live too long in the present—frivolous people, I mean; others, too much in the future, ever anxious and full of care. It is seldom that a man holds the right balance between the two extremes. Those who strive and hope and live only in the future, always looking ahead and impatiently anticipating what is coming, as something which will make them happy when they get it, are, in spite of their very clever airs, exactly like those donkeys one sees in Italy, whose pace may be hurried by fixing a stick on their heads with a wisp of hay at the end of it; this is always just in front of them, and they keep on trying to get it. Such people are in a constant state of illusion as to their whole existence; they go on living *ad interim*,[1] until at last they die.

Instead, therefore, of always thinking about our plans and anxiously looking to the future, or of giving ourselves up to regret for the past, we should never forget that the present is the only reality, the only certainty; that the future almost always turns out contrary to our expectations; that the past, too, was very different from what we suppose it to have been. But the past and the future are, on the whole, of less consequence than we think. Distance, which makes objects look small to the outward eye, makes them look big to the eye of thought. The present alone is true and actual; it is the only time which possesses full reality, and our existence lies in it exclusively. Therefore we should always be glad of it, and give it the welcome it deserves, and enjoy every hour that is bearable by its freedom from pain and annoyance with a full consciousness of its value. We shall hardly be able to do this if we make a wry face over the failure of our hopes in the past or over our anxiety for the future. It is the height of folly to refuse the present hour of happiness, or wantonly to spoil it by vexation at bygones or uneasiness about what is to come. There is a time, of course, for forethought, nay, even for repentance; but when it is over let us think of what is past as of something to which we have said farewell, of necessity subduing our hearts—

> But however much it mortified us, we will
>   let bygones be bygones;
> And hard as it may be for us, we will
>   subdue the peevishness in our hearts.[2]

and of the future as of that which lies beyond our power, in the lap of the gods—

---

[1] Literally, "In the time between." Means "In the meantime" or "temporarily."
[2] *Iliad*, XIX, 65.

> all aetoi men tauta theon en gounasi keitai.[1]

But in regard to the present let us remember Seneca's advice, and live each day as if it were our whole life—*singulas dies singulas vitas puta*:[2] let us make it as agreeable as possible, it is the only real time we have.

Only those evils which are sure to come at a definite date have any right to disturb us; and how few there are which fulfil this description. For evils are of two kinds; either they are possible only, at most probable; or they are inevitable. Even in the case of evils which are sure to happen, the time at which they will happen is uncertain. A man who is always preparing for either class of evil will not have a moment of peace left him. So, if we are not to lose all comfort in life through the fear of evils, some of which are uncertain in themselves, and others, in the time at which they will occur, we should look upon the one kind as never likely to happen, and the other as not likely to happen very soon.

Now, the less our peace of mind is disturbed by fear, the more likely it is to be agitated by desire and expectation. This is the true meaning of that song of Goethe's which is such a favourite with everyone: *Ich hab' mein' Sach' auf nichts gestellt*.[3] It is only after a man has got rid of all pretension, and taken refuge in mere unembellished existence, that he is able to attain that peace of mind which is the foundation of human happiness. Peace of mind!—that is something essential to any enjoyment of the present moment; and unless its separate moments are enjoyed, there is an end of life's happiness as a whole. We should always collect that *Today* comes only once, and never returns. We fancy that it will come again tomorrow; but *Tomorrow* is another day, which, in its turn, comes once only. We are apt to forget that every day is an integral, and therefore irreplaceable portion of life,

---

1 *Iliad*, XVII, 514. "This lies in the lap of the gods."
2 "Regard each particular day as a special life."
3 "On nothing have I set my hopes."

and to look upon life as though it were a collective idea or name which does not suffer if one of the individuals it covers is destroyed.

We should be more likely to appreciate and enjoy the present if, in those good days when we are well and strong, we did not fail to reflect how, in sickness and sorrow, every past hour that was free from pain and privation seemed in our memory so infinitely to be envied—as it were, a lost paradise, or some one who was only then seen to have acted as a friend. But we live through our days of happiness without noticing them; it is only when evil comes upon us that we wish them back. A thousand gay and pleasant hours are wasted in ill-humour; we let them slip by unenjoyed, and sigh for them in vain when the sky is overcast. Those present moments that are bearable, be they never so trite and common—passed by in indifference, or, it may be, impatiently pushed away—those are the moments we should honour; never failing to remember that the ebbing tide is even now hurrying them into the past, where memory will store them transfigured and shining with an imperishable light—in some after-time—and above all, when our days are evil, to raise the veil and present them as the object of our fondest regret.

VI

Limitations always make for happiness. We are happy in proportion as our range of vision, our sphere of work, our points of contact with the world, are restricted and circumscribed. We are more likely to feel worried and anxious if these limits are wide; for it means that our cares, desires and terrors are increased and intensified. That is why the blind are not so unhappy as we might be inclined to suppose; otherwise there would not be that gentle and almost serene expression of peace in their faces.

Another reason why limitation makes for happiness is that the second half of life proves even more dreary that the first. As the years wear on, the horizon of our aims and our points of contact with the world become more extended. In childhood our horizon is limited to the narrowest sphere about us; in youth there is already a very considerable widening of our view; in manhood it comprises the whole range of our activity, often stretching out over a very distant sphere—the care, for instance, of a State or a nation; in old age it embraces posterity.

But even in the affairs of the intellect, limitation is necessary if we are to be happy. For the less the will is excited, the less we suffer. We have seen that suffering is something positive, and that happiness is only a negative condition. To limit the sphere of outward activity is to relieve the will of external stimulus: to limit the sphere of our intellectual efforts is to relieve the will of internal sources of excitement. This latter kind of limitation is attended by the disadvantage that it opens the door to boredom, which is a direct source of countless sufferings; for to banish boredom, a man will have recourse to any means that may be handy—dissipation, society, extravagance, gaming, and drinking, and the like, which in their turn bring mischief, ruin, and misery in their train. *Difficiles in otio quies*—it is difficult to keep quiet if you have nothing to do. That limitation in the sphere of outward activity is conducive, nay, even necessary to human happiness, such as it is, may be seen in the fact that the only kind of poetry which depicts men in a happy state of life—Idyllic poetry, I mean—always aims, as an intrinsic part of its treatment, at representing them in very simple and restricted circumstances. It is this feeling, too, which is at the bottom of the pleasure we take in what are called *genre* pictures.

Simplicity, therefore, as far as it can be attained, and even *monotony*, in our manner of life, if it does not mean that we are bored, will contribute to happiness; just because, under such circumstances, life, and consequently the burden which is the essential concomitant of life, will be least felt. Our existence will glide on peacefully like a stream which no waves or whirlpools disturb.

VII

Whether we are in a pleasant or a painful state depends, ultimately, upon the kind of matter that pervades and engrosses our consciousness. In this respect, purely intellectual occupation, for the mind that is capable of it, will, as a rule, do much more in the way of happiness than any form of practical life, with its constant alternations of success and failure, and all the shocks and torments it produces. But it must be confessed that for such occupation a preeminent amount of intellectual capacity is necessary. And in this connection it may be noted that, just as a life devoted to outward activity will distract and divert a man from study, and also deprive him of that quiet concentration of mind which is necessary for such work; so, on the other hand, a long course of thought will make him more or less unfit for the noisy pursuits of real life. It is advisable, therefore, to suspend mental work for a while, if circumstances happen which demand any degree of energy in affairs of a practical nature.

VIII

To live a life that shall be entirely prudent and discreet, and to draw from experience all the instruction it contains, it is requisite to be constantly thinking back—to make a kind of recapitulation of what we have done, of our impressions and sensations, to compare our former with our present judgments—what we set before us and struggle to achieve, with the actual result and satisfaction we have obtained. To do this is to get a repetition of the private lessons of experience—lessons which are given to everyone.

Experience of the world may be looked upon as a kind of text, to which reflection and knowledge form the commentary. Where there is great deal of reflection and intellectual knowledge, and very little experience, the result is like those books which have on each page two lines of text to forty lines of commentary. A great deal of experience with little reflection and scant knowledge, gives us books like those of the *editio Bipontina* where there are no notes and much that is unintelligible.

The advice here given is on a par with a rule recommended by Pythagoras—to review, every night before going to sleep, what we have done during the day. To live at random, in the hurly-burly of business or pleasure, without ever reflecting upon the past—to go on, as it were, pulling cotton off the reel of life—is to have no clear idea of what we are about; and a man who lives in this state will have chaos in his emotions and certain confusion in his thoughts; as is soon manifest by the abrupt and fragmentary character of his conversation, which becomes a kind of mincemeat. A man will be all the more exposed to this fate in proportion as he lives a restless life in the world, amid a crowd of various impressions and with a correspondingly small amount of activity on the part of his own mind.

And in this connection it will be in place to observe that, when events and circumstances which have influenced us pass away in the course of time, we are unable to bring back and renew the particular mood or state of feeling which they aroused in us: but we can remember what we were led to say and do in regard to them; and thus form, as it were, the result, expression and measure of those events. We should, therefore, be careful to preserve the memory of our thoughts at important points in our life; and herein lies the great advantage of keeping a journal.

IX

To be self-sufficient, to be all in all to oneself, to want for nothing, to be able to say *omnia mea mecum porto*[1]—that is assuredly the chief qualification for happiness. Hence Aristotle's remark, "to be happy means to be self-sufficient,"[2] cannot be too often repeated. It is, at bottom, the same thought as is present in the very well-turned sentence from Chamfort: *Le*

---

[1] "All that is mine I carry with me."
[2] *Eudemian Ethics*, VII, 2.

bonheur n'est pas chose aisée: il est très difficile de le trouver en nous, et impossible de le trouver ailleurs.[1]

For while a man cannot reckon with certainty upon anyone but himself, the burdens and disadvantages, the dangers and annoyances, which arise from having to do with others, are not only countless but unavoidable.

There is no more mistaken path to happiness than worldliness, revelry, *high life*: for the whole object of it is to transform our miserable existence into a succession of joys, delights and pleasures—a process which cannot fail to result in disappointment and delusion; on a par, in this respect, with its *obligato* accompaniment, the interchange of lies.[2]

All society necessarily involves, as the first condition of its existence, mutual accommodation and restraint upon the part of its members. This means that the larger it is, the more insipid will be its tone. A man can be *himself* only so long as he is alone; and if he does not love solitude, he will not love freedom; for it is only when he is alone that he is really free. Constraint is always present in society, like a companion of whom there is no riddance; and in proportion to the greatness of a man's individuality, it will be hard for him to bear the sacrifices which all intercourse with others demands. Solitude will be welcomed or endured or avoided, according as a man's personal value is large or small—the wretch feeling, when he is alone, the whole burden of his misery; the great intellect delighting in its greatness; and everyone, in short, being just what he is.

Further, if a man stands high in Nature's lists, it is natural and inevitable that he should feel solitary. It will be an advantage to him if his surroundings do not interfere with this feeling; for if he has to see a great deal of other people who are not of like character with himself, they will exercise a

---

[1] "Happiness is not an easy thing: it is very difficult to find it within ourselves, and impossible to find it elsewhere."

[2] Author's Footnote: As our body is concealed by the clothes we wear, so our mind is veiled in lies. The veil is always there, and it is only through it that we can sometimes guess at what a man really thinks; just as from his clothes we arrive at the general shape of his body.

disturbing influence upon him, adverse to his peace of mind; they will rob him, in fact, of himself, and give him nothing to compensate for the loss.

But while Nature sets very wide differences between man and man in respect both of morality and of intellect, society disregards and effaces them; or, rather, it sets up artificial differences in their stead—gradations of rank and position, which are very often diametrically opposed to those which Nature establishes. The result of this arrangement is to elevate those whom Nature has placed low, and to depress the few who stand high. These latter, then, usually withdraw from society, where, as soon as it is at all numerous, vulgarity reigns supreme.

What offends a great intellect in society is the equality of rights, leading to equality of pretensions, which everyone enjoys; while at the same time, inequality of capacity means a corresponding disparity of social power. So-called *good society* recognizes every kind of claim but that of intellect, which is a contraband article; and people are expected to exhibit an unlimited amount of patience towards every form of folly and stupidity, perversity and dullness; while personal merit has to beg pardon, as it were, for being present, or else conceal itself altogether. Intellectual superiority offends by its very existence, without any desire to do so.

The worst of what is called good society is not only that it offers us the companionship of people who are unable to win either our praise or our affection, but that it does not allow of our being that which we naturally are; it compels us, for the sake of harmony, to shrivel up, or even alter our shape altogether. Intellectual conversation, whether grave or humorous, is only fit for intellectual society; it is downright abhorrent to ordinary people, to please whom it is absolutely necessary to be commonplace and dull. This demands an act of severe self-denial; we have to forfeit three-fourths of ourselves in order to become like other people. No doubt their company may be set down against our loss in this respect; but the more a man is worth, the more he will find that what he gains does not cover what he loses, and that the balance is on the debit side of the account; for the people with whom he deals are generally bankrupt—that is to say, there is nothing to be got from their society which can compensate either for its boredom, annoyance and disagreeableness, or for the self-denial which it renders necessary. Accordingly, most society is so constituted as to offer a good profit to anyone who will exchange it for solitude.

Nor is this all. By way of providing a substitute for real—I mean intellectual—superiority, which is seldom to be met with, and intolerable when it is found, society has capriciously adopted a false kind of superiority, conventional in its character, and resting upon arbitrary principles—a tradition, as it were, handed down in the higher circles, and, like a password, subject to alteration; I refer to *bon-ton* fashion. Whenever this kind of superiority comes into collision with the real kind, its weakness is manifest. Moreover, the presence of *good tone* means the absence of *good sense*.

No man can be in *perfect accord* with anyone but himself—not even with a friend or the partner of his life; differences of individuality and temperament are always bringing in some degree of discord, though it may be a very slight one. That genuine, profound peace of mind, that perfect tranquillity of soul, which, next to health, is the highest blessing the earth can give, is to be attained only in solitude, and, as a permanent mood, only in complete retirement; and then, if there is anything great and rich in the man's own self, his way of life is the happiest that may be found in this wretched world.

Let me speak plainly. However close the bond of friendship, love, marriage—a man, ultimately, looks to himself, to his own welfare alone; at most, to his child's too. The less necessity there is for you to come into contact with mankind in general, in the relations whether of business or of personal intimacy, the better off you are. Loneliness and solitude have their evils, it is true; but if you cannot feel them all at once, you can at least see where they lie; on the other hand, society is *insidious* in this respect; as in offering you what appears to be the pastime of pleasing social intercourse, it works great and often irreparable mischief. The young should early be trained to bear being left alone; for it is a source of happiness and peace of mind.

It follows from this that a man is best off if he be thrown upon his own resources and can be all in all to himself; and Cicero goes so far as to say that a man who is in this condition cannot fail to be very happy—*nemo potest non beatissimus esse qui est totus aptus ex sese, quique in se uno ponit omnia.*[1] The more a man has in himself, the less others can be to him. The feeling of self-sufficiency!—it is that which restrains those whose personal value is in itself great riches, from such considerable sacrifices as are demanded by intercourse with the world, let alone, then, from actually practicing self-denial by going out of their way to seek it. Ordinary people are sociable and complaisant just from the very opposite feeling: to bear others' company is easier for them than to bear their own. Moreover, respect is not paid in this world to that which has real merit; it is reserved for that which has none. So retirement is at once a proof and a result of being distinguished by the possession of meritorious qualities. It will therefore show real wisdom on the part of anyone who is worth anything in himself, to limit his requirements as may be necessary, in order to preserve or extend his freedom, and—since a man must come into some relations with his fellow-men—to admit them to his intimacy as little as possible.

I have said that people are rendered sociable by their inability to endure solitude, that is to say, their own society. They become sick of themselves. It is this vacuity of soul which drives them to intercourse with others—to travels in foreign countries. Their mind is wanting in elasticity; it has no movement of its own, and so they try to give it some—by drink, for instance. How much drunkenness is due to this cause alone! They are always looking for some form of excitement, of the strongest kind they can bear—the excitement of being with people of like nature with themselves; and if they fail in

---

[1] *Paradoxa Stoidorum,* II. "It is impossible for anyone not to be perfectly happy who depends entirely on himself and possesses in himself alone all that he calls *him.*"

this, their mind sinks by its own weight, and they fall into a grievous lethargy.[1] Such people, it may be said, possess only a small fraction of humanity in themselves; and it requires a great many of them put together to make up a fair amount of it—to attain any degree of consciousness as men. A man, in the full sense of the word—a man *par excellence*—does not represent a fraction, but a whole number: he is complete in himself.

Ordinary society is, in this respect, very like the kind of music to be obtained from an orchestra composed of Russian horns. Each horn has only one note; and the music is produced by each note coming in just at the right moment. In the monotonous sound of a single horn, you have a precise illustration of the effect of most people's minds. How often there seems to be only one thought there! and no room for any other. It is easy to see why people are so bored; and also why they are sociable, why they like to go about in crowds—why mankind is so *gregarious*. It is the monotony of his own nature that makes a man find solitude intolerable. *Omnis stultitia laborat fastidio sui*: folly is truly its own burden. Put a great many men together, and you may get some result—some music from your horns!

A man of intellect is like an artist who gives a concert without any help from anyone else, playing on a single instrument—a

---

[1] Author's Footnote: It is a well-known fact, that we can more easily bear up under evils which fall upon a great many people besides ourselves. As boredom seems to be an evil of this kind, people band together to offer it a common resistance. The love of life is at bottom only the fear of death; and, in the same way, the social impulse does not rest directly upon the love of society, but upon the fear of solitude; it is not alone the charm of being in others' company that people seek, it is the dreary oppression of being alone—the monotony of their own consciousness—that they would avoid. They will do anything to escape it,—even tolerate bad companions, and put up with the feeling of constraint which all society involves, in this case a very burdensome one. But if aversion to such society conquers the aversion to being alone, they become accustomed to solitude and hardened to its immediate effects. They no longer find solitude to be such a very bad thing, and settle down comfortably to it without any hankering after society;—and this, partly because it is only indirectly that they need others' company, and partly because they have become accustomed to the benefits of being alone.

piano, say, which is a little orchestra in itself. Such a man is a little world in himself; and the effect produced by various instruments together, he produces single-handed, in the unity of his own consciousness. Like the piano, he has no place in a symphony: he is a soloist and performs by himself—in solitude, it may be; or, if in company with other instruments, only as principal; or for setting the tone, as in singing. However, those who are fond of society from time to time may profit by this simile, and lay it down as a general rule that deficiency of quality in those we meet may be to some extent compensated by an increase in quantity. One man's company may be quite enough, if he is clever; but where you have only ordinary people to deal with, it is advisable to have a great many of them, so that some advantage may accrue by letting them all work together—on the analogy of the horns; and may Heaven grant you patience for your task!

That mental vacuity and barrenness of soul to which I have alluded, is responsible for another misfortune. When men of the better class form a society for promoting some noble or ideal aim, the result almost always is that the innumerable mob of humanity comes crowding in too, as it always does everywhere, like vermin—their object being to try and get rid of boredom, or some other defect of their nature; and anything that will effect that, they seize upon at once, without the slightest discrimination. Some of them will slip into that society, or push themselves in, and then either soon destroy it altogether, or alter it so much that in the end it comes to have a purpose the exact opposite of that which it had at first.

[...]

X

Envy is natural to man; and still, it is at once a vice and a source of misery.[1] We should treat it as the enemy of our happiness, and stifle it like an evil thought. This is the advice

---

[1] Author's Footnote: Envy shows how unhappy people are; and their constant attention to what others do and leave undone, how much they are bored.

given by Seneca; as he well puts it, we shall be pleased with what we have, if we avoid the self-torture of comparing our own lot with some other and happier one—*nostra nos sine comparatione delectent; nunquam erit felix quem torquebit felicior.*[1] And again, *quum adspexeris quot te antecedent, cogita quot sequantur*[2]—if a great many people appear to be better off than yourself, think how many there are in a worse position. It is a fact that if real calamity comes upon us, the most effective consolation—though it springs from the same source as envy—is just the thought of greater misfortunes than ours; and the next best is the society of those who are in the same luck as we—the partners of our sorrows.

So much for the envy which we may feel towards others. As regards the envy which we may excite in them, it should always be remembered that no form of hatred is so implacable as the hatred that comes from envy; and therefore we should always carefully refrain from doing anything to rouse it; nay, as with many another form of vice, it is better altogether to renounce any pleasure there may be in it, because of the serious nature of its consequences.

Aristocracies are of three kinds: (1) of birth and rank; (2) of wealth; and (3) of intellect. The last is really the most distinguished of the three, and its claim to occupy the first position comes to be recognized, if it is only allowed time to work. So eminent a king as Frederick the Great admitted it—*les âmes privilegiées rangent à l'égal des souverains,*[3] as he said to his chamberlain, when the latter expressed his surprise that Voltaire should have a seat at the table reserved for kings and princes, while ministers and generals were relegated to the chamberlain's.

Every one of these aristocracies is surrounded by a host of envious persons. If you belong to one of them, they will be

---

[1] *De Ira*, III, 30. "We will find pleasure in what we have got without making comparisons. We shall never be happy if we are worried that someone else is luckier than we."
[2] *Epistles*, XV. "If you see many who are better off than you, think of how many who are worse off."
[3] "Privileged minds have equal rank with sovereigns."

secretly embittered against you; and unless they are restrained by fear, they will always be anxious to let you understand that *you are no better than they*. It is by their anxiety to let you know this, that they betray how greatly they are conscious that the opposite is the truth.

The line of conduct to be pursued if you are exposed to envy, is to keep the envious persons at a distance, and, as far as possible, avoid all contact with them, so that there may be a wide gulf fixed between you and them; if this cannot be done, to bear their attacks with the greatest composure. In the latter case, the very thing that provokes the attack will also neutralize it. This is what appears to be generally done.

The members of one of these aristocracies usually get on very well with those of another, and there is no call for envy between them, because their several privileges effect an equipoise.

XI

Give mature and repeated consideration to any plan before you proceed to carry it out; and even after you have thoroughly turned it over in your mind, make some concession to the incompetency of human judgment; for it may always happen that circumstances which cannot be investigated or foreseen, will come in and upset the whole of your calculation. This is a reflection that will always influence the negative side of the balance—a kind of warning to refrain from unnecessary action in matters of importance—*quieta non movere*.[1] But having once made up your mind and begun your work, you must let it run its course and abide the result—not worry yourself by fresh reflections on what is already accomplished, or by a renewal of your scruples on the score of possible danger: free your mind from the subject altogether, and refuse to go into it again, secure in the thought that you gave it mature attention at the proper time. This is the same advice as is given by an Italian proverb—*legala bene e poi lascia la*

---

[1] "Not to set in motion what is at rest."

andare[1]—which Goethe has translated thus: See well to your girths, and then ride on boldly.[2]

And if, notwithstanding that, you fail, it is because human affairs are the sport of chance and error. Socrates, the wisest of men, needed the warning voice of his good genius, or *daimonion*, to enable him to do what was right in regard to his own personal affairs, or at any rate, to avoid mistakes; which argues that the human intellect is incompetent for the purpose. There is a saying—which is reported to have originated with one of the Popes—that when misfortune happens to us, the blame of it, at least in some degree, attaches to ourselves. If this is not true absolutely and in every instance, it is certainly true in the great majority of cases. It even looks as if this truth had a great deal to do with the effort people make as far as possible to conceal their misfortunes, and to put the best face they can upon them, for fear lest their misfortunes may show how much they are to blame.

XII

In the case of a misfortune which has already happened and therefore cannot be altered, you should not allow yourself to think that it might have been otherwise; still less, that it might have been avoided by such and such means; for reflections of this kind will only add to your distress and make it intolerable, so that you will become a tormentor to yourself—*heautontimoroumeaeos*.[3] It is better to follow the example of King David, who, as long as his son lay on the bed of sickness, assailed Jehovah with unceasing supplications and entreaties for his recovery; but when he was dead, snapped his fingers and thought no more of it. If you are not light-hearted enough for that, you can take refuge in fatalism, and have the great

---

[1] "Harness the horse and send him off."
[2] Author's Footnote: It may be observed, in passing, that a great many of the maxims which Goethe puts under the head of Proverbial, are translations from the Italian.
[3] Greek: literally, "executioner of oneself."

truth revealed to you that everything which happens is the result of necessity, and therefore inevitable.

However good this advice may be, it is one-sided and partial. In relieving and quieting us for the moment, it is no doubt effective enough; but when our misfortunes have resulted—as is usually the case—from our own carelessness or folly, or, at any rate, partly by our own fault, it is a good thing to consider how they might have been avoided, and to consider it often in spite of its being a tender subject—a salutary form of self-discipline, which will make us wiser and better men for the future. If we have made obvious mistakes, we should not try, as we generally do, to gloss them over, or to find something to excuse or extenuate them; we should admit to ourselves that we have committed faults, and open our eyes wide to all their enormity, in order that we may firmly resolve to avoid them in time to come. To be sure, that means a great deal of self-inflicted pain, in the shape of discontent, but it should be remembered that to spare the rod is to spoil the child—*ho mae dareis anthropos ou paideuetai.*[1]

XIII

In all matters affecting our weal or woe, we should be careful not to let our imagination run away with us, and build no castles in the air. In the first place, they are expensive to build, because we have to pull them down again immediately, and that is a source of grief. We should be still more on our guard against distressing our hearts by depicting possible misfortunes. If these were misfortunes of a purely imaginary kind, or very remote and unlikely, we should at once see, on awaking from our dream, that the whole thing was mere illusion; we should rejoice all the more in a reality better than our dreams, or at most, be warned against misfortunes which, though very remote, were still possible. These, however, are not the sort of playthings in which imagination delights; it

---

[1] Menander. *Monost*, 422. "Whoever is not chastised is not properly brought up."

is only in idle hours that we build castles in the air, and they are always of a pleasing description. The matter which goes to form gloomy dreams are mischances which to some extent really threaten us, though it be from some distance; imagination makes them look larger and nearer and more terrible than they are in reality. This is a kind of dream which cannot be so readily shaken off on awaking as a pleasant one; for a pleasant dream is soon dispelled by reality, leaving, at most, a feeble hope lying in the lap of possibility. Once we have abandoned ourselves to a fit of the blues, visions are conjured up which do not so easily vanish again; for it is always just possible that the visions may be realized. But we are not always able to estimate the exact degree of possibility: possibility may easily pass into probability; and thus we deliver ourselves up to torture. Therefore we should be careful not to be over-anxious on any matter affecting our weal or our woe, not to carry our anxiety to unreasonable or injudicious limits; but coolly and dispassionately to deliberate upon the matter, as though it were an abstract question which did not touch us in particular. We should give no play to imagination here; for imagination is not judgment—it only conjures up visions, inducing an unprofitable and often very painful mood.

The rule on which I am here insisting should be most carefully observed towards evening. For as darkness makes us timid and apt to see terrifying shapes everywhere, there is something similar in the effect of indistinct thought; and uncertainty always brings with it a sense of danger. Hence, towards evening, when our powers of thought and judgment are relaxed—at the hour, as it were, of subjective darkness—the intellect becomes tired, easily confused, and unable to get at the bottom of things; and if, in that state, we meditate on matters of personal interest to ourselves, they soon assume a dangerous and terrifying aspect. This is mostly the case at night, when we are in bed; for then the mind is fully relaxed, and the power of judgment quite unequal to its duties; but imagination is still awake. Night gives a black look to everything, whatever it may be. This is why our thoughts, just before we go to sleep, or as we lie awake through the hours of the night, are usually such confusions and perversions of facts as dreams themselves; and when our thoughts at that time are concentrated upon our own concerns, they are generally as black and monstrous as possible. In the morning all such nightmares vanish like dreams: as the Spanish proverb has it, *noche tinta, bianco el dia*—the night is coloured, the day is white. But even towards nightfall, as soon as the candles are lit, the mind, like the eye, no longer sees things so clearly as by day: it is a time unsuited to serious meditation, especially on unpleasant subjects. The morning is the proper time for that—as indeed for all efforts without exception, whether mental or bodily. For the morning is the youth of the day, when everything is bright, fresh, and easy of attainment; we feel strong then, and all our faculties are completely at our disposal. Do not shorten the morning by getting up late, or waste it in unworthy occupations or in talk; look upon it as the quintessence of life, as to a certain extent sacred. Evening is like old age: we are languid, talkative, silly. Each day is a little life: every waking and rising a little birth, every fresh morning a little youth, every going to rest and sleep a little death.

But condition of health, sleep, nourishment, temperature, weather, surroundings, and much else that is purely external, have, in general, an important influence upon our mood and therefore upon our thoughts. Hence both our view of any matter and our capacity for any work are very much subject to time and place. So it is best to profit by a good mood—for how seldom it comes!—*Nehmt die gute Stimmung wahr, Denn sie kommt so selten.*[1]

We are not always able to form new ideas about our surroundings, or to command original thoughts: they come if they will, and when they will. And so, too, we cannot always succeed in completely considering some personal matter at the precise time at which we have determined beforehand to consider it, and just when we set ourselves to do so. For

---

[1] Goethe, *Generalbeichte*. "To the true good mood pay heed, because it comes so seldom."

the peculiar train of thought which is favourable to it may suddenly become active without any special call being made upon it, and we may then follow it up with keen interest. In this way reflection, too, chooses its own time.

This reining-in of the imagination which I am recommending will also forbid us to summon up the memory of the past misfortune, to paint a dark picture of the injustice or harm that has been done us, the losses we have sustained, the insults, slights and annoyances to which we have been exposed: for to do that is to rouse into fresh life all those hateful passions long laid asleep—the anger and resentment which disturb and pollute our nature. In an excellent parable, Proclus, the Neoplatonist, points out how in every town the mob dwells side by side with those who are rich and distinguished: so, too, in every man, be he ever so noble and dignified, there is, in the depth of his nature, a mob of low and vulgar desires which constitute him an animal. It will not do to let this mob revolt or even so much as peep forth from its hiding-place; it is hideous of mien, and its rebel leaders are those flights of imagination which I have been describing. The smallest annoyance, whether it comes from our fellow-men or from the things around us, may swell up into a monster of dreadful aspect, putting us at our wits' end—and all because we go on brooding over our troubles and painting them in the most glaring colours and on the largest scale. It is much better to take a very calm and prosaic view of what is disagreeable; for that is the easiest way of bearing it.

If you hold small objects close to your eyes, you limit your field of vision and shut out the world. And, in the same way, the people or the things which stand nearest, even though they are of the very smallest consequence, are apt to claim an amount of attention much beyond their due, occupying us disagreeably, and leaving no room for serious thoughts and affairs of importance. We ought to work against this tendency.

XIV

The sight of things which do not belong to us is very apt

to raise the thought: *Ah, if that were only mine!* making us sensible of our privation. Instead of that we should do better by more frequently putting to ourselves the opposite case: *Ah, if that were not mine.* What I mean is that we should sometimes try to look upon our possessions in the light in which they would appear if we had lost them; whatever they may be, property, health, friends, a wife or child or someone else we love, our horse or our dog—it is usually only when we have lost them that we begin to find out their value. But if we come to look at things in the way I recommend, we shall be doubly the gainers; we shall at once get more pleasure out of them than we did before, and we shall do everything in our power to prevent the loss of them; for instance, by not risking our property, or angering our friends, or exposing our wives to temptation, or being careless about our children's health, and so on.

We often try to banish the gloom and despondency of the present by speculating upon our chances of success in the future; a process which leads us to invent a great many chimerical hopes. Every one of them contains the germ of illusion, and disappointment is inevitable when our hopes are shattered by the hard facts of life.

It is less hurtful to take the chances of misfortune as a theme for speculation; because, in doing so, we provide ourselves at once with measures of precaution against it, and a pleasant surprise when it fails to make its appearance. Is it not a fact that we always feel a marked improvement in our spirits when we begin to get over a period of anxiety? I may go further and say that there is some use in occasionally looking upon terrible misfortunes—such as might happen to us—as though they had actually happened, for then the trivial reverses which subsequently come in reality, are much easier to bear. It is a source of consolation to look back upon those great misfortunes which never happened. But in following out this rule, care must be taken not to neglect what I have said in the preceding section.

XV

The things which engage our attention—whether they are matters of business or ordinary events—are of such diverse kinds, that, if taken quite separately and in no fixed order or relation, they present a medley of the most glaring contrasts, with nothing in common, except that they one and all affect us in particular. There must be a corresponding abruptness in the thoughts and anxieties which these various matters arouse in us, if our thoughts are to be in keeping with their various subjects. Therefore, in setting about anything, the first step is to withdraw our attention from everything else: this will enable us to attend to each matter at its own time, and to enjoy or put up with it, quite apart from any thought of our remaining interests. Our thoughts must be arranged, as it were, in little drawers, so that we may open one without disturbing any of the others.

In this way we can keep the heavy burden of anxiety from weighing upon us so much as to spoil the little pleasures of the present, or from robbing us of our rest; otherwise the consideration of one matter will interfere with every other, and attention to some important business may lead us to neglect many affairs which happen to be of less moment. It is most important for everyone who is capable of higher and nobler thoughts to keep their mind from being so completely engrossed with private affairs and vulgar troubles as to let them take up all his attention and crowd out worthier matters; for that is, in a very real sense, to lose sight of the true end of life—*propter vitam vivendi perdere causas.*[1]

Of course for this—as for so much else—self-control is necessary; without it, we cannot manage ourselves in the way I have described. And self-control may not appear so very difficult, if we consider that every man has to submit to a great deal of very severe control on the part of his surroundings, and that without it no form of existence is possible. Further, a little self-control at the right moment may prevent much

---

1 "To ruin the purpose of life in order to live."

subsequent compulsion at the hands of others; just as a very small section of a circle close to the centre may correspond to a part near the circumference a hundred times as large. Nothing will protect us from external compulsion so much as the control of ourselves; and, as Seneca says, to submit yourself to reason is the way to make everything else submit to you—*si tibi vis omnia subjicere, te subjice rationi.*[1] Self-control, too, is something which we have in our own power; and if the worst comes to the worst, and it touches us in a very sensitive part, we can always relax its severity. But other people will pay no regard to our feelings, if they have to use compulsion, and we shall be treated without pity or mercy. Therefore it will be prudent to anticipate compulsion by self-control.

XVI

We must set limits to our wishes, curb our desires, moderate our anger, always remembering that an individual can attain only an infinitesimal share in anything that is worth having; and that, on the other hand, everyone must incur many of the ills of life; in a word, we must bear and forbear—*abstinere et sustinere*; and if we fail to observe this rule, no position of wealth or power will prevent us from feeling wretched. This is what Horace means when he recommends us to study carefully and inquire diligently what will best promote a tranquil life—not to be always agitated by fruitless desires and fears and hopes for things, which, after all, are not worth very much:—

> Inter cuncta leges et percontabere doctos
> Qua ratione queas traducere leniter
>   aevum;
> Ne te semper inops agitet vexetque
>   cupido,
> Ne pavor, et rerum mediocriter utilium

---

[1] Seneca, *Epistles* XXXVII: "If you want to subject everything to yourself, then subject yourself to reason."

spes.[1]

XVII

Life consists in movement, says Aristotle; and he is obviously right. We exist, physically, because our organism is the seat of constant motion; and if we are to exist intellectually, it can only be by means of continual occupation—no matter with what so long as it is some form of practical or mental activity. You may see that this is so by the way in which people who have no work or nothing to think about, immediately begin to beat the devil's tattoo with their knuckles or a stick or anything that comes handy. The truth is, that our nature is essentially *restless* in its character: we very soon get tired of having nothing to do; it is intolerable boredom. This impulse to activity should be regulated, and some sort of method introduced into it, which of itself will enhance the satisfaction we obtain. Activity!—doing something, if possible creating something, at any rate learning something—how fortunate it is that men cannot exist without that! A man wants to use his strength, to see, if he can, what effect it will produce; and he will get the most complete satisfaction of this desire if he can make or construct something—be it a book or a basket. There is a direct pleasure in seeing work grow under one's hands day by day, until at last it is finished. This is the pleasure attaching to a work of art or a manuscript, or even mere manual labour; and, of course, the higher the work, the greater pleasure it will give.

From this point of view, those are happiest of all who are conscious of the power to produce great works animated by some significant purpose: it gives a higher kind of interest—a sort of rare flavour—to the whole of their life, which, by its absence from the life of the ordinary man, makes it, in com-

---

[1] *Epistles*, I, xviii, 97: "Always read between the lines of what you are doing, and ask the wise men how you may pass your life with an easy mind, so that you may not be tormented by desire, fear, or the hope for things that are of little use."

parison, something very insipid. For richly endowed natures, life and the world have a special interest beyond the mere everyday personal interest which so many others share; and something higher than that—a formal interest. It is from life and the world that they get the material for their works; and as soon as they are freed from the pressure of personal needs, it is to the diligent collection of material that they devote their whole existence. So with their intellect: it is to some extent of a two-fold character, and devoted partly to the ordinary affairs of every day—those matters of will which are common to them and the rest of mankind, and partly to their peculiar work—the pure and objective contemplation of existence. And while, on the stage of the world, most men play their little part and then pass away, the genius lives a double life, at once an actor and a spectator.

Let everyone, then, do something, according to the measure of his capacities. To have no regular work, no set sphere of activity—what a miserable thing it is! How often long travels undertaken for pleasure make a man downright unhappy; because the absence of anything that can be called occupation forces him, as it were, out of his right element. Effort, struggles with difficulties! that is as natural to a man as grubbing in the ground is to a mole. To have all his wants satisfied is something intolerable—the feeling of stagnation which comes from pleasures that last too long. To overcome difficulties is to experience the full delight of existence, no matter where the obstacles are encountered; whether in the affairs of life, in commerce or business; or in mental effort—the spirit of inquiry that tries to master its subject. There is always something pleasurable in the struggle and the victory. And if a man has no opportunity to excite himself, he will do what he can to create one, and according to his individual bent, he will hunt or play Cup and Ball: or led on by this unsuspected element in his nature, he will pick a quarrel with someone, or hatch a plot or intrigue, or take to swindling and rascally courses generally—all to put an end to a state of repose which is intolerable. As I have remarked, *difficilis in otio quies*—it is difficult to keep quiet if you have nothing to do.

XVIII

A man should avoid being led on by the phantoms of his imagination. This is not the same thing as to submit to the guidance of ideas clearly thought out: and yet these are rules of life which most people pervert. If you examine closely into the circumstances which, in any deliberation, ultimately turn the scale in favour of some particular course, you will generally find that the decision is influenced, not by any clear arrangement of ideas leading to a formal judgment, but by some fanciful picture which seems to stand for one of the alternatives in question.

In one of Voltaire's or Diderot's romances—I forget the precise reference—the hero, standing like a young Hercules at the parting of ways, can see no other representation of Virtue than his old tutor holding a snuff-box in his left hand, from which he takes a pinch and moralizes; whilst Vice appears in the shape of his mother's chambermaid. It is in youth, more especially, that the goal of our efforts comes to be a fanciful picture of happiness, which continues to hover before our eyes sometimes for half and even for the whole of our life—a sort of mocking spirit; for when we think our dream is to be realized, the picture fades away, leaving us the knowledge that nothing of what it promised is actually accomplished. How often this is so with the visions of domesticity—the detailed picture of what our home will be like; or, of life among our fellow-citizens or in society; or, again, of living in the country—the kind of house we shall have, its surroundings, the marks of honour and respect that will be paid to us, and so on—whatever our hobby may be; *chaque fou a sa marotte.*[1] It is often the same, too, with our dreams about one we love. And this is all quite natural; for the visions we conjure up affect us directly, as though they were real objects; and so they exercise a more immediate influence upon our will than an abstract idea, which gives merely a vague, general outline, devoid of details; and the details are just the real part of it. We

---

1 "Every fool has his cap and bells."

can be only indirectly affected by an abstract idea, and yet it is the abstract idea alone which will do as much as it promises; and it is the function of education to teach us to put our trust in it. Of course the abstract idea must be occasionally explained—paraphrased, as it were—by the aid of pictures; but discreetly, *cum grano salis*.[1]

XIX

The preceding rule may be taken as a special case of the more general maxim, that a man should never let himself be mastered by the impressions of the moment, or indeed by outward appearances at all, which are incomparably more powerful in their effects than the mere play of thought or a train of ideas; not because these momentary impressions are rich in virtue of the data they supply—it is often just the contrary—but because they are something palpable to the senses and direct in their working; they forcibly invade our mind, disturbing our repose and shattering our resolutions.

It is easy to understand that the thing which lies before our very eyes will produce the whole of its effect at once, but that time and leisure are necessary for the working of thought and the appreciation of argument, as it is impossible to think of everything at one and the same moment. This is why we are so allured by pleasure, in spite of all our determination to resist it; or so much annoyed by a criticism, even though we know that its author it totally incompetent to judge; or so irritated by an insult, though it comes from some very contemptible quarter. In the same way, to mention no other instances, ten reasons for thinking that there is no danger may be outweighed by one mistaken notion that it is actually at hand. All this shows the radical unreason of human nature. Women frequently succumb altogether to this predominating influence of present impressions, and there are few men so overweighted with reason as to escape suffering from a similar cause.

[1] "With a grain of salt."

If it is impossible to resist the effects of some external influence by the mere play of thought, the best thing to do is to neutralize it by some contrary influence; for example, the effect of an insult may be overcome by seeking the society of those who have a good opinion of us; and the unpleasant sensation of imminent danger may be avoided by fixing our attention on the means of warding it off.

Leibnitz[1] tells of an Italian who managed to bear up under the tortures of the rack by never for a moment ceasing to think of the gallows which would have awaited him, had he revealed his secret; he kept on crying out: *I see it! I see it!*—afterwards explaining that this was part of his plan.

It is from some such reason as this, that we find it so difficult to stand alone in a matter of opinion—not to be made irresolute by the fact that everyone else disagrees with us and acts accordingly, even though we are quite sure that they are in the wrong. Take the case of a fugitive king who is trying to avoid capture; how much consolation he must find in the ceremonious and submissive attitude of a faithful follower, exhibited secretly so as not to betray his master's strict *incognito*; it must be almost necessary to prevent him doubting his own existence.

XXX

No man is so formed that he can be left entirely to himself, to go his own ways; everyone needs to be guided by a preconceived plan, and to follow certain general rules. But if this is carried too far, and a man tries to take on a character which is not natural or innate in him, but is artificially acquired and evolved merely by a process of reasoning, he will very soon discover that Nature cannot be forced, and that if you drive it out, it will return despite your efforts: *Naturam expelles furca, tamen usque recurret.*[2]

---

[1] *Nouveaux Essais*, I, ii, 11.
[2] Horace, *Epistles*, I, x, 24. "Expel Nature with a pitchfork, she still comes back."

To understand a rule governing conduct towards others, even to discover it for oneself and to express it neatly, is easy enough; and still, very soon afterwards, the rule may be broken in practice. But that is no reason for despair; and you need not fancy that as it is impossible to regulate your life in accordance with abstract ideas and maxims, it is better to live just as you please. Here, as in all theoretical instruction that aims at a practical result, the first thing to do is to understand the rule; the second thing is to learn the practice of it. The theory may be understand at once by an effort of reason, and yet the practice of it acquired only in course of time.

A pupil may learn the various notes on an instrument of music, or the different position in fencing; and when he makes a mistake, as he is sure to do, however hard he tries, he is apt to think it will be impossible to observe the rules, when he is set to read music at sight or challenged to a furious duel. But for all that, gradual practice makes him perfect, through a long series of slips, blunders and fresh efforts. It is just the same in other things; in learning to write and speak Latin, a man will forget the grammatical rules; it is only by long practice that a blockhead turns into a courtier, that a passionate man becomes shrewd and worldly-wise, or a frank person reserved, or a noble person ironical. But though self-discipline of this kind is the result of long habit, it always works by a sort of external compulsion, which Nature never ceases to resist and sometimes unexpectedly overcomes. The difference between action in accordance with abstract principles, and action as the result of original, innate tendency, is the same as that between a work of art, say a watch—where form and movement are impressed upon shapeless and inert matter—and a living organism, where form and matter are one, and each is inseparable from the other.

There is a maxim attributed to the Emperor Napoleon, which expresses this relation between acquired and innate character, and confirms what I have said: *everything that is unnatural is imperfect*—a rule of universal application, whether in the physical or in the moral sphere. The only exception I can think of to this rule is aventurine, a substance known to mineralogists, which in its natural state cannot compare with the artificial preparation of it.

And in this connection let me utter a word of protest against any and every form of *affectation*. It always arouses contempt; in the first place, because it argues deception, and the deception is cowardly, for it is based on fear; and, secondly, it argues self-condemnation, because it means that a man is trying to appear what he is not, and therefore something which he thinks better than he actually is. To affect a quality, and to plume yourself upon it, is just to confess that you have not got it. Whether it is courage, or learning, or intellect, or wit, or success with women, or riches, or social position, or whatever else it may be that a man boasts of, you may conclude by his boasting about it that that is precisely the direction in which he is rather weak; for if a man really possesses any faculty to the full, it will not occur to him to make a great show of affecting it; he is quite content to know that he has it. That is the application of the Spanish proverb: *herradura que chacolotea clavo le falta*—a clattering hoof means a nail gone. To be sure, as I said at first, no man ought to let the reins go quite loose, and show himself just as he is; for there are many evil and bestial sides to our nature which require to be hidden away out of sight; and this justifies the negative attitude of dissimulation, but it does not justify a positive feigning of qualities which are not there. It should also be remembered that affectation is recognized at once, even before it is clear what it is that is being affected. And, finally, affectation cannot last very long, and one day the mask will fall off. *Nemo potest personam diu ferre fictam*, says Seneca;[1] *ficta cito in naturam suam recidunt*—no one can persevere long in a fictitious character; for nature will soon reassert itself.

XXXI

A man bears the weight of his own body without knowing it, but he soon feels the weight of any other, if he tries to move it;

[1] *De Clementia*, I, 1.

in the same way, a man can see other people's shortcoming's and vices, but he is blind to his own. This arrangement has one advantage: it turns other people into a kind of mirror, in which a man can see clearly everything that is vicious, faulty, ill-bred and loathsome in his own nature; only, it is generally the old story of the dog barking at his own image; it is himself that he sees and not another dog, as he fancies.

He who criticizes others, works at the reformation of himself. Those who form the secret habit of scrutinizing other people's general behaviour, and passing severe judgment upon what they do and leave undone, thereby improve themselves, and work out their own perfection: for they will have sufficient sense of justice, or at any rate enough pride and vanity, to avoid in their own case that which they condemn so harshly elsewhere. But tolerant people are just the opposite, and claim for themselves the same indulgence that they extend to others—*hanc veniam damus petimusque vicissim.*[1] It is all very well for the Bible to talk about the mote in another's eye and the beam in one's own. The nature of the eye is to look not at itself but at other things; and therefore to observe and blame faults in another is a very suitable way of becoming conscious of one's own. We require a looking-glass for the due dressing of our morals.

The same rule applies in the case of style and fine writing. If, instead of condemning, you applaud some new folly in these matters, you will imitate it. That is just why literary follies have such vogue in Germany. The Germans are a very tolerant people—everybody can see that! Their maxim is—*Hanc veniam damns petimusque vicissim.*

XXXII

When he is young, a man of noble character fancies that the relations prevailing amongst mankind, and the alliances to which these relations lead, are at bottom and essentially, *ideal*

---

[1] Horace, *Ars Poetica*, II. "We beg this freedom for ourselves and likewise grant it to others."

in their nature; that is to say, that they rest upon similarity of disposition or sentiment, or taste, or intellectual power, and so on.

But, later on, he finds out that it is a *real* foundation which underlies these alliances; that they are based upon some *material* interest. This is the true foundation of almost all alliances: nay, most men have no notion of an alliance resting upon any other basis. Accordingly we find that a man is always measured by the office he holds, or by his occupation, nationality, or family relations—in a word, by the position and character which have been assigned him in the conventional arrangements of life, where he is ticketed and treated as so much goods. Reference to what he is in himself, as a man—to the measure of his own personal qualities—is never made unless for convenience' sake: and so that view of a man is something exceptional, to be set aside and ignored, the moment that anyone finds it disagreeable; and this is what usually happens. But the more of personal worth a man has, the less pleasure he will take in these conventional arrangements; and he will try to withdraw from the sphere in which they apply. The reason why these arrangements exist at all, is simply that in this world of ours misery and need are the chief features: therefore it is everywhere the essential and paramount business of life to devise the means of alleviating them.

XXXIV

A man must be still a greenhorn in the ways of the world, if he imagines that he can make himself popular in society by exhibiting intelligence and discernment. With the immense majority of people, such qualities excite hatred and resentment, which are rendered all the harder to bear by the fact that people are obliged to suppress—even from themselves—the real reason of their anger.

What actually takes place is this. A man feels and perceives that the person with whom he is conversing is intellectually very much his superior.[1]

He thereupon secretly and half unconsciously concludes that his interlocutor must form a proportionately low and limited estimate of his abilities. That is a method of reasoning—an enthymeme—which rouses the bitterest feelings of sullen and rancorous hatred. And so Gracian is quite right in saying that the only way to win affection from people is to show the most animal-like simplicity of demeanour—*para ser bien quisto, el unico medio vestirse la piel del mas simple de los brutos*.[2]

To show your intelligence and discernment is only an indirect way of reproaching other people for being dull and incapable. And besides, it is natural for a vulgar man to be violently agitated by the sight of opposition in any form; and in this case envy comes in as the secret cause of his hostility. For it is a matter of daily observation that people take the greatest pleasure in that which satisfies their vanity; and vanity cannot be satisfied without comparison with others. Now, there is nothing of which a man is prouder than of intellectual ability, for it is this that gives him his commanding place in the animal world. It is an exceedingly rash thing to let anyone see that you are decidedly superior to him in this respect, and to let other people see it too; because he will then thirst for vengeance, and generally look about for an opportunity of taking it by means of insult, because this is to pass from the sphere of *intellect* to that of *will*—and there, all are on an equal footing as regards the feeling of hostility. Hence, while rank and riches may always reckon upon deferential treatment in society, that is something which intellectual ability can never expect; to be ignored is the greatest favour shown to it; and

---

[1] Author's Footnote: See *The World as Will and Representation*, Book II, where I quote from Dr. Johnson and from Goethe's friend, Merck. The former says, "There is nothing by which a man exasperates most people more, than by displaying a superior ability of brilliancy in conversation. They seem pleased at the time, but their envy makes them curse him at their hearts." (Boswell's *Life of Johnson.*)

[2] "The only way to be popular is for us to be clad in the skin of the stupidest of animals."

if people notice it at all, it is because they regard it as a piece of impertinence, or else as something to which its possessor has no legitimate right, and upon which he dares to pride himself; and in retaliation and revenge for his conduct, people secretly try and humiliate him in some other way; and if they wait to do this, it is only for a fitting opportunity. A man may be as humble as possible in his demeanour, and yet hardly ever get people to overlook his crime in standing intellectually above them. In the *Garden of Roses*, Sadi makes the remark, "You should know that foolish people are a hundredfold more averse to meeting the wise than the wise are indisposed to the company of the foolish."

On the other hand, it is a real recommendation to be stupid. For just as warmth is agreeable to the body, so it does the mind good to feel its superiority; and a man will seek company likely to give him this feeling, as instinctively as he will approach the fireplace or walk in the sun if he wants to get warm. But this means that he will be disliked on account of his superiority; and if a man is to be liked, he must really be inferior in point of intellect; and the same thing holds good of a woman in point of beauty. To give proof of real and unfeigned inferiority to some of the people you meet—that is a very difficult business indeed!

Consider how kindly and heartily a girl who is passably pretty will welcome one who is downright ugly. Physical advantages are not thought so much of in the case of man, though I suppose you would rather a little man sat next to you than one who was bigger than yourself. This is why, amongst men, it is the dull and ignorant, and amongst women, the ugly, who are always popular and in request.[1] It is likely to be said

---

[1] Author's Footnote: If you desire to get on in the world, friends and acquaintances are by far the best passport to fortune. The possession of a great deal of ability makes a man proud, and therefore not apt to flatter those who have very little, and from whom, on that account, the possession of great ability should be carefully concealed. The consciousness of small intellectual power has just the opposite effect, and is very compatible with a humble, affable, and companionable nature, and with respect for what is mean and wretched. This is why an inferior sort of man has so many friends to befriend and encourage

of such people that they are extremely good-natured, because every one wants to find a pretext for caring about them—a pretext which will blind both himself and other people to the real reason why he likes them. This is also why mental superiority of any sort always tends to isolate its possessor; people run away from him out of pure hatred, and say all manner of bad things about him by way of justifying their action. Beauty, in the case of women, has a similar effect: very pretty girls have no friends of their own sex, and they even find it hard to get another girl to keep them company. A handsome woman should always avoid applying for a position as companion, because the moment she enters the room, her prospective mistress will scowl at her beauty, as a piece of folly with which, both for her own and for her daughter's sake, she can very well dispense. But if the girl has advantages of rank, the case is very different; because rank, unlike personal qualities which work by the force of mere contrast, produces its effect by a process of reflection; much in the same way as the particular hue of a person's complexion depends upon the prevailing tone of his immediate surroundings.

XXXVI

Politeness—which the Chinese hold to be a cardinal virtue—is based upon two considerations of policy. I have explained one of these considerations in my *Ethics*; the other is as follows: Politeness is a tacit agreement that people's miserable defects, whether moral or intellectual, shall on either side be ignored and not made the subject of reproach; and since these defects are thus rendered somewhat less obtrusive, the result is mutually advantageous.

It is a wise thing to be polite; consequently, it is a stupid

---

him. These remarks are applicable not only to advancement in political life, but to all competition for places of honour and dignity, nay, even for reputation in the world of science, literature and art. In learned societies, for example, mediocrity—that very acceptable quality—is always to the fore, while merit meets with tardy recognition, or with none at all. So it is in everything.

thing to be rude. To make enemies by unnecessary and wilful incivility, is just as insane a proceeding as to set your house on fire. For politeness is like a counter—an avowedly false coin, with which it is foolish to be stingy. A sensible man will be generous in the use of it. It is customary in every country to end a letter with the words *your most obedient servant—votre très-humble serviteur—suo devotissimo servo*. (The Germans are the only people who suppress the word *servant—Diener*—because, of course, it is not true!) However, to carry politeness to such an extent as to damage your prospects, is like giving money where only counters are expected.

Wax, a substance naturally hard and brittle, can be made soft by the application of a little warmth, so that it will take any shape you please. In the same way, by being polite and friendly, you can make people pliable and obliging, even though they are apt to be crabbed and malevolent. Hence politeness is to human nature what warmth is to wax.

Of course, it is no easy matter to be polite; insofar, I mean, as it requires us to show great respect for everybody, whereas most people deserve none at all; and again in so far as it demands that we should feign the most lively interest in people, when we must be very glad that we have nothing to do with them. To combine politeness with pride is a masterpiece of wisdom.

We should be much less ready to lose our temper over an insult—which, in the strict sense of the word, means that we have not been treated with respect—if, on the one hand, we have not such an exaggerated estimate of our value and dignity—that is to say, if we were not so immensely proud of ourselves; and, on the other hand, if we had arrived at any clear notion of the judgment which, in his heart, one man generally passes upon another. If most people resent the slightest hint that any blame attaches to them, you may imagine their feelings if they were to overhear what their acquaintance say about them. You should never lose sight of the fact that ordinary politeness is only a grinning mask: if it shifts its place a little, or is removed for a moment, there is no use raising a hue and cry. When a man is downright rude, it is as though he had taken off all his clothes, and stood before you *in puris naturalibus*.[1] Like most men in this condition, he does not present a very attractive appearance.

XXXVII

You ought never to take any man as a model for what you should do or leave undone; because position and circumstances are in no two cases alike, and difference of character gives a peculiar, individual tone to what a man does. Hence *duo cum faciunt idem, non est idem*—two persons may do the same thing with a different result. A man should act in accordance with his own character, as soon as he has carefully deliberated on what he is about to do.

The outcome of this is that *originality* cannot be dispensed with in practical matters: otherwise, what a man does will not accord with what he is.

XXXVIII

Never combat any man's opinion; for though you reached the age of Methuselah, you would never have done setting him right upon all the absurd things that he believes.

It is also well to avoid correcting people's mistakes in conversation, however good your intentions may be; for it is easy to offend people, and difficult, if not impossible, to mend them.

If you feel irritated by the absurd remarks of two people whose conversation you happen to overhear, you should imagine that you are listening to a dialogue of two fools in a comedy. *Probatum est.*[2]

The man who comes into the world with the notion that he is really going to instruct in matters of the highest importance, may thank his stars if he escapes with a whole skin.

---

1 "Naked."
2 "It is tested and proved."

XXXIX

If you want your judgment to be accepted, express it coolly and without passion. All violence has its seat in the *will*; and so, if your judgment is expressed with vehemence, people will consider it an effort of will, and not the outcome of knowledge, which is in its nature cold and unimpassioned. Since the will is the primary and radical element in human nature, and *intellect* merely supervenes as something secondary, people are more likely to believe that the opinion you express with so much vehemence is due to the excited state of your will, rather than that the excitement of the will comes only from the ardent nature of your opinion.

XL

Even when you are fully justified in praising yourself, you should never be seduced into doing so. For vanity is so very common, and merit so very uncommon, that even if a man appears to be praising himself, though very indirectly, people will be ready to lay a hundred to one that he is talking out of pure vanity, and that he has not sense enough to see what a fool he is making of himself.

Still, for all that, there may be some truth in Bacon's remark that, as in the case of calumny, if you throw enough dirt, some of it will stick, so it is also in regard to self-praise; with the conclusion that self-praise, in small doses, is to be recommended.

XLI

If you have reason to suspect that a person is telling you a lie, look as though you believed every word he said. This will give him courage to go on; he will become more vehement in his assertions, and in the end betray himself.

Again, if you perceive that a person is trying to conceal something from you, but with only partial success, look as though you did not believe him. This opposition on your part will provoke him into leading out his reserve of truth and bringing the whole force of it to bear upon your incredulity.

XLII

You should regard all your private affairs as secrets, and, in respect of them, treat your acquaintances, even though you are on good terms with them, as perfect strangers, letting them know nothing more than they can see for themselves. For in course of time, and under altered circumstances, you may find it a disadvantage that they know even the most harmless things about you.

And, as a general rule, it is more advisable to show your intelligence by saying nothing than by speaking out; for silence is a matter of prudence, while speech has something in it of vanity. The opportunities for displaying the one or the other quality occur equally often; but the fleeting satisfaction afforded by speech is often preferred to the permanent advantage secured by silence.

The feeling of relief which lively people experience in speaking aloud when no one is listening, should not be indulged, lest it grow into a habit; for in this way thought establishes such very friendly terms with speech, that conversation is apt to become a process of thinking aloud. Prudence exacts that a wide gulf should be fixed between what we think and what we say.

At times we fancy that people are utterly unable to believe in the truth of some statement affecting us personally, whereas it never occurs to them to doubt it; but if we give them the slightest opportunity of doubting it, they find it absolutely impossible to believe it any more. We often betray ourselves into revealing something, simply because we suppose that people cannot help noticing it—just as a man will throw himself down from a great height because he loses his head, in other words, because he fancies that he cannot retain a firm footing any longer; the torment of his position is so great, that he thinks it better to put an end to it at once. This is the kind of insanity which is called *acrophobia*.

But it should not be forgotten how clever people are in regard to affairs which do not concern them, even though they show no particularly sign of acuteness in other matters. This is a kind of algebra in which people are very proficient: give them a single fact to go upon, and they will solve the most complicated problems. So, if you wish to relate some event that happened long ago, without mentioning any names, or otherwise indicating the persons to whom you refer, you should be very careful not to introduce into your narrative anything that might point, however distantly, to some definite fact, whether it is a particular locality, or a date, or the name of someone who was only to a small extent implicated, or anything else that was even remotely connected with the event; for that at once gives people something positive to go upon, and by the aid of their talent for this sort of algebra, they will discover all the rest. Their curiosity in these matters becomes a kind of enthusiasm: their will spurs on their intellect, and drives it forward to the attainment of the most remote results. For however unsusceptible and different people may be to general and universal truths, they are very ardent in the matter of particular details.

In keeping with what I have said, it will be found that all those who profess to give instructions in the wisdom of life are specially urgent in commending the practice of silence, and assign manifold reasons why it should be observed; so it is not necessary for me to enlarge upon the subject any further. However, I may just add one or two little known Arabian proverbs, which occur to me as peculiarly appropriate:

> Do not tell a friend anything that you
> would conceal from an enemy.

> A secret is in my custody, if I keep it; but
> should it escape me, it is I who am the
> prisoner.

> The tree of silence bears the fruit of peace.

XLIII

Money is never spent to so much advantage as when you have been cheated out of it; for at one stroke you have purchased prudence.

XLIV

If possible, no animosity should be felt for anyone. But carefully observe and remember the manner in which a man conducts himself, so that you may take the measure of his value—at any rate in regard to yourself—and regulate your bearing towards him accordingly; never losing sight of the fact that character is unalterable, and that to forget the bad features in a man's disposition is like throwing away hard-won money. Thus you will protect yourself against the results of unwise intimacy and foolish friendship.

Give way neither to love nor to hate, is one-half of worldly wisdom: *say nothing and believe nothing*, the other half. Truly, a world where there is need of such rules as this and the following, is one upon which a man may well turn his back.

XLV

To speak angrily to a person, to show your hatred by what you say or by the way you look, is an unnecessary proceeding—dangerous, foolish, ridiculous, and vulgar.

Anger and hatred should never be shown otherwise than in what you do; and feelings will be all the more effective in action, insofar as you avoid the exhibition of them in any other way. It is only cold-blooded animals whose bite is poisonous.

XLVI

To speak without emphasizing your words—*parler sans accent*—is an old rule with those who are wise in the world's ways. It means that you should leave other people to discover what it is that you have said; and as their minds are slow, you can make your escape in time. On the other hand, to emphasize your meaning—*parler avec accent*—is to address their feelings; and the result is always the opposite of what you expect. If you are polite enough in your manner and courteous in your tone there are many people whom you may abuse outright, and yet run no immediate risk of offending them.

Chapter Four: Worldly Fortune

XLVII

However varied the forms that human destiny may take, the same elements are always present; and so life is everywhere much of a piece, whether it passed in the cottage or in the palace, in the barrack or in the cloister. Alter the circumstance as much as you please! point to strange adventures, successes, failures! life is like a sweet-shop, where there is a great variety of things, odd in shape and diverse in colour—one and all made from the same paste. And when men speak of someone's success, the lot of the man who has failed is not so very different as it seems. The inequalities in the world are like the combinations in a kaleidoscope; at every turn a fresh picture strikes the eye; and yet, in reality, you see only the same bits of glass as you saw before.

XLVIII

An ancient writer says, very truly, that there are three great powers in the world: *Sagacity, Strength*, and *Luck*. I think the last is the most efficacious.

A man's life is like the voyage of a ship, where luck—*secunda aut adversa fortuna*[1]—acts the part of the wind, and speeds the vessel on its way or drives it far out of its course. All that the man can do for himself is of little avail; like the

---

[1] "Favourable or adverse fortune."

rudder, which, if worked hard and continuously, may help in the navigation of the ship; and yet all may be lost again by a sudden squall. But if the wind is only in the right quarter, the ship will sail on so as not to need any steering. The power of luck is nowhere better expressed than in a certain Spanish proverb: *Da Ventura a tu hijo, y echa lo en el mar*—give your son luck and throw him into the sea.

Still, chance, it may be said, is a malignant power, and as little as possible should be left to its agency. And yet where is there any giver who, in dispensing gifts, tells us quite clearly that we have no right to them, and that we owe them not to any merit on our part, but wholly to the goodness and grace of the giver—at the same time allowing us to cherish the joyful hope of receiving, in all humility, further undeserved gifts from the same hands—where is there any giver like that, unless it be *Chance*?—who understands the kingly art of showing the recipient that all merit is powerless and unavailing against the royal grace and favour.

On looking back over the course of his life—that *labyrinthine way of error*—a man must see many points where luck failed him and misfortune came; and then it is easy to carry self-reproach to an unjust excess. For the course of a man's life is in no wise entirely of his own making; it is the product of two factors—the series of things that happened, and his own resolves in regard to them, and these two are constantly interacting upon and modifying each other. And besides these, another influence is at work in the very limited extent of a man's horizon, whether it is that he cannot see very far ahead in respect of the plans he will adopt, or that he is still less able to predict the course of future events: his knowledge is strictly confined to present plans and present events. Hence, as long as a man's goal is far off, he cannot steer straight for it; he must be content to make a course that is approximately right; and in following the direction in which he thinks he ought to go, he will often have occasion to tack.

All that a man can do is to form such resolves as from time to time accord with the circumstances in which he is placed, in the hope of thus managing to advance a step nearer towards the final goal. It is usually the case that the position in which we stand, and the object at which we aim, resemble two tendencies working with dissimilar strength in different directions; and the course of our life is represented by their diagonal, or resultant force.

Terence makes the remark that life is like a game at dice, where if the number that turns up is not precisely the one you want, you can still contrive to use it equally: *in vita est hominum quasi cum ludas tesseris; si illud quod maxime opus est jactu non cadit, illud quod cecidit forte, id arte ut corrigas.*[1] Or, to put the matter more shortly, life is a game of cards, when the cards are shuffled and dealt by fate. But for my present purpose, the most suitable simile would be that of a game of chess, where the plan we determined to follow is conditioned by the play of our rival—in life, by the caprice of fate. We are compelled to modify our tactics, often to such an extent that, as we carry them out, hardly a single feature of the original plan can be recognized.

But above and beyond all this, there is another influence that makes itself felt in our lives. It is a trite saying—only too frequently true—that we are often more foolish than we think. On the other hand, we are often wiser than we fancy ourselves to be. This, however, is a discovery which only those can make, of whom it is really true; and it takes them a long time to make it. Our brains are not the wisest part of us. In the great moments of life, when a man decides upon an important step, his action is directed not so much by any clear knowledge of the right thing to do, as by an inner impulse—you may almost call it an instinct—proceeding from the deepest foundations of his being. If, later on, he attempts to criticize his action by the light of hard and fast ideas of what is right in the abstract—those unprofitable ideas which are learnt by rote, or, it may be, borrowed from other people—if he begins to apply general rules, the principles which have guided oth-

---

[1] "Human life is like a game of dice. If the dice does not turn up as you want it, then skill must improve what chance has offered." Author's Footnote: He seems to have been referring to a game something like backgammon.

ers, to his own case, without sufficiently weighing the maxim that one man's meat is another's poison, then he will run great risk of doing himself an injustice. The result will show where the right course lay. It is only when a man has reached the happy age of wisdom that he is capable of just judgment in regard either to his own actions or to those of others.

It may be that this impulse or instinct is the unconscious effect of a kind of prophetic dream which is forgotten when we awake—lending our life a uniformity of tone, a dramatic unity, such as could never result from the unstable moments of consciousness, when we are so easily led into error, so liable to strike a false note. It is in virtue of some such prophetic dream that a man feels himself called to great achievements in a special sphere, and works in that direction from his youth up out of an inner and secret feeling that that is his true path, just as by a similar instinct the bee is led to build up its cells in the comb. This is the impulse which Balthazar Gracian calls *la gran sindéresis*—the great power of moral discernment: it is something that a man instinctively feels to be his salvation without which he were lost.

To act in accordance with abstract principles is a difficult matter, and a great deal of practice will be required before you can be even occasionally successful; it often happens that the principles do not fit in with your particular case. But every man has certain innate *concrete principles*—a part, as it were, of the very blood that flows in his veins, the sum or result, in fact, of all his thoughts, feelings and volitions. Usually he has no knowledge of them in any abstract form; it is only when he looks back upon the course his life has taken, that he becomes aware of having been always led on by them—as though they formed an invisible clue which he had followed unawares.

XLIX

That Time works great changes, and that all things are in their nature fleeting—these are truths that should never be forgotten. Hence, in whatever case you may be, it is well to picture to yourself the opposite: in prosperity, to be mindful of misfortune; in friendship, of enmity; in good weather, of days when the sky is overcast; in love, of hatred; in moments of trust, to imagine the betrayal that will make you regret your confidence; and so, too, when you are in evil plight, to have a lively sense of happier times—what a lasting source of true worldly wisdom were there! We should then always reflect, and not be so very easily deceived; because, in general, we should anticipate the very changes that the years will bring.

Perhaps in no form of knowledge is personal experience so indispensable as in learning to see that all things are unstable and transitory in this world. There is nothing that, in its own place and for the time it lasts, is not a product of necessity, and therefore capable of being fully justified; and it is this fact that makes circumstances of every year, every month, even of every day, seem as though they might maintain their right to last to all eternity. But we know that this can never be the case, and that in a world where all is fleeting, change alone endures. He is a prudent man who is not only undeceived by apparent stability, but is able to forecast the lines upon which movement will take place.[1]

But people generally think that present circumstances will last, and that matters will go on in the future as they have done in the past. Their mistakes arises from the fact that they do not understand the cause of the things they see—causes which, unlike the effects they produce, contain in themselves the germ of future change. The effects are all that people know, and they hold fast to them on the supposition that those unknown causes, which were sufficient to bring them

---

1 Author's Footnote: *Chance* plays so great a part in all human affairs that when a man tries to ward off a remote danger by present sacrifice, the danger often vanishes under some new and unforeseen development of events; and then the sacrifice, in addition to being a complete loss, brings about such an altered state of things as to be in itself a source of positive danger in the face of this new development. In taking measures of precaution, then, it is well not to look too far ahead, but to reckon with chance; and often to oppose a courageous front to a danger, in the hope that, like many a dark thunder-cloud, it may pass away without breaking.

about, will also be able to maintain them as they are. This is a very common error; and the fact that it is common is not without its advantage, for it means that people always err in unison; and hence the calamity which results from the error affects all alike, and is therefore easy to bear; whereas, if a philosopher makes a mistake, he is alone in his error, and so at a double disadvantage.[1]

But in saying that we should anticipate the effects of time, I mean that we should mentally forecast what they are likely to be; I do not mean that we should practically forestall them, by demanding the immediate performance of promises which time alone can fulfil. The man who makes this demand will find out that there is no worse or more exacting usurer than Time; and that, if you compel Time to give money in advance, you will have to pay a rate of interest more ruinous than any banker would require. It is possible, for instance, to make a tree burst forth into leaf, blossom, or even bear fruit within a few days, by the application of unslaked lime and artificial heat; but after that the tree will wither away. So a young man may abuse his strength—it may be only for a few weeks—by trying to do at nineteen what he could easily manage at thirty, and Time may give him the loan for which he asks; but the interest he will have to pay comes out of the strength of his later years; nay, it is part of his very life itself.

There are some kinds of illness in which entire restoration to health is possible only by letting the complaint run its natural course; after which it disappears without leaving any trace of its existence. But if the sufferer is very impatient, and, while he is still affected, insists that he is completely well, in this case, too, Time will grant the loan, and the complaint may be shaken off; but life-long weakness and chronic mischief will be the interest paid upon it.

Again, in time of war or general disturbance, a man may

---

[1] Author's Footnote: I may remark, parenthetically, that all this is a confirmation of the principle laid down in *The World as Will and Representation*, Book I, that error always consists in making a wrong inference, that is, in ascribing a given effect to something that did not cause it.

require ready money at once, and have to sell out his investments in land or government stock for a third or even a still smaller fraction of the sum he would have received from them, if he could have waited for the market to right itself, which would have happened in due course; but he compels Time to grant him a loan, and his loss is the interest he has to pay. Or perhaps he wants to go on a long journey and requires the money: in one or two years he could lay by a sufficient sum out of his income, but he cannot afford to wait; and so he either borrows it or deducts it from his capital; in other words, he gets Time to lend him the money in advance. The interest he pays is a disordered state of his accounts, and permanent and increasing deficits, which he can never make good.

Such is Time's usury; and all who cannot wait are its victims. There is no more thriftless proceeding than to try and mend the measured pace of Time. Be careful, then, not to become its debtor.

XI

Whatever fate befalls you, do not give way to great rejoicings or great lamentations; partly because all things are full of change, and your fortune may turn at any moment; partly because men are so apt to be deceived in their judgment as to what is good or bad for them.

Almost every one in his turn has lamented over something which afterwards turned out to be the very best thing for him that could have happened—or rejoiced at an event which became the source of his greatest sufferings. The right state of mind has been finely portrayed by Shakespeare:

> I have felt so many quirks of joy and grief
> That the first face of neither, on the start,
> Can woman me unto't.[1]

---

[1] *All's Well that Ends Well*, Act II, Sc. ii.

And, in general, it may be said that if a man takes misfortunes quietly, it is because he knows that very many dreadful things may happen in the course of life; and so he looks upon the trouble of the moment as only a very small part of that which might come. This is the Stoic temper—never to be unmindful of the sad fate of humanity—*condicionis humanoe oblitus*;[1] but always to remember that our existence is full of woe and misery: and that the ills to which we are exposed are innumerable. Wherever he be, a man need only cast a look around, to revive the sense of human misery: there before his eyes he can see mankind struggling and floundering in torment—all for the sake of a wretched existence, barren and unprofitable!

If he remembers this, a man will not expect very much from life, but learn to accommodate himself to a world where all is relative and no perfect state exists—always looking misfortune in the face, and if he cannot avoid it, meeting it with courage.

It should never be forgotten that misfortune, be it great or small, is the element in which we live. But that is no reason why a man should indulge in fretful complaints, and, like Beresford, pull a long face over the *Miseries of Human Life*—and not a single hour is free from them; or still less, call upon the Deity at every flea-bite—*in pulicis morsu Deum invocare*.[2] Our aim should be to look well about us, to ward off misfortune by going to meet it, to attain such perfection and refinement in averting the disagreeable things of life—whether they come from our fellow-men or from the physical world—that, like a clever fox, we may slip out of the way of every mishap, great or small; remembering that a mishap is generally only our own awkwardness in disguise.

The main reason why misfortune falls less heavily upon us, if we have looked upon its occurrence as not impossible, and, as the saying is, prepared ourselves for it, may be this: if, before this misfortune comes, we have quietly thought over

---

[1] "To forget the condition of man."
[2] "To invoke the Deity for every flea-bite."

it as something which may or may not happen, the whole of its extent and range is known to us, and we can, at least, determine how far it will affect us; so that, if it really arrives, it does not depress us unduly—its weight is not felt to be greater than it actually is. But if no preparation has been made to meet it, and it comes unexpectedly, the mind is in a state of terror for the moment and unable to measure the full extent of the calamity; it seems so far-reaching in its effects that the victim might well think there was no limit to them; in any case, its range is exaggerated. In the same way, darkness and uncertainty always increase the sense of danger. And, of course, if we have thought over the possibility of misfortune, we have also at the same time considered the sources to which we shall look for help and consolation; or, at any rate, we have accustomed ourselves to the idea of it.

There is nothing that better fits us to endure the misfortunes of life with composure, than to know for certain that *everything that happens—from the smallest up to the greatest facts of existence—happens of necessity.*[1] A man soon accommodates himself to the inevitable—to something that must be; and if he knows that nothing can happen except of necessity, he will see that things cannot be other than they are, and that even the strangest chances in the world are just as much a product of necessity as phenomena which obey well-known rules and turn out exactly in accordance with expectation. Let me here refer to what I have said elsewhere on the soothing effect of the knowledge that all things are inevitable and a product of necessity.

If a man is steeped in the knowledge of this truth, he will, first of all, do what he can, and then readily endure what he must.

We may regard the petty vexations of life that are constantly happening, as designed to keep us in practice for bearing great misfortunes, so that we may not become completely enervated

---

1 Author's Footnote: This is a truth which I have firmly established in my prize-essay on the *Freedom of the Will*, where the reader will find a detailed explanation of the grounds on which it rests.

by a career of prosperity. A man should be as Siegfried, armed *cap-à-pie*,[1] towards the small troubles of every day—those little differences we have with our fellow-men, insignificant disputes, unbecoming conduct in other people, petty gossip, and many other similar annoyances of life; he should not feel them at all, much less take them to heart and brood over them, but hold them at arm's length and push them out of his way, like stones that lie in the road, and upon no account think about them and give them a place in his reflections.

LII

What people commonly call *Fate* is, as a general rule, nothing but their own stupid and foolish conduct. There is a fine passage in Homer,[2] illustrating the truth of this remark, where the poet praises *maetis*—shrewd council; and his advice is worthy of all attention. For if wickedness is atoned for only in another world, stupidity gets its reward here—although, now and then, mercy may be shown to the offender.

It is not ferocity but cunning that strikes fear into the heart and forebodes danger; so true it is that the human brain is a more terrible weapon than the lion's paw.

The most finished man of the world would be one who was never irresolute and never in a hurry.

LIII

Courage comes next to prudence as a quality of mind very essential to happiness. It is quite true that no one can endow himself with either, since a man inherits prudence from his mother and courage from his father; still, if he has these qualities, he can do much to develop them by means of resolute exercise.

In this world, *where the game is played with loaded dice*,

---

1 "From head to foot." Siegfried is a German mythical hero. He wore a cloak of invisibility that gave him the strength of twelve men.
2 *Iliad*, XXIII, 313.

a man must have a temper of iron, with armor proof to the blows of fate, and weapons to make his way against men. Life is one long battle; we have to fight at every step; and Voltaire very rightly says that if we succeed, it is at the point of the sword, and that we die with the weapon in our hand—on *ne réussit dans ce monde qu'à la pointe de l'épee, et on meurt les armes à la main.*[1] It is a cowardly soul that shrinks or grows faint and despondent as soon as the storm begins to gather, or even when the first cloud appears on the horizon. Our motto should be *No Surrender*; and far from yielding to the ills of life, let us take fresh courage from misfortune:

Tu ne cede malis sed contra audentior ito.[2]

As long as the issue of any matter fraught with peril is still in doubt, and there is yet some possibility left that all may come right, no one should ever tremble or think of anything but resistance—just as a man should not despair of the weather if he can see a bit of blue sky anywhere. Let our attitude be such that we should not quake even if the world fell in ruins about us:

*Si fractus illabatur orbis Impavidum
ferient ruinae.*[3]

Our whole life itself—let alone its blessings—would not be worth such a cowardly trembling and shrinking of the heart. Therefore, let us face life courageously and show a firm front to every ill: *Quocirca vivite fortes Fortiaque adversis opponite pectora rebus.*[4]

Still, it is possible for courage to be carried to an excess and to degenerate into rashness. It may even be said that some

---

[1] "In this world we succeed only at the point of the sword and we die with weapons in hand."
[2] Virgil, *Aeneid*, VI, 95. "Do not give way to the evil, but face it more boldly."
[3] Horace, *Odes*, III, 3. "Even if the world collapses over him, the ruins still leave him undismayed."
[4] Horace, *Satires*, II, 2. "Therefore he lives bravely and presents a bold front to the blows of fate."

amount of fear is necessary, if we are to exist at all in the world, and cowardice is only the exaggerated form of it. This truth has been very well expressed by Bacon, in his account of *Terror Panicus*; and the etymological account which he gives of its meaning is very superior to the ancient explanation preserved for us by Plutarch.[1] He connects the expression with *Pan*, the personification of Nature, and observes that fear is innate in every living thing, and, in fact, tends to its preservation, but that it is apt to come into play without due cause, and that man is especially exposed to it. The chief feature of this *Panic Terror* is that there is no clear notion of any definite danger bound up with it; that it presumes rather than knows that danger exists; and that, in case of need, it pleads fright itself as the reason for being afraid.

Chapter Five: The Ages of Life

There is a very fine saying of Voltaire's to the effect that every age of life has its own peculiar mental character, and that a man will feel completely unhappy if his mind is not in accordance with his years: *Qui n'a pas l'esprit de son âge, De son âge a tout le malheur.*[2]

It will, therefore, be a fitting close to our speculations upon the nature of happiness, if we glance at the changes which the various periods of life produce in us.

Our whole life long it is *the present*, and the present alone, that we actually possess: the only difference is that at the beginning of life we look forward to a long future, and that towards the end we look back upon a long past; also that our temperament, but not our character, undergoes certain well-known changes, which make *the present* wear a different colour at each period of life.

I have elsewhere stated that in childhood we are more given to using our *intellect* than our *will*; and I have explained why

---

1 *De Iside et Osiride*, XIV.
2 "Who has not the spirit of his age, Has all the misfortune of his age."

this is so.[1] It is just for this reason that the first quarter of life is so happy: as we look back upon it in after years, it seems a sort of lost paradise. In childhood our relations with others are limited, our wants are few—in a word, there is little stimulus for the will; and so our chief concern is the extension of our knowledge. The intellect—like the brain, which attains its full size in the seventh year, is developed early, though it takes time to mature; and it explores the whole world of its surroundings in its constant search for nutriment: it is then that existence is in itself an ever fresh delight, and all things sparkle with the charm of novelty.

This is why the years of childhood are like a long poem. For the function of poetry, as of all art, is to grasp the *Idea*—in the Platonic sense; in other words, to apprehend a particular object in such a way as to perceive its essential nature, the characteristics it has in common with all other objects of the same kind; so that a single object appears as the representative of a class, and the results of one experience hold good for a thousand.

It may be thought that my remarks are opposed to fact, and that the child is never occupied with anything beyond the individual objects or events which are presented to it from time to time, and then only in so far as they interest and excite its will for the moment; but this is not really the case. In those early years, life—in the full meaning of the word, is something so new and fresh, and its sensations are so keen and unblunted by repetition, that, in the midst of all its pursuits and without any clear consciousness of what it is doing, the child is always silently occupied in grasping the nature of life itself—in arriving at its fundamental character and general outline by means of separate scenes and experiences; or, to use Spinoza's phraseology, the child is learning to see the things and persons about it *sub specie aeternitatis*—as particular manifestations of universal law.

---

[1] In *The World as Will and Representation*, Book II, Chapter 31, Schopenhauer explains that this is because in that period of life the brain and nervous system are much more developed than any other part of the organism.

The younger we are, then, the more does every individual object represent for us the whole class to which it belongs; but as the years increase, this becomes less and less the case. That is the reason why youthful impressions are so different from those of old age. And that it also why the slight knowledge and experience gained in childhood and youth afterwards come to stand as the permanent rubric, or heading, for all the knowledge acquired in later life—those early forms of knowledge passing into categories, as it were, under which the results of subsequent experience are classified; though a clear consciousness of what is being done does not always attend upon the process.

In this way the earliest years of a man's life lay the foundation of his view of the world, whether it be shallow or deep; and although this view may be extended and perfected later on, it is not materially altered. It is an effect of this purely objective and therefore poetical view of the world—essential to the period of childhood and promoted by the as yet undeveloped state of the volitional energy—that, as children, we are concerned much more with the acquisition of pure knowledge than with exercising the power of will. Hence that grave, fixed look observable in so many children, of which Raphael makes such a happy use in his depiction of cherubs, especially in the picture of the *Sistine Madonna*. The years of childhood are thus rendered so full of bliss that the memory of them is always coupled with longing and regret.

While we thus eagerly apply ourselves to learning the outward aspect of things, as the primitive method of understanding the objects about us, education aims at instilling into us *ideas*. But ideas furnish no information as to the real and essential nature of objects, which, as the foundation and true content of all knowledge, can be reached only by the process called *intuition*. This is a kind of knowledge which can in no wise be instilled into us from without; we must arrive at it by and for ourselves.

Hence a man's intellectual as well as his moral qualities proceed from the depths of his own nature, and are not the result of external influences; and no educational scheme—of

Pestalozzi, or of any one else—can turn a born simpleton into a man of sense. The thing is impossible! He was born a simpleton, and a simpleton he will die.

It is the depth and intensity of this early intuitive knowledge of the external world that explain why the experiences of childhood take such a firm hold on the memory. When we were young, we were completely absorbed in our immediate surroundings; there was nothing to distract our attention from them; we looked upon the objects about us as though they were the only ones of their kind, as though, indeed, nothing else existed at all. Later on, when we come to find out how many things there are in the world, this primitive state of mind vanishes, and with it our patience.

I have said elsewhere that the world, considered as *object*—in other words, as it is *presented* to us objectively—wears in general a pleasing aspect; but that in the world, considered as *subject*—that is, in regard to its inner nature, which is *will*—pain and trouble predominate. I may be allowed to express the matter, briefly, thus: *the world is glorious to look at, but dreadful in reality.*

Accordingly, we find that, in the years of childhood, the world is much better known to us on its outer or objective side, namely, as the presentation of will, than on the side of its inner nature, namely, as the will itself. Since the objective side wears a pleasing aspect, and the inner or subjective side, with its tale of horror, remains as yet unknown, the youth, as his intelligence develops, takes all the forms of beauty that he sees, in nature and in art, for so many objects of blissful existence; they are so beautiful to the outward eye that, on their inner side, they must, he thinks, be much more beautiful still. So the world lies before him like another Eden; and this is the Arcadia in which we are all born.

A little later, this state of mind gives birth to a thirst for real life—the impulse to do and suffer—which drives a man forth into the hurly-burly of the world. There he learns the other side of existence—the inner side, the will, which is thwarted at every step. Then comes the great period of disillusion, a period of very gradual growth; but once it has fairly begun, a man will tell you that he has got over all his false notions—*l*'âge des illusions est passé;[1] and yet the process is only beginning, and it goes on extending its sway and applying more and more to the whole of life.

So it may be said that in childhood, life looks like the scenery in a theatre, as you view it from a distance; and that in old age it is like the same scenery when you come up quite close to it.

And, lastly, there is another circumstance that contributes to the happiness of childhood. As spring commences, the young leaves on the trees are similar in colour and much the same in shape; and in the first years of life we all resemble one another and harmonize very well. But with puberty divergence begins; and, like the radii of a circle, we go further and further apart.

The period of youth, which forms the remainder of this earlier half of our existence—and how many advantages it has over the later half!—is troubled and made miserable by the pursuit of happiness, as though there were no doubt that it can be met with somewhere in life—a hope that always ends in failure and leads to discontent. An illusory image of some vague future bliss—born of a dream and shaped by fancy—floats before our eyes; and we search for the reality in vain. So it is that the young man is generally dissatisfied with the position in which he finds himself, whatever it may be; he ascribes his disappointment solely to the state of things that meets him on his first introduction to life, when he had expected something very different; whereas it is only the vanity and wretchedness of human life everywhere that he is now for the first time experiencing.

It would be a great advantage to a young man if his early training could eradicate the idea that the world has a great deal to offer him. But the usual result of education is to strengthen this delusion; and our first ideas of life are generally taken from fiction rather than from fact.

In the bright dawn of our youthful days, the poetry of life spreads out a gorgeous vision before us, and we torture

---

[1] "The age of illusions has passed."

ourselves by longing to see it realized. We might as well wish to grasp the rainbow! The youth expects his career to be like an interesting romance; and there lies the germ of that disappointment which I have been describing. What lends a charm to all these visions is just the fact that they are visionary and not real, and that in contemplating them we are in the sphere of pure knowledge, which is sufficient in itself and free from the noise and struggle of life. To try and realize those visions is to make them an object of *will*—a process which always involves pain.

If the chief feature of the earlier half of life is a never-satisfied longing after happiness, the later half is characterized by the dread of misfortune. For, as we advance in years, it becomes in a greater or less degree clear that all happiness is chimerical in its nature, and that pain alone is real. Accordingly, in later years, we, or, at least, the more prudent amongst us, are more intent upon eliminating what is painful from our lives and making our position secure, than on the pursuit of positive pleasure. I may observe, by the way, that in old age, we are better able to prevent misfortunes from coming, and in youth better able to bear them when they come.

In my young days, I was always pleased to hear a ring at my door: ah! thought I, now for something pleasant. But in later life my feelings on such occasions were rather akin to dismay than to pleasure: heaven help me! thought I, what am I to do? A similar revulsion of feeling in regard to the world of men takes place in all persons of any talent or distinction. For that very reason they cannot be said properly to belong to the world; in a greater or less degree, according to the extent of their superiority, they stand alone. In their youth they have a sense of being abandoned by the world; but later on, they feel as though they had escaped it. The earlier feeling is an unpleasant one, and rests upon ignorance; the second is pleasurable—for in the meantime they have come to know what the world is.

The consequence of this is that, as compared with the earlier, the later half of life, like the second part of a musical period, has less of passionate longing and more restfulness about it. And why is this the case? Simply because, in youth, a man fancies that there is a prodigious amount of happiness and pleasure to be had in the world, only that it is difficult to come by it; whereas, when he becomes old, he knows that there is nothing of the kind; he makes his mind completely at ease on the matter, enjoys the present hour as well as he can, and even takes a pleasure in trifles.

The chief result gained by experience of life is *clearness of view*. This is what distinguishes the man of mature age, and makes the world wear such a different aspect from that which it presented in his youth or boyhood. It is only then that he sees things quite plain, and takes them for that which they really are; while in earlier years he saw a phantom-world, put together out of the whims and crotchets of his own mind, inherited prejudice, and strange delusion: the real world was hidden from him, or the vision of it distorted. The first thing that experience finds to do is to free us from the phantoms of the brain—those false notions that have been put into us in youth.

To prevent their entrance at all would, of course, be the best form of education, even though it were only negative in aim: but it would be a task full of difficulty. At first the child's horizon would have to be limited as much as possible, and yet within that limited sphere none but clear and correct notions would have to be given; only after the child had properly appreciated everything within it, might the sphere be gradually enlarged; care being always taken that nothing was left obscure, or half or wrongly understood. The consequence of this training would be that the child's notions of men and things would always be limited and simple in their character; but, on the other hand, they would be clear and correct, and only need to be extended, not to be rectified. The same line might be pursued on into the period of youth. This method of education would lay special stress upon the prohibition of novel reading; and the place of novels would be taken by suitable biographical literature—the life of Franklin, for instance, or Moritz' *Anton Reiser*.

In our early days we fancy that the leading events in our life, and the persons who are going to play an important part in it, will make their entrance to the sound of drums and trumpets; but when, in old age, we look back, we find that they all came in quite quietly, slipped in, as it were, by the side-door, almost unnoticed.

From the point of view we have been taking up until now, life may be compared to a piece of embroidery, of which, during the first half of his time, a man gets a sight of the right side, and during the second half, of the wrong. The wrong side is not so pretty as the right, but it is more instructive; it shows the way in which the threads have been worked together.

Intellectual superiority, even if it is of the highest kind, will not secure for a man a preponderating place in conversation until after he is forty years of age. For age and experience, though they can never be a substitute for intellectual talent, may far outweigh it; and even in a person of the meanest capacity, they give a certain counterpoise to the power of an extremely intellectual man, so long as the latter is young. Of course I allude here to personal superiority, not to the place a man may gain by his works.

And on passing his fortieth year, any man of the slightest power of mind—any man, that is, who has more than the sorry share of intellect with which Nature has endowed five-sixths of mankind—will hardly fail to show some trace of misanthropy. For, as is natural, he has by that time inferred other people's character from an examination of his own; with the result that he has been gradually disappointed to find that in the qualities of the head or in those of the heart—and usually in both—he reaches a level to which they do not attain; so he gladly avoids having anything more to do with them. For it may be said, in general, that every man will love or hate solitude—in other words, his own society—just in proportion as he is worth anything in himself. Kant has some remarks upon this kind of misanthropy in his *Critique of the Faculty of Judgment*.[1]

In a young man, it is a bad sign, as well from an intel-

---

[1] *Critique of the Faculty of Judgment*, Part I, §29, Note ad fin.

lectual as from a moral point of view, if he is precocious in understanding the ways of the world, and in adapting himself to its pursuits; if he at once knows how to deal with men, and enters upon life, as it were, fully prepared. It argues a vulgar nature. On the other hand, to be surprised and astonished at the way people act, and to be clumsy and cross-grained in having to do with them, indicates a character of the nobler sort.

The cheerfulness and vivacity of youth are partly due to the fact that, when we are ascending the hill of life, death is not visible: it lies down at the bottom of the other side. But once we have crossed the top of the hill, death comes in view—death—which, until then, was known to us only by hearsay. This makes our spirits droop, for at the same time we begin to feel that our vital powers are on the ebb. A grave seriousness now takes the place of that early extravagance of spirit; and the change is noticeable even in the expression of a man's face. As long as we are young, people may tell us what they please!—we look upon life as endless and use our time recklessly; but the older we become, the more we practice economy. For towards the close of life, every day we live gives us the same kind of sensation as the criminal experiences at every step on his way to be tried.

From the standpoint of youth, life seems to stretch away into an endless future; from the standpoint of old age, to go back but a little way into the past; so that, at the beginning, life presents us with a picture in which the objects appear a great way off, as though we had reversed our telescope; while in the end everything seems so close. To see how short life is, a man must have grown old, that is to say, he must have lived long.

On the other hand, as the years increase, things look smaller, one and all; and Life, which had so firm and stable a base in the days of our youth, now seems nothing but a rapid flight of moments, every one of them illusory: we have come to see that the whole world is vanity!

Time itself seems to go at a much slower pace when we are young; so that not only is the first quarter of life the happiest, it is also the longest of all; it leaves more memories behind it. If a man were put to it, he could tell you more out of the first quarter of his life than out of two of the remaining periods. Nay, in the spring of life, as in the spring of the year, the days reach a length that is positively tiresome; but in the autumn, whether of the year or of life, though they are short, they are more genial and uniform.

But why is it that to an old man his past life appears so short? For this reason: his memory is short; and so he fancies that his life has been short too. He no longer remembers the insignificant parts of it, and much that was unpleasant is now forgotten; how little, then, there is left! For, in general, a man's memory is as imperfect as his intellect; and he must make a practice of reflecting upon the lessons he has learned and the events he has experienced, if he does not want them both to sink gradually into the gulf of oblivion. Now, we are unaccustomed to reflect upon matters of no importance, or, as a rule, upon things that we have found disagreeable, and yet that is necessary if the memory of them is to be preserved. But the class of things that may be called insignificant is continually receiving fresh additions: much that wears an air of importance at first, gradually becomes of no consequence at all from the fact of its frequent repetition; so that in the end we actually lose count of the number of times it happens. Hence we are better able to remember the events of our early than of our later years. The longer we live, the fewer are the things that we can call important or significant enough to deserve further consideration, and by this alone can they be fixed in the memory; in other words, they are forgotten as soon as they are past. Thus it is that time runs on, leaving always fewer traces of its passage.

Further, if disagreeable things have happened to us, we do not care to ruminate upon them, least of all when they touch our vanity, as is usually the case; for few misfortunes fall upon us for which we can be held entirely blameless. So people are very ready to forget many things that are disagreeable, as well as many that are unimportant.

It is from this double cause that our memory is so short; and a man's recollection of what has happened always becomes proportionately shorter, the more things that have occupied him in life. The things we did in years gone by, the events that happened long ago, are like those objects on the coast which, to the seafarer on his outward voyage, become smaller every minute, more unrecognizable and harder to distinguish.

Again, it sometimes happens that memory and imagination will call up some long past scene as vividly as if it had occurred only yesterday; so that the event in question seems to stand very near to the present time. The reason of this is that it is impossible to call up all the intervening period in the same vivid way, as there is no one figure pervading it which can be taken in at a glance; and besides, most of the things that happened in that period are forgotten, and all that remains of it is the general knowledge that we have lived through it—a mere notion of abstract existence, not a direct vision of some particular experience. It is this that causes some single event of long ago to appear as though it took place but yesterday: the intervening time vanishes, and the whole of life looks incredibly short. Nay, there are occasional moments in old age when we can scarcely believe that we are so advanced in years, or that the long past lying behind us has had any real existence—a feeling which is mainly due to the circumstance that the present always seems fixed and immovable as we look at it. These and similar mental phenomena are ultimately to be traced to the fact that it is not our nature in itself, but only the outward presentation of it, that lies in time, and that the present is the point of contact between the world as subject and the world as object.[1]

Again, why is it that in youth we can see no end to the years that seem to lie before us? Because we are obliged to find room for all the things we hope to attain in life. We cram the

---

[1] By this remark Schopenhauer means that the *will*, which, as he argues, forms the inner reality underlying all the phenomena of life and nature, is not in itself affected by time; but that, on the other hand, time is necessary for the objectification of the will, for the will as presented in the passing phenomena of the world. Time is thus definable as the condition of change, and the present time as the only point of contact between reality and appearance.

years so full of projects that if we were to try and carry them all out, death would come prematurely though we reached the age of Methuselah.

Another reason why life looks so long when we are young, is that we are apt to measure its length by the few years we have already lived. In those early years things are new to us, and so they appear important; we dwell upon them after they have happened and often call them to mind; and thus in youth life seems replete with incident, and therefore of long duration.

Sometimes we credit ourselves with a longing to be in some distant spot, whereas, in truth, we are only longing to have the time back again which we spent there—days when we were younger and fresher than we are now. In those moments Time mocks us by wearing the mask of space; and if we travel to the spot, we can see how much we have been deceived.

There are two ways of reaching a great age, both of which presuppose a sound constitution as a *conditio sine quâ non*.[1] They may be illustrated by two lamps, one of which burns a long time with very little oil, because it has a very thin wick; and the other just as long, though it has a very thick one, because there is plenty of oil to feed it. Here, the oil is the vital energy, and the difference in the wick is the manifold way in which the vital energy is used.

Up to our thirty-sixth year, we may be compared, in respect of the way in which we use our vital energy, to people who live on the interest of their money: what they spend today, they have again tomorrow. But from the age of thirty-six onwards, our position is like that of the investor who begins to entrench upon his capital. At first he hardly notices any difference at all, as the greater part of his expenses is covered by the interest of his securities; and if the deficit is but slight, he pays no attention to it. But the deficit goes on increasing, until he awakes to the fact that it is becoming more serious every day: his position becomes less and less secure, and he feels himself growing poorer and poorer, while he has no expectation of

---

1 "An indispensable condition."

this drain upon his resources coming to an end. His fall from wealth to poverty becomes faster every moment—like the fall of a solid body in space, until at last he has absolutely nothing left. A man is truly in a woeful plight if both the terms of this comparison—his vital energy and his wealth—really begin to melt away at one and the same time. It is the dread of this calamity that makes love of possession increase with age.

On the other hand, at the beginning of life, in the years before we come of age, and for some little time afterwards—the state of our vital energy puts us on a level with those who each year lay by a part of their interest and add it to their capital: in other words, not only does their interest come in regularly, but the capital is constantly receiving additions. This happy condition of affairs is sometimes brought about—with health as with money—under the watchful care of some honest guardian. O happy youth, and sad old age!

Nevertheless, a man should economize his strength even when he is young. Aristotle[1] observes that amongst those who were victors at Olympia only two or three gained a prize at two different periods, once in boyhood and then again when they came to be men; and the reason of this was that the premature efforts which the training involved, so completely exhausted their powers that they failed to last on into manhood. As this is true of muscular, so it is still more true of nervous energy, of which all intellectual achievements are the manifestation. Hence, those infant prodigies—*ingenia praecoda*—the fruit of a hot-house education, who surprise us by their cleverness as children, afterwards turn out very ordinary folk. Nay, the manner in which boys are forced into an early acquaintance with the ancient tongues may, perhaps, be to blame for the dullness and lack of judgment which distinguish so many learned persons.

I have said that almost every man's character seems to be specially suited to some one period of life, so that on reaching it the man is at his best. Some people are charming so long as they are young, and afterwards there is nothing attractive

[1] *Politics.*

about them; others are vigorous and active in manhood, and then lose all the value they possess as they advance in years; many appear to best advantage in old age, when their character assumes a gentler tone, as becomes men who have seen the world and take life easily. This is often the case with the French.

This peculiarity must be due to the fact that the man's character has something in it akin to the qualities of youth or manhood or old age—something which accords with one or another of these periods of life, or perhaps acts as a corrective to its special failings.

The mariner observes the progress he makes only by the way in which objects on the coast fade away into the distance and apparently decrease in size. In the same way a man becomes conscious that he is advancing in years when he finds that people older than himself begin to seem young to him.

It has already been remarked that the older a man becomes, the fewer are the traces left in his mind by all that he sees, does or experiences, and the cause of this has been explained. There is thus a sense in which it may be said that it is only in youth that a man lives with a full degree of consciousness, and that he is only half alive when he is old. As the years advance, his consciousness of what goes on about him dwindles, and the things of life hurry by without making any impression upon him, just as none is made by a work of art seen for the thousandth time. A man does what his hand finds to do, and afterwards he does not know whether he has done it or not.

As life becomes more and more unconscious, the nearer it approaches the point at which all consciousness ceases, the course of time itself seems to increase in rapidity. In childhood all the things and circumstances of life are novel; and that is sufficient to awake us to the full consciousness of existence: hence, at that age, the day seems of such immense length. The same thing happens when we are travelling: one month seems longer then than four spent at home. Still, though time seems to last longer when we are young or on a journey, the sense of novelty does not prevent it from now and then in reality hanging heavily upon our hands under both these circumstances, at any rate more than is the case when we are old or staying at home. But the intellect gradually becomes so rubbed down and blunted by long habituation to such impressions that things have a constant tendency to produce less and less impression upon us as they pass by; and this makes time seem increasingly less important, and therefore shorter in duration: the hours of the boy are longer than the days of the old man. Accordingly, time goes faster and faster the longer we live, like a ball rolling down a hill. Or, to take another example: as in a revolving disc, the further a point lies from the centre, the more rapid is its rate of progression, so it is in the wheel of life; the further you stand from the beginning, the faster time moves for you. Hence it may be said that as far as concerns the immediate sensation that time makes upon our minds, the length of any given year is in direct proportion to the number of times it will divide our whole life: for instance, at the age of fifty the year appears to us only one-tenth as long as it did at the age of five.

This variation in the rate at which time appears to move, exercises a most decided influence upon the whole nature of our existence at every period of it. First of all, it causes childhood—even though it embrace only a span of fifteen years—to seem the longest period of life, and therefore the richest in reminiscences. Next, it brings it about that a man is apt to be bored just in proportion as he is young. Consider, for instance, that constant need of occupation—whether it is work or play—that is shown by children: if they come to an end of both work and play, a terrible feeling of boredom ensues. Even in youth people are by no means free from this tendency, and dread the hours when they have nothing to do. As manhood approaches, boredom disappears; and old men find the time too short when their days fly past them like arrows from a bow. Of course, I must be understood to speak of *men*, not of decrepit *brutes*. With this increased rapidity of time, boredom mostly passes away as we advance in life; and as the passions with all their attendant pain are then laid asleep, the burden of life is, on the whole, appreciably lighter in later years than in youth, provided, of course, that health remains. So it is that the period immediately preceding the weakness and troubles of old age, receives the name of a man's *best years*.

That may be a true appellation, in view of the comfortable feeling which those years bring; but for all that the years of youth, when our consciousness is lively and open to every sort of impression, have this privilege—that then the seeds are sown and the buds come forth; it is the springtime of the mind. Deep truths may be perceived, but can never be excogitated—that is to say, the first knowledge of them is immediate, called forth by some momentary impression. This knowledge is of such a kind as to be attainable only when the impressions are strong, lively and deep; and if we are to be acquainted with deep truths, everything depends upon a proper use of our early years. In later life, we may be better able to work upon other people—upon the world, because our natures are then finished and rounded off, and no more a prey to fresh views; but then the world is less able to work upon us. These are the years of action and achievement; while youth is the time for forming fundamental conceptions, and laying down the ground-work of thought.

In youth it is the outward aspect of things that most engages us; while in age, thought or reflection is the predominating quality of the mind. Hence, youth is the time for poetry, and age is more inclined to philosophy. In practical affairs it is the same: a man shapes his resolutions in youth more by the impression that the outward world makes upon him; whereas, when he is old, it is thought that determines his actions. This is partly to be explained by the fact that it is only when a man is old that the results of outward observation are present in sufficient numbers to allow of their being classified according to the ideas they represent—a process which in its turn causes those ideas to be more fully understood in all their bearings, and the exact value and amount of trust to be placed in them, fixed and determined; while at the same time he has grown accustomed to the impressions produced by the various phenomena of life, and their effects on him are no longer what they were. Contrarily, in youth, the impressions that things make, that is to say, the outward aspects of life, are so overpoweringly strong, especially in the case of people of lively and imaginative disposition, that they view the world like a picture; and their chief concern is the figure they cut in it, the appearance they present; nay, they are unaware of the extent to which this is the case. It is a quality of mind that shows itself—if in no other way—in that personal vanity, and that love of fine clothes, which distinguish young people.

There can be no doubt that the intellectual powers are most capable of enduring great and sustained efforts in youth, up to the age of thirty-five at latest; from which period their strength begins to decline, though very gradually. Still, the later years of life, and even old age itself, are not without their intellectual compensation. It is only then that a man can be said to be really rich in experience or in learning; he has then had time and opportunity enough to enable him to see and think over life from all its sides; he has been able to compare one thing with another, and to discover points of contact and connecting links, so that only then are the true relations of things rightly understood. Further, in old age there comes an increased depth in the knowledge that was acquired in youth; a man has now many more illustrations of any ideas he may have attained; things which he thought he knew when he was young, he now knows in reality. And besides, his range of knowledge is wider; and in whatever direction it extends, it is thorough, and therefore formed into a consistent and connected whole; whereas in youth knowledge is always defective and fragmentary.

A complete and adequate notion of life can never be attained by any one who does not reach old age; for it is only the old man who sees life whole and knows its natural course; it is only he who is acquainted—and this is most important—not only with its entrance, like the rest of mankind, but with its exit too; so that he alone has a full sense of its utter vanity; while the others never cease to labour under the false notion that everything will come right in the end.

On the other hand, there is more conceptive power in youth, and at that time of life a man can make more out of the little that he knows. In age, judgment, penetration and thoroughness predominate. Youth is the time for amassing the material for a knowledge of the world that shall be distinctive and peculiar—for an original view of life, in other words, the legacy that a man of genius leaves to his fellow-men; it is, however, only in later years that he becomes master of his material. Accordingly it will be found that, as a rule, a great writer gives his best work to the world when he is about fifty years of age. But though the tree of knowledge must reach its full height before it can bear fruit, the roots of it lie in youth.

Every generation, no matter how paltry its character, thinks itself much wiser than the one immediately preceding it, let alone those that are more remote. It is just the same with the different periods in a man's life; and yet often, in the one case no less than in the other, it is a mistaken opinion. In the years of physical growth, when our powers of mind and our stores of knowledge are receiving daily additions, it becomes a habit for today to look down with contempt upon yesterday. The habit strikes root, and remains even after the intellectual powers have begun to decline—when today should rather look up with respect to yesterday. So it is that we often unduly depreciate the achievements as well as the judgments of our youth. This seems the place for making the general observation, that, although in its main qualities a man's *intellect* or *head*, as well as his *character* or *heart*, is innate, yet the former is by no means so unalterable in its nature as the latter. The fact is that the intellect is subject to very many transformations, which, as a rule, do not fail to make their actual appearance; and this is so, partly because the intellect has a deep foundation in the physique, and partly because the material with which it deals is given in experience. And so, from a physical point of view, we find that if a man has any peculiar power, it first gradually increases in strength until it reaches its acme, after which it enters upon a path of slow decadence, until it ends in imbecility. But, on the other hand, we must not lose sight of the fact that the material which gives employment to a man's powers and keeps them in activity—the subject-matter of thought and knowledge, experience, intellectual attainments, the practice of seeing to the bottom of things, and so a perfect mental vision, form in themselves a mass which continues to increase in size, until the time comes when weakness shows itself, and the man's powers suddenly fail. The way in which these two distinguishable elements combine in the same nature—the one absolutely unalterable, and the other subject to change in two directions opposed to each other—explains the variety of mental attitude and the dissimilarity of value which attach to a man at different periods of life.

The same truth may be more broadly expressed by saying that the first forty years of life furnish the text, while the remaining thirty supply the commentary; and that without the commentary we are unable to understand aright the true sense and coherence of the text, together with the moral it contains and all the subtle application of which it admits.

Towards the close of life, much the same thing happens as at the end of a *bal masqué*—the masks are taken off. Then you can see who the people really are, with whom you have come into contact in your passage through the world. For by the end of life characters have come out in their true light, actions have borne fruit, achievements have been rightly appreciated, and all shams have fallen to pieces. For this, Time was in every case requisite.

But the most curious fact is that it is also only towards the close of life than a man really recognizes and understands his own true self—the aims and objects he has followed in life, more especially the kind of relation in which he has stood to other people and to the world. It will often happen that as a result of this knowledge, a man will have to assign himself a lower place than he formerly thought was his due. But there are exceptions to this rule; and it will occasionally be the case that he will take a higher position than he had before. This will be owing to the fact that he had no adequate notion of the *baseness* of the world, and that he set up a higher aim for himself than was followed by the rest of mankind.

The progress of life shows a man the stuff of which he is made.

It is customary to call youth the happy, and age the sad part of life. This would be true if it were the passions that made a man happy. Youth is swayed to and fro by them; and they give a great deal of pain and little pleasure. In age the passions cool and leave a man at rest, and then forthwith his mind takes a contemplative tone; the intellect is set free and attains the upper hand. And since, in itself, intellect is beyond the range of pain, a man feels happy just insofar as his intellect is the predominating part of him.

It need only be remembered that all pleasure is negative, and that pain is positive in its nature, in order to see that the passions can never be a source of happiness, and that age is not the less to be envied on the ground that many pleasures are denied it. For every sort of pleasure is never anything more than the quieting of some need or longing; and that pleasure should come to an end as soon as the need ceases, is no more a subject of complaint than that a man cannot go on eating after he has had his dinner, or fall asleep again after a good night's rest.

So far from youth being the happiest period of life, there is much more truth in the remark made by Plato, at the beginning of the *Republic*, that the prize should rather be given to old age, because then at last a man is freed from the animal passion which has hitherto never ceased to disquiet him. Nay, it may even be said that the countless and manifold humours which have their source in this passion, and the emotions that spring from it, produce a mild state of madness; and this lasts as long as the man is subject to the spell of the impulse—this evil spirit, as it were, of which there is no riddance—so that he never really becomes a reasonable being until the passion is extinguished.

There is no doubt that, in general, and apart from individual circumstances and particular dispositions, youth is marked by a certain melancholy and sadness, while genial sentiments attach to old age; and the reason for this is nothing but the fact that the young man is still under the service, nay, the forced labour, imposed by that evil spirit, which scarcely ever leaves him a moment to himself. To this source may be traced, directly or indirectly, almost all and every ill that befalls or menaces mankind. The old man is genial and cheerful because, after long lying in the bonds of passion, he can now move about in freedom.

Still, it should not be forgotten that, when this passion is extinguished, the true kernel of life is gone, and nothing remains but the hollow shell; or, from another point of view, life then becomes like a comedy, which, begun by real actors, is continued and brought to an end by automata dressed in their clothes.

However that may be, youth is the period of unrest, and age of repose; and from that very circumstance, the relative degree of pleasure belonging to each may be inferred. The child stretches out its little hands in the eager desire to seize all the pretty things that meet its sight, charmed by the world because all its senses are still so young and fresh. Much the same thing happens with the youth, and he displays greater energy in his quest. He, too, is charmed by all the pretty things and the many pleasing shapes that surround him; and forthwith his imagination conjures up pleasures which the world can never realize. So he is filled with an ardent desire for he knows not what delights—robbing him of all rest and making happiness impossible. But when old age is reached, all this is over and done with, partly because the blood runs cooler and the senses are no longer so easily allured; partly because experience has shown the true value of things and the futility of pleasure, whereby illusion has been gradually dispelled, and the strange fancies and prejudices which previously concealed or distorted a free and true view of the world, have been dissipated and put to flight; with the result that a man can now get a juster and clearer view, and see things as they are, and also in a measure attain more or less insight into the nullity of all things on this earth.

It is this that gives almost every old man, no matter how ordinary his faculties may be, a certain tincture of wisdom, which distinguishes him from the young. But the chief result of all this change is the peace of mind that ensues—a great element in happiness, and, in fact, the condition and essence of it. While the young man fancies that there is a vast amount of good things in the world, if he could only come at them, the old man is steeped in the truth of the Preacher's words, that *all things are vanity*—knowing that, however gilded the shell, the nut is hollow.

In these later years, and not before, a man comes to a true appreciation of Horace's maxim: *Nil admirari*.[1] He is directly and sincerely convinced of the vanity of everything and that all the glories of the world are as nothing: his illusions are gone. He is no more beset with the idea that there is any particular amount of happiness anywhere, in the palace or in the cottage, any more than he himself enjoys when he is free from bodily or mental pain. The worldly distinctions of great and small, high and low, exist for him no longer; and in this blissful state of mind the old man may look down with a smile upon all false notions. He is completely undeceived, and knows that whatever may be done to adorn human life and deck it out in finery, its paltry character will soon show through the glitter of its surroundings; and that, paint and bejewel it as one may, it remains everywhere much the same—an existence which has no true value except in freedom from pain, and is never to be estimated by the presence of pleasure, let alone, then, of display.

Disillusion is the chief characteristic of old age; for by that time the fictions are gone which gave life its charm and spurred on the mind to activity; the splendours of the world have been proved null and vain; its pomp, grandeur and magnificence are faded. A man has then found out that behind most of the things he wants, and most of the pleasures he longs for, there is very little after all; and so he comes by degrees to see that our existence is all empty and void. It is only when he is seventy years old that he quite understands the first words of the Preacher; and this again explains why it is that old men are sometimes fretful and morose.

It is often said that the common lot of old age is disease and weariness of life. Disease is by no means essential to old age; especially where a really long span of years is to be attained;

---

[1] "To be surprised by nothing."

for as life goes on, the conditions of health and disorder tend to increase—*crescente vita, crescit sanitas et morbus.*[1] And as far as weariness or boredom is concerned, I have stated above why old age is even less exposed to that form of evil than youth. Nor is boredom by any means to be taken as a necessary accompaniment of that solitude, which, for reasons that do not require to be explained, old age certainly cannot escape; it is rather the fate that awaits those who have never known any other pleasures but the gratification of the senses and the delights of society—who have left their minds unenlightened and their faculties unused. It is quite true that the intellectual faculties decline with the approach of old age; but where they were originally strong, there will always be enough left to combat the onslaught of boredom. And then again, as I have said, experience, knowledge, reflection, and skill in dealing with men, combine to give an old man an increasingly accurate insight into the ways of the world; his judgment becomes keen and he attains a coherent view of life: his mental vision embraces a wider range. Constantly finding new uses for his stores of knowledge and adding to them at every opportunity, he maintains uninterrupted that inward process of self-education, which gives employment and satisfaction to the mind, and thus forms the due reward of all its efforts.

All this serves in some measure as a compensation for decreased intellectual power. And besides, Time, as I have remarked, seems to go much more quickly when we are advanced in years; and this is in itself a preventive of boredom. There is no great harm in the fact that a man's bodily strength decreases in old age, unless, indeed, he requires it to make a living. To be poor when one is old, is a great misfortune. If a man is secure from that, and retains his health, old age may be a very passable time of life. Its chief necessity is to be comfortable and well off; and, in consequence, money is then prized more than ever, because it is a substitute for failing strength. Deserted by Venus, the old man likes to turn to Bac-

---

[1] "With increasing age health and sickness increase."

chus to make him merry. In the place of wanting to see things, to travel and learn, comes the desire to speak and teach. It is a piece of good fortune if the old man retains some of his love of study or of music or of the theatre—if, in general, he is still somewhat susceptible to the things about him; as is, indeed, the case with some people to a very late age. At that time of life, *what a man has in himself* is of greater advantage to him than ever it was before.

There can be no doubt that most people who have never been anything but dull and stupid, become more and more of automata as they grow old. They have always thought, said, and done the same things as their neighbours; and nothing that happens now can change their disposition, or make them act otherwise. To talk to old people of this kind is like writing on the sand; if you produce any impression at all, it is gone almost immediately; old age is here nothing but the *caput mortuum*[1] of life—all that is essential to manhood is gone. There are cases in which nature supplies a third set of teeth in old age, thereby apparently demonstrating the fact that that period of life is a second childhood.

It is certainly a very melancholy thing that all a man's faculties tend to waste away as he grows old, and at a rate that increases in rapidity: but still, this is a necessary, nay, a beneficial arrangement, as otherwise death, for which it is a preparation, would be too hard to bear. So the greatest boon that follows the attainment of extreme old age is *euthanasia*—an easy death, not ushered in by disease, and free from all pain and struggle. For let a man live as long as he may, he is never conscious of any moment but the present, one and indivisible; and in those late years the mind loses more every day by sheer forgetfulness than ever it gains anew.

The main difference between youth and age will always be that youth looks forward to life, and old age to death; and that while the one has a short past and a long future before it, the case is just the opposite with the other. It is quite true that

---

[1] "Dead head" or "dead residue." An expression from ancient chemistry, denoting the dry residue that remains after heating certain substances in retorts.

when a man is old, to die is the only thing that awaits him; while if he is young, he may expect to live; and the question arises which of the two fates is the more hazardous, and if life is not a matter which, on the whole, it is better to have behind one than before? Does not the Preacher say: *the day of death [is better] than the day of one's birth.*[1] It is certainly a rash thing to wish for long life;[2] for as the Spanish proverb has it, it means to see much evil—*Quien larga vida vive mucho mal vide.*[3]

A man's individual career is not, as Astrology wishes to make out, to be predicted from observation of the planets; but the course of human life in general, as far as the various periods of it are concerned, may be likened to the succession of the planets: so that we may be said to pass under the influence of each one of them in turn.

---

1 *Ecclesiastes* 7:1.
2 Author's Footnote: The life of man cannot, strictly speaking, be called either long or short, since it is the ultimate standard by which duration of time in regard to all other things is measured. In one of the Vedic Upanishads (Oupnekhat, II) the natural length of human life is put down at one hundred years. And I believe this to be right. I have observed, as a matter of fact, that it is only people who exceed the age of ninety who attain euthanasia—who die, that is to say, of no disease, apoplexy or convulsion, and pass away without agony of any sort; nay, who sometimes even show no pallor, but expire generally in a sitting attitude, and often after a meal—or, I may say, simply cease to live rather than die. To come to one's end before the age of ninety, means to die of disease—in other words, prematurely.

Now the Old Testament (Psalms 90:10) puts the limit of human life at seventy, and if it is very long, at eighty years; and what is more noticeable still, Herodotus (I, 32 and III, 22) says the same thing. But this is wrong; and the error is due simply to a rough and superficial estimate of the results of daily experience. For if the natural length of life were from seventy to eighty years, people would die, about that time, of mere old age. Now this is certainly not the case. If they die then, they die, like younger people, of disease; and disease is something abnormal. Therefore it is not natural to die at that age. It is only when they are between ninety and a hundred that people die of old age; die, I mean, without suffering from any disease, or showing any special signs of their condition, such as a struggle, death-rattle, convulsion, pallor—the absence of all which constitutes euthanasia. The natural length of human life is a hundred years; and in assigning that limit the Upanishads are right once more.
3 "Whoever lives long experiences much evil."

At ten, *Mercury* is in the ascendant; and at that age, a youth, like this planet, is characterized by extreme mobility within a narrow sphere, where trifles have a great effect upon him; but under the guidance of so crafty and eloquent a god, he easily makes great progress. *Venus* begins her sway during his twentieth year, and then a man is wholly given up to the love of women. At thirty, *Mars* comes to the front, and he is now all energy and strength—daring, pugnacious and arrogant.

When a man reaches the age of forty, he is under the rule of the four *Asteroids*; that is to say, his life has gained something in extension. He is frugal; in other words, by the help of *Ceres*, he favours what is useful; he has his own hearth, by the influence of *Vesta*; *Pallas* has taught him that which is necessary for him to know; and his wife—his *Juno*—rules as the mistress of his house.

But at the age of fifty, *Jupiter* is the dominant influence. At that period a man has outlived most of his contemporaries, and he can feel himself superior to the generation about him. He is still in the full enjoyment of his strength, and rich in experience and knowledge; and if he has any power and position of his own, he is endowed with authority over all who stand in his immediate surroundings. He is no more inclined to receive orders from others; he wants to take command himself. The work most suitable to him now is to guide and rule within his own sphere. This is the point where Jupiter culminates, and where the man of fifty years is at his best.

Then comes *Saturn*, at about the age of sixty, a weight as of *lead*, dull and slow:—

> But old folks, many feign as they were dead;
> Unwieldy, slow, heavy and pale as lead.[1]

Last of all, Uranus; or, as the saying is, a man goes to heaven.

I cannot find a place for *Neptune*, as this planet has been very thoughtlessly named; because I may not call it as it should

---

1 *Romeo and Juliet*, Act II, Sc. v.

be called—*Eros*. Otherwise I should point out how Beginning and End meet together, and how closely and intimately Eros is connected with Death: how Orcus, or Amenthes, as the Egyptians called him, is not only the receiver but the giver of all things—*lambanon kai didous*.[1] Death is the great reservoir of Life. Everything comes from Orcus; everything that is alive now was once there. Could we but understand the great trick by which that is done, all would be clear!

---

[1] "The taker and giver."

from
THE BHAGAVAD GITA

Third Discourse: Karma Yoga
(Selfless Action)

Arjuna:
> ¹If you say that knowledge is superior to action, O Krishna, then why do you direct me to wage this terrible war?
> ²Your perplexing speech confuses my understanding. Tell me with certainty the one path to follow to the Supreme Good.

Krishna:
> ³In this world, at the beginning, I taught a twofold path, O sinless one: *jnana yoga*, the path of knowledge, and *karma yoga*, the path of selfless action.
> ⁴Not by abstaining from action does a man win actionlessness, nor by mere renunciation does he attain perfection.
> ⁵No one, verily, even for an instant, ever remains doing no action; for everyone is helplessly driven to action by his own nature.
> ⁶He who, while restraining the body, sits thinking of objects of the senses, is self-deluded, and said to be one of false conduct.
> ⁷But he who, restraining the senses through the mind, engages the body in *karma yoga* while remaining unattached,

he is esteemed.

⁸Perform your fated duty; for action is superior to inaction. And even the maintenance of the body would not be possible by inaction.

⁹Action is always enslaving us in this world, except in the case of selfless action. Therefore act selflessly, O Arjuna, free from attachment.

¹⁰Having first created mankind together with selfless service, the Prajapati[1] said, "By this shall ye propagate; let this be to you the cow of plenty."

¹¹With this do you nourish the Gods, and the Gods shall nourish you; thus nourishing one another, you shall attain the Supreme Good.

¹²Nourished by your selfless service, the Gods shall indeed bestow on you the enjoyments you desire. But he who enjoys—without offering to Them Their gifts—he is verily a thief.

¹³The righteous, who eat the remnant of the sacrifice, are freed from all sins; but the impious, who cook only for themselves, they verily eat sin.

¹⁴Food comes forth from creatures; the production of food is from the rain; rain comes forth from sacrifice; sacrifice is born of action.

¹⁵Know, however, that action comes from Brahman,[2] and that Brahman comes from the Imperishable. Therefore, the

---

[1] The Lord of Offspring. In one Indian myth, Prajapati, the great father, is responsible for creation. In other myths, many fathers or sages work together to create all living beings.

[2] Brahman is the ultimate, unchanging reality behind all life, the divine ground of existence, the eternal and infinite God.

all-pervading Brahman is ever-present in selfless action.

[16] He who does not follow the wheel thus set in motion, who leads a sinful life, indulging the senses, he lives in vain, Arjuna.

[17] That man, verily, who rejoices only in the Self,[1] who is satisfied with the Self, who is content in the Self alone—he is fulfilled.

[18] For him, there is no interest whatever in what is done or not done in the external world. Nor does he depend on any other being for his joy and security.

[19] Therefore, without attachment, always do what must be done; for in performing action without attachment, man reaches the Supreme.

[20] By action only did Janaka[2] and others attain perfection. With a view to the welfare of the masses, you should perform action.[3]

[21] Whatever a great man does, other men will try to do; whatever he sets up as the standard, that is what the world will follow.

[22] I have nothing whatsoever to achieve in the three worlds, O Arjuna, nor is there anything unattained that I should attain; and yet I engage in action.

[23] For should I ever cease to engage in action, men would in all matters follow

---

[1] This capitalized "Self" denotes Atman, the *true* self that is beyond body and mind and phenomena—the individual's essence. Salvation means attaining Self-knowledge, knowledge of Atman, who is identical to the transcendent self, Brahman.

[2] An ancient King who was at once a successful ruler and a holy sage.

[3] The *Bhagavad Gita* was Mahatma Ghandi's personal guide for living.

My path, O Arjuna.

²⁴These worlds would be ruined if I stopped performing action; I would be the cause of chaos and confusion, and of the destruction of these creatures.

²⁵Ignorant men work for their own gain, and are attached, Arjuna; but wise men work for the welfare of the world, and are unattached.

²⁶Let no wise man abstain from action, and thus cause confusion in the minds of the ignorant who are attached to action; let him inspire them to fulfil their duties, as he fulfils his own with devotion.

²⁷Actions are wrought in all cases by the energies of Nature. He whose mind is deluded by egoism thinks, "I am the doer."

²⁸But he who knows the truth, O Arjuna, about the divisions of the energies and their functions, is not attached, and knows that the energies act upon the energies.

²⁹Those deluded by the energies of Nature are attached to the functions of the energies. He who knows the All should not unsettle the unwise who know not the All.

³⁰Renouncing all action in me, with your thought resting on the Self, free from hope, free from selfishness, fight!—but do not succumb to the fever of the ego.

³¹Those who constantly practice this teaching with faith and without complaining, they are liberated from *karma*.

³²But those who carp at my teaching, who violate and renounce these laws—know them as deluded in all knowledge, as

senseless men doomed to destruction.
³³Even the man of knowledge acts in conformity with his own nature; all beings follow their nature; so what is the use of trying to change others?
³⁴Love and hate lie toward the object of each sense; let none become subject to these two; for they are his enemies.
³⁵Better to struggle in one's own *dharma*,[1] though devoid of merit, than to flourish in the *dharma* of another, though praised. Better is death in one's own *dharma* than life in another's, for such a life invites fear and danger.

Arjuna:

³⁶But what is the force, O Krishna, that drags a man, though reluctant, to commit sin?

Krishna:

³⁷It is desire, it is wrath, born of the energy of *rajas*[2]—all-devouring, all-sinful; that, Arjuna, is the foe here.
³⁸As fire is surrounded by smoke, as a mirror by rust, as the foetus is enclosed in the womb, so is knowledge covered by passion.
³⁹Wisdom is covered, O Arjuna, by this

---

1 Dharma is the universal law that holds the world together. It is also the true duty and authentic nature of the individual. When a person acts in accordance with their own dharma, they are in harmony with the Whole. Those who suppress or defy their own dharma invite suffering and danger.

2 One of the three *gunas*—qualities that make up the phenomenal world: *sattva guna* is harmony, purity and goodness; *tamas guna* is ignorance, inertia, destruction; *raja guna* is energy and passion. Therefore *raja guna* is responsible for all craving, lust, greed, as well as the passions that arise from these, such as wrath, anger, hatred. One might compare *raja guna* to Schopenhauer's *will to live*, which is at once the driving force of life and the ultimate cause of suffering.

constant enemy of the wise—*desire*—
which is greedy and insatiable.
⁴⁰The senses, mind, and reason are said to
be its seat; veiling wisdom through these,
desire deludes the understanding.
⁴¹Therefore, O Arjuna, restrain the senses
first, so that you can cast off this wretched
destroyer of knowledge and wisdom.
⁴²They say that the senses are superior
to the body; superior to the senses is the
mind; superior to the mind is reason; and
the one who is even superior to reason is
Atman.
⁴³Then knowing Him who is superior to
reason, subduing the self by the self, slay,
O mighty-armed Arjuna, the formidable
enemy that is desire.

Fourth Discourse: Jnana Yoga (Wisdom)

Krishna:
¹⁹He whose engagements are all devoid of
desires and motives, and whose actions
have been burnt by the fire of wisdom,
him the wise call a sage.
²⁰Having abandoned attachment to the
fruits of action, ever content, dependent
on none, though engaged in actions, he
really does nothing.
²¹Free from desire, with the mind and the
self controlled, having relinquished all
possessions, doing mere bodily action, he
incurs no sin.
²²Satisfied with what comes to him by
chance, rising above the pairs of opposites,

free from envy, equanimous in success and failure, though he acts, he is not bound.

²³The man whose attachment is gone, who is liberated, whose mind is established in knowledge, who acts for the sake of sacrifice—the burden of his action melts away.

²⁴Brahman is the offering, Brahman is the oblation; by Brahman the oblation is poured into the fire of Brahman; Brahman verily shall be reached by him who always sees Brahman in action.

[. . .]

³²Thus manifold sacrifices are spread at the mouth of Brahman. Know them all as born of action. Thus knowing, you shall be liberated.

³³Wisdom-sacrifice is superior to the sacrifice of objects, O Arjuna. And the goal of all action, without exception, is wisdom.

³⁴Know this: by long prostration, by inquiry, by service, you will be taught wisdom by those men of wisdom who have realized the truth.

³⁵Knowing this, you shall not again fall into error, O Arjuna; and you will see all beings in your Self and also in Me.

³⁶Even should you be the most sinful of all the sinful, you shall verily cross all sin by the bark of wisdom.

³⁷As kindled fire reduces fuel to ashes, O Arjuna, so does wisdom-fire reduce all actions to ashes.

³⁸Verily, there exists no purifier equal to wisdom. He who is perfect in yoga finds it in time in himself by himself.

³⁹He obtains wisdom who is full of

faith, who is devoted to it, and who has subdued the senses. Having obtained wisdom, he before long attains the Supreme Peace.

⁴⁰The ignorant, the faithless, and the one of doubting self, are ruined. There is neither this world, nor the other, nor happiness, for one of doubting self.

⁴¹He who has renounced selfish attachment to actions, whose doubts have been cloven asunder by wisdom, who is self-possessed—he is not enslaved by actions.

⁴²Therefore, with the sword of wisdom cleave asunder this doubt of the self lying in the heart and born of ignorance, and take the path of yoga. Arise, O Arjuna.

Fifth Discourse: Sannyasa Yoga (Renunciation)

Arjuna:

¹O Krishna, you praise the path of selfless action in *karma yoga*, but you also praise *sannyasa*, the path of renunciation of actions. Tell me conclusively which is the better of the two.

Krishna:

²Both renunciation of action and selfless action lead to the highest bliss: but, of the two, the path of action is esteemed more than renunciation of action.

³He should be known as a perpetual renouncer who neither hates nor desires: for, free from the pairs of opposites, he is

easily set free from bondage.
⁴Children, not the wise, speak of wisdom and action as distinct. He who is rightly devoted to even one obtains the fruits of both.
⁵That state which is reached by *sannyasa* is reached by *karma yoga* also. He who sees, sees wisdom and selfless action as one.
⁶But renunciation, O Arjuna, is hard to attain except by performing action; the sage, following the path of *karma yoga*, before long reaches Brahman.
⁷He who follows the path of service, whose mind is pure, who has conquered the self, whose senses have been subdued, whose Self has become the Self of all beings—though doing, he is not tainted.
⁸"I am not the doer": thus would the truth-knower always think—though seeing, hearing, touching, smelling, eating, going, sleeping, breathing,
⁹speaking, letting go, seizing, opening and closing the eyes—remembering that the senses move among sense-objects.
¹⁰He who performs actions, offering them to Brahman, abandoning attachment, is not tainted by sin, as a lotus leaf floats clean and dry in the water.
¹¹By the body, by the mind, by the intellect, by mere senses also, yogis perform action, without attachment, for the purification of the self.
¹²The steady-minded one, abandoning the fruit of action, attains the peace born of devotion. The unsteady one, attached to the fruit through the action of desire, is firmly enslaved.

¹³Renouncing all actions by thought, and self-controlled, the embodied one rests happily in the nine-gated city, neither at all acting nor causing to act.

¹⁴Neither agency nor objects does the Lord create for the world, nor union with the fruits of actions. But it is the nature that acts.

¹⁵The Lord partakes in neither the evil nor even the good deed of any; wisdom is enveloped by ignorance; thereby mortals are deluded.

¹⁶But he whose ignorance is destroyed by knowledge of the Self, his wisdom shines like the sun, illuminating the Supreme Brahman.

¹⁷With his consciousness in That, his Self being That, intent on That, with That for his supreme goal, he joins with That, never again to return, his sins shaken off by means of wisdom.

¹⁸One endued with wisdom and humility sees the same Self in the wise and the ignorant, in a cow, in an elephant, as also in a dog and in a dog-eater.

¹⁹Even here birth is overcome by those whose minds rest on equality. Spotless, indeed, and equal is Brahman; so in Brahman they rest.

²⁰He who knows Brahman can neither rejoice on obtaining the pleasant, nor grieve on obtaining the unpleasant—he is steady-minded, undeluded, resting in Brahman.

²¹With the self unattached to external contacts, he finds the joy which is in the Self; with the self engaged in the contemplation of Brahman he attains the

endless joy.
²²For those delights born of the world
of the senses are only generators of pain,
having a beginning and an end, O Arjuna;
a wise man does not rejoice in them.
²³He who is able, while still here, before
liberation from the body, to withstand
the impulse of desire and anger, he is a
yogi—he is a happy man.
²⁴Whoever find his joy within, and his rest
within, and who has his light only within,
that yogi attains Brahman's bliss, himself
becoming Brahman.
²⁵The sages whose sins and doubts have
been destroyed, who are self-controlled
and intent on the welfare of all beings,
attain Brahman's bliss.
²⁶To the devotees who are free from desire
and anger, who have controlled their
thought, and who have known the Self,
Brahman's bliss exists everywhere.
²⁷Shutting out all external contacts and
fixing the sight between the eyebrows,
equalizing the out-going and in-going
breaths that pass through the nostrils,
²⁸controlling the senses, mind, and intellect,
having self-realization as his highest goal,
free from desire, fear, and anger—the sage
who ever remains thus is verily liberated.
²⁹On knowing Me—the Lord of all
sacrifices and austerities, the Great Lord
of all Worlds, the Friend of all beings—he
goes to Peace.

Sixth Discourse: *Dhyana Yoga* (Meditation)

Krishna:

¹He who, without depending on the fruits of action, performs his bounden duty, he is a *sannyasin* and a yogi: not he who is without fire and without action.

²Therefore, Arjuna, know yoga to be that which they call renunciation: no one, verily, becomes a yogi who has not renounced attachments.

³For a devotee who wishes to attain yoga, action is said to be the path. For the same devotee, when he has attained yoga, the path is stillness and tranquillity.

⁴When a man, renouncing all thoughts, is not attached to sense-objects and actions, then he is said to have attained yoga.

⁵Let a man raise himself by himself, let him not lower himself; for the will is the only friend of the self, and the will is the only enemy of the self.

⁶To those who have conquered themselves, the will is a friend; but to those who have not conquered themselves, the will is an enemy, like an external foe.

⁷The self-controlled and serene man's Supreme Self is steadfast in cold and heat, in pleasure and pain, in honour and disgrace.

⁸The yogi who is steadfast with knowledge and wisdom, who remains unshaken, who has conquered the senses, he is said to be a saint. For him a lump of earth, a stone, and gold are all the same.

⁹He is esteemed who is of the same mind

to friends and foes, relatives and strangers, the good-hearted, the indifferent, the neutral, the hateful, the righteous, and the unrighteous.

¹⁰Let the yogi try constantly to keep the soul steady, remaining in seclusion, with the mind and body controlled, free from desire, and having no possessions.

¹¹Find a clean spot and make yourself a seat, neither too high nor too low, with cloth, skin, and kusha grass;

¹²Once seated, make the mind one-pointed, with the actions of the body and the senses controlled, and practice yoga for the purification of the self.

¹³Hold the body, head, and neck firmly, in a straight line, gazing on the tip of the nose, without looking around;

¹⁴Serene-minded, fearless, firm in the vow of godly life, having restrained the mind and fixed it on Me, sit and meditate on Me as the Supreme.

¹⁵Thus always keeping the mind balanced, the yogi, with the senses controlled, attains the Peace abiding in Me, which culminates in Nirvana.

¹⁶Yoga is not possible for him who eats too much, nor for him who does not eat at all, nor for him who is addicted to too much sleep, nor for him who is ever wakeful, O Arjuna.

¹⁷To him whose food and recreation are moderate, whose exertion in action is moderate, whose sleep and waking are moderate, to him accrues yoga, and thus the destruction of suffering.

¹⁸When his well-restrained thought is established in the Self only, without

longing for any of the objects of desire, then he is said to be a Saint.

[19] "As a lamp in a sheltered spot does not flicker"—this has been thought as the simile of a yogi of subdued thought, practicing meditation in the Self.

[20] When thought is quiet, restrained by the practice of meditation; when, seeing the Self by the self, he is satisfied in his own self;

[21] When he knows the Infinite Joy which, transcending the senses, can be grasped by reason; when, steady in the Self, he never moves from the Reality;

[22] When, having obtained it, he thinks no other acquisition superior to it; when, therein established, he is not moved even by great pain;

[23] This severance from union with pain, be it known, is called *union* yoga. That yoga must be practiced with determination and with undepressed heart.

[24] Abandoning without reserve all fancy-born desires, well-restraining all the senses from all quarters by force of will;

[25] Little by little let him withdraw, by firm reason and through practice; keeping the mind established in the Self, let him not think of anything.

[26] By whatever cause the wavering and unsteady mind wanders away, from that let him restrain it and bring it back directly under the control of the Self.

[27] Supreme Bliss verily comes to this yogi, whose mind is tranquil, whose passion is quieted, who has become Brahman, who is blemishless.

[28] Thus always keeping the self steadfast,

the yogi, freed from sins, attains with ease the infinite bliss of contact with the Supreme Brahman.

29. He whose self has been made steadfast by yoga, who sees the same thing everywhere, sees the Self abiding in all beings, and all beings abiding in the Self.

30. He who sees Me everywhere and sees everything in Me, to him I do not vanish, nor to Me does he vanish.

31. Whoever, intent on unity, worships Me who abides in all beings, that yogi dwells in Me, whatever his mode of life.

32. Whoever, by comparison with himself, sees the same everywhere, O Arjuna, be it pleasure or pain, he is deemed the highest yogi.

Arjuna:

33. This yoga of equanimity you teach, O Krishna—I cannot achieve its steady continuance, due to the restlessness of the mind.

34. The mind verily is restless, O Krishna, turbulent, strong, and obstinate. Trying to restrain it is like trying to repress the wind.

Krishna:

35. Doubtless, O Arjuna, the mind is restless and hard to restrain; but by practice, and by detachment, it can be conquered.

36. Yoga is hard to attain for a man of uncontrolled self; but by him who strives by the proper means and is self-controlled, it can be acquired.

Arjuna:

37. He who has faith, but whose mind

wanders away from yoga, who lacks self-control—having failed to attain perfection in yoga, what end, O Krishna, does he meet?

38 Having failed in both worlds, perplexed in the path to Brahman, does he not perish like a scattered cloud, with no support from this world or the other?

39 Dispel completely this worry of mine, O Krishna; for none other than you can possibly remove my doubt.

Krishna:

40 O Arjuna, neither in this world nor in the next is there destruction in him; none, verily, who does good, my son, ever comes to grief.

41 Having attained to the worlds of the righteous and having dwelt there for eternal years, he who failed in yoga is reborn in a house of the pure and wealthy.

42 Else, he is born in a family of wise yogis. Verily, a birth like this is hard to obtain in this world.

43 There he gains touch with the knowledge that was acquired in the former body and strives more than before for perfection, O Arjuna.

44 He is driven on by the strength of that former practice, though unknowingly. Even he who merely wishes to know of yoga meditation rises superior to he who merely follows rituals.

45 Verily, a yogi who strives with focus, purified from sins and perfected in the course of many births, finally reaches the Supreme Goal.

46 The yogi who achieves perfection

through meditation is deemed superior to men of extreme asceticism, and superior even to men of wisdom; he is also superior to men of action; therefore be a yogi, O Arjuna.
⁴⁷But of all yogis, he who worships me with perfect faith, fully absorbed in me, he is the most devout.

Sixteenth Discourse: Two Paths (Spirituality and Materialism)

Krishna:
¹Fearlessness, purity of heart, steadfastness in knowledge, and yoga; alms-giving, self-restraint, worship, study of one's own scriptures, austerity, uprightness;
²Harmlessness, truth, absence of anger, renunciation, serenity, absence of calumny, compassion to creatures, uncovetousness, gentleness, modesty, absence of fickleness;
³Energy, forgiveness; fortitude, purity, absence of hatred, absence of pride: these belong to one born for a divine lot, O Arjuna.
⁴Ostentation, arrogance and self-conceit, anger and insolence, cruelty and ignorance, belong to one born for a demonic lot.
⁵The divine qualities lead to liberation; the demonic lead to bondage. Grieve not, Arjuna; you are born for a divine lot.
⁶There are two types of beings in this world, the divine and the demonic. The divine has been described at length; hear from me now, O Arjuna, of the demonic.

⁷The demonic men do things they ought to shun, and shun the things they ought to do. Neither action nor inaction do they know; neither purity nor good conduct nor truth is found in them.

⁸They say, "there is no God, no truth, no moral law, no spiritual order, only pleasure brought about by lust. What else?"

⁹Holding this view, these ruined souls of small intellect, of wicked deeds, rise as the enemies of the world for its destruction.

¹⁰Filled with insatiable desires, full of hypocrisy, pride, and arrogance, holding unwholesome views through delusion, they work with unholy persistence.

¹¹Beset with immense cares ending only in death, sensual enjoyment their highest aim, they are assured that is the best life the universe has to offer.

¹²Bound by a hundred chains of hope, given over to lust and wrath, they strive to secure by unjust means hoards of wealth for sensual enjoyment.

¹³"I have gotten this today," they say, "tomorrow I will get that. This wealth is mine, and that wealth will be mine in future.

¹⁴"I have destroyed this enemy, and I will destroy others too. I am like a God, I enjoy what I want, I am successful, I am powerful, and I am happy.

¹⁵"I am rich and well-born. Who else is equal to me? I will sacrifice, I will give gifts, and I will rejoice in my own generosity." Thus they are deluded by ignorance.

¹⁶Bewildered by their many fancies,

entangled in the snare of delusion, addicted to the gratification of lust, they fall into a foul hell.

17 Self-important, stubborn, filled with pride and intoxicated by wealth, they perform sacrifices with ostentation and hypocrisy, without regard for their purpose.

18 Egotistical, arrogant, power-hungry, lustful, angry, and jealous of everyone, these malicious people hate Me in their own and others' bodies.

19 These cruel haters, worst of men, I hurl these evil-doers, life after life, into the wombs of demons.

20 Entering demonic wombs, in birth after birth the deluded ones fail to reach Me, O Arjuna, and fall lower still.

21 There are three gates to this self-destructive hell: LUST, WRATH, and GREED. Therefore, you should renounce these three.

22 A man who is released from these three gates to darkness, O Arjuna, does good to the Self, and thereby reaches the Supreme Goal.

23 He who, neglecting the scriptural teaching, acts under the impulse of desire, attains not perfection, nor happiness, nor the Supreme Goal.

24 Therefore, the scripture is your authority in deciding what you ought to do and not do. Now, you should know and perform your duty according to these teachings.

Eighteenth Discourse: Conclusion

Arjuna:
¹O Krishna, please explain to me the truth of *sannyasa* and *tyaga*, and how these two types of renunciation differ from one another.

Krishna:
²Sages understand *sannyasa* to be the renunciation of self-interested acts. To renounce the fruits of all action is called *tyaga*.
³Some philosophers declare that all action should be abandoned as evil; while others declare that acts of sacrifice, giving, and austerity should not be given up.
⁴Learn from Me the truth about this abandonment, O Arjuna; abandonment verily has been declared to be of three kinds.
⁵Practice of worship, giving, and austerity should not be given up, for they are purifiers of the soul.
⁶But even those actions should be performed without selfish desire for rewards; this, Arjuna, is my firm and highest belief.
⁷Verily, to renounce a required duty is not proper; such renunciation, stemming from ignorance, is declared to be *tamasic*.
⁸He who renounces an act because it is painful, difficult, or uncomfortable, practices *rajasic* renunciation, and he shall obtain no reward whatsoever for this renunciation.
⁹But to do your required work, O Arjuna,

simply because it ought to be done, while desiring no personal reward and remaining unattached to the results, that is deemed to be *sattvic* renunciation.

[10] He who is pervaded by *sattva* knows the wisdom of renunciation, and his doubts are cut asunder; he hates not unpleasant work, nor is he attached to pleasant work.

[11] Verily, it is not possible for an embodied being to renounce action completely; but to renounce the fruits of action is verily said to be true renunciation.

[12] The threefold fruit of action—evil, good, and mixed—accrues after death to non-renouncers, but never to renouncers.

[13] Now hear from me, O Arjuna, of the five factors necessary in the accomplishment of all action, as taught by the Sankhya[1]:

[14] The means, the ego, the body, the performance of the act, and the divine will.

[15] Whatever action a man does by the body, speech, or mind, right or wrong, these five are its causes.

[16] Those who are untrained in wisdom look upon themselves as separate agents; their crude intelligence cannot grasp the truth.

[17] He who is free from ego, whose mind is not tainted—though he kills these creatures, he kills not, and he is not bound by his action.

[18] Knowledge, the object known, and the knower, form the threefold impulse to action; the means, the action, and the agent, form the threefold basis of action.

---

[1] *Sankhya* is a branch of Hindu philosophy which seeks to liberate the individual spirit (*Purusha*) from mind/matter (*prakriti*).

[19] Knowledge, action, and the agent, are said to be of three kinds only, in accordance with the *gunas*. Listen, now, to these:

[20] The knowledge by which man sees the one Indestructible Reality in all beings, the inseparate in the separated—that knowledge is known as *sattvic*.

[21] But the knowledge of differentiation, that sees in all creation various entities of distinct kinds, that knowledge is known as *rajasic*.

[22] And the knowledge that clings to one single effect as if it were the whole, lacking perspective, narrow, and having no real object, that knowledge is declared to be *tamasic*.

[23] An action that is performed to fulfil one's duty, without attachment or aversion, without concern for personal reward, that action is declared to be *sattvic*.

[24] But the action that is done by one longing for pleasures, prompted by egotism, involving much stress, that action is declared to be *rajasic*.

[25] The action that is undertaken from delusion, without regard for the consequences, waste, injury to others, or one's own abilities, that action is declared to be *tamasic*.

[26] Free from attachment, not given to egotism, endued with firmness and vigour, unaffected by success and failure, such an agent is said to be *sattvic*.

[27] Passionate, desiring to attain the fruit of action, greedy, cruel, impure, subject to joy and sorrow, such an agent is said to be

rajasic.

²⁸Unsteady, vulgar, unbending, deceptive, wicked, indolent, desponding, and procrastinating, such an agent is said to be *tamasic.*

²⁹Listen, Arjuna, as I teach you of the three types of intellect and will.

³⁰The intellect that knows when to act and when to abstain from action, what ought to be done and what ought not to be done, what brings fear and what brings an absence of fear, what brings bondage and what brings freedom, that intellect is *sattvic*, O Arjuna.

³¹The intellect that wrongly understands dharma, confusing what ought to be done and not done, that intellect, O Arjuna, is *rajasic.*

³²The intellect that, enveloped in darkness, sees non-dharma as dharma, and sees all things perverted, that intellect, O Arjuna, is *tamasic.*

³³The will that is ever accompanied by yoga meditation, and by which the activities of thought, of life-breaths, and sense-organs are kept in harmony, such a will is *sattvic.*

³⁴But the will which pursues pleasures, wealth, and reputation, driven by selfish desire, that will is *rajasic.*

³⁵The will with which the stupid man clings to sloth, fear, grift, depression, and lust, that will is *tamasic.*

³⁶And now hear from me, Arjuna, of the threefold pleasures, in which one delights by practice and surely comes to the end of pain.

³⁷The pleasure that is like poison at first,

but in the end like nectar, that pleasure is declared to be *sattvic*, born of the purity of one's own mind.

³⁸The pleasure that arises from the contact of the sense-organ with the object, at first like nectar, in the end like poison, that pleasure is declared to be *rajasic*.

³⁹The pleasure that at the beginning and end is delusive to the self, arising from sleep, indolence, and intoxication, that pleasure is declared to be *tamasic*.

⁴⁰There is no being on earth or in heaven that can be free from these three gunas born of *prakriti*.[1]

⁴¹The duties of *brahmins*[2], *kshatriyas*[3], *vaishyas*[4], and *shudras*[5], are divided according to these qualities born of nature.

⁴²Serenity, self-restraint, austerity, purity, forgiveness, patience, humility, knowledge, wisdom, and faith—these are the duties of the *brahmins*, born of nature.

⁴³Bravery, boldness, fortitude, promptness, not flying from battle, generosity, and leadership—these are the duties of the *kshatriyas*, born of nature.

⁴⁴Ploughing, cattle-rearing, and trade are the duties of the *vaishyas*, born of nature. And service is the duty of the *shudras*, born of nature.

⁴⁵Each devoted to his own duty, man attains perfection; how one, devoted to one's own duty, attains success, hear now

---

[1] *Prakriti* is nature, or the essential energy from which the mental/physical world takes shape.
[2] Members of the learned class; literally, persons who strive to know Brahman.
[3] Warriors or princes.
[4] Landowners, traders, and moneylenders.
[5] Servants to the other three social classes.

from me, O Arjuna.

⁴⁶By performing his own duty, man attains perfection, for he is worshipping Him from whom arises the evolution of all beings, who inhabits every creature.

⁴⁷It is better to perform one's own duty, though devoid of merits, than to master the duty of another. Fulfilling the duty ordained by nature, one incurs no suffering.

⁴⁸The duty born with oneself, O Arjuna, though faulty, one ought not to abandon; for all undertakings are surrounded with faults, as fire is surrounded with smoke.

⁴⁹He who is free from selfish attachments, who has mastered himself and banished all desire, he by renunciation attains the supreme state of freedom from action.

⁵⁰Listen, O Arjuna, to how one who has attained perfection reaches Brahman— that supreme consummation of wisdom.

⁵¹Endued with pure reason, controlling the passions and senses, abandoning the clamour of life, and laying aside love and hatred;

⁵²Resorting to a sequestered spot, eating but little, speech and body and mind subdued, always engaged in meditation and concentration, endued with tranquillity;

⁵³Having abandoned egotism, aggression, arrogance, desire, enmity, property, free from the notion of "mine," he is at peace and fit for becoming Brahman.

⁵⁴Becoming Brahman, of serene self, he neither grieves nor desires, treating all beings alike; he attains supreme devotion to Me.

⁵⁵By Devotion he knows Me truly, what and who I am; then, knowing Me truly, he forthwith enters into Me.
⁵⁶Doing continually all actions in service to Me, taking refuge in Me—by My Grace he reaches the eternal undecaying Abode.
⁵⁷Mentally resign all deeds to Me, regard Me as the Supreme, practice inner discipline, and meditate ever on Me.
⁵⁸Fixing your heart in Me, you shall, by My Grace, cross over all difficulties; but if from egotism you will not hear Me, you shall perish.
⁵⁹If, indulging egotism, you think, "I will not fight this battle," your resolve is in vain: your own nature will impel you.
⁶⁰Bound as you are, O Arjuna, your own karma, born of your own nature, will impel you to do even that which, out of delusion, you wish not to do.
⁶¹The Lord dwells in the hearts of all beings, O Arjuna, whirling them around on the wheel of Maya.
⁶²Fly to Him for refuge with all your being, and by His Grace you shall obtain supreme peace and the eternal resting place.
⁶³Thus has wisdom, more secret than all that is secret, been declared to you by Me; reflect over it all and act as you please.
⁶⁴Hear again My Word Supreme, the most secret of all; because you are my firm friend, I will tell you what is good.
⁶⁵Fix your thought on Me, be devoted to Me, worship Me, pay homage to Me, and you shall reach Me. I declare the truth to you, for you are dear to Me.
⁶⁶Abandoning all righteous deeds, seek me

as your sole Refuge; I will liberate you from all sins; do not grieve.

⁶⁷This which has been taught to you is never to be taught to one who is devoid of self-control, nor to one who is not devoted, nor to one who does not do service, nor to one who speaks ill of Me.

⁶⁸He who with supreme devotion to Me will teach this Supreme Secret to my devotees, shall doubtless come to Me.

⁶⁹Nor is there any among men who does dearer service to Me; nor shall there be another on earth dearer to Me.

⁷⁰I deem highest those who will study this sacred dialogue of ours, who worship Me with the sacrifice of wisdom.

⁷¹And even those who listen, full of faith and free from malice, even they will be liberated, and shall attain the happy worlds where the righteous dwell.

⁷²Have you listened, O Arjuna, with an attentive mind? Has the delusion of ignorance been destroyed?

Arjuna:

⁷³Destroyed is delusion, and I have gained awareness through Thy Grace, O Krishna. I am firm now, with all my doubts gone. I will do Thy will.

from
THE KING JAMES BIBLE

Matthew

V

¹And seeing the multitudes, he went up into a mountain: and when he was set, his disciples came unto him:
²And he opened his mouth, and taught them, saying,
³Blessed are the poor in spirit: for theirs is the kingdom of heaven.
⁴Blessed are they that mourn: for they shall be comforted.
⁵Blessed are the meek: for they shall inherit the earth.
⁶Blessed are they which do hunger and thirst after righteousness: for they shall be filled.
⁷Blessed are the merciful: for they shall obtain mercy.
⁸Blessed are the pure in heart: for they shall see God.
⁹Blessed are the peacemakers: for they shall be called the children of God.
¹⁰Blessed are they which are persecuted for righteousness' sake: for theirs is the kingdom of heaven.
¹¹Blessed are ye, when men shall revile you, and persecute you, and shall say all manner of evil against you falsely, for my sake.

¹²Rejoice, and be exceeding glad: for great is your reward in heaven: for so persecuted they the prophets which were before you.

¹³Ye are the salt of the earth: but if the salt have lost his savour, wherewith shall it be salted? it is thenceforth good for nothing, but to be cast out, and to be trodden under foot of men.

¹⁴Ye are the light of the world. A city that is set on an hill cannot be hid.

¹⁵Neither do men light a candle, and put it under a bushel, but on a candlestick; and it giveth light unto all that are in the house.

¹⁶Let your light so shine before men, that they may see your good works, and glorify your Father which is in heaven.

¹⁷Think not that I am come to destroy the law, or the prophets: I am not come to destroy, but to fulfil.

¹⁸For verily I say unto you, Till heaven and earth pass, one jot or one tittle shall in no wise pass from the law, till all be fulfilled.

¹⁹Whosoever therefore shall break one of these least commandments, and shall teach men so, he shall be called the least in the kingdom of heaven: but whosoever shall do and teach them, the same shall be called great in the kingdom of heaven.

²⁰For I say unto you, That except your righteousness shall exceed the righteousness of the scribes and Pharisees, ye shall in no case enter into the kingdom of heaven.

²¹Ye have heard that it was said by them of old time, Thou shalt not kill; and whosoever shall kill shall be in danger of

the judgment:

²²But I say unto you, That whosoever is angry with his brother without a cause shall be in danger of the judgment: and whosoever shall say to his brother, Raca, shall be in danger of the council: but whosoever shall say, Thou fool, shall be in danger of hell fire.

²³Therefore if thou bring thy gift to the altar, and there rememberest that thy brother hath ought against thee;

²⁴Leave there thy gift before the altar, and go thy way; first be reconciled to thy brother, and then come and offer thy gift.

²⁵Agree with thine adversary quickly, whiles thou art in the way with him; lest at any time the adversary deliver thee to the judge, and the judge deliver thee to the officer, and thou be cast into prison.

²⁶Verily I say unto thee, Thou shalt by no means come out thence, till thou hast paid the uttermost farthing.

²⁷Ye have heard that it was said by them of old time, Thou shalt not commit adultery:

²⁸But I say unto you, That whosoever looketh on a woman to lust after her hath committed adultery with her already in his heart.

²⁹And if thy right eye offend thee, pluck it out, and cast it from thee: for it is profitable for thee that one of thy members should perish, and not that thy whole body should be cast into hell.

³⁰And if thy right hand offend thee, cut it off, and cast it from thee: for it is profitable for thee that one of thy members should perish, and not that thy

whole body should be cast into hell.

31 It hath been said, Whosoever shall put away his wife, let him give her a writing of divorcement:

32 But I say unto you, That whosoever shall put away his wife, saving for the cause of fornication, causeth her to commit adultery: and whosoever shall marry her that is divorced committeth adultery.

33 Again, ye have heard that it hath been said by them of old time, Thou shalt not forswear thyself, but shalt perform unto the Lord thine oaths:

34 But I say unto you, Swear not at all; neither by heaven; for it is God's throne:

35 Nor by the earth; for it is his footstool: neither by Jerusalem; for it is the city of the great King.

36 Neither shalt thou swear by thy head, because thou canst not make one hair white or black.

37 But let your communication be, Yea, yea; Nay, nay: for whatsoever is more than these cometh of evil.

38 Ye have heard that it hath been said, An eye for an eye, and a tooth for a tooth:

39 But I say unto you, That ye resist not evil: but whosoever shall smite thee on thy right cheek, turn to him the other also.

40 And if any man will sue thee at the law, and take away thy coat, let him have thy cloak also.

41 And whosoever shall compel thee to go a mile, go with him twain.

42 Give to him that asketh thee, and from him that would borrow of thee turn not thou away.

43 Ye have heard that it hath been said,

Thou shalt love thy neighbour, and hate thine enemy.

44 But I say unto you, Love your enemies, bless them that curse you, do good to them that hate you, and pray for them which despitefully use you, and persecute you;

45 That ye may be the children of your Father which is in heaven: for he maketh his sun to rise on the evil and on the good, and sendeth rain on the just and on the unjust.

46 For if ye love them which love you, what reward have ye? do not even the publicans the same?

47 And if ye salute your brethren only, what do ye more than others? do not even the publicans so?

48 Be ye therefore perfect, even as your Father which is in heaven is perfect.

VI

1 Take heed that ye do not your alms before men, to be seen of them: otherwise ye have no reward of your Father which is in heaven.

2 Therefore when thou doest thine alms, do not sound a trumpet before thee, as the hypocrites do in the synagogues and in the streets, that they may have glory of men. Verily I say unto you, They have their reward.

3 But when thou doest alms, let not thy left hand know what thy right hand doeth:

4 That thine alms may be in secret: and thy Father which seeth in secret himself shall reward thee openly.

⁵And when thou prayest, thou shalt not be as the hypocrites are: for they love to pray standing in the synagogues and in the corners of the streets, that they may be seen of men. Verily I say unto you, They have their reward.

⁶But thou, when thou prayest, enter into thy closet, and when thou hast shut thy door, pray to thy Father which is in secret; and thy Father which seeth in secret shall reward thee openly.

⁷But when ye pray, use not vain repetitions, as the heathen do: for they think that they shall be heard for their much speaking.

⁸Be not ye therefore like unto them: for your Father knoweth what things ye have need of, before ye ask him.

⁹After this manner therefore pray ye: Our Father which art in heaven, Hallowed be thy name.

¹⁰Thy kingdom come. Thy will be done in earth, as it is in heaven.

¹¹Give us this day our daily bread.

¹²And forgive us our debts, as we forgive our debtors.

¹³And lead us not into temptation, but deliver us from evil: For thine is the kingdom, and the power, and the glory, for ever. Amen.

¹⁴For if ye forgive men their trespasses, your heavenly Father will also forgive you:

¹⁵But if ye forgive not men their trespasses, neither will your Father forgive your trespasses.

¹⁶Moreover when ye fast, be not, as the hypocrites, of a sad countenance: for they disfigure their faces, that they may appear unto men to fast. Verily I say unto you,

They have their reward.

¹⁷But thou, when thou fastest, anoint thine head, and wash thy face;

¹⁸That thou appear not unto men to fast, but unto thy Father which is in secret: and thy Father, which seeth in secret, shall reward thee openly.

¹⁹Lay not up for yourselves treasures upon earth, where moth and rust doth corrupt, and where thieves break through and steal:

²⁰But lay up for yourselves treasures in heaven, where neither moth nor rust doth corrupt, and where thieves do not break through nor steal:

²¹For where your treasure is, there will your heart be also.

²²The light of the body is the eye: if therefore thine eye be single, thy whole body shall be full of light.

²³But if thine eye be evil, thy whole body shall be full of darkness. If therefore the light that is in thee be darkness, how great is that darkness!

²⁴No man can serve two masters: for either he will hate the one, and love the other; or else he will hold to the one, and despise the other. Ye cannot serve God and mammon.

²⁵Therefore I say unto you, Take no thought for your life, what ye shall eat, or what ye shall drink; nor yet for your body, what ye shall put on. Is not the life more than meat, and the body than raiment?

²⁶Behold the fowls of the air: for they sow not, neither do they reap, nor gather into barns; yet your heavenly Father feedeth them. Are ye not much better than they?

²⁷Which of you by taking thought can add one cubit unto his stature?
²⁸And why take ye thought for raiment? Consider the lilies of the field, how they grow; they toil not, neither do they spin:
²⁹And yet I say unto you, That even Solomon in all his glory was not arrayed like one of these.
³⁰Wherefore, if God so clothe the grass of the field, which to day is, and to morrow is cast into the oven, shall he not much more clothe you, O ye of little faith?
³¹Therefore take no thought, saying, What shall we eat? or, What shall we drink? or, Wherewithal shall we be clothed?
³²For after all these things do the Gentiles seek: for your heavenly Father knoweth that ye have need of all these things.
³³But seek ye first the kingdom of God, and his righteousness; and all these things shall be added unto you.
³⁴Take therefore no thought for the morrow: for the morrow shall take thought for the things of itself. Sufficient unto the day is the evil thereof.

VII

¹Judge not, that ye be not judged.
²For with what judgment ye judge, ye shall be judged: and with what measure ye mete, it shall be measured to you again.
³And why beholdest thou the mote that is in thy brother's eye, but considerest not the beam that is in thine own eye?
⁴Or how wilt thou say to thy brother, Let me pull out the mote out of thine eye; and, behold, a beam is in thine own eye?

⁵Thou hypocrite, first cast out the beam out of thine own eye; and then shalt thou see clearly to cast out the mote out of thy brother's eye.

⁶Give not that which is holy unto the dogs, neither cast ye your pearls before swine, lest they trample them under their feet, and turn again and rend you.

⁷Ask, and it shall be given you; seek, and ye shall find; knock, and it shall be opened unto you:

⁸For every one that asketh receiveth; and he that seeketh findeth; and to him that knocketh it shall be opened.

⁹Or what man is there of you, whom if his son ask bread, will he give him a stone?

¹⁰Or if he ask a fish, will he give him a serpent?

¹¹If ye then, being evil, know how to give good gifts unto your children, how much more shall your Father which is in heaven give good things to them that ask him?

¹²Therefore all things whatsoever ye would that men should do to you, do ye even so to them: for this is the law and the prophets.

¹³Enter ye in at the strait gate: for wide is the gate, and broad is the way, that leadeth to destruction, and many there be which go in thereat:

¹⁴Because strait is the gate, and narrow is the way, which leadeth unto life, and few there be that find it.

¹⁵Beware of false prophets, which come to you in sheep's clothing, but inwardly they are ravening wolves.

¹⁶Ye shall know them by their fruits. Do men gather grapes of thorns, or figs of

thistles?

17 Even so every good tree bringeth forth good fruit; but a corrupt tree bringeth forth evil fruit.

18 A good tree cannot bring forth evil fruit, neither can a corrupt tree bring forth good fruit.

19 Every tree that bringeth not forth good fruit is hewn down, and cast into the fire.

20 Wherefore by their fruits ye shall know them.

21 Not every one that saith unto me, Lord, Lord, shall enter into the kingdom of heaven; but he that doeth the will of my Father which is in heaven.

22 Many will say to me in that day, Lord, Lord, have we not prophesied in thy name? and in thy name have cast out devils? and in thy name done many wonderful works?

23 And then will I profess unto them, I never knew you: depart from me, ye that work iniquity.

24 Therefore whosoever heareth these sayings of mine, and doeth them, I will liken him unto a wise man, which built his house upon a rock:

25 And the rain descended, and the floods came, and the winds blew, and beat upon that house; and it fell not: for it was founded upon a rock.

26 And every one that heareth these sayings of mine, and doeth them not, shall be likened unto a foolish man, which built his house upon the sand:

27 And the rain descended, and the floods came, and the winds blew, and beat upon that house; and it fell: and great was the

fall of it.

²⁸And it came to pass, when Jesus had ended these sayings, the people were astonished at his doctrine:

²⁹For he taught them as one having authority, and not as the scribes.

XIII

¹⁰And the disciples came, and said unto him, Why speakest thou unto them in parables?

¹¹He answered and said unto them, Because it is given unto you to know the mysteries of the kingdom of heaven, but to them it is not given.

¹²For whosoever hath, to him shall be given, and he shall have more abundance: but whosoever hath not, from him shall be taken away even that he hath.

¹³Therefore speak I to them in parables: because they seeing see not; and hearing they hear not, neither do they understand.

¹⁴And in them is fulfilled the prophecy of Esaias, which saith, By hearing ye shall hear, and shall not understand; and seeing ye shall see, and shall not perceive:

¹⁵For this people's heart is waxed gross, and their ears are dull of hearing, and their eyes they have closed; lest at any time they should see with their eyes, and hear with their ears, and should understand with their heart, and should be converted, and I should heal them.

¹⁶But blessed are your eyes, for they see: and your ears, for they hear.

¹⁷For verily I say unto you, That many prophets and righteous men have desired

to see those things which ye see, and have not seen them; and to hear those things which ye hear, and have not heard them.
[18] Hear ye therefore the parable of the sower.
[19] When any one heareth the word of the kingdom, and understandeth it not, then cometh the wicked one, and catcheth away that which was sown in his heart. This is he which received seed by the way side.
[20] But he that received the seed into stony places, the same is he that heareth the word, and anon with joy receiveth it;
[21] Yet hath he not root in himself, but dureth for a while: for when tribulation or persecution ariseth because of the word, by and by he is offended.
[22] He also that received seed among the thorns is he that heareth the word; and the care of this world, and the deceitfulness of riches, choke the word, and he becometh unfruitful.
[23] But he that received seed into the good ground is he that heareth the word, and understandeth it; which also beareth fruit, and bringeth forth, some an hundredfold, some sixty, some thirty.

XVI

[24] Then said Jesus unto his disciples, If any man will come after me, let him deny himself, and take up his cross, and follow me.
[25] For whosoever will save his life shall lose it: and whosoever will lose his life for my sake shall find it.

²⁶For what is a man profited, if he shall gain the whole world, and lose his own soul? or what shall a man give in exchange for his soul?

XVIII

²¹Then came Peter to him, and said, Lord, how oft shall my brother sin against me, and I forgive him? till seven times?
²²Jesus saith unto him, I say not unto thee, Until seven times: but, Until seventy times seven.

XIX

¹⁶And, behold, one came and said unto him, Good Master, what good thing shall I do, that I may have eternal life?
¹⁷And he said unto him, Why callest thou me good? there is none good but one, that is, God: but if thou wilt enter into life, keep the commandments.
¹⁸He saith unto him, Which? Jesus said, Thou shalt do no murder, Thou shalt not commit adultery, Thou shalt not steal, Thou shalt not bear false witness,
¹⁹Honour thy father and thy mother: and, Thou shalt love thy neighbour as thyself.
²⁰The young man saith unto him, All these things have I kept from my youth up: what lack I yet?
²¹Jesus said unto him, If thou wilt be perfect, go and sell that thou hast, and give to the poor, and thou shalt have treasure in heaven: and come and follow me.
²²But when the young man heard that

saying, he went away sorrowful: for he had great possessions.

23 Then said Jesus unto his disciples, Verily I say unto you, That a rich man shall hardly enter into the kingdom of heaven.

24 And again I say unto you, It is easier for a camel to go through the eye of a needle, than for a rich man to enter into the kingdom of God.

Mark

VII

1 Then came together unto him the Pharisees, and certain of the scribes, which came from Jerusalem.

2 And when they saw some of his disciples eat bread with defiled, that is to say, with unwashen, hands, they found fault.

3 For the Pharisees, and all the Jews, except they wash their hands oft, eat not, holding the tradition of the elders.

4 And when they come from the market, except they wash, they eat not. And many other things there be, which they have received to hold, as the washing of cups, and pots, brasen vessels, and of tables.

5 Then the Pharisees and scribes asked him, Why walk not thy disciples according to the tradition of the elders, but eat bread with unwashen hands?

6 He answered and said unto them, Well hath Esaias prophesied of you hypocrites, as it is written, This people honoureth me with their lips, but their heart is far from me.

⁷Howbeit in vain do they worship me, teaching for doctrines the commandments of men.

⁸For laying aside the commandment of God, ye hold the tradition of men, as the washing of pots and cups: and many other such like things ye do.

⁹And he said unto them, Full well ye reject the commandment of God, that ye may keep your own tradition.

¹⁰For Moses said, Honour thy father and thy mother; and, Whoso curseth father or mother, let him die the death:

¹¹But ye say, If a man shall say to his father or mother, It is Corban, that is to say, a gift, by whatsoever thou mightest be profited by me; he shall be free.

¹²And ye suffer him no more to do ought for his father or his mother;

¹³Making the word of God of none effect through your tradition, which ye have delivered: and many such like things do ye.

¹⁴And when he had called all the people unto him, he said unto them, Hearken unto me every one of you, and understand:

¹⁵There is nothing from without a man, that entering into him can defile him: but the things which come out of him, those are they that defile the man.

¹⁶If any man have ears to hear, let him hear.

¹⁷And when he was entered into the house from the people, his disciples asked him concerning the parable.

¹⁸And he saith unto them, Are ye so without understanding also? Do ye not perceive, that whatsoever thing from without entereth into the man, it cannot

defile him;

¹⁹Because it entereth not into his heart, but into the belly, and goeth out into the draught, purging all meats?

²⁰And he said, That which cometh out of the man, that defileth the man.

²¹For from within, out of the heart of men, proceed evil thoughts, adulteries, fornications, murders,

²²Thefts, covetousness, wickedness, deceit, lasciviousness, an evil eye, blasphemy, pride, foolishness:

²³All these evil things come from within, and defile the man.

X

⁴³But so shall it not be among you: but whosoever will be great among you, shall be your minister:

⁴⁴And whosoever of you will be the chiefest, shall be servant of all.

⁴⁵For even the Son of man came not to be ministered unto, but to minister, and to give his life a ransom for many.

XI

²⁵And when ye stand praying, forgive, if ye have ought against any: that your Father also which is in heaven may forgive you your trespasses.

²⁶But if ye do not forgive, neither will your Father which is in heaven forgive your trespasses.

XII

38 And he said unto them in his doctrine, Beware of the scribes, which love to go in long clothing, and love salutations in the marketplaces,
39 And the chief seats in the synagogues, and the uppermost rooms at feasts:
40 Which devour widows' houses, and for a pretence make long prayers: these shall receive greater damnation.
41 And Jesus sat over against the treasury, and beheld how the people cast money into the treasury: and many that were rich cast in much.
42 And there came a certain poor widow, and she threw in two mites, which make a farthing.
43 And he called unto him his disciples, and saith unto them, Verily I say unto you, That this poor widow hath cast more in, than all they which have cast into the treasury:
44 For all they did cast in of their abundance; but she of her want did cast in all that she had, even all her living.

Luke

X

23 And he turned him unto his disciples, and said privately, Blessed are the eyes which see the things that ye see:
24 For I tell you, that many prophets and kings have desired to see those things which ye see, and have not seen them; and

to hear those things which ye hear, and have not heard them.

²⁵And, behold, a certain lawyer stood up, and tempted him, saying, Master, what shall I do to inherit eternal life?

²⁶He said unto him, What is written in the law? how readest thou?

²⁷And he answering said, Thou shalt love the Lord thy God with all thy heart, and with all thy soul, and with all thy strength, and with all thy mind; and thy neighbour as thyself.

²⁸And he said unto him, Thou hast answered right: this do, and thou shalt live.

²⁹But he, willing to justify himself, said unto Jesus, And who is my neighbour?

³⁰And Jesus answering said, A certain man went down from Jerusalem to Jericho, and fell among thieves, which stripped him of his raiment, and wounded him, and departed, leaving him half dead.

³¹And by chance there came down a certain priest that way: and when he saw him, he passed by on the other side.

³²And likewise a Levite, when he was at the place, came and looked on him, and passed by on the other side.

³³But a certain Samaritan, as he journeyed, came where he was: and when he saw him, he had compassion on him,

³⁴And went to him, and bound up his wounds, pouring in oil and wine, and set him on his own beast, and brought him to an inn, and took care of him.

³⁵And on the morrow when he departed, he took out two pence, and gave them to the host, and said unto him, Take care of

him; and whatsoever thou spendest more, when I come again, I will repay thee.

36 Which now of these three, thinkest thou, was neighbour unto him that fell among the thieves?

37 And he said, He that shewed mercy on him. Then said Jesus unto him, Go, and do thou likewise.

XII

13 And one of the company said unto him, Master, speak to my brother, that he divide the inheritance with me.

14 And he said unto him, Man, who made me a judge or a divider over you?

15 And he said unto them, Take heed, and beware of covetousness: for a man's life consisteth not in the abundance of the things which he possesseth.

16 And he spake a parable unto them, saying, The ground of a certain rich man brought forth plentifully:

17 And he thought within himself, saying, What shall I do, because I have no room where to bestow my fruits?

18 And he said, This will I do: I will pull down my barns, and build greater; and there will I bestow all my fruits and my goods.

19 And I will say to my soul, Soul, thou hast much goods laid up for many years; take thine ease, eat, drink, and be merry.

20 But God said unto him, Thou fool, this night thy soul shall be required of thee: then whose shall those things be, which thou hast provided?

21 So is he that layeth up treasure for

himself, and is not rich toward God.

²²And he said unto his disciples, Therefore I say unto you, Take no thought for your life, what ye shall eat; neither for the body, what ye shall put on.

²³The life is more than meat, and the body is more than raiment.

²⁴Consider the ravens: for they neither sow nor reap; which neither have storehouse nor barn; and God feedeth them: how much more are ye better than the fowls?

²⁵And which of you with taking thought can add to his stature one cubit?

²⁶If ye then be not able to do that thing which is least, why take ye thought for the rest?

²⁷Consider the lilies how they grow: they toil not, they spin not; and yet I say unto you, that Solomon in all his glory was not arrayed like one of these.

²⁸If then God so clothe the grass, which is to day in the field, and to morrow is cast into the oven; how much more will he clothe you, O ye of little faith?

²⁹And seek not ye what ye shall eat, or what ye shall drink, neither be ye of doubtful mind.

³⁰For all these things do the nations of the world seek after: and your Father knoweth that ye have need of these things.

³¹But rather seek ye the kingdom of God; and all these things shall be added unto you.

³²Fear not, little flock; for it is your Father's good pleasure to give you the kingdom.

³³Sell that ye have, and give alms; provide yourselves bags which wax not old, a

treasure in the heavens that faileth not, where no thief approacheth, neither moth corrupteth.

³⁴For where your treasure is, there will your heart be also.

³⁵Let your loins be girded about, and your lights burning;

³⁶And ye yourselves like unto men that wait for their lord, when he will return from the wedding; that when he cometh and knocketh, they may open unto him immediately.

³⁷Blessed are those servants, whom the lord when he cometh shall find watching: verily I say unto you, that he shall gird himself, and make them to sit down to meat, and will come forth and serve them.

³⁸And if he shall come in the second watch, or come in the third watch, and find them so, blessed are those servants.

³⁹And this know, that if the goodman of the house had known what hour the thief would come, he would have watched, and not have suffered his house to be broken through.

⁴⁰Be ye therefore ready also: for the Son of man cometh at an hour when ye think not.

XVI

¹³No servant can serve two masters: for either he will hate the one, and love the other; or else he will hold to the one, and despise the other. Ye cannot serve God and mammon.

¹⁴And the Pharisees also, who were covetous, heard all these things: and they derided him.

[15] And he said unto them, Ye are they which justify yourselves before men; but God knoweth your hearts: for that which is highly esteemed among men is abomination in the sight of God.

[16] The law and the prophets were until John: since that time the kingdom of God is preached, and every man presseth into it.

[17] And it is easier for heaven and earth to pass, than one tittle of the law to fail.

[18] Whosoever putteth away his wife, and marrieth another, committeth adultery: and whosoever marrieth her that is put away from her husband committeth adultery.

[19] There was a certain rich man, which was clothed in purple and fine linen, and fared sumptuously every day:

[20] And there was a certain beggar named Lazarus, which was laid at his gate, full of sores,

[21] And desiring to be fed with the crumbs which fell from the rich man's table: moreover the dogs came and licked his sores.

[22] And it came to pass, that the beggar died, and was carried by the angels into Abraham's bosom: the rich man also died, and was buried;

[23] And in hell he lift up his eyes, being in torments, and seeth Abraham afar off, and Lazarus in his bosom.

[24] And he cried and said, Father Abraham, have mercy on me, and send Lazarus, that he may dip the tip of his finger in water, and cool my tongue; for I am tormented in this flame.

²⁵But Abraham said, Son, remember that thou in thy lifetime receivedst thy good things, and likewise Lazarus evil things: but now he is comforted, and thou art tormented.

²⁶And beside all this, between us and you there is a great gulf fixed: so that they which would pass from hence to you cannot; neither can they pass to us, that would come from thence.

²⁷Then he said, I pray thee therefore, father, that thou wouldest send him to my father's house:

²⁸For I have five brethren; that he may testify unto them, lest they also come into this place of torment.

²⁹Abraham saith unto him, They have Moses and the prophets; let them hear them.

³⁰And he said, Nay, father Abraham: but if one went unto them from the dead, they will repent.

³¹And he said unto him, If they hear not Moses and the prophets, neither will they be persuaded, though one rose from the dead.

John

VIII

³⁰As he spake these words, many believed on him.

³¹Then said Jesus to those Jews which believed on him, If ye continue in my word, then are ye my disciples indeed;

³²And ye shall know the truth, and the

truth shall make you free.

33 They answered him, We be Abraham's seed, and were never in bondage to any man: how sayest thou, Ye shall be made free?

34 Jesus answered them, Verily, verily, I say unto you, Whosoever committeth sin is the servant of sin.

35 And the servant abideth not in the house for ever: but the Son abideth ever.

36 If the Son therefore shall make you free, ye shall be free indeed.

37 I know that ye are Abraham's seed; but ye seek to kill me, because my word hath no place in you.

38 I speak that which I have seen with my Father: and ye do that which ye have seen with your father.

39 They answered and said unto him, Abraham is our father. Jesus saith unto them, If ye were Abraham's children, ye would do the works of Abraham.

40 But now ye seek to kill me, a man that hath told you the truth, which I have heard of God: this did not Abraham.

41 Ye do the deeds of your father. Then said they to him, We be not born of fornication; we have one Father, even God.

42 Jesus said unto them, If God were your Father, ye would love me: for I proceeded forth and came from God; neither came I of myself, but he sent me.

43 Why do ye not understand my speech? even because ye cannot hear my word.

44 Ye are of your father the devil, and the lusts of your father ye will do. He was a murderer from the beginning, and abode not in the truth, because there is no

truth in him. When he speaketh a lie, he speaketh of his own: for he is a liar, and the father of it.

⁴⁵And because I tell you the truth, ye believe me not.

⁴⁶Which of you convinceth me of sin? And if I say the truth, why do ye not believe me?

⁴⁷He that is of God heareth God's words: ye therefore hear them not, because ye are not of God.

IX

¹And as Jesus passed by, he saw a man which was blind from his birth.

²And his disciples asked him, saying, Master, who did sin, this man, or his parents, that he was born blind?

³Jesus answered, Neither hath this man sinned, nor his parents: but that the works of God should be made manifest in him.

⁴I must work the works of him that sent me, while it is day: the night cometh, when no man can work.

⁵As long as I am in the world, I am the light of the world.

from
PENSÉES

by

BLAISE PASCAL

66

One must know oneself. If this does not help us discover truth, it at least serves as a guide to living our life, and there is nothing better.

110

The consciousness of the falsity of present pleasures, and the ignorance of the vanity of absent pleasures, cause inconstancy.

128

The weariness we feel in leaving pursuits to which we are attached. A man dwells at home with pleasure; but if he sees a charming woman, or if he enjoys himself in gambling for five or six days, he is miserable if he returns to his former way of living. Nothing is more common than that.

129

Our nature consists in motion; complete rest is death.

130

Restlessness. If a soldier or labourer complains of the hardship of his lot, set him to do nothing.

131

Weariness. Nothing is so insufferable to man as to be completely at rest, without passions, without business, without diversion, without study. He then feels his nothingness, his forlornness, his insufficiency, his dependence, his weakness, his emptiness. There will immediately arise from the depth of his heart weariness, gloom, sadness, fretfulness, vexation, despair.

135

The struggle alone pleases us, not the victory. We love to see animals fighting, not the victor triumphing over the vanquished. We only want to see the victorious end; and, as soon as it comes, we are satiated. It is the same in play, and the same in the search for truth. In disputes we like to see the clash of opinions, but not at all to contemplate the truth when it is found. To observe anything with pleasure, we have to see it emerge out of strife. So in the passions, there is pleasure in seeing the collision of two contraries; but when one acquires the mastery, it becomes only brutality. We never seek things for themselves, but for the search. Likewise in plays, scenes which do not rouse the emotion of fear are worthless, and so are scenes of extreme and hopeless misery, brutal lust, and cruelty.

136

A mere trifle consoles us, for a mere trifle distresses us.

137

Without examining every particular pursuit, it is enough to comprehend them under the rubric of *diversion*.

139

Diversion. When I set myself to considering the different distractions of man, the pains and perils to which he exposes himself at court or in war, whence arise so many quarrels, passions, bold and often bad ventures, etc., I discover that all the unhappiness of man arises from one single fact: that he cannot stay quietly in his room. A man who has enough wealth to live on, if he knew how to stay with pleasure at home, would not leave it to go to sea or to besiege a town. A commission in the army would not be so attractive were it not insufferable to stay in the same town; and men only seek conversation and the diversion of gambling because they cannot remain with pleasure at home.

But on further consideration, when, after finding the cause of all our ills, I have sought to discover the reason for it, I have found that there is one very real reason, namely, the natural poverty of our feeble and mortal condition, so wretched that nothing can comfort us when we think about it.

Whatever condition we picture to ourselves, if we muster all the good things which are possible to possess, royalty is the finest position in the world. Yet, when we imagine a king attended with every pleasure he can feel, if he is without diversion, and is left to consider and reflect on what he is, this feeble happiness will not sustain him; he will necessarily fall into forebodings of dangers, of revolutions which may happen, and, finally, of inevitable disease and death; so that if he is without what is called diversion, he is unhappy, and more unhappy than the least of his subjects who plays and diverts himself.

Hence it comes that gambling, the society of women, war, and high posts, are so sought after. It is not that they bring happiness in and of themselves, or that men imagine true bliss to consist in the money won in gambling or the hare that is hunted—they would not even take it for free. What people want is not that easy and peaceful lot which allows us to think of our unhappy condition, nor is it the dangers of war or the labour of office, but rather the activity and agitation that takes our minds off of these thoughts and diverts us. That is why we like the chase better than the quarry.

Hence it comes that men love noise and stir; hence it comes that the prison is so horrible a punishment; hence it comes that the pleasure of solitude is a thing incomprehensible. And it is in fact the greatest source of happiness in the condition of kings that men try incessantly to divert them and to procure for them all kinds of pleasures.

The king is surrounded by persons whose only thought is to divert the king, and to prevent his thinking of self. For he is unhappy, king though he be, if he thinks of himself.

This is all that men have been able to discover to make themselves happy. And those who philosophize on the matter, and who think men unreasonable for spending a whole day chasing a hare which they would not have bought, scarce know our nature. The hare in itself would not screen us from the sight of death and calamities; but the chase which turns away our attention from these, does screen us.

The advice given to Pyrrhus to take the rest which he was about to seek with so much labour, was full of difficulties.

To bid a man live quietly is to bid him live happily. It is to advise him to be in a state perfectly happy, in which he can think at leisure without finding therein a cause of distress. This is to misunderstand nature.

As men who naturally understand their own condition avoid nothing so much as rest, so there is nothing they leave undone in seeking turmoil. Not that they have an instinctive knowledge of true happiness . . .

So we are wrong in blaming them. Their error does not lie in seeking excitement, if they seek it only as a diversion; the evil is that they seek it as if the possession of the objects of their quest would make them really happy. In this respect it is right to call their quest a vain one. Hence in all this both the censurers and the censured do not understand man's true nature.

And thus, when we take the exception against them, that what they seek with such fervour cannot satisfy them, if they replied—as they should do if they considered the matter thoroughly—that they sought in it only a violent and impetuous occupation which turned their thoughts from self, and that they therefore chose an attractive object to charm and ardently attract them, they would leave their opponents without a reply. But they do not make this reply, because they do not know themselves. They do not know that it is the chase, and not the quarry, which they seek.

Dancing: we must consider rightly where to place our feet.—A gentleman sincerely believes that hunting is great and royal sport; but a beater is not of this opinion.

They imagine that if they obtained such a post, they would then rest with pleasure, and are insensible of the insatiable nature of their desire. They think they are truly seeking quiet, and they are only seeking excitement.

They have a secret instinct which impels them to seek amusement and occupation abroad, and which arises from the sense of their constant unhappiness. They have another secret instinct, a remnant of the greatness of our original nature, which teaches them that happiness in reality consists only in rest, and not in stir. And of these two contrary instincts they form within themselves a confused idea, which hides itself from their view in the depths of their soul, inciting them to aim at rest through excitement, and always to fancy that the satisfaction which they lack will come to them, if, by surmounting whatever difficulties confront them, they can thereby open the door to rest.

Thus passes away all man's life. Men seek rest in a struggle against difficulties; and when they have conquered these, rest becomes insufferable. For we think either of the misfortunes we have or of those which threaten us. And even if we should see ourselves sufficiently sheltered on all sides, weariness of its own accord would not fail to arise from the depths of the heart wherein it has its natural roots, and to fill the mind with its poison.

Thus so wretched is man that he would weary even without any cause for weariness, from the peculiar state of his disposition; and so frivolous is he that, though full of a thousand reasons for weariness, the least thing, such as playing billiards or hitting a ball, is sufficient to amuse him.

But will you say what object he has in all this? The pleasure of bragging tomorrow among his friends that he has played better than another. So others sweat in their own rooms to show to the learned that they have solved a problem in algebra, which no one had hitherto been able to solve. Many more expose themselves to extreme perils, in my opinion as foolishly, in order to boast afterwards that they have captured a town. Lastly, others wear themselves out in studying all these things, not in order to become wiser, but only in order to prove that they know them; and these are the most senseless of the band, since they are so knowingly, whereas one may suppose of the others, that if they knew it, they would no longer be foolish.

This man spends his life without weariness in playing every day for a small stake. Give him each morning the money he can win each day, on condition he does not play; you make him miserable. It will perhaps be said that he seeks the amusement of play and not the winnings. Make him then play for nothing; he will not become excited over it, and will feel bored. It is then not the amusement alone that he seeks; a languid and passionless amusement will weary him. He must get excited over it, and deceive himself by the fancy that he will be happy to win what he would not have as a gift on condition of not playing; and he must make for himself an object of passion, and excite over it his desire, his anger, his fear, to obtain his imagined end, as children are frightened at the face they have blackened.

Whence comes it that this man, who lost his only son a few months ago, or who this morning was in such trouble through being distressed by lawsuits and quarrels, now no longer thinks of them? Do not wonder; he is quite taken up in looking out for the boar which his dogs have been hunting so hotly for the last six hours. He requires nothing more. However full of sadness a man may be, he is happy for the time, if you can prevail upon him to enter into some amusement; and however happy a man may be, he will soon be discontented and wretched, if he is not diverted and occupied by some passion or pursuit which prevents weariness from overcoming him. Without amusement there is no joy; with amusement there is no sadness. And this also constitutes the happiness of persons in high position, that they have a number of people to amuse them, and have the power to keep themselves in this state.

Consider this. What is it to be superintendent, chancellor, first president, but to be in a condition wherein from early morning a large number of people come from all quarters to see them, so as not to leave them an hour in the day in which they can think of themselves? And when they are in disgrace and sent back to their country houses, where they lack neither wealth nor servants to help them on occasion, they do not fail to be wretched and desolate, because no one prevents them from thinking of themselves.

140

How does it happen that this man, so distressed at the death of his wife and his only son, or who has some great lawsuit which annoys him, is not at this moment sad, and that he seems so free from all painful and disquieting thoughts? We need not wonder; for a ball has been served him, and he must return it to his companion. He is occupied in catching it in its fall from the roof, to win a game. How can he think of his own affairs, pray, when he has this other matter in hand? Here is a care worthy of occupying this great soul, and taking away from him every other thought of the mind. This man, born to know the universe, to judge all causes, to govern a whole state, is altogether occupied and taken up with the business of catching a hare. And if he does not lower himself to this, and wants always to be on the strain, he will be more foolish still, because he would raise himself above humanity; and after all he is only a man, that is to say capable of little and of much, of all and of nothing; he is neither angel nor brute, but man.

141

Men spend their time in following a ball or a hare; it is the pleasure even of kings.

142

Diversion. Is not the royal dignity sufficiently great in itself to make its possessor happy by the mere contemplation of what he is? Must he be diverted from this thought like ordinary folk? I see well that a man is made happy by diverting him from the view of his domestic sorrows so as to occupy all his thoughts with the care of dancing well. But will it be the same with a king, and will he be happier in the pursuit of these idle amusements than in the contemplation of his greatness? And what more satisfactory object could be presented to his mind? Would it not be a deprivation of his delight for him to occupy his soul with the thought of how to adjust his steps to the cadence of an air, or of how to throw a ball skilfully, instead of leaving it to enjoy quietly the contemplation of the majestic glory which encompasses him? Let us make the trial; let us leave a king all alone to reflect on himself quite at leisure, without any gratification of the senses, without any care in his mind, without society; and we will see that a king without diversion is a man full of wretchedness. So this is carefully avoided, and near the persons of kings there never fail to be a great number of people who see to it that amusement follows business, and who watch all the time of their leisure to supply them with delights and games, so that there is no blank in it. In fact, kings are surrounded with persons who are wonderfully attentive in taking care that the king be not alone and in a state to think of himself, knowing well that he will be miserable, king though he be, if he meditate on self.

In all this I am not talking of Christian kings as Christians, but only as kings.

143

Diversion. Men are entrusted from infancy with the care of their honour, their property, their friends, and even with the property and the honour of their friends. They are overwhelmed with business, with the study of languages, and with physical exercise; and they are made to understand that they cannot be happy unless their health, their honour, their fortune and that of their friends is in good condition, and that a single thing wanting will make them unhappy. Thus they are given cares and business which make them bustle about from the break of day. "It is," you will exclaim, "a strange way to make them happy! What more could be done to make them miserable?"—Indeed!, what could be done? We should only have to relieve them from all these cares; for then they would see themselves: they would reflect on what they are, whence they came, whither they go, and thus we cannot employ and divert them too much. And this is why, after having given them so much business, we advise them, if they have some time for relaxation, to employ it in amusement, in play, and to be always fully occupied.

How hollow and full of ribaldry is the heart of man!

144

I spent a long time in the study of the abstract sciences, and was disheartened by the small number of fellow-students in them. When I commenced the study of man, I saw that these abstract sciences are not suited to man, and that I was wandering farther from my own state in examining them, than others in not knowing them. I pardoned their little knowledge; but I thought at least to find many companions in the study of man, and that it was the true study which is suited to him. I have been deceived; still fewer study it than geometry. It is only from the want of knowing how to study this that we seek the other studies. But is it not the case that even this is not the knowledge which man should have, and that for the purpose of happiness it is better for him not to know himself?

145

One thought alone occupies us; we cannot think of two things at the same time. This is lucky for us according to the world, not according to God.

146

Man is obviously made to think. It is his whole dignity and his whole merit; and his whole duty is to think as he ought. Now, the order of thought is to begin with self, and with its Author and its end.

Now, of what does the world think? Never of this, but of dancing, playing the lute, singing, making verses, running at the ring, etc., fighting, making oneself king, without thinking what it is to be a king and what it is to be a man.

147

We do not content ourselves with the life we have in ourselves and in our own being; we desire to live an imaginary life in the mind of others, and for this purpose we endeavour to shine. We labour unceasingly to adorn and preserve this imaginary existence, and neglect the real. And if we possess calmness, or generosity, or truthfulness, we are eager to make it known, so as to attach these virtues to that imaginary existence. We would rather separate them from ourselves to join them to it; and we would willingly be cowards in order to acquire the reputation of being brave. A great proof of the nothingness of our being, not to be satisfied with the one without the other, and to renounce the one for the other! For he would be infamous who would not die to preserve his honour.

148

We are so presumptuous that we would wish to be known by all the world, even by people who shall come after, when we shall be no more; and we are so vain that the esteem of five or six neighbours delights and contents us.

149

We do not trouble ourselves about being esteemed in the towns through which we pass. But if we are to remain a little while there, we are so concerned. How long is necessary? A time commensurate with our vain and paltry life.

150

Vanity is so anchored in the heart of man that a soldier, a soldier's servant, a cook, a porter brags, and wishes to have his admirers. Even philosophers wish for them. Those who write against it want to have the glory of having written well;[1] and those who read it desire the glory of having read it. I who write this have perhaps this desire, and perhaps those who will read it . . .

164

He who does not see the vanity of the world is himself very vain. Indeed who do not see it but youths who are absorbed in fame, diversion, and the thought of the future? But take away diversion, and you will see them dried up with weariness. They feel then their nothingness without knowing it; for it is indeed to be unhappy to be in insufferable sadness as soon as we are reduced to thinking of our self, and have no diversion.

165

Thoughts. In omnibus requiem quaesivi.[2] If our condition

---

[1] A thought of Cicero's in *Pro Archia*, mentioned by Montaigne in his *Essays*, I, 41.
[2] "I have sought everywhere for peace." From a quote attributed to Thomas à Kempis, *"In omnibus requiem quaesivi, sed non inveni, nisi in hoexkens ende boexkens"* ("I have sought everywhere for peace, and I have only found it in

were truly happy, we would not need diversion from thinking of it in order to make ourselves happy.

166

Diversion. Death is easier to bear without thinking of it, than is the thought of death without peril.

167

The miseries of human life have established all this: as men have seen this, they have taken up diversion.

168

Diversion. As men are not able to fight against death, misery, ignorance, they have taken it into their heads, in order to be happy, not to think of them at all.

169

Despite these miseries, man wishes to be happy, and only wishes to be happy, and cannot wish not to be so. But how will he set about it? To be happy he would have to make himself immortal; but, not being able to do so, it has occurred to him to prevent himself from thinking of death.

170

Diversion. If man were happy, he would be the more so, the less he was diverted, like the Saints and God. "Yes," you say, "but is it not to be happy to have a faculty of being amused by diversion?"—No, for that comes from elsewhere and from without, and thus is dependent, and therefore subject to be disturbed by a thousand accidents, which bring inevitable griefs.

---

nooks and in books.")

171

Misery. The only thing which consoles us for our miseries is diversion, and yet this is the greatest of our miseries. For it is this which principally hinders us from reflecting upon ourselves, and which makes us insensibly ruin ourselves. Without this we should be in a state of weariness, and this weariness would spur us to seek a more solid means of escaping from it. But diversion amuses us, and leads us unconsciously to death.

172

We do not rest satisfied with the present. We anticipate the future as too slow in coming, as if in order to hasten its course; or we recall the past, to stop its too rapid flight. So imprudent are we that we wander in the times which are not ours, and do not think of the only one which belongs to us; and so idle are we that we dream of those times which are no more, and thoughtlessly overlook that which alone exists. For the present is generally painful to us. We conceal it from our sight, because it troubles us; and if it be delightful to us, we regret to see it pass away. We try to sustain it by the future, and think of arranging matters which are not in our power, for a time which we have no certainty of reaching.

Let each one examine his thoughts, and he will find them all occupied with the past and the future. We scarcely ever think of the present; and if we think of it, it is only to take light from it to arrange the future. The present is never our end. The past and the present are our means; the future alone is our end. So we never live, but we hope to live; and, as we are always preparing to be happy, it is inevitable we should never be so.

181

We are so unfortunate that we can only take pleasure in a thing on condition of being annoyed if it turn out ill, as a thousand things can do, and do every hour. He who should find the secret of rejoicing in the good, without troubling himself with its contrary evil, would have hit the mark. It is perpetual motion.

240

"I would soon have renounced pleasure," they say, "if I had faith." For my part I tell you, "You would soon have faith, if you renounced pleasure." Now, it is for you to begin. If I could, I would give you faith. I cannot do so, nor therefore test the truth of what you say. But you can well renounce pleasure, and test whether what I say is true.

345

Reason commands us far more imperiously than a master; for in disobeying the one we are unhappy, and in disobeying the other we are fools.

409

The greatness of man. The greatness of man is so evident, that it is even proved by his wretchedness. For what in animals is nature we call in man wretchedness; by which we recognize that, his nature being now like that of animals, he has fallen from a better nature which once was his.

For who is unhappy at not being a king, except a deposed king? Was Paulus Emilius unhappy at being no longer consul? On the contrary, everybody thought him happy in having been consul, because the office could only be held for a time. But men thought Perseus so unhappy in being no longer king, because the condition of kingship implied his being always king, that they thought it strange that he endured life. Who is unhappy at having only one mouth? And who is not unhappy at having only one eye? Probably no man ever ventured to mourn at not having three eyes. But anyone is inconsolable at having none.

425

Man without faith cannot know the true good, nor justice.

All men seek happiness. This is without exception. Whatever different means they employ, they all tend to this end. The cause of some going to war, and of others avoiding it, is the same desire in both, attended with different views. The will never takes the least step but to this object. This is the motive of every action of every man, even of those who hang themselves.

And yet after such a great number of years, no one without faith has reached the point to which all continually look. All complain, princes and subjects, noblemen and commoners, old and young, strong and weak, learned and ignorant, healthy and sick, of all countries, all times, all ages, and all conditions.

A trial so long, so continuous, and so uniform, should certainly convince us of our inability to reach the good by our own efforts. But example teaches us little. No resemblance is ever so perfect that there is not some slight difference; and hence we expect that our hope will not be deceived on this occasion as before. And thus, while the present never satisfies us, experience dupes us, and from misfortune to misfortune leads us to death, their eternal crown.

What is it then that this desire and this inability proclaim to us, but that there was once in man a true happiness of which there now remain to him only the mark and empty trace, which he in vain tries to fill from all his surroundings, seeking from things absent the help he does not obtain in things present? But these are all inadequate, because the infinite abyss can only be filled by an infinite and immutable object, that is to say, only by God Himself.

He only is our true good, and since we have forsaken Him, it is a strange thing that there is nothing in nature which has not been serviceable in taking His place; the stars, the heavens, earth, the elements, plants, cabbages, leeks, animals, insects, calves, serpents, fever, pestilence, war, famine, vices, adultery, incest. And since man has lost the true good, everything can appear equally good to him, even his own destruction, though so opposed to God, to reason, and to the whole course of nature.

Some seek good in authority, others in scientific research, others in pleasure. Others, who are in fact nearer the truth, have considered it necessary that the universal good, which all men desire, should not consist in any of the particular things which can only be possessed by one man, and which, when shared, afflict their possessor more by the want of the part he has not, than they please him by the possession of what he has. They have learned that the true good should be such as all can possess at once, without diminution and without envy, and which no one can lose against his will. And their reason is that this desire being natural to man, since it is necessarily in all, and that it is impossible not to have it, they infer from it . . .

447

Will it be said that, as men have declared that righteousness has departed the earth, they therefore knew of original sin?—*Nemo ante obitum beatus est*[1]—that is to say, they knew death to be the beginning of eternal and essential happiness?

458

"All that is in the world is the lust of the flesh, or the lust of the eyes, or the pride of life;" *libido sentiendi, libido sciendi, libido dominandi.*[2] Wretched is the cursed land which these three rivers of fire enflame rather than water! Happy they who, on these rivers, are not overwhelmed nor carried away, but are immovably fixed, not standing but seated on a low and secure base, whence they do not rise before the light, but, having rested in peace, stretch out their hands to Him, who

---

[1] "No one is happy until he is dead." See Ovid's Metamorphosis, III, 135, and Montaigne's *Essays*, I, 18.
[2] 1 John, 2:16.

must lift them up, and make them stand upright and firm in the porches of the holy Jerusalem! There pride can no longer assail them nor cast them down; and yet they weep, not to see all those perishable things swept away by the torrents, but at the remembrance of their loved country, the heavenly Jerusalem, which they remember without ceasing during their prolonged exile.

11[1]

All great diversions are dangerous to the Christian life; but among all those which the world has invented there is none more to be feared than the theatre. It is a representation of the passions so natural and so delicate that it excites them and gives birth to them in our hearts, and, above all, to that of love, principally when it is represented as very chaste and virtuous. For the more innocent it appears to innocent souls, the more they are likely to be touched by it. Its violence pleases our self-love, which immediately forms a desire to produce the same effects which are seen so well represented; and, at the same time, we make ourselves a conscience founded on the propriety of the feelings which we see there, by which the fear of pure souls is removed, since they imagine that it cannot hurt their purity to love with a love which seems to them so reasonable.

So we depart from the theatre with our heart so filled with all the beauty and tenderness of love, the soul and the mind so persuaded of its innocence, that we are quite ready to receive its first impressions, or rather to seek an opportunity of awakening them in the heart of another, in order that we may receive the same pleasures and the same sacrifices which we have seen so well represented in the theatre.

---

1 I have moved this aphorism toward the end so that it can be properly appreciated in the context of the discussion on diversion. It is remarkable how much this passage still applies to our lives today, i.e. the insidious influence of Hollywood films, etc.

541

The Christian religion alone makes man altogether *lovable and happy*. In honesty, perhaps we cannot be altogether lovable and happy.

549

I love poverty because He loved it. I love riches because they afford me the means of helping the very poor. I keep faith with everybody; I do not render evil to those who wrong me, but I wish them a lot like mine, in which I receive neither evil nor good from men. I try to be just, true, sincere, and faithful to all men; I have a tender heart for those to whom God has more closely united me; and whether I am alone, or seen of men, I do all my actions in the sight of God, who must judge of them, and to whom I have consecrated them all.

These are my sentiments; and every day of my life I bless my Redeemer, who has implanted them in me, and who, of a man full of weakness, of miseries, of lust, of pride, and of ambition, has made a man free from all these evils by the power of His grace, to which all the glory of it is due, as of myself I have only misery and error.

from
MORAL EPISTLES

by

SENECA

XXVIII

ON TRAVEL AS A CURE FOR DISCONTENT

Do you suppose that you alone have had this experience? Are you surprised, as if it were a novelty, that after such long travel and so many changes of scene you have not been able to shake off the gloom and heaviness of your mind? You need a change of soul rather than a change of climate. Though you may cross vast spaces of sea, and though, as our Virgil remarks,

> Lands and cities are left astern,

your faults will follow you wherever you travel. Socrates made the same remark to one who complained; he said: "Why do you wonder that globe-trotting does not help you, seeing that you always take yourself with you? The reason which set you wandering is ever at your heels." What pleasure is there in seeing new lands? Or in surveying cities and spots of interest? All your bustle is useless. Do you ask why such flight does not help you? It is because you flee along with yourself. You must lay aside the burdens of the mind; until you do this, no place will satisfy you. Reflect that your present behaviour is like that of the prophetess whom Virgil describes: she is excited and goaded into fury, and contains within herself much inspiration that is not her own: "The priestess raves, if haply she may shake / The great god from her heart." You wander here and there, to rid yourself of the burden that rests upon you, though it becomes more troublesome by reason of your very restlessness, just as in a ship the cargo when stationary makes no trouble, but when it shifts to this side or that, it causes the vessel to heel more quickly in the direction where it has settled. Anything you do tells against you, and you hurt yourself by your very unrest; for you are shaking up a sick man.

That trouble once removed, all change of scene will become pleasant; though you may be driven to the uttermost ends of the earth, in whatever corner of a savage land you may find yourself, that place, however forbidding, will be to you a hospitable abode. The person you are matters more than the place to which you go; for that reason we should not make the mind a bondsman to any one place. Live in this belief: "I am not born for any one corner of the universe; this whole world is my country." If you saw this fact clearly, you would not be surprised at getting no benefit from the fresh scenes to which you roam each time through weariness of the old scenes. For the first would have pleased you in each case, had you believed it wholly yours. As it is, however, you are not journeying; you are drifting and being driven, only exchanging one place for another, although that which you seek—to live well—is found everywhere. Can there be any spot so full of confusion as the Forum? Yet you can live quietly even there, if necessary. Of course, if one were allowed to make one's own arrangements, I should flee far from the very sight and neighbourhood of the Forum. For just as pestilential places assail even the strongest constitution, so there are some places which are also unwholesome for a healthy mind which is not yet quite sound, though recovering from its ailment. I disagree with those who strike out into the midst of the billows and, welcoming a stormy existence, wrestle daily in hardihood of soul with life's problems. The wise man will endure all that, but will not choose it; he will prefer to be at peace rather than at war. It helps little to have cast out your own faults if you must quarrel with those of others. Says one: "There were thirty tyrants surrounding Socrates, and yet they could not break his spirit"; but what does it matter how many masters a man has? "Slavery" has no plural; and he who has scorned it is free—no matter amid how large a mob of over-lords he stands.

It is time to stop, but not before I have paid duty. "The knowledge of sin is the beginning of salvation." This saying of Epicurus seems to me to be a noble one. For he who does not know that he has sinned does not desire correction; you must discover yourself in the wrong before you can reform yourself. Some boast of their faults. Do you think that the man has any thought of mending his ways who counts over his vices as if they were virtues? Therefore, as far as possible, prove yourself guilty, hunt up charges against yourself; play the part, first of accuser, then of judge, last of intercessor. At times be harsh with yourself.

Farewell.

LIX

ON PLEASURE AND JOY

I received great pleasure from your letter; kindly allow me to use these words in their everyday meaning, without insisting upon their Stoic import. For we Stoics hold that pleasure is a vice. Very likely it is a vice; but we are accustomed to use the word when we wish to indicate a happy state of mind. I am aware that if we test words by our formula, even pleasure is a thing of ill repute, and joy can be attained only by the wise. For "joy" is an elation of spirit, of a spirit which trusts in the goodness and truth of its own possessions. The common usage, however, is that we derive great "joy" from a friend's position as consul, or from his marriage, or from the birth of his child; but these events, so far from being matters of joy, are more often the beginnings of sorrow to come. No, it is a characteristic of real joy that it never ceases, and never changes into its opposite.

Accordingly, when our Virgil speaks of "The evil joys of

the mind," his words are eloquent, but not strictly appropriate. For no "joy" can be evil. He has given the name "joy" to pleasures, and has thus expressed his meaning. For he has conveyed the idea that men take delight in their own evil. Nevertheless, I was not wrong in saying that I received great "pleasure" from your letter; for although an ignorant man may derive "joy" if the cause be an honourable one, yet, since his emotion is wayward, and is likely soon to take another direction, I call it "pleasure"; for it is inspired by an opinion concerning a spurious good; it exceeds control and is carried to excess.

But, to return to the subject, let me tell you what delighted me in your letter. You have your words under control. You are not carried away by your language, or borne beyond the limits which you have determined upon. Many writers are tempted by the charm of some alluring phrase to some topic other than that which they had set themselves to discuss. But this has not been so in your case; all your words are compact, and suited to the subject. You say all that you wish, and you mean still more than you say. This is a proof of the importance of your subject matter, showing that your mind, as well as your words, contains nothing superfluous or bombastic.

I do, however, find some metaphors, not, indeed, daring ones, but the kind which have stood the test of use. I find similes also; of course, if anyone forbids us to use them, maintaining that poets alone have that privilege, he has not, apparently, read any of our ancient prose writers, who had not yet learned to affect a style that should win applause. For those writers, whose eloquence was simple and directed only towards proving their case, are full of comparisons; and I think that these are necessary, not for the same reason which makes them necessary for the poets, but in order that they may serve as props to our feebleness, to bring both speaker and listener face to face with the subject under discussion. For example, I am at this very moment reading Sextius; he is a keen man, and a philosopher who, though he writes in Greek, has the Roman standard of ethics. One of his similes appealed especially to me, that of an army marching in hollow square, in a place where the enemy might be expected to appear from any quarter, ready for battle. "This," said he, "is just what the wise man ought to do; he should have all his fighting qualities deployed on every side, so that wherever the attack threatens, there his supports may be ready to hand and may obey the captain's command without confusion." This is what we notice in armies which serve under great leaders; we see how all the troops simultaneously understand their general's orders, since they are so arranged that a signal given by one man passes down the ranks of cavalry and infantry at the same moment. This, he declares, is still more necessary for men like ourselves; for soldiers have often feared an enemy without reason, and the march which they thought most dangerous has in fact been most secure; but folly brings no repose, fear haunts it both in the front and in the rear of the column, and both flanks are in a panic. Folly is pursued, and confronted, by peril. It blenches at everything; it is unprepared; it is frightened even by auxiliary troops. But the wise man is fortified against all inroads; he is alert; he will not retreat before the attack of poverty, or of sorrow, or of disgrace, or of pain. He will walk undaunted both against them and among them.

We human beings are fettered and weakened by many vices; we have wallowed in them for a long time and it is hard for us to be cleansed. We are not merely defiled; we are dyed by them. But, to refrain from passing from one figure to another, I will raise this question, which I often consider in my own heart: why is it that folly holds us with such an insistent grasp? It is, primarily, because we do not combat it strongly enough, because we do not struggle towards salvation with all our might; secondly, because we do not put sufficient trust in the discoveries of the wise, and do not drink in their words with open hearts; we approach this great problem in too trifling a spirit. But how can a man learn, in the struggle against his vices, an amount that is enough, if the time which he gives to learning is only the amount left over from his vices?

None of us goes deep below the surface. We skim the top only, and we regard the smattering of time spent in the search for wisdom as enough and to spare for a busy man. What hinders us most of all is that we are too readily satisfied with ourselves; if we meet with someone who calls us good men, or sensible men, or holy men, we see ourselves in his description, not content with praise in moderation, we accept everything that shameless flattery heaps upon us, as if it were our due. We agree with those who declare us to be the best and wisest of men, although we know that they are given to much lying. And we are so self-complacent that we desire praise for certain actions when we are especially addicted to the very opposite. Yonder person hears himself called "most gentle" when he is inflicting tortures, or "most generous" when he is engaged in looting, or "most temperate" when he is in the midst of drunkenness and lust. Thus it follows that we are unwilling to be reformed, just because we believe ourselves to be the best of men.

Alexander was roaming as far as India, ravaging tribes that were but little known, even to their neighbours. During the blockade of a certain city., while he was reconnoitring the walls and hunting for the weakest spot in the fortifications, he was wounded by an arrow. Nevertheless, he long continued the siege, intent on finishing what he had begun. The pain of his wound, however, as the surface became dry and as the flow of blood was checked, increased; his leg gradually became numb as he sat his horse; and finally, when he was forced to withdraw, he exclaimed: "All men swear that I am the son of Jupiter, but this wound cries out that I am mortal." Let us also act in the same way.

Each man, according to his lot in life, is stultified by flattery. We should say to him who flatters us: "You call me a man of sense, but I understand how many of the things which I crave are useless, and how many of the things which I desire will do me harm. I have not even the knowledge, which satiety teaches to animals, of what should be the measure of my food or my drink. I do not yet know how much I can hold."

I shall now show you how you may know that you are not wise. The wise man is joyful, happy and calm, unshaken—he lives on a plane with the gods. Now go, question yourself; if you are never downcast, if your mind is not harassed by apprehension through anticipation of what is to come, if day and night your soul keeps on its even and unswerving course, upright and content with itself, then you have attained the greatest good that mortals can possess. If, however, you seek pleasures of all kinds in all directions, you must know that you are as far short of wisdom as you are short of joy. Joy is the goal which you desire to reach, but you are wandering from the path if you expect to reach your goal while you are in the midst of riches and official titles—in other words, if you seek joy in the midst of cares. These objects for which you strive so eagerly, as if they would give you happiness and pleasure, are merely causes of grief.

All men of this stamp, I maintain, are pressing on in pursuit of joy, but they do not know where they may obtain a joy that is both great and enduring. One person seeks it in feasting and self-indulgence; another, in canvassing for honours and in being surrounded by a throng of clients; another, in his mistress; another, in idle display of culture and in literature that has no power to heal; all these men are led astray by delights which are deceptive and short-lived—like drunkenness for example, which pays for a single hour of hilarious madness by a sickness of many days, or like applause and the popularity of enthusiastic approval which are gained, and atoned for, at the cost of great mental disquietude.

Reflect, therefore, on this, that the effect of wisdom is a joy that is unbroken and continuous. The mind of the wise man is like the ultra-lunar firmament; eternal calm pervades that region. You have, then, a reason for wishing to be wise, if the wise man is never deprived of joy. This joy springs only from the knowledge that you possess the virtues. None but the brave, the just, the self-restrained, can rejoice. And when you query: "What do you mean? Do not the foolish and the wicked also rejoice?" I reply, no more than lions who have caught their prey. When men have wearied themselves with wine and lust, when night fails them before their debauch is done, when the pleasures which they have heaped upon a body that is too small to hold them begin to fester, at such times they utter in their wretchedness those lines of Virgil:

> Thou knowest how, amid false-glittering
>   joys,
> We spent that last of nights.

Pleasure-lovers spend every night amid false-glittering joys, and just as if it were their last. But the joy which comes to the gods, and to those who imitate the gods, is not broken off, nor does it cease; but it would surely cease were it borrowed from without. Just because it is not in the power of another to bestow, neither is it subject to another's whims. That which Fortune has not given, she cannot take away.

Farewell.

XCII

ON THE HAPPY LIFE

You and I will agree, I think, that outward things are sought for the satisfaction of the body, that the body is cherished out of regard for the soul, and that in the soul there are certain parts which minister to us, enabling us to move and to sustain life, bestowed upon us just for the sake of the primary part of us. In this primary part there is something irrational, and something rational. The former obeys the latter, while the latter is the only thing that is not referred back to another, but rather refers all things to itself. For the divine reason also is set in supreme command over all things, and is itself subject to none; and even this reason which we possess is the same, because it is derived from the divine reason. Now if we are agreed on this point, it is natural that we shall be agreed on the following also—namely, that the happy life depends upon this and this alone: our attainment of perfect reason. For it is naught but this that keeps the soul from being bowed down, that stands its ground against Fortune; whatever the condition of their affairs may be, it keeps men untroubled. And that alone is a good which is never subject to impairment. That man, I declare, is happy whom nothing makes less strong than he is; he keeps to the heights, leaning upon none but himself; for one who sustains himself by any prop may fall. If the case is otherwise, then things which do not pertain to us will begin to have great influence over us. But who desires Fortune to have the upper hand, or what sensible man prides himself upon that which is not his own?

What is the happy life? It is peace of mind, and lasting tranquillity. This will be yours if you possess greatness of soul; it will be yours if you possess the steadfastness that resolutely clings to a good judgment just reached. How does a man reach this condition? By gaining a complete view of truth, by maintaining, in all that he does, order, measure, fitness, and a will that is inoffensive and kindly, that is intent upon reason and never departs therefrom, that commands at the same time love and admiration. In short, to give you the principle in brief compass, the wise man's soul ought to be such as would be proper for a god. What more can one desire who possesses all honourable things? For if dishonourable things can contribute to the best estate, then there will be the possibility of a happy life under conditions which do not include an honourable life. And what is more base or foolish than to connect the good of a rational soul with things irrational? Yet there are certain philosophers who hold that the Supreme Good admits of increase because it is hardly complete when the gifts of fortune are adverse. Even Antipater, one of the great leaders of this school, admits that he ascribes some influence to externals, though only a very slight influence. You see, however, what absurdity lies in not being content with the daylight unless it is increased by a tiny fire. What importance can a spark have in the midst of this clear sunlight? If you are not contented with only that which is honourable, it must follow that you desire in addition either the kind of quiet which the Greeks call "undisturbedness," or else pleasure. But the former may be attained in any case. For the mind is free from disturbance when it is fully free to contemplate the universe, and nothing distracts it from the contemplation of nature. The second, pleasure, is simply the good of cattle. We are but adding the irrational to the rational, the dishonourable to the honourable. A pleasant physical sensation affects this life of ours; why, therefore, do you hesitate to say that all is well with a man just because all is well with his appetite? And do you rate, I will not say among heroes, but among men, the person whose Supreme Good is a matter of flavours and colours and sounds? Nay, let him withdraw from the ranks of this, the noblest class of living beings, second only to the gods; let him herd with the dumb brutes—an animal whose delight is in fodder!

The irrational part of the soul is twofold: the one part is spirited, ambitious, uncontrolled; its seat is in the passions; the other is lowly, sluggish, and devoted to pleasure. Philosophers have neglected the former, which, though unbridled, is yet better, and is certainly more courageous and more worthy of a man, and have regarded the latter, which is nerveless and ignoble, as indispensable to the happy life. They have ordered reason to serve this latter; they have made the Supreme Good of the noblest living being an abject and mean affair, and a monstrous hybrid, too, composed of various members which harmonize but ill. For as our Virgil, describing Scylla, says

> Above, a human fate and maiden's
>   breast,—
> A beauteous breast,—below, a monster
>   huge
> Of bulk and shapeless, with a dolphin's
>   tail
> Joined to a wolf-like belly.

And yet to this Scylla are tacked on the forms of wild animals, dreadful and swift; but from what monstrous shapes have these wiseacres compounded wisdom! Man's primary art is virtue itself; there is joined to this the useless and fleeting flesh, fitted only for the reception of food, as Posidonius remarks. This divine virtue ends in foulness, and to the higher parts, which are worshipful and heavenly, there is fastened a sluggish and flabby animal. As for the second desideratum—quiet—although it would indeed not of itself be of any benefit to the soul, yet it would relieve the soul of hindrances; pleasure, on the contrary, actually destroys the soul and softens all its vigour. What elements so inharmonious as these can be found united? To that which is most vigorous is joined that which is most sluggish, to that which is austere that which is far from serious, to that which is most holy that which is unrestrained even to the point of impurity. "What, then," comes the retort, "if good health, rest, and freedom from pain are not likely to hinder virtue, shall you not seek all these?" Of course I shall seek them, but not because they are goods—I shall seek them because they are according to nature and because they will be acquired through the exercise of good judgment on my part. What, then, will be good in them? This alone—that it is a good thing to choose them. For when I don suitable attire, or walk as I should, or dine as I ought to dine, it is not my dinner, or my walk, or my dress that are goods, but the deliberate choice which I show in regard to them, as I observe, in each thing I do, a mean that conforms with reason. Let me also add that the choice of neat clothing is a fitting object of a man's efforts; for man is by nature a neat and well-groomed animal. Hence the choice of neat attire, and not neat attire in itself, is a good; since the good is not in the thing selected, but in the quality of the selection. Our actions are honourable, but not the actual things which we do. And you may assume that what I have said about dress applies also to the body. For nature has surrounded our soul with the body as with a sort of garment; the body is its cloak. But who has ever reckoned the value of clothes by the wardrobe which contained them? The scabbard does not make the sword good or bad. Therefore, with regard to the body I shall return the same answer to you—that, if I have the choice, I shall choose health and strength, but that the good involved will be my judgment regarding these things, and not the things themselves.

Another retort is: "Granted that the wise man is happy; nevertheless, he does not attain the Supreme Good which we have defined, unless the means also which nature provides for its attainment are at his call. So, while one who possesses virtue cannot be unhappy, yet one cannot be perfectly happy if one lacks such natural gifts as health, or soundness of limb."

But in saying this, you grant the alternative which seems the more difficult to believe—that the man who is in the midst of unremitting and extreme pain is not wretched, nay, is even happy; and you deny that which is much less serious—that he is completely happy. And yet, if virtue can keep a man from being wretched, it will be an easier task for it to render him completely happy. For the difference between happiness and complete happiness is less than that between wretchedness and happiness. Can it be possible that a thing which is so powerful as to snatch a man from disaster, and place him among the happy, cannot also accomplish what remains, and render him supremely happy? Does its strength fail at the very top of the climb? There are in life things which are advantageous and disadvantageous—both beyond our control. If a good man, in spite of being weighed down by all kinds of disadvantages, is not wretched, how is he not supremely happy, no matter if he does lack certain advantages? For as he is not weighted down to wretchedness by his burden of disadvantages, so he is not withdrawn from supreme happiness through lack of any advantages; nay, he is just as supremely happy without the advantages as he is free from wretchedness though under the load of his disadvantages. Otherwise, if his good can be impaired, it can be snatched from him altogether.

A short space above, I remarked that a tiny fire does not add to the sun's light. For by reason of the sun's brightness any light that shines apart from the sunlight is blotted out. "But," one may say, "there are certain objects that stand in the way even of the sunlight." The sun, however, is unimpaired even in the midst of obstacles, and, though an object may intervene and cut off our view thereof, the sun sticks to his work and goes on his course. Whenever he shines forth from amid the clouds, he is no smaller, nor less punctual either, than when he is free from clouds; since it makes a great deal of difference whether there is merely something in the way of his light or something which interferes with his shining. Similarly, obstacles take nothing away from virtue; it is no smaller, but merely shines with less brilliancy. In our eyes, it may perhaps be less visible and less luminous than before;

but as regards itself it is the same and, like the sun when he is eclipsed, is still, though in secret, putting forth its strength. Disasters, therefore, and losses, and wrongs, have only the same power over virtue that a cloud has over the sun.

We meet with one person who maintains that a wise man who has met with bodily misfortune is neither wretched nor happy. But he also is in error, for he is putting the results of chance upon a parity with the virtues, and is attributing only the same influence to things that are honourable as to things that are devoid of honour. But what is more detestable and more unworthy than to put contemptible things in the same class with things worthy of reverence! For reverence is due to justice, duty, loyalty, bravery, and prudence; on the contrary, those attributes are worthless with which the most worthless men are often blessed in fuller measure—such as a sturdy leg, strong shoulders, good teeth, and healthy and solid muscles. Again, if the wise man whose body is a trial to him shall be regarded as neither wretched nor happy, but shall be left in a sort of half-way position, his life also will be neither desirable nor undesirable. But what is so foolish as to say that the wise man's life is not desirable? And what is so far beyond the bounds of credence as the opinion that any life is neither desirable nor undesirable? Again, if bodily ills do not make a man wretched, they consequently allow him to be happy. For things which have no power to change his condition for the worse, have not the power, either, to disturb that condition when it is at its best.

"But," someone will say, "we know what is cold and what is hot; a lukewarm temperature lies between. Similarly, A is happy, and B is wretched, and C is neither happy nor wretched." I wish to examine this figure, which is brought into play against us. If I add to your lukewarm water a larger quantity of cold water, the result will be cold water. But if I pour in a larger quantity of hot water, the water will finally become hot. In the case, however, of your man who is neither wretched nor happy, no matter how much I add to his troubles, he will not be unhappy, according to your argument; hence your figure offers no analogy. Again, suppose that I set before you a man who is neither miserable nor happy. I add blindness to his misfortunes; he is not rendered unhappy. I cripple him; he is not rendered unhappy. I add afflictions which are unceasing and severe; he is not rendered unhappy. Therefore, one whose life is not changed to misery by all these ills is not dragged by them, either, from his life of happiness. Then if, as you say, the wise man cannot fall from happiness to wretchedness, he cannot fall into non-happiness. For how, if one has begun to slip, can one stop at any particular place? That which prevents him from rolling to the bottom, keeps him at the summit. Why, you urge, may not a happy life possibly be destroyed? It cannot even be disjointed; and for that reason virtue is itself of itself sufficient for the happy life.

"But," it is said, "is not the wise man happier if he has lived longer and has been distracted by no pain, than one who has always been compelled to grapple with evil fortune?" Answer me now—is he any better or more honourable? If he is not, then he is not happier either. In order to live more happily, he must live more rightly; if he cannot do that, then he cannot live more happily either. Virtue cannot be strained tighter, and therefore neither can the happy life, which depends on virtue. For virtue is so great a good that it is not affected by such insignificant assaults upon it as shortness of life, pain, and the various bodily vexations. For pleasure does not deserve that virtue should even glance at it. Now what is the chief thing in virtue? It is the quality of not needing a single day beyond the present, and of not reckoning up the days that are ours; in the slightest possible moment of time virtue completes an eternity of good. These goods seem to us incredible and transcending man's nature; for we measure its grandeur by the standard of our own weakness, and we call our vices by the name of virtue. Furthermore, does it not seem just as incredible that any man in the midst of extreme suffering should say, "I am happy"? And yet this utterance was heard in the very factory of pleasure, when Epicurus said: "Today and one other day have been the happiest of all!"—although in the one case he was tortured by strangury, and in the other by the incurable pain of an ulcerated stomach. Why, then, should those goods which virtue bestows be incredible in the sight of us, who cultivate virtue, when they are found even in those who acknowledge pleasure as their mistress? These also, ignoble and base-minded as they are, declare that even in the midst of excessive pain and misfortune the wise man will be neither wretched nor happy. And yet this also is incredible—nay, still more incredible, than the other case. For I do not understand how, if virtue falls from her heights, she can help being hurled all the way to the bottom. She either must preserve one in happiness, or, if driven from this position, she will not prevent us from becoming unhappy. If virtue only stands her ground, she cannot be driven from the field; she must either conquer or be conquered.

But some say: "Only to the immortal gods is given virtue and the happy life; we can attain but the shadow, as it were, and semblance of such goods as theirs. We approach them, but we never reach them." Reason, however, is a common attribute of both gods and men; in the gods it is already perfected, in us it is capable of being perfected. But it is our vices that bring us to despair; for the second class of rational being, man, is of an inferior order—a guardian, as it were, who is too unstable to hold fast to what is best, his judgment still wavering and uncertain. He may require the faculties of sight and hearing, good health, a bodily exterior that is not loathsome, and, besides, greater length of days conjoined with an unimpaired constitution. Though by means of reason be can lead a life which will not bring regrets, yet there resides in this imperfect creature, man, a certain power that makes for badness, because he possesses a mind which is easily moved to perversity. Suppose, however, the badness which is in full view, and has previously been stirred to activity, to be removed; the man is still not a good man, but he is being moulded to goodness. One, however, in whom there is lacking any quality that makes for goodness, is bad.

But

>He in whose body virtue dwells, and spirit
>E'er present

is equal to the gods; mindful of his origin, he strives to return thither. No man does wrong in attempting to regain the heights from which he once came down. And why should you not believe that something of divinity exists in one who is a part of God? All this universe which encompasses us is one, and it is God; we are associates of God; we are his members. Our soul has capabilities, and is carried thither, if vices do not hold it down. Just as it is the nature of our bodies to stand erect and look upward to the sky, so the soul, which may reach out as far as it will, was framed by nature to this end, that it should desire equality with the gods. And if it makes use of its powers and stretches upward into its proper region it is by no alien path that it struggles toward the heights. It would be a great task to journey heavenwards; the soul but returns thither. When once it has found the road, it boldly marches on, scornful of all things. It casts no backward glance at wealth; gold and silver—things which are fully worthy of the gloom in which they once lay—it values not by the sheen which smites the eyes of the ignorant, but by the mire of ancient days, whence our greed first detached and dug them out.

The soul, I affirm, knows that riches are stored elsewhere than in men's heaped-up treasure-houses; that it is the soul, and not the strong-box, which should be filled. It is the soul that men may set in dominion over all things, and may install as owner of the universe, so that it may limit its riches only by the boundaries of East and West, and, like the gods, may possess all things; and that it may, with its own vast resources, look down from on high upon the wealthy, no one of whom rejoices as much in his own wealth as he resents the wealth of another. When the soul has transported itself to this lofty height, it regards the body also as a burden which must be borne: not as a thing to love, but as a thing to oversee; nor is it subservient to that over which it is set in mastery. For no man is free who is a slave to his body. Indeed, omitting all the other masters which are brought into being by excessive care for the body, the sway which the body itself exercises is captious and fastidious. Forth from this body the soul issues, now with unruffled spirit, now with exultation, and, when once it has gone forth, asks not what shall be the end of the deserted day. No; just as we do not take thought for the clippings of the hair and the beard, even so that divine soul, when it is about to issue forth from the mortal man, regards the destination of its earthly vessel—whether it be consumed by fire, or shut in by a stone, or buried in the earth, or torn by wild beasts—as being of no more concern to itself than is the afterbirth to a child just born. And whether this body shall be cast out and plucked to pieces by birds, or devoured when thrown to the sea-dogs as prey, how does that concern him who is nothing? Nay even when it is among the living, the soul fears nothing that may happen to the body after death; for though such things may have been threats, they were not enough to terrify the soul previous to the moment of death. It says, "I am not frightened by the executioner's hook, nor by the revolting mutilation of the corpse which is exposed to the scorn of those who would witness the spectacle. I ask no man to perform the last rites for me; I entrust my remains to none. Nature has made provision that none shall go unburied. Time will lay away one whom cruelty has cast forth." Those were eloquent words which Maecenas uttered:

> I want no tomb; for Nature doth provide
> For outcast bodies burial.

You would imagine that this was the saying of a man of strict principles. He was indeed a man of noble and robust native gifts, but in prosperity he impaired these gifts by laxness.
Farewell.

CIV

ON THE QUALITY AS CONTRASTED WITH THE LENGTH OF LIFE

I have run off to my villa at Nomentum, for what purpose, do you suppose? To escape the city? No; to shake off a fever which was surely working its way into my system. It had already got a grip upon me. My physician kept insisting that when the circulation was upset and irregular, disturbing the natural poise, the disease was under way. I therefore ordered my carriage to be made ready at once, and insisted on departing in spite of my wife Paulina's efforts to stop me; for I remembered master Gallio's words, when he began to develop a fever in Achaia and took ship at once, insisting that the disease was not of the body but of the place. That is what I remarked to my dear Paulina, who always urges me to take care of my health. I know that her very life-breath comes and goes with my own, and I am beginning, in my solicitude for her, to be solicitous for myself. And although old age has made me braver to bear many things, I am gradually losing this boon that old age bestows. For it comes into my mind that in this old man there is a youth also, and youth needs tenderness. Therefore, since I cannot prevail upon her to love me any more heroically, she prevails upon me to cherish myself more carefully. For one must indulge genuine emotions; sometimes, even in spite of weighty reasons, the breath of life must be called back and kept at our very lips even at the price of great suffering, for the sake of those whom we hold dear; because the good man should not live as long as it pleases him, but as long as he ought. He who does not value his wife, or his friend, highly enough to linger longer in life—he who obstinately persists in dying is a voluptuary.

The soul should also enforce this command upon itself whenever the needs of one's relatives require; it should pause and humour those near and dear, not only when it desires, but even when it has begun, to die. It gives proof of a great heart to return to life for the sake of others; and noble men have often done this. But this procedure also, I believe, indicates the highest type of kindness: that although the greatest advantage of old age is the opportunity to be more negligent regarding self-preservation and to use life more adventurously, one should watch over one's old age with still greater care if one knows that such action is pleasing, useful, or desirable in the eyes of a person whom one holds dear. This is also a source of no mean joy and profit; for what is sweeter than to be so valued by one's wife that one becomes more valuable to oneself for this reason? Hence my dear Paulina is able to make me responsible, not only for her fears, but also for my own. So you are curious to know the outcome of this prescription of travel? As soon as I escaped from the oppressive atmosphere of the city, and from that awful odour of reeking kitchens which, when in use, pour forth a ruinous mess of steam and soot, I perceived at once that my health was mending. And how much stronger do you think I felt when I reached my vineyards! Being, so to speak, let out to pasture, I regularly walked into my meals! So I am my old self again, feeling now no wavering languor in my system, and no sluggishness in my brain. I am beginning to work with all my energy.

But the mere place avails little for this purpose. unless the mind is fully master of itself, and can, at its pleasure, find seclusion even in the midst of business; the man, however, who is always selecting resorts and hunting for leisure, will find something to distract his mind in every place. Socrates is reported to have replied, when a certain person complained of having received no benefit from his travels: "It serves you right! You travelled in your own company!" O what a blessing it would be for some men to wander away from themselves! As it is, they cause themselves vexation, worry, demoralization, and fear! What profit is there in crossing the sea and in going from one city to another? If you would escape your troubles, you need not another place but another personality. Perhaps you have reached Athens, or perhaps Rhodes; choose any state you fancy, how does it matter what its character may be? You will be bringing to it your own.

Suppose that you hold wealth to be a good: poverty will then distress you, and—which is most pitiable—it will be an imaginary poverty. For you may be rich, and nevertheless, because your neighbour is richer, you suppose yourself to be poor exactly by the same amount in which you fall short of your neighbour. You may deem official position a good; you will be vexed at another's appointment or re-appointment to the consulship; you will be jealous whenever you see a name several times in the state records. Your ambition will be so frenzied that you will regard yourself last in the race if there is anyone in front of you. Or you may rate death as the worst of evils, although there is really no evil therein except that which precedes death's coming fear. You will be frightened out of your wits, not only by real, but by fancied dangers, and will be tossed forever on the sea of illusion. What benefit will it be to

> Have threaded all the towns of Argolis,
> A fugitive through midmost press of foes?

For peace itself will furnish further apprehension. Even in the midst of safety you will have no confidence if your mind has once been given a shock; once it has acquired the habit of blind panic, it is incapable of providing even for its own safety. For it does not avoid danger, but runs away. Yet we are more exposed to danger when we turn our backs.

You may judge it the most grievous of ills to lose any of those you love; while all the same this would be no less foolish than weeping because the trees which charm your eye and adorn your home lose their foliage. Regard everything that pleases you as if it were a flourishing plant; make the most of it while it is in leaf, for different plants at different seasons must fall and die. But just as the loss of leaves is a light thing, because they are born afresh, so it is with the loss of those whom you love and regard as the delight of your life; for they can be replaced even though they cannot be born afresh. "New friends, however, will not be the same." No, nor will you yourself remain the same; you change with every day and every hour. But in other men you more readily see what time plunders; in your own case the change is hidden, because it will not take place visibly. Others are snatched from sight; we ourselves are being stealthily filched away from ourselves. You will not think about any of these problems, nor will you apply remedies to these wounds. You will of your own volition be sowing a crop of trouble by alternate hoping and despairing. If you are wise, mingle these two elements: do not hope without despair, or despair without hope. What benefit has travel of itself ever been able to give anyone? No restraint upon pleasure, no bridling of desire, no checking of bad temper, no crushing of the wild assaults of passion, no opportunity to rid the soul of evil. Travelling cannot give us judgment, or shake off our errors; it merely holds our attention for a moment by a certain novelty, as children pause to wonder at something unfamiliar. Besides, it irritates us, through the wavering of a mind which is suffering from an acute attack of sickness; the very motion makes it more fitful and nervous. Hence the spots we had sought most eagerly we quit still more eagerly, like birds that flit and are off as soon as they have alighted. What travel will give is familiarity with other nations: it will reveal to you mountains of strange shape, or unfamiliar tracts of plain, or valleys that are watered by ever-flowing springs, or the characteristics of some river that comes to our attention. We observe how the Nile rises and swells in summer, or how the Tigris disappears, runs underground through hidden spaces, and then appears with unabated sweep; or how the Maeander, that oft-rehearsed theme and plaything of the poets, turns in frequent bendings, and often in winding comes close to its own channel before resuming its course. But this sort of information will not make better or sounder men of us. We ought rather to spend our time in study, and to cultivate those who are masters of wisdom, learning something which has been investigated, but not settled; by this means the mind can be relieved of a most wretched serfdom, and won over to freedom. Indeed, as long as you are ignorant of what you should avoid or seek, or of what is necessary or superfluous, or of what is right or wrong, you will not be travelling, but merely wandering. There will be no benefit to you in this hurrying to and fro; for you are travelling with your emotions and are followed by your afflictions. Would that they were indeed following you! In that case, they would be farther away; as it is, you are carrying and not leading them. Hence they press about you on all sides, continually chafing and annoying you. It is medicine, not scenery, for which the sick man must go searching. Suppose that someone has broken a leg or dislocated a joint: he does not take carriage or ship for other regions, but he calls in the physician to set the fractured limb, or to move it back to its proper place in the socket. What then? When the spirit is broken or wrenched in so many places, do you think that change of place can heal it? The complaint is too deep-seated to be cured by a journey. Travel does not make a physician or an orator; no art is acquired by merely living in a certain place. Where lies the truth, then? Can wisdom, the greatest of all the arts, be picked up on a journey? I assure you, travel as far as you like, you can never establish yourself beyond the reach of desire, beyond the reach of bad temper, or beyond the reach of fear; had it been so, the human race would long ago have banded together and made a pilgrimage to the spot. Such ills, as long as you carry with you their causes, will load you down and worry you to skin and bone in your wanderings over land and sea. Do you wonder that it is of no use to run away from them? That from which you are running, is within you. Accordingly, reform your own self, get the burden off your own shoulders, and keep within safe limits the cravings which ought to be removed. Wipe out from your soul all trace of sin. If you would enjoy your travels, make healthy the companion of your travels. As long as this companion is avaricious and mean, greed will stick to you; and while you consort with an overbearing man, your puffed-up ways will also stick close. Live with a hangman, and you will never be rid of your cruelty. If an adulterer be your club-mate, he will kindle the baser passions. If you would be stripped of your faults leave far behind you the patterns of the faults. The miser, the swindler, the bully, the cheat, who will do you much harm merely by being near you, are within you. Change therefore to better associations: live with the Catos, with Laelius, with Tubero. Or, if you enjoy living with Greeks also, spend your time with Socrates and with Zeno: the former will show you how to die if it be necessary; the latter how to die before it is necessary. Live with Chrysippus, with Posidonius: they will make you acquainted with things earthly and things heavenly; they will bid you work hard over something more than neat turns of language and phrases mouthed forth for the entertainment of listeners; they will bid you be stout of heart and rise superior to threats. The only harbour safe from the seething storms of this life is scorn of the future, a firm stand, a readiness to receive Fortune's missiles full in the breast, neither skulking nor turning the back. Nature has brought us forth brave of spirit, and, as she has implanted in certain animals a spirit of ferocity, in others craft, in others terror, so she has gifted us with an aspiring and lofty spirit, which prompts us to seek a life of the greatest honour, and not of the greatest security, that most resembles the soul of the universe, which it follows and imitates as far as our mortal steps permit. This spirit thrusts itself forward, confident of commendation and esteem. It is superior to all, monarch of all it surveys; hence it should be subservient to nothing, finding no task too heavy, and nothing strong enough to weigh down the shoulders of a man.

> Shapes dread to look upon, of toil or
> death

are not in the least dreadful, if one is able to look upon them with unflinching gaze, and is able to pierce the shadows. Many a sight that is held a terror in the night-time, is turned to ridicule by day. "Shapes dread to look upon, of toil or death": our Vergil has excellently said that these shapes are dread, not in reality, but only "to look upon"—in other words, they seem terrible, but are not. And in these visions what is there, I say, as fear-inspiring as rumour has proclaimed? Why, pray, my dear Lucilius, should a man fear toil, or a mortal death? Countless cases occur to my mind of men who think that what they themselves are unable to do is impossible, who maintain that we utter words which are too big for man's nature to carry out. But how much more highly do I think of these men! They can do these things, but decline to do them. To whom that ever tried have these tasks proved false? To what man did they not seem easier in the doing? Our lack of confidence is not the result of difficulty. The difficulty comes from our lack of confidence.

If, however, you desire a pattern, take Socrates, a long-suffering old man, who was sea-tossed amid every hardship and yet was unconquered both by poverty (which his troubles at home made more burdensome) and by toil, including the drudgery of military service. He was much tried at home, whether we think of his wife, a woman of rough manners and shrewish tongue, or of the children whose intractability showed them to be more like their mother than their father. And if you consider the facts, he lived either in time of war, or under tyrants, or under a democracy, which is more cruel than wars and tyrants. The war lasted for twenty-seven years; then the state became the victim of the Thirty Tyrants, of whom many were his personal enemies. At the last came that climax of condemnation under the gravest of charges: they accused him of disturbing the state religion and corrupting the youth, for they declared that he had influenced the youth to defy the gods, to defy the council, and to defy the state in general. Next came the prison, and the cup of poison. But all these measures changed the soul of Socrates so little that they did not even change his features. What wonderful and rare distinction! He maintained this attitude up to the very end, and no man ever saw Socrates too much elated or too much depressed. Amid all the disturbance of Fortune, he was undisturbed.

Do you desire another case? Take that of the younger Marcus Cato, with whom Fortune dealt in a more hostile and more persistent fashion. But he withstood her, on all occasions, and in his last moments, at the point of death, showed that a brave man can live in spite of Fortune, can die in spite of her. His whole life was passed either in civil warfare, or under a political regime which was soon to breed civil war. And you may say that he, just as much as Socrates, declared allegiance to liberty in the midst of slavery—unless perchance you think that Pompey, Caesar, and Crassus were the allies of liberty! No one ever saw Cato change, no matter how often the state changed: he kept himself the same in all circumstances—in the praetorship, in defeat, under accusation, in his province, on the platform, in the army, in death. Furthermore, when the republic was in a crisis of terror, when Caesar was on one side with ten embattled legions at his call, aided by so many foreign nations. and when Pompey was on the other, satisfied to stand alone against all comers, and when the citizens were leaning towards either Caesar or Pompey, Cato alone established a definite party for the Republic. If you would obtain a mental picture of that period, you may imagine on one side the people and the whole proletariat eager for revolution—on the other the senators and knights, the chosen and honoured men of the commonwealth; and there were left between them but these two—the Republic and Cato. I tell you, you will marvel when you see

> Atreus' son, and Priam, and Achilles,
> wroth at both.

Like Achilles, he scorns and disarms each faction. And this is the vote which he casts concerning them both: "If Caesar wins, I slay myself; if Pompey, I go into exile." What was there for a man to fear who, whether in defeat or in victory, had assigned to himself a doom which might have been assigned to him by his enemies in their utmost rage? So he died by his own decision.

You see that man can endure toil: Cato, on foot, led an army through African deserts. You see that thirst can be endured: he marched over sun-baked hills, dragging the remains of a beaten army and with no train of supplies, undergoing lack of water and wearing a heavy suit of armour; always the last to drink of the few springs which they chanced to find. You see that honour, and dishonour too, can be despised: for they report that on the very day when Cato was defeated at the elections, he played a game of ball. You see also that man can be free from fear of those above him in rank: for Cato attacked Caesar and Pompey simultaneously, at a time when none dared fall foul of the one without endeavouring to oblige the other. You see that death can be scorned as well as exile: Cato inflicted exile upon himself and finally death, and war all the while.

And so, if only we are willing to withdraw our necks from

the yoke, we can keep as stout a heart against such terrors as these. But first and foremost, we must reject pleasures; they render us weak and womanish; they make great demands upon us, and, moreover, cause us to make great demands upon Fortune. Second, we must spurn wealth: wealth is the diploma of slavery. Abandon gold and silver, and whatever else is a burden upon our richly-furnished homes; liberty cannot be gained for nothing. If you set a high value on liberty, you must set a low value on everything else.

Farewell.

CXXIII

ON THE CONFLICT BETWEEN PLEASURE AND VIRTUE

Wearied with the discomfort rather than with the length of my journey, I have reached my Alban villa late at night, and I find nothing in readiness except myself. So I am getting rid of fatigue at my writing-table: I derive some good from this tardiness on the part of my cook and my baker. For I am communing with myself on this very topic—that nothing is heavy if one accepts it with a light heart, and that nothing need provoke one's anger if one does not add to one's pile of troubles by getting angry. My baker is out of bread; but the overseer, or the house-steward, or one of my tenants can supply me therewith. "Bad bread!" you say. But just wait for it; it will become good. Hunger will make even such bread delicate and of the finest flavour. For that reason I must not eat until hunger bids me; so I shall wait and shall not eat until I can either get good bread or else cease to be squeamish about it. It is necessary that one grow accustomed to slender fare: because there are many problems of time and place which will cross the path even of the rich man and one equipped for pleasure, and bring him up with a round turn. To have whatsoever he wishes is in no man's power; it is in his power not to wish for what he has not, but cheerfully to employ what comes to him. A great step towards independence is a good-humoured stomach, one that is willing to endure rough treatment.

You cannot imagine how much pleasure I derive from the fact that my weariness is becoming reconciled to itself; I am asking for no slaves to rub me down, no bath, and no other restorative except time. For that which toil has accumulated, rest can lighten. This repast, whatever it may be, will give me more pleasure than an inaugural banquet. For I have made trial of my spirit on a sudden—a simpler and a truer test. Indeed, when a man has made preparations and given himself a formal summons to be patient, it is not equally clear just how much real strength of mind he possesses; the surest proofs are those which one exhibits off-hand, viewing one's own troubles not only fairly but calmly, not flying into fits of temper or wordy wranglings, supplying one's own needs by not craving something which was really due, and reflecting that our habits may be unsatisfied, but never our own real selves. How many things are superfluous we fail to realize until they begin to be wanting; we merely used them not because we needed them but because we had them. And how much do we acquire simply because our neighbours have acquired such things, or because most men possess them! Many of our troubles may be explained from the fact that we live according to a pattern, and, instead of arranging our lives according to reason, are led astray by convention. There are things which, if done by the few, we should refuse to imitate; yet when the majority have begun to do them, we follow along—as if anything were more honourable just because it is more frequent! Furthermore, wrong views, when they have become prevalent, reach, in our eyes, the standard of righteousness. Everyone now travels with Numidian outriders preceding him, with a troop of slave-runners to clear the way; we deem it disgraceful to have no attendants who will elbow crowds from the road, or will prove, by a great cloud of dust, that a high dignitary is approaching! Everyone now possesses mules that are laden with crystal and myrrhine cups carved by skilled artists of great renown; it is disgraceful for all your baggage to be made up of that which can be rattled along without danger. Everyone has pages who ride along with ointment-covered faces so that the heat or the cold will not harm their tender complexions; it is disgraceful that none of your attendant slave-boys should show a healthy cheek, not covered with cosmetics.

You should avoid conversation with all such persons: they are the sort that communicate and engraft their bad habits from one to another. We used to think that the very worst variety of these men were those who vaunted their words; but there are certain men who vaunt their wickedness. Their talk is very harmful; for even though it is not at once convincing, yet they leave the seeds of trouble in the soul, and the evil which is sure to spring into new strength follows us about even when we have parted from them. Just as those who have attended a concert carry about in their heads the melodies and the charm of the songs they have heard—a proceeding which interferes with their thinking and does not allow them to concentrate upon serious subjects—even so the speech of flatterers and enthusiasts over that which is depraved sticks in our minds long after we have heard them talk. It is not easy to rid the memory of a catching tune; it stays with us, lasts on, and comes back from time to time. Accordingly, you should close your ears against evil talk, and right at the outset, too; for when such talk has gained an entrance and the words are admitted and are in our minds, they become more shameless. And then we begin to speak as follows: "Virtue, Philosophy, Justice—this is a jargon of empty words. The only way to be happy is to do yourself well. To eat, drink, and spend your money is the only real life, the only way to remind yourself that you are mortal. Our days flow on, and life—which we cannot restore—hastens away from us. Why hesitate to come to our senses? This life of ours will not always admit pleasures; meantime, while it can do so, while it clamours for them, what profit lies in imposing thereupon frugality? Therefore get ahead of death, and let anything that death will filch from you be squandered now upon yourself. You have no mistress, no favourite slave to make your mistress envious; you are sober when you make your daily appearance in public; you dine as if you had to show your account-book to 'Papa'; but that is not living, it is merely going shares in someone else's existence. And what madness it is to be looking out for the interests of your heir, and to deny yourself everything, with the result that you turn friends into enemies by the vast amount of the fortune you intend to leave! For the more the heir is to get from you, the more he will rejoice in your taking-off! All those sour fellows who criticize other men's lives in a spirit of priggishness and are real enemies to their own lives, playing schoolmaster to the world—you should not consider them as worth a farthing, nor should you hesitate to prefer good living to a good reputation."

These are voices which you ought to shun just as Ulysses did; he would not sail past them until he was lashed to the mast. They are no less potent; they lure men from country, parents, friends, and virtuous ways; and by a hope that, if not base, is ill-starred, they wreck them upon a life of baseness.

How much better to follow a straight course and attain a goal where the words "pleasant" and "honourable" have the same meaning! This end will be possible for us if we understand that there are two classes of objects which either attract us or repel us. We are attracted by such things as riches, pleasures, beauty, ambition, and other such coaxing and pleasing objects; we are repelled by toil, death, pain, disgrace, or lives of greater frugality. We ought therefore to train ourselves so that we may avoid a fear of the one or a desire for the other. Let us fight in the opposite fashion: let us retreat from the objects that allure, and rouse ourselves to meet the objects that attack.

Do you not see how different is the method of descending a mountain from that employed in climbing upwards? Men coming down a slope bend backwards; men ascending a steep place lean forward. For, my dear Lucilius, to allow yourself to put your body's weight ahead when coming down, or, when climbing up, to throw it backward is to comply with vice. The pleasures take one down hill but one must work upwards toward that which is rough and hard to climb; in the one case let us throw our bodies forward, in the others let us put the check-rein on them.

Do you believe me to be stating now that only those men bring ruin to our ears, who praise pleasure, who inspire us with fear of pain—that element which is in itself provocative of fear? I believe that we are also in injured by those who masquerade under the disguise of the Stoic school and at the same time urge us on into vice. They boast that only the wise man and the learned is a lover. "He alone has wisdom in this art; the wise man too is best skilled in drinking and feasting. Our study ought to be this alone: up to what age the bloom of love can endure!" All this may be regarded as a concession to the ways of Greece; we ourselves should preferably turn our attention to words like these: "No man is good by chance. Virtue is something which must be learned. Pleasure is low, petty, to be deemed worthless, shared even by dumb animals—the tiniest and meanest of whom fly towards pleasure. Glory is an empty and fleeting thing, lighter than air. Poverty is an evil to no man unless he kick against the goads. Death is not an evil; why need you ask? Death alone is the equal privilege of mankind. Superstition is the misguided idea of a lunatic; it fears those whom it ought to love; it is an outrage upon those whom it worships. For what difference is there between denying the gods and dishonouring them?"

You should learn such principles as these, nay rather you should learn them by heart; philosophy ought not to try to explain away vice. For a sick man, when his physician bids him live recklessly, is doomed beyond recall.

Farewell.

from
THE DHAMMAPADA

I

THE TWIN-VERSES

¹All that we are is the result of what we have thought: it is founded on our thoughts, it is made up of our thoughts. If a man speaks or acts with an evil thought, pain follows him, as the wheel follows the foot of the ox that draws the carriage.

²All that we are is the result of what we have thought: it is founded on our thoughts, it is made up of our thoughts. If a man speaks or acts with a pure thought, happiness follows him, like a shadow that never leaves him.

³"He abused me, he beat me, he defeated me, he robbed me." In those who harbour such thoughts hatred will never cease.

⁴"He abused me, he beat me, he defeated me, he robbed me." In those who do not harbour such thoughts hatred will cease.

⁵For hatred will never cease by hatred: hatred ceases by love— this is a timeless law.

⁶People forget that their lives must soon come to an end—but those who remember, their quarrels cease at once.

⁷He who lives looking for pleasures only, his senses uncontrolled, immoderate in his food, idle and weak—Mara the Tempter will certainly overthrow him, as the wind throws down a weak tree.

⁸He who lives without looking for pleasures, his senses well

controlled, moderate in his food, faithful and strong—Mara will certainly not overthrow him, any more than the wind throws down a rocky mountain.

9He who wishes to put on the saffron robe without having cleansed himself from sin, who lacks self-control and truth—he is unworthy of the saffron robe.

10But he who has cleansed himself from sin, is well grounded in all virtues, and also possesses self-control and truth—he is indeed worthy of the saffron robe.

11The deluded, who see truth in untruth, and see untruth in truth, never arrive at truth, but follow vain desires.

12But the wise, who know truth in truth, and untruth in untruth, arrive at truth, and follow true desires.

13As rain breaks through an ill-thatched house, passion will break through an untrained mind.

14As rain does not break through a well-thatched house, passion will not break through a well-trained mind.

15The evil-doer suffers in this world, and he suffers in the next; in both worlds, he suffers from the evil results of his own actions.

16The virtuous man delights in this world, and he delights in the next; in both worlds, he delights in the good results of his own actions.

17The selfish man suffers in this world, and he suffers in the next. He suffers when he thinks of the evil he has done, and he suffers more in continuing on the evil path in this life and the next.

18The selfless man is happy in this world, and he is happy in the next. He is happy when he thinks of the good he has done, and he is still happier in continuing on the good path in this life and the next.

[19] The thoughtless man who, though he can recite many of the scriptures, does not practice their teachings, has no share in the joys of truth, but is like a cowherd counting the cows of others.

[20] The follower of the law who, though he can recite only a few of the scriptures, has overcome all lust, hatred, and delusion, possesses true knowledge and serenity of mind; he, attached to nothing in this world or the world to come, has indeed a share in the joys of truth.

III

THOUGHT

[33] As an archer aims his arrow, a wise man aims his trembling and unsteady thought, which is difficult to control, difficult to restrain.

[34] As a fish, taken from his watery home and thrown on dry ground, thrashes around and suffers, so the mind trembles all over and struggles to escape the dominion of Mara the Tempter.

[35] It is good to tame the mind, which is difficult to restrain and rushes wherever it likes: a tamed mind brings happiness.

[36] Let the wise man guard his thoughts, for they are difficult to perceive, very artful, and they rush wherever they like: thoughts well guarded bring happiness.

[37] Those who bridle their mind—which wanders aimlessly and far, moves about alone, is without a body, and hides in the chamber of the heart—will be free from the bonds of Mara.

³⁸If a man's thoughts are unsteady, if he does not know the dharma, if his peace of mind is troubled, he will never be truly wise.

³⁹If a man's thoughts are not dissipated, if his mind is not perplexed, if he has ceased to think of good or evil, then he will have no fear, as long as he remains watchful.

⁴⁰Knowing that this body is fragile like a clay pot, and making this thought firm like a fortress, we should attack Mara the Tempter with the weapon of wisdom—and we should watch him when conquered, never relaxing our vigilance.

⁴¹Before long—alas!—this body will lie on the earth, despised, without understanding, like a useless log.

⁴²Whatever a hater may do to a hater, or an enemy to an enemy, a wrongly-directed mind will do us greater mischief.

⁴³Not a mother, nor a father, nor any other relative or friend, will do us greater service than a well-directed mind.

XIV

THE AWAKENED ONE (BUDDHA)

¹⁷⁹He whose conquest is not conquered again, into whose conquest no one in this world can enter, by what track can you lead him, the Awakened, the Omniscient, the one who is free from all conditioning?

¹⁸⁰He who cannot be led astray by the snares and poisons of desire, by what track can you lead him, the Awakened, the Omniscient, the one who is free from all conditioning?

¹⁸¹Even the gods envy those who are awakened and not forgetful, who are given to meditation, who are wise, and who delight in the repose of retirement from the world.

¹⁸²Difficult it is to obtain a human birth, difficult is the life of mortals, difficult it is to understand dharma, but most difficult of all is to become Awakened—to attain Nirvana.

¹⁸³Commit no evil actions, do good, purify your mind: so teach all Awakened Ones.

¹⁸⁴The Awakened call patience the highest penance, and long-suffering the path to Nirvana, which is the highest good; for he is not a spiritual aspirant who injures or insults others.

¹⁸⁵Not to blame, not to strike, to live in accordance with dharma, to be moderate in eating, to sleep and sit alone, and to meditate on the highest thoughts—this is the teaching of the Awakened.

¹⁸⁶There is no satisfying lusts, even by a shower of gold pieces; he is wise who knows that lusts have a short taste and bring much pain in their wake.

¹⁸⁷Even in heavenly pleasures the lustful finds no satisfaction, while the disciple who is fully awakened delights only in the destruction of all desires.

¹⁸⁸Men, driven by fear, go to many a refuge, to mountains and forests, to groves and sacred trees.

¹⁸⁹But none of these is a safe refuge, because it cannot deliver a man from fear.

¹⁹⁰He who takes refuge with Buddha, the law of dharma, and the sangha[1]—he, with clear understanding, sees the Four Noble Truths:

¹⁹¹Suffering, the origin of suffering, the destruction of suffering, and the Noble Eightfold Path that leads to going beyond

---

[1] The spiritual community or church.

suffering.

¹⁹²That is the safe refuge, that is the best refuge; having gone to that refuge, a man is delivered from all pain.

¹⁹³A supernatural person like the Buddha is not easily found—he is not born everywhere. Wherever such a sage is born, that race prospers.

¹⁹⁴Happy is the birth of the Awakened, happy is the teaching of the dharma, happy is peace in the sangha, happy is the devotion of those who live in harmony.

¹⁹⁵⁻¹⁹⁶He who pays homage to those who deserve homage, whether the Awakened or his disciples; he who has overcome the host of evils and crossed the flood of sorrow; he who pays homage to those who have found deliverance and know no fear: he is happy beyond measure.

XV

HAPPINESS

¹⁹⁷Let us live happily then, not hating those who hate us! Among men who hate us, let us dwell free from hatred!

¹⁹⁸Let us live happily then, free from sickness among the sick! Among men who are ailing, let us dwell free from ailments!

¹⁹⁹Let us live happily then, free from greed among the greedy! Among men who are greedy, let us dwell free from greed!

²⁰⁰Let us live happily then, free from possessions among the hoarders! We shall be like the bright gods, feeding on happiness!

²⁰¹Victory breeds hatred, for the defeated are unhappy. He who has given up both victory and defeat lives in peace and

happiness.

[202] There is no fire like lust; there is no sickness like hatred; there is no suffering like this separate body; there is no happiness higher than peace.

[203] Craving is the worst of diseases, ego the greatest of pains; he who knows this attains Nirvana, the highest happiness.

[204] Health is the greatest of gifts, contentedness the best riches; trust is the best of relationships, Nirvana the highest happiness.

[205] He who has tasted the sweetness of solitude and tranquillity is free of fear and free of sin—for he tastes the sweetness of drinking in the dharma.

[206] To meet the wise is good, to live with them is happiness; if a man does not see fools, he will be truly happy.

[207] He who walks in the company of fools suffers a long way; company with fools, as with an enemy, is always painful; company with the wise is a pleasure, like meeting with one's true family.

[208] Therefore, one ought to follow the wise, the intelligent, the learned, the patient, the dutiful, and the noble; one ought to follow a good and wise man, as the moon follows the path of the stars.

XV

PLEASURE

[209] He who indulges his vanity, who neglects to practice meditation, who forgets the true aim of life and always grasps at pleasure, will in time envy him who has exerted himself in meditation.

210 One must go beyond pleasure and pain: for the absence of what is pleasant brings pain, and the presence of what is painful is unpleasant.

211 Therefore, avoid selfish attachment to anything, for its loss will bring pain. They are free who are attached to nothing and averse to nothing.

212 Pleasure brings pain; pleasure brings fear: he who is free from pleasure knows neither pain nor fear.

213 Attachment brings grief; attachment brings fear: he who is free from attachment knows neither grief nor fear.

214 Lust brings torment; lust brings anxiety: he who is free from lust knows neither torment nor anxiety.

215 Possessive love brings hatred; possessive love brings envy: he who is free from possessive love knows neither hatred nor envy.

216 Greed causes wretchedness; greed causes fear; he who is free from greed knows neither wretchedness nor fear.

217 He who possesses virtue and intelligence, who is good and honest, and who follows the dharma—him the world holds dear.

218 He who seeks Nirvana, who resists temptations, who is not bewildered by attachments—he is carried upwards by the stream.

219 Family, friends, and lovers greet with joy a man who returns safely from a long journey.

220 In like manner, a man's good deeds receive him when he has gone from this life to the next, as kinsmen receive a friend on his return.

XX

THE EIGHTFOLD PATH

²⁷³The best path is the Eightfold; the best truths are the Noble Four; the best virtue is detachment; the best person is the illumined one.

²⁷⁴This is the path; there is no other that leads to the purifying of the mind. Follow this path! Everything else is the deceit of Mara the Tempter.

²⁷⁵If you follow this path, you will put an end to suffering! I preached this path after the thorns of sorrow fell from my flesh.

²⁷⁶You yourself must make an effort. The Buddhas are only preachers, showing you the way. The thoughtful who follow the path are freed from the bondage of Mara.

²⁷⁷*All created things perish*. He who knows and sees this is freed from suffering. This is the way to pure wisdom.

²⁷⁸*All created beings feel grief and pain*. He who knows and sees this is freed from suffering. This is the way that leads to pure wisdom.

²⁷⁹*All forms are without a separate self*. He who knows and sees this is freed from suffering. This is the way that leads to pure wisdom.

²⁸⁰He who does not rouse himself when it is time to rise, who, though young and strong, is full of sloth, whose will and thought are weak—that lazy and idle man will never find the way to wisdom.

²⁸¹Restrain your mind, guard your speech, and commit no wrong with your body. Keep but these three roads of action

clear, and you will speed along the path to wisdom.

²⁸²Wisdom is brought by meditation; wisdom is lost through lack of meditation. Know this double path of gain and loss, and choose the path that leads to wisdom.

²⁸³Cut down the whole forest of lust, not just one tree! Great danger comes out of this forest. When you have cut down both the forest and its undergrowth, then you will be liberated!

²⁸⁴As long as a man's love of women is not destroyed—without a trace!—his mind remains in bondage, as the calf that drinks milk is in bondage to its mother.

²⁸⁵Cut out the love of self with your own hand, as you would an autumn lotus. Cherish the road of detachment: the path to Nirvana has been shown by the Buddha.

²⁸⁶"I will live here during monsoon season, I will have another house for winter, and still another for summer." Thus the fool meditates, and does not think of his death.

²⁸⁷Death comes and carries off the man who is mindlessly absorbed in his family and possessions, as a flood carries off a sleeping village.

²⁸⁸Neither children, nor parents, nor relations can rescue one who has been seized by death.

²⁸⁹A wise and good man who knows the meaning of this should quickly clear the path that leads to Nirvana.

XXI

MISCELLANEOUS

²⁹⁰If, while enjoying a small pleasure, one sees a greater pleasure, let him, if he is wise, leave the small pleasure and look

to the great.

²⁹¹He who, by causing pain to others, wishes to obtain pleasure for himself, he, entangled in the bonds of hatred, will never be free from hatred.

²⁹²What ought to be done is neglected, what ought not to be done is done; the desires of unruly, thoughtless people are always increasing.

²⁹³But they whose whole watchfulness is always directed to their body, who do not follow wrong actions, and who steadfastly do what ought to be done—the desires of such watchful and wise people will come to an end.

²⁹⁴A true Brahmin is blameless, though he once killed father and mother, and two valiant kings, though he destroyed a kingdom with all its subjects.

²⁹⁵A true Brahmin is blameless, though he once killed father and mother, and two holy kings, and an eminent man besides.

²⁹⁶The disciples of Gautama[1] are always well awake, and their thoughts day and night are always set on Buddha.

²⁹⁷The disciples of Gautama are always well awake, and their thoughts day and night are always set on dharma.

²⁹⁸The disciples of Gautama are always well awake, and their thoughts day and night are always set on the sangha.

²⁹⁹The disciples of Gautama are always well awake, and day and night they are always training the senses.

³⁰⁰The disciples of Gautama are always well awake, and their mind day and night always delights in compassion.

---

1 The Buddha.

301 The disciples of Gautama are always well awake, and their mind day and night always delights in meditation.

302 It is hard to leave the world and hard to live in it; hard is the monastery, but painful are the houses of the world; it is painful to live among the worldly, and painful to be a vagabond. Therefore attain the highest goal, and you will be a vagabond no more.

303 Whatever place a faithful, virtuous, celebrated, and wealthy man chooses, there he is respected.

304 Good people shine from afar, like the snowy Himalayas; bad people are not seen, like arrows shot at night.

305 He alone who, without ceasing, practices the duty of sitting alone and sleeping alone—he, subduing himself, will alone rejoice in the destruction of all desires, as if living in a forest.

XXIV

THIRST

334 The thirst of a thoughtless man grows like a creeper; he jumps from life to life, like a monkey seeking fruit in the forest.

335 Whoever is overcome by this fierce craving becomes full of poison in this world, and his sufferings increase like the abundant Birana grass.

336 He who overcomes this fierce craving cannot be conquered in this world, and his sufferings fall from him like water-drops from a lotus leaf.

337 Therefore I tell you, "Dig up this craving—as he who wants the sweet-scented Usira root must dig up the Birana grass—so that Mara the Tempter may not crush you again and again, as the stream crushes the reeds."

338As a tree, even though it has been cut down, is firm as long as its root is safe, and grows again, so, unless the feeders of thirst are destroyed, the pain of life will return again and again.

339He whose thirst for pleasure rages in the thirty-six streams—that wretched man will be washed away by his own desires.

340The streams run everywhere, the creeper of passion sprouts endlessly; if you see one springing up in your mind, cut its root by means of wisdom.

341Man's pleasures are extravagant and luxurious; sunk in lust and looking for pleasure, men undergo again and again birth and decay.

342Men, driven on by thirst, run about like a hunted hare; held in fetters and bonds, they suffer pain again and again for a long time.

343Men, driven on by thirst, run about like a hunted hare; be like the mendicant, then, and drive out thirst by striving for detachment.

344He who, having quit the forest of lust, runs into another forest—look at that man! Though free, he runs into bondage.

345The wise say, fetters made of iron, wood, and hemp are not as strong as our attachment to wealth, luxuries, and possessive love.

346The wise say a fetter is strong when it drags us down, allows us some restricted movement, yet is difficult to break altogether; but having broken it at last, we become free from cares, leaving desires and pleasures behind.

347Those who are slaves to their passions run down with the stream of desires, as a spider runs down the web which he has made himself; when they have cut this at last, the wise become free from cares, leaving all lust behind.

³⁴⁸If you want to reach the other shore of existence, give up what is before, give up what is behind, give up what is in the middle; if your mind is fully free, you will never again enter into birth and decay.

³⁴⁹If a man is tossed about by doubts, full of strong passions, and yearning only for what is delightful, his thirst will grow more and more, and he will only make his fetters stronger.

³⁵⁰If a man delights in quieting doubts, and reflects on what is not delightful (for instance, the impurity of the body), he will certainly break the fetter of Mara.

³⁵¹He who has reached the consummation, who does not tremble, who is without thirst and without sin, he has removed all the thorns of life: this body will be his last.

³⁵²He who is without craving and without lust, who understands the meaning of the words of scripture, he has received his last body—he is called the great sage, the great man.

³⁵³"I have conquered all, I know all, I am untainted in all conditions of life, I have left everything behind, and through the destruction of thirst I am free. Having learned myself, whom shall I teach?"

³⁵⁴The gift of dharma exceeds all gifts; the sweetness of dharma exceeds all sweetness; the delight in dharma exceeds all delights; through it, you put an end to craving, and overcome all suffering.

³⁵⁵Pleasures destroy the foolish, if they do not seek the other shore. The foolish, by their thirst for pleasures, destroy themselves as if they are their own worst enemy.

³⁵⁶The fields are ruined by weeds, mankind is ruined by greed: therefore, it is wise to honour those who are without greed.

³⁵⁷The fields are ruined by weeds, mankind is ruined by hatred: therefore, it is wise to honour those who are without hatred.

³⁵⁸The fields are ruined by weeds, mankind is ruined by vanity: therefore, it is wise to honour those who are without vanity.

³⁵⁹The fields are ruined by weeds, mankind is ruined by lust: therefore, it is wise to honour those who are without lust.

XXV

THE BHIKSHU (MENDICANT)

³⁶⁰Restraint in the eye is good, good is restraint in the ear; restraint in the nose is good, good is restraint in the tongue.

³⁶¹In the body restraint is good, good is restraint in speech; restraint in thought is good, good is restraint in all things. A Bhikshu, restrained in all things, is freed from all suffering.

³⁶²He who controls his hand, he who controls his feet, he who controls his speech, he who is well controlled, he who delights inwardly, he who is collected, he who is solitary and content—him they call Bhikshu.

³⁶³The Bhikshu who controls his mouth, who speaks wisely and calmly, who teaches the meaning and the dharma, his word is sweet.

³⁶⁴He who dwells in dharma, delights in dharma, meditates on dharma, follows the dharma, that Bhikshu will never fall away from the true law.

³⁶⁵Let him not despise what he has received, nor ever envy others: a mendicant who envies others does not obtain peace

of mind.

³⁶⁶A Bhikshu who, though he receives little, does not despise what he has received, even the gods will praise him, if his life is pure, and if he is not slothful.

³⁶⁷He who never identifies himself with name and form, and does not grieve over what is no more, he indeed is called a Bhikshu.

³⁶⁸The Bhikshu who acts with kindness, who is calm in the doctrine of Buddha, will achieve quietude in Nirvana, the cessation of natural desires, and happiness.

³⁶⁹O Bhikshu, empty this boat! If emptied, it will go quickly; having cut off passion and hatred, you will go to Nirvana.

³⁷⁰Cut off the five senses, leave the five senses, rise above the five senses. A Bhikshu who has escaped from the five fetters is called Oghatinna, "saved from the flood."

³⁷¹Meditate, O Bhikshu, and be not heedless! Do not direct your thought to what gives pleasure, so that you may not, for your heedlessness, have to swallow the iron ball in hell, and so that you may not cry out when burning, "This is pain!"

³⁷²Without knowledge there is no meditation, without meditation there is no knowledge: he who has knowledge and meditation is close to Nirvana.

³⁷³A Bhikshu who has entered his empty house, and whose mind is tranquil, feels a more than human delight when he sees the dharma clearly.

³⁷⁴As soon as he has considered the origin and destruction of the elements of the body, he finds the happiness and joy that belong to those who know the Immortal.

375And this is the beginning for a wise Bhikshu: watchfulness over the senses, contentedness, restraint under the dharma, and keeping noble friends whose lives are pure, and who are not slothful.

376Let him live in charity, let him be perfect in his duties; then in the fullness of delight he will bring an end to suffering.

377As the Vassika plant sheds its withered flowers, a Bhikshu must shed passion and hatred.

378He is called a Bhikshu whose body and tongue and mind are quieted, who is collected, and who has rejected the baits of the world.

379Rouse yourself by yourself, examine yourself by yourself; thus, self-protected and attentive, you will live happily, O Bhikshu!

380For the self is the lord of the self, the self is the refuge of the self; therefore, bridle yourself as the merchant bridles a good horse.

381The Bhikshu, full of delight, who is calm in the doctrine of Buddha, will attain the quiet place, the cessation of natural desires, and happiness.

382He who, even as a young Bhikshu, applies himself to the doctrine of Buddha, brightens up this world, like the moon when free from clouds.

XXVI

THE BRAHMIN

383Stop the stream valiantly, drive away the desires, O Brahmin! When you have understood the destruction of all that was made, you will understand that which was not made.

384 If the Brahmin reaches the other shore in both laws—in restraint and contemplation—all bonds vanish, for he has obtained knowledge.

385 He for whom there is neither this nor that shore, nor both—him, the fearless and unshackled, I call indeed a Brahmin.

386 He who is thoughtful, blameless, settled, dutiful, without passions, and who has attained the highest end, him I call indeed a Brahmin.

387 The sun is bright by day, the moon shines by night, the warrior is bright in his armour, the Brahmin is bright in his meditation; but Buddha, the Awakened, is bright with splendour day and night.

388 Because a man is rid of evil, he is therefore called a Brahmin; because he walks quietly, he is therefore called an ascetic; because he has sent away his own impurities, he is therefore called a pilgrim.

389 No one should attack a Brahmin, but no Brahmin, if attacked, should let himself fly at his aggressor! Woe to him who strikes a Brahmin, but more woe to him who flies at his aggressor!

390 It benefits a Brahmin to hold his mind back from the pleasures of life. And when all wish to injure has vanished, pain will cease.

391 Him I call a Brahmin who does not offend by body, word, or thought, and is controlled on these three points.

392 After a man has understood the dharma as taught by the Awakened, let him worship it carefully, as the Brahmin worships the sacrificial fire.

393 A man does not become a Brahmin by his platted hair, by

his family, or by birth: he is a Brahmin, he is blessed, in whom there is truth and righteousness.

³⁹⁴What is the use of platted hair, O fool! What good is the goat-skin on which you sit and meditate? Within you there is filth, but the outside you make clean.

³⁹⁵The man who wears dirty raiments, who is emaciated and covered with veins, who lives alone in the forest and meditates, him I call indeed a Brahmin.

³⁹⁶I do not call a man a Brahmin because of his origin or his mother: he is arrogant, and he is wealthy: but the poor, who is free from all attachments, him I call indeed a Brahmin.

³⁹⁷Him I call a Brahmin who has cut all fetters, who never trembles, who is independent and unshackled.

³⁹⁸Him I call a Brahmin who has cut the strap and thong and chain of karma, who has burst through the bars, and who is awakened.

³⁹⁹Him I call a Brahmin who, though he has committed no offence, endures reproach, prison, and even death, who can endure his own force, and who has the strength of an army.

⁴⁰⁰Him I call a Brahmin who is free from anger, dutiful, virtuous, without appetite, who is subdued, and has received his last body.

⁴⁰¹Him I call a Brahmin who does not cling to pleasures any more than water clings to a lotus leaf, or a mustard seed clings to the point of a needle.

⁴⁰²Him I call a Brahmin who, even here, knows the end of his suffering, has put down his burden, and is unshackled.

⁴⁰³Him I call a Brahmin whose knowledge is deep, who pos-

sesses wisdom, who knows the right way and the wrong, and has attained the highest end.

⁴⁰⁴Him I call a Brahmin who keeps aloof both from laymen and from mendicants, who frequents no houses, and has but few desires.

⁴⁰⁵Him I call a Brahmin who finds no fault with other beings, whether feeble or strong, and does not kill nor cause slaughter.

⁴⁰⁶Him I call a Brahmin who is tolerant with the intolerant, mild with fault-finders, and free from passion among the passionate.

⁴⁰⁷Him I call a Brahmin from whom anger, hatred, pride, and envy have dropped like a mustard seed from the point of a needle.

⁴⁰⁸Him I call a Brahmin who utters true speech, instructive and free from harshness, so that he offend no one.

⁴⁰⁹Him I call a Brahmin who takes nothing in the world that is not given him, be it long or short, small or large, good or bad.

⁴¹⁰Him I call a Brahmin who harbours no desires for this world or the next, has no inclinations, and is unshackled.

⁴¹¹Him I call a Brahmin who has no doubts, and who, when he has understood the truth, does not say, "How, how?" For such a one has reached the depth of the Immortal.

⁴¹²Him I call a Brahmin who in this world is above good and evil, above the bondage of both, and who is free from grief, from sin, and from impurity.

⁴¹³Him I call a Brahmin who is bright like the moon, pure, serene, undisturbed, and in whom all gaiety is extinct.

⁴¹⁴Him I call a Brahmin who has traversed this miry road, the impassable world and its vanity, who has gone through and reached the other shore, who is thoughtful, guileless, free from doubts, free from attachment, and content.

⁴¹⁵Him I call a Brahmin who in this world, leaving all desires, travels about without a home, and in whom all lust is extinct.

⁴¹⁶Him I call a Brahmin who, leaving all longings, travels about without a home, and in whom all covetousness is extinct.

⁴¹⁷Him I call a Brahmin who, after leaving all bondage to men, has risen above all bondage to the gods, and is free from all and every bondage.

⁴¹⁸Him I call a Brahmin who has left what gives pleasure and what gives pain, who is cool, who is free from the germ of rebirth—the hero who has conquered all the worlds.

⁴¹⁹Him I call a Brahmin who knows the destruction and the return of beings everywhere, who is free from bondage, who is generous and awakened.

⁴²⁰Him I call a Brahmin whose path no one can know—not gods, nor spirits, nor men—whose passions are extinct, and who is free from future and past, decay and death.

⁴²¹Him I call a Brahmin who is free from *I*, *me*, and *mine*, who is poor, and who is free from the love of the world.

⁴²²Him I call a Brahmin: the manly, the noble, the hero, the great sage, the conqueror, the impassable, the accomplished, the awakened.

⁴²³Him I call a Brahmin who knows his former abodes, who sees heaven and hell, who has reached the end of births, who is perfect in knowledge, a sage, and one whose perfections are all perfect.

from
MEDITATIONS

by

MARCUS AURELIUS

Book Two

I

Begin the morning by saying to yourself, "Today I will meet with the meddlesome, the ungrateful, the arrogant, the deceitful, the envious, and the selfish." All these people are such because they are ignorant of what is good and evil. But I have long known the nature of good and its beauty, and the nature of evil and its ugliness, and I know the nature of the evildoer, for he is my brother; he may not be of the same blood or seed, but he is a fellow-being with Reason and an equal share of the divine; I can neither be injured by my brother (because no one can implicate me in ugliness), nor be angry with him, nor hate him. For we are made for cooperation, like feet, like hands, like eyelids, like the rows of the upper and lower teeth. To obstruct one another is contrary to Nature; and irritation and aversion are a form of obstruction.

II

What am I? A little flesh, some breath, and a Reason to rule all. Throw away your books—distract yourself no more—they are no part of you. Instead, as if you were right now on the brink of death, begin to despise your flesh, with its blood and bones, its network of nerves, veins, and arteries. Your breath, now: what sort of thing is it? Wind . . . and not always the same, but every moment blown out and sucked in anew. The third, then, the Reason—consider this: You are old now—let it be a slave no more—shaking like a puppet to every selfish whim. And cease to lament your present lot or shrink from the future.

III

All that is from the gods is full of Providence. Even Fortune is part of Nature's plan—the interweaving and turning of things ordered by Providence. Providence is the source from which all things flow; and beside it there is Necessity, and all that is for the welfare of the whole Universe, of which you are a part. And what the nature of the Whole brings about is good for every part of the whole, and sustains it. The Universe is preserved by the changes of the elements, and so also by the changes of things composed of the elements. Let these principles be enough for you; let them always be fixed in your mind. But cast away your thirst for books, so that you may not die murmuring, but die cheerfully, truly, and sincerely grateful to the gods.

IV

Remember how long you have been putting off these things, and how often you have received an opportunity from the gods, and yet did not use it. You must now at last recognize the Universe of which you are a part, the administrating Power from which your existence flows, and that a limit of time is fixed for you, which if you do not use for clearing away the clouds from your mind, will pass, and you will pass, and will never return.

V

Every moment resolve firmly, as a Roman and as a man, to do what comes to hand with perfect and natural dignity, with compassion, freedom, and justice. Relieve your mind from all other cares. This you can do if you perform every action as if it were your last, dismissing the wayward thought, the passions that divert you from the commands of Reason, the desire to make an impression, the admiration of self, the dissatisfaction with your lot. See how little a man needs in order to live a life that flows in quiet, like the existence of the gods. And the gods, for their part, will require nothing more from him who observes these counsels.

VI

Violence! You are doing violence to yourself, my soul; and soon you will no longer have the chance do to yourself honour. Every man has but one life. Yours is nearly finished, yet your soul has no eye to its own honour, but places its happiness in the souls of others.

VII

Are you distracted by what befalls you from outside? Then find yourself a quiet space, where you can add to your knowledge of the Good, and cease to be whirled around in restlessness. Watch that you do not fall into another kind of error: the folly of triflers who busy themselves in life with much activity, but who have no object toward which they direct their whole effort, and no aim upon which they focus their whole thought.

VIII

By being indifferent to the workings of another's soul, seldom is a man made unhappy; but a man who does not observe the movements of his own soul will certainly be unhappy.

IX

You must always bear this in mind: what is the nature of the Whole, and what is my nature, and how are the two related, and what is my part in the Whole? And ensure that no one hinders you from always doing and saying the things that are in accordance with that Nature of which you are a part.

X

Theophrastus, in his comparison of evil acts, says truly that the offenses committed through desire are more blameable than those committed through anger. For he who is excited by anger seems to turn away from Reason with a certain pain and unconscious constraint; but he who offends through desire, being overpowered by pleasure, seems to be in a way more self-indulgent and more womanish in his offences. Rightly, then, he says that an offence committed with pleasure is more blameable than an offense committed with pain; for in the one case the offender is like a man provoked to anger after having been wronged, but in the other, the man is moved by his own impulse and desire to do wrong.

XI

Since you may depart from life at any moment, regulate every act and thought accordingly. If gods exist, there is nothing to fear in taking leave of men, for the gods will not involve you in evil; but if indeed gods do not exist, or if they are not concerned human affairs, what is it to me to live in a universe devoid of gods or devoid of Providence? But in truth they do exist, and they do care about human things, and they have put all the means in man's power to enable him not to fall into true evils. In all of life, avoidance of evil is within the ability of every man. Now if something does not make a man worse, how can it make his life worse? But neither through ignorance nor through a want of power could the Universe have overlooked this matter; nor is it possible that it has made so great a mistake, either through want of power or want of skill, that good and evil should be visited indiscriminately on the virtuous and sinful alike. Yet living and dying, honour and dishonour, pain and pleasure, riches and poverty—all these things are equally the lot good men and bad, for they make us neither better nor worse. Therefore they are neither good nor evil.

XII

How quickly all things disappear—in the Universe the bodies themselves, but in time even the memory of them. What is the nature of all objects of sense, and particularly those that attract us with the bait of pleasure or terrify us with pain, or are noised afar by vapoury fame; how worthless, and contemptible, and sordid, and perishable, and dead they are: all this is apparent to our intellect. And who are these people whose opinions and voices give reputation? And what is death? For if a man looks at it plainly, and mentally examines all its parts and how these present themselves to the imagination, he will come to see it as just another operation of Nature; and only children are afraid of natural phenomena. This, however, is not only an operation of Nature, but it is also a thing that contributes to the well-being of Nature. Finally, observe too how man has contact with the Divine, and by what part of him, and what happens to this part after its disposal.

XIII

Nothing is more wretched than a man who traverses the whole of creation, "probing into the depths of the earth", as the poet[1] says, and seeks by conjecture what is in the minds of his neighbours, without perceiving that it is enough to attend to the divine spirit within himself, and to serve it loyally. And reverence of the divine spirit consists in keeping it pure from passion and mindlessness and dissatisfaction with what comes from gods and men. For the things from the gods deserve veneration for their excellence; and the things from men should be dear to us by reason of kinship, and they even arouse our pity because of men's ignorance of good and evil—

[1] Pindar, in the *Theaetetus* of Plato.

an impairment as crippling as the inability to distinguish black from white.

XIV

Were you to live three thousand years, or even thirty thousand, still remember that the only life a man can lose is that which is being lived at that moment, and there is no life other than that which he now loses. Therefore the longest life and the shortest life amount to the same thing. For the present is the same to all, though that which has passed is not the same. Our loss, then, is limited to a single fleeting moment, for a man cannot lose what is already past or what might have been. And so that which is lost is a mere moment. And how can anyone take from a man that which he does not possess? These two things, then, you must bear in mind: first, that all things from eternity are of like forms and come round in a circle, and that it makes no difference whether a man sees the same things over the course of a hundred years, or two hundred, or an infinite amount of time; and second, that when the longest- and shortest-lived among us come to die, their loss is exactly equal. For the only thing a man can be deprived of is the present, since this is all he has, and a man cannot lose what is not his.

XV

Remember that all is opinion. For what was said by the Cynic Monimus is clear, that "things are determined by the view taken of them." And clear too is the value of what he said, if we admit that it contains some truth.

XVI

A man's soul does violence to itself first of all when it becomes an abscess or tumour on the Universe, so far as it can. For to be vexed at anything that happens is a separation of ourselves from Nature, which contains within it the nature of all its parts. Second, the soul does violence to itself when it turns away from any man, or even moves towards him with the intention of injuring him, as men do when they are angry. Third, the soul does violence to itself when it is overpowered by pleasure or by pain. Fourth, when it dissembles, and does or says anything with insincerity or dishonesty. Fifth, when it allows any act of its own to be aimless, and does anything mindlessly and without considering what it is, for even the least of our activities should have some end in view—and the end of rational animals is to follow the Reason and the law of the eternal City and Commonwealth.

XVII

In a man's life his time is but a moment, his substance is in constant flux, his perception is dull, his body is prey to worms, his soul is a whirlwind, his fortune is impossible to predict, and his fame is nothing. And, in a word, everything that belongs to the body is a stream, and what belongs to the soul is a dream, and life is warfare, a brief sojourn in an alien land; and after fame: oblivion. What power, then, is able to guide a man? One thing, and only one: philosophy. But this consists in keeping the divine spirit within a man free from harm and violence, above pain and pleasure, so that it does nothing without a purpose, does nothing falsely or with hypocrisy, does not depend on another man's actions or inactions, and accepts all that happens as coming from the same Source from which he himself has come; and finally, he must wait for death with a cheerful mind, viewing it as nothing but a dissolution of the elements that form every living being. But if there is no harm in the elements themselves continually forming and re-forming, why should a man have any fear about the change and dissolution of all the elements? For it is according to Nature, and nothing is evil which is according to Nature.

Book Three

I

The daily wasting away of our life, and how it leaves us with a smaller portion yet to live, is not the only thing we need to consider. Because even if a man lives longer, we must still take into account that it is uncertain whether his understanding will remain sufficient for the comprehension of things, and retain the power of contemplation which strives to acquire the knowledge of the divine and the human. For if he becomes senile, he will still be able to breathe and eat, to have senses and impulses and imagination, and so forth; but the ability to make full use of his faculties, to assess and fulfil his duty, to make judgments, to decide whether the time has come to depart from life, and to make any of the other decisions that require a disciplined Reason—all this is already extinguished. We must make haste, then, not only because every moment brings us closer to death, but because even before then our powers of perception and understanding are always in decline.

II

We ought to observe also the beauty and fascination of even the incidental processes of Nature. For instance, when bread is baked, some parts are split at the surface, and these parts open in a certain way that is contrary to the baker's purpose, but they are beautiful and peculiar in a manner that excites a desire for eating. And again, figs, when they are quite ripe, gape open; and in ripe olives, their approaching rottenness adds a peculiar beauty to the fruit. And the ears of corn bending down, and the lion's eyebrows, and the foam that flows from the mouth of wild boars, and many other things—though they are far from being beautiful by themselves—still, as the consequences of other processes of Nature, they add their own charm and please the mind; so if a man has a feeling and deeper insight for the things produced in the Universe, there is hardly one that, even if it is merely a byproduct of something else, does not seem designed to give pleasure. And so he will see the real gaping jaws of wild beasts with no less pleasure than the painter's or sculptor's imitation of them; and in an old woman and an old man he will be able to see a certain maturity and charm; and the attractive loveliness of young persons he will be able to enjoy with chaste eyes; and many such things will present themselves, not pleasing to every man, but only to him who has become truly familiar with Nature and her works.

III

Hippocrates, after curing many illnesses, himself fell sick and died. The Chaldeans foretold the deaths of many, and then fate caught them too. Alexander and Pompey and Julius Caesar, after destroying whole cities, and in battle cutting to pieces many thousands of cavalry and infantry, themselves too departed from life. Heraclitus, after so many speculations on the conflagration of the universe, was in the end saturated with water and died smeared all over with mud. And vermin destroyed Democritus; and other vermin killed Socrates. So what does this all mean? You have embarked, you have made the voyage, you have come to shore: now get out. If indeed to another life, then gods are everywhere, even there; but if to a state without sensation, you will cease to be gripped by pains and pleasures, and to be a slave to the vessel, which is so immeasurably inferior to that which ministers it. For the one is intelligence and divinity; the other is dirt and corruption.

IV

Do not waste what remains of your life in thoughts about others, unless with an eye to some mutual benefit. For you lose the opportunity to do something worthwhile when you have such thoughts as, "What is such-and-such doing, and why, and what is he saying, and what is he thinking of, and what is he contriving," and anything else of the like, which makes us wander away from the observation of our own ruling power. We must see to it then that our thoughts are free of everything that is idle and useless, and particularly those of a prying or malignant nature. And a man should accustom himself to such a way of thinking that if suddenly asked, "What is in your mind right now?" he could respond openly and without hesitation; so from your words it should be clear that everything in you is simple and benevolent, and such as befits a social animal and one who cares not at all for thoughts of pleasure or sensual enjoyments, nor has any rivalry or envy or suspicion, or anything else that would cause him to blush if he had to acknowledge thinking it. The man who is such, and who no longer delays being among the best of men, is like a priest and minister of the gods, for he is making full use of the divine which is planted within him, and so he is uncontaminated by pleasure, unharmed by any pain, untouched by any insult, impervious to evil; he is a fighter in the noblest struggle against passion's mastery, imbued with justice, accepting with all his soul everything that falls to his lot; and rarely, and only out of great necessity and for the general interest, does he wonder what another is saying, or doing, or thinking. His whole activity is confined to his own concerns, and his whole attention is fixed on his place in the Whole. And he sees to it that his own actions are honourable, and he is convinced that whatever befalls him is for the best; for the lot assigned to each man is carried along with him and carries him along with it. And he remembers also that every rational animal is his kinsman, and that to care for all men is according to man's nature; and a man should not concern himself with the opinion of the world, but only of those whose own lives are in accord with Nature. But as for others whose lives are not in accord with Nature, he reminds himself constantly what kind of men they are both at home and in public, by night and by day, and what character they have, and what society they frequent, and what impure lives they lead. Accordingly, he does not value at all the praise that comes from such men, since they are not even satisfied with themselves.

V

Labour not unwillingly, nor without regard to the common interest, nor without due consideration, nor with distraction; nor let studied pretensions set off your thoughts, and be neither a man of many words, nor busy doing too many things. Let the Divine that is in you be the guardian of a being that is mature and virile, a statesman, a Roman, and a ruler, who has taken his post like a man waiting for the signal which summons him from life, and ready to go; a man whose credit need not be sworn to by himself or by others. Therein lies the secret of cheerfulness: depending on no external help and needing from no one the tranquillity they offer. A man then must stand erect, not be kept erect by others.

VI

If you find in human life anything better than justice, truth, temperance, fortitude, and, in a word, anything better than your own mind's self-satisfaction in the things that enable you to conduct yourself according to right Reason, and in the condition that is assigned to you without your choice—if, I say, you see anything better than this, turn to it with all your soul, and enjoy that which you have found to be the best. But if nothing appears to be better than the Divine that is in you, that has subjected to itself all your appetites and carefully examines all the impressions, and, as Socrates said, has detached itself from the persuasions of sense, and has submitted itself to the gods, and cares for mankind—if you find everything else smaller and of less value than this, give place to nothing else, for if you once diverge and incline to it, you will no longer without distraction be able to give the preference to that Good thing which is your proper possession and your own; for it is not right that anything of any other kind, such as praise from the many, or power, or enjoyment of pleasure, should come into competition with that which is rationally and practically good. All these things, even though they may seem to adapt themselves to the better things in a small degree, obtain the advantage all at once, and carry us away. But do you, I say, simply and freely choose the better, and hold to it?—"But what is best for myself is the highest," you say.—Well, then, if it is best for you as a rational being, keep to it; but if it is only best for you as an animal, then say so outright, and maintain your view with the proper humility. Only take care that you make the inquiry rightly.

VII

Never value any profit to yourself that compels you to break your promise, to lose your self-respect, to hate any man, to suspect others, to curse, to be insincere, or to desire anything that needs walls and curtains: for he who has preferred to everything else his own mind and divine spirit and the worship of its excellence, acts no tragic part, does not groan, does not need either solitude or much company; and, what is most important, he will live without either pursuing or flying from death. Whether his soul will be enclosed in the body for a longer or shorter time does not concern him: for even if he must leave immediately, he will depart as readily as if he were going to do anything else that can be done with decency and order. He has no other care in life but to keep his mind from straying in directions not befitting an intelligent and social being.

VIII

In the mind of one who is chastened and purified you will find no corrupt matter, nor uncleanness, nor any sore skinned over. Nor is his life incomplete when fate overtakes him, as one may say of an actor who leaves the stage before finishing the play. Besides, there is in him nothing servile, nor affected, nor too closely bound to other things, nor yet detached, nothing worthy of blame, nothing which seeks a hiding-place.

IX

Respect the power you have to form opinion. On this faculty depends whether there will exist in your ruling part any opinion inconsistent with Nature and the constitution of the rational animal. And this faculty promises freedom from hasty judgment, and friendship towards men, and obedience to the gods.

X

Throwing away then all things, hold to these few truths. Remember that man lives only in the present, which is an indivisible point, and that all the rest of his life is either past or is uncertain. Short then is the time which every man lives, and small the nook of the earth where he lives; and short too the longest posthumous fame, as even this is only continued by a succession of poor human beings, who will very soon die as well, and who know not even themselves, much less him who died long ago.

XI

To these maxims add one more: make for yourself a definition or description of anything that is presented to you, so as to see distinctly what kind of a thing it is in its substance, in its nudity, in its complete entirety, and tell yourself its proper name, and the names of the things it is made of and into which it will be dissolved. For nothing elevates the mind as much as to be able to examine methodically and truly every object that is presented to you in life, and always to look at things so as to see at the same time what kind of universe this is, and what kind of use everything performs in it, and what value everything has with reference to the whole and with reference to man, who is a citizen of the supreme City, of which all other cities are like families. Take, for instance, the thing that is producing an impression on me at this moment: what is it? what is it made of? how long is it designed to last?

what virtue do I need in response to it: gentleness, fortitude, truth, fidelity, simplicity, contentment, or something else? Wherefore, on every occasion a man should say: this comes from God; and this is according to the apportionment and spinning of the thread of destiny; and this is the work of man, who is of the same stock, a kinsman and partner, but who is ignorant of what Nature requires of him. But I know. And for this reason I behave towards him according to the natural law of fellowship with benevolence and justice. At the same time, however, in things not involving good or evil, I attempt to ascertain the value of each.

XII

If you work at that which is before you, following right Reason seriously, vigorously, calmly, without allowing anything else to distract you, but keeping your divine part pure, as if you should be bound to give it back immediately; if you hold to this, expecting nothing, fearing nothing, but satisfied with your present activity according to Nature, and with heroic truth in every word and sound that you utter, you will live happy. And there is no man who can hold you back.

XIII

As physicians always have their lancets and scalpels ready for cases that suddenly require their skill, so must you have principles ready for the understanding of things divine and human, and for doing everything, even the smallest, with a recollection of the bond which unites the divine and human to one another. For neither will you do anything well that pertains to man without at the same time having a reference to the divine, nor the contrary.

XIV

No longer wander at hazard. For neither will you read your own memoirs, nor the acts of the ancient Romans and Hellenes, nor the selections from books that you were reserving for your old age. Hasten then to the end that you have before you, and, throwing away idle hopes, come to your own aid, if you care at all for yourself, and do it while it is still in your power.

XV

They know not how many things are signified by the words stealing, sowing, buying, keeping quiet, seeing what ought to be done; for this is not effected by the eyes, but by another kind of vision.

XVI

Body, soul, mind: to the body belong sensation, to the soul appetites, to the mind principles. To receive the impressions of forms by means of appearances belongs even to animals; to be pulled by the strings of desire belongs both to wild beasts and to men who have made themselves into women, and to a Phalaris and a Nero; and to have the mind that guides us to the things that appear suitable belongs equally to those who do not believe in the gods, and who betray their country, and who do their impure deeds when they have shut the doors. If, then, everything else is common to all that I have mentioned, there remains that which is peculiar to the good man: to be pleased and content with what happens, and with the thread which is spun for him; and not to defile the divinity that is planted in his breast, nor disturb it with a crowd of images, but to keep it tranquil, following it obediently as a god, neither saying anything contrary to the truth, nor doing anything contrary to justice. And if all others refuse to believe that he lives a simple, modest, and contented life, he is neither angry with any of them, nor does he deviate from the way that leads to the end of life, to which a man ought to come pure, tranquil, ready to depart, and without any compulsion, perfectly reconciled to his lot.

Book Four

I

That which rules within, when it is according to Nature, is so affected with respect to the events that happen, that it always easily adapts itself to that which is possible and is presented to it. For it requires no definite material, but it moves towards its purpose; and it makes a material for itself out of that which opposes it, as fire lays hold of what falls into it, by which a small light would be extinguished; but when the fire is strong, it soon appropriates to itself the matter which is heaped on it, and consumes it, and rises higher by means of this very material.

II

Let no act be done without a purpose, nor otherwise than according to the perfect principles governing its proper execution.

III

Men seek seclusion in the country, sea-shores, and mountains; and you too are accustomed to desire such things very much. But this is altogether a mark of the most common sort of men, since it is in your power whenever you choose to retire into yourself. Nowhere can a man find a more quiet retreat, and more freedom from trouble, than in his own soul, particularly when he has within him such thoughts that, being contemplated, immediately bring on perfect tranquillity; and I affirm that tranquillity is nothing else than the good ordering of the mind. Constantly, then, avail yourself of this retreat, and renew yourself; and let your principles be brief and fundamental, so that as soon as you refer to them, they will be sufficient to cleanse the soul completely, and to send you back free from all discontent with the things to which you return. For with what are you discontented? With the badness of men? Recall to your mind this conclusion, that rational animals exist for one another, and that to endure is a part of justice, and that men do wrong involuntarily; and consider how many already, after mutual enmity, suspicion, hatred, and fighting, have been stretched dead, reduced to ashes; and be tranquil at last.—But perhaps you are dissatisfied with your lot in the universe.—Recall to your mind this alternative; either there is Providence, or atoms, and so a fortuitous concurrence of things; or remember the arguments which have proved that the world is a kind of political community, and be quiet at last.—But perhaps corporeal things will still fasten upon you.—Consider then further that the mind mingles not with the breath, whether moving gently or violently, when it has once drawn itself apart and discovered its own power, and think also of all that you have heard and assented to about pain and pleasure.—But perhaps desire for the thing called fame is what torments you.—See how soon everything is forgotten, and look at the chaos of infinite time on each side of the present, and the emptiness of applause, and the changeableness and want of judgment in those who pretend to give praise, and the narrowness of the space within which it is circumscribed, and be tranquil at last. For the whole earth is a point, and how small a nook it is in this great dwelling; and how few are in it, and what kind of people are they who will praise you?

This then remains: Remember to retire into this little territory of your own, and above all do not distract or strain yourself, but be free, and look at things as a man, as a human being, as a citizen, as a mortal. But among the things readiest to your hand to which you turn, let there be these, which are two: first, things do not touch the soul, for they are external and remain immovable, and our disturbances come only from our opinion; and second, all these things that you see are already in the midst of change and will soon no longer be; and constantly bear in mind how many of these changes you have already witnessed. The universe is transformation: life is opinion.[1]

IV

If our intellectual part is common, the Reason too, by way of which we are rational beings, is common: if this is so, common too is the Reason that commands us what to do and what not to do; if this is so, there is a common law also; if this is so, we are fellow-citizens; if this is so, we are members of some political community; if this is so, the world is in a manner a state. For of what other common political community will anyone say that the whole human race are members? And from this common political community comes also our very intellectual faculty and reasoning faculty and our capacity for law; or whence do they come? For as my earthly part is a portion given to me from certain earth, and that which is watery from another element, and that which is hot and fiery from some peculiar source (for nothing comes out of nothing, as nothing returns to nothing), so also the mind comes from some source.

VII

Put away your opinion, and then is taken away the complaint, "I have been harmed." Take away the complaint, "I have been harmed," and the harm is taken away.

VIII

That which does not make a man worse than he was, also does not make his life worse, nor does it harm him either from without or from within.

---

[1] Cf. Hamlet (Act II, scene ii): "For there is nothing either good or bad but thinking makes it so."

X

Consider that everything which happens, happens justly, and if you observe carefully, you will find it to be so. I do not say this only with respect to the continuity of things, but with respect to what is just, and as if it were done by one who assigns to each thing its value. Observe then as you have begun; and whatever you do, let goodness accompany you, "goodness" in the proper sense of the word. Keep to this in every action.

XI

Do not have the same opinions of things as he has who does you wrong, or the opinions he wishes you to have, but look at things as they are in truth.

XII

A man should always have these two rules in readiness: first, to do only whatever Reason, our king and lawgiver, may suggest for the common good of men; and second, to change your opinion if there is anyone at hand who sets you right and moves you from any opinion. But this change of opinion must proceed only from a certain persuasion, with regard to what is just or for the common good, and not because it appears pleasant or brings reputation.

XVII

Do not act as if you are going to live a thousand years. Death hangs over you. While you live, while it is in your power, make yourself good.

XVIII

He avoids much trouble who does not look to see what his neighbour says or does or thinks, but only to what he does himself, that it may be pure and just; or, as Agathon says, look not around at the depraved morals of others, but run straight along the line without deviating from it.

XIX

He who has a great desire for posthumous fame does not consider that every one of those who remember him will himself also die very soon, and not long after, the generation after that, until the whole remembrance has been extinguished, as it is transmitted through men who foolishly admire and then perish. But suppose that those who will remember are even immortal, and that the remembrance will be immortal, what then is this to you? And I say not what is it to the dead, but what is it to the living? What is praise, unless it has a certain utility? For you are rejecting unseasonably the gift that Nature has given you today, and you are clinging to what men will say of you tomorrow.

XXIV

"Occupy yourself with few things," says the sage, "if you wish to be happy."—But would it not be better to say, "Do what is necessary, in accordance with the Reason of a social animal, and as Reason demands." For this brings not only the tranquillity that comes from doing well, but also that which comes from doing few things. For the greatest part of what we say and do is unnecessary, and if a man puts this away, he will have more leisure and less uneasiness. Accordingly, on every occasion a man should ask himself, "Is this one of the unnecessary things?" Now a man should put away not only unnecessary acts, but also unnecessary thoughts, for then superfluous acts will not follow either.

XXV

See for yourself how the life of the good man suits you—the life of him who is satisfied with his portion out of the Whole, and satisfied with his own just acts and benevolent disposition.

XXVI

You have seen all the unpleasantness? Now look also at these. Your part is to be serene, to be simple. Is someone doing wrong? It is to himself that he does the wrong. Has anything happened to you? Good. It was your part in the Universe's spinning web, assigned to you when time itself began. In a word, your life is short. You must snatch your profit from the present moment, by the aid of Reason and Justice. Relax, but be temperate.

XXIX

If he is a stranger to the Universe who does not know what is in it, no less is he a stranger who does not know what is happening in it. He is a runaway, who flies from social Reason; he is blind, who shuts the eyes of understanding; he is poor, who has need of another, and has not from himself all things that are needed for life. He is an abscess on the universe who withdraws and separates himself from the Reason of our common nature by being displeased with the things that happen, for the same Nature that produces this has produced him too: he is a piece rent asunder from the State, who tears his own soul from the unified soul of reasonable animals.

XXXI

Love the trade that you have learned, poor as it may be, and be content with it; and pass through the rest of life like one who has wholly entrusted everything to the gods, thus making himself neither the tyrant nor the slave of any man.

XXXII

Consider, for a moment, the times of Vespasian: and what do you see? You will see people marrying, bringing up children, becoming sick, dying, warring, feasting, bargaining, cultivating the ground, flattering, bragging, suspecting, plotting, wishing for some to die, grumbling about the present, loving, heaping up treasure, desiring consulship and kingly power. Well, then, the life of those people no longer exists at all. Or come forward to the times of Trajan. Again, it is all the same. And their life too is gone. In the same manner, view also the other epochs of time and of whole nations, and see how many after great efforts soon fell and were resolved into the elements. But mainly you should think of those you have personally known, distracting themselves about idle things, neglecting to do what is in accordance with their proper constitution—and hold firmly to this and be content with it. And here it is necessary to remember that the attention given to everything has its proper value and proportion. In this way you will avoid discouragement, if you never become unduly invested in small matters.

XXXIII

The words that were once familiar are now antiquated, as are the names of those who were once famous: Camillus, Caeso, Volesus, Leonnatus, and a little after also Scipio, Cato, Augustus, then also Hadrianus and Antoninus. For all things soon pass away and become a mere tale, and complete oblivion soon buries them. This is true even of those who have shone in a wondrous way. For the rest, as soon as they have breathed out their breath, they are gone, and no man speaks of them. And, finally, what is even an eternal remembrance? A mere nothing. To what then should we devote our serious pains? Only this: just thoughts, unselfish acts, words that never lie, and a disposition that gladly accepts all that happens as something necessary, expected, and flowing from the One origin and source.

XXXVI

Observe constantly that all things take place by change, and accustom yourself to considering that the nature of the Universe loves nothing more than to change the things which are and to make new things like them. For everything that exists is in a manner the seed of that which will be. But you are thinking only of seeds that are cast into the earth or into a womb: but this is a very narrow view.

XXXIX

What is evil to you does not come from the mind of another, nor in any turning and mutation of your corporeal covering. Where is it then? It is in that part of you that contains the power of forming opinions about evils. Let this power then not form opinions, and all is well. And if that which is nearest to it, the poor body, is cut, burnt, filled with matter and rottenness, nevertheless let the part that forms opinions about these things be quiet; that is, let it judge that nothing is either bad or good that can happen equally to the bad man and the good. For that which happens equally to him who lives contrary to Nature and to him who lives according to Nature, is neither according to nature nor contrary to nature.

XLIV

Everything that happens is as familiar and expected as the rose in spring and the fruit in summer; this is true of disease, and death, and slander and treachery, and whatever else delights or troubles fools.

XLVII

If a god told you that you will die either tomorrow or the day after tomorrow, you would not care much whether it was on the latter day or on the morrow, unless you were the most pathetic of men; for how small is the difference! In the same way, do not consider it of much consequence if death is to come many years from now, or tomorrow.

XLIX

Be like the promontory against which the waves continually break: it stands firm and tames the fury of the water around it. "I am happy because *this* has happened to me?" Not so, but rather, " I am happy, though *this* has happened to me, because I continue free from pain, neither crushed by the present nor fearing the future." For such a thing as *this* might have happened to every man; but every man would not have continued free from pain on such an occasion. Why then is one misfortune and the other good fortune? Can a man call anything at all a misfortune if it is not a deviation from his own nature? And can it be a deviation from nature if it is not contrary to Nature's will? Well, you have learned to know the will of Nature. Does *this* which has happened prevent you from being just, magnanimous, temperate, prudent, truthful, and compassionate? Does it prevent you from having modesty, freedom, and everything else by which man's nature comes to its fulfilment? On every occasion that leads you to feel troubled or vexed, apply this principle: not that this is a misfortune, but that to bear it nobly is good fortune.

LI

Always run the short way; and the short way is the natural: accordingly, say and do everything in conformity with the soundest Reason. For such a purpose frees a man from trouble, and warfare, and all artifice and ostentatious display.

from
NICOMACHEAN ETHICS

by

ARISTOTLE

Book One

I

Every art and every inquiry, and similarly every action and moral choice, is thought to aim at some good; and for this reason the *Ultimate Good* has rightly been declared to be *the end at which all things aim*.

But a certain difference is found among ends; some are *activities*, and others are *products* apart from the activities that produce them. Where there are ends apart from the actions, *it is the nature of the products to be better than the activities*. Now, as there are many actions, arts, and sciences, their ends also are many; the end of the medical art is health, the end of shipbuilding is a vessel, the end of strategy is victory, the end of economics is wealth. But where such arts fall under a single capacity—as bridle-making and the other arts concerned with the equipment of horses fall under the art of riding, and this and every military action fall under the art of strategy, in the same way other arts are subsidiary to others—and in all of these *the ends of the master arts are to be preferred to all the subordinate ends*, because it is for the sake of the former that the latter are pursued. (It makes no difference whether the activities themselves are the ends of the actions, or if the ends are something else apart from the activities, as is the case with the sciences just mentioned.)

II

Since, then, of all things that may be done there is some final End that we desire for its own sake, with a view to which we desire everything else; and since we do not desire everything for the sake of something else (for then men would go on without limit, and so the desire would be unsatisfied and fruitless), this final End plainly must be the Ultimate Good, i.e. *the best thing of all.*

Will not the knowledge of it, then, have a great influence on life?—shall we not, like archers who have a mark to aim at, be more likely to hit upon what is right? If so, we must try to determine, in outline at least, what the Ultimate Good is, and of which of the sciences or capacities it is the object.

The Ultimate Good would seem to belong to the most authoritative art and that which is most truly the master art. And political science appears to be of this nature; for it is this that ordains which of the sciences should be studied in a state, and which sciences each class of citizens should learn, and up to what point they should learn them; and we see that even the most highly esteemed of capacities, e.g. strategy, economics, rhetoric, fall under this art. Now, since political science uses the rest of the sciences, and since, again, it legislates as to what we are to do and what we are to abstain from, the end of this science must include those of the others, so that its end must be *The Good* of Man. And even if the end is the same for the individual and for the community, yet surely that of the latter is obviously greater and more perfect to discover and preserve: for to do this even for a single individual is a matter for contentment; but to do it for a whole nation, and for communities generally, is more noble and godlike.

These, then, are the ends at which our inquiry aims, since it is political science, in one sense of that term.

III

Our discussion will be adequate if it has as much clearness as the subject-matter allows, for precision is not to be sought for in all discussions alike, any more than in all the works of handicraft. Now the notions of nobility and justice, which political science investigates, admit of much variety and fluctuation of opinion, so that they may be thought to exist only by convention, and not by nature. And "goods" also give rise to a similar controversy because some of them bring harm to many people; for many men have been undone by their wealth, and others by their courage.

We must be content, then, in speaking of such subjects and with such premises, to indicate the truth roughly and in outline; in other words, since we are speaking of general matters and from general data, we must be content to draw conclusions that are also merely general. And in the same spirit should each person receive what we say: for the man of education will seek exactness in each subject only so far as the nature of the subject admits; it is obviously equally foolish to accept probable reasoning from a mathematician and to demand from a rhetorician scientific proofs.

Now each man judges well the things he knows, and of these he is a good judge. And so the man who has been educated in a subject is a good judge of *that subject*, and the man who has received an all-round education is a good judge of things *in general*.

Hence a young man is not a fit student of Moral Philosophy, for he is inexperienced in the actions that occur in life, though the discussions of Moral Philosophy start from these and are about these; and, further, since he tends to follow his passions, he will hear as though he heard not, and his study will be vain and unprofitable, because the end aimed at is not knowledge but *action*. And it makes no difference whether he is young in years or young in temper and disposition; the defect does not depend on time, but on his living at the beck and call of passion, and following each object as it arises. For to such persons, as to those who lack self-control, knowledge brings no profit; but, to those who form their desires and act in accordance with reason, knowledge of such matters will be of great benefit.

These remarks about the student, the spirit in which our

observations should be received, and the purpose of the inquiry, may be taken as our preface.

IV

Let us resume our inquiry and state, in view of the fact that all knowledge and every moral choice aims at some *good*, what it is that we say political science aims at—that is, *what is the highest of all goods achievable by action?*

As far as the name goes, there is a very general agreement; for both the general run of men and people of superior refinement say that the Ultimate Good is *Happiness*, and equate "living well" and "doing well" with being happy; but they differ with regard to *what Happiness is*, and the multitude do not give the same account as the wise. For the former think it is some plain and obvious thing, like pleasure, wealth, or honour; they differ, however, from one another—and often even the same man identifies Happiness with different things: with health when he is ill, with wealth when he is poor, etc.; yet, conscious of their ignorance, men admire those who proclaim Happiness to be some great ideal that is above their comprehension. Now some think that apart from these many goods there is another which is self-subsistent and causes the goodness of all these as well. To examine all the opinions that have been held is perhaps somewhat fruitless; it is enough to examine those that are most prevalent or that seem to have some reason in them.

And here we must not forget the difference between reasoning *from* principles, and reasoning *to* principles. For Plato, too, was right in raising this question and asking, "are we on the way *from* or *to* the first principles?" There is a difference, as there is in a race-course between the course from the judges to the turning-point and the way back.

Of course, we must begin with what is known; but then this is of two kinds, what we *do* know, and what we *may* know: perhaps then as individuals we must begin with what we *do* know. Hence anyone who is to listen intelligently to lectures about what is noble and just, and generally, about the subjects of Moral Philosophy, must have been brought up in good habits. For a principle is a matter of fact, and if the fact is sufficiently plain to a man, he will not need the reason for the fact as well; and the man who has been well brought up either has principles already, or can easily acquire them. And as for him who neither has nor can get them, let him hear his sentence from Hesiod:

> Far best is he who knows all things
>   himself;
> Good, he that hearkens when men
>   counsel right;
> But he who neither knows, nor lays to
>   heart
> Another's wisdom, is a useless wight.

V

Now of the Ultimate Good (i.e. Happiness) men seem to form their notions from the different modes of life, as we might naturally expect: most men, and those of the most vulgar type, conceive it to be *Pleasure*, and hence they are content with the life of sensual enjoyment. For there are three lines of life which stand out prominently to view: *the life of pleasure, the life in society*, and, thirdly, *the life of contemplation*.

Now the mass of mankind are plainly quite slavish in their tastes, choosing a life like that of brute animals, but they get some ground for their view from the fact that many of those in high places share the tastes of Sardanapalus.[1] The refined and active men conceive the Ultimate Good to be *Honour*: for this may be said to be the end of the life in society: but it seems too superficial to be what we are looking for, since it is thought to depend on those who bestow Honour rather than on him who receives it, whereas we instinctively feel that the

---

[1] Sardanapalus was, according to ancient Greek historians, the last king of Assyria, famous for his decadence, self-indulgence, sloth, and luxury. He had male and female concubines, wore women's clothes, and in his epitaph, which he wrote himself, proclaimed that sexual gratification is the only purpose of life.

Ultimate Good must be *something which is our own*, and not easily to be taken from us.

Further, men seem to pursue Honour in order that they may be assured of their goodness; for instance, they seek to be honoured by the wise, and by those among whom they are known—and they desire to be honoured for their *virtue*: clearly then, in the opinion at least of these men, Virtue is a higher good than Honour. And perhaps one might even suppose Virtue, rather than Honour, to be the end of the life in society. But even this appears somewhat incomplete; for it is conceivable that a man possessed of Virtue might sleep or be inactive all through his life, or suffer the greatest evils and misfortunes: and no one would call such a man happy, except for mere disputation's sake.

But enough of this; for the subject has been sufficiently treated even in the current discussions.

Third comes the contemplative life, which we shall consider later.

As for the life of money-making, it is one of constraint, undertaken under compulsion, and *wealth* is evidently not the Good we are seeking, because it is merely useful and for the sake of something else. And hence one would rather conceive the aforementioned ends to be the right ones, for men rest content with them for their own sake. But it is evident that even these are not final ends, though many words have been wasted on them.

So much then for these.

VII

Let us again return to the Good we are seeking, and ask what it can be. It seems different in different actions and arts; it is different in medicine, in strategy, and in the other arts likewise. What then is the Good of each? Surely that for whose sake everything else is done. In medicine it is health, in strategy it is victory, in architecture it is a house, in any other sphere it is something else, and every action and moral choice has its own end; because it is for the sake of this end that all men do whatever else they do. Therefore, if there is *one End for all that we do*, this will be the Good achievable by action, and if there are more than one, then these will be the Goods.

Thus the argument has by a different course reached the same point; but we must try to state this even more clearly. Since there are evidently many different ends, and we choose some of these (e.g. wealth) for the sake of something else, clearly not all ends are final ends; but the Ultimate Good is evidently something *final*. Therefore, if there is only one final end, this must be what we are seeking, and if there are more than one, the most final of these will be what we are seeking. Now we call that which is worthy of pursuit *in itself* more final than that which is worthy of pursuit for the sake of something else; and we call that which is not desirable for the sake of something else more final than the things that are desirable both in themselves and for the sake of something else; and therefore we say that an end is final without qualification if *it is always desirable in itself and never for the sake of something else*.

Now such a thing, above all else, is *Happiness*; for we desire this always for its own sake and never for the sake of something else: whereas Honour, Pleasure, Intellect, and in fact every Excellence we desire for their own sakes, it is true (because we would desire each of these even if no result were to follow), but we desire them also for the sake of *Happiness*, believing that by means of them we shall be happy: On the other hand, no one desires Happiness for the sake of these, nor, in general, for the sake of anything other than itself.

The same result is seen to follow also from the notion of self-sufficiency, a quality thought to belong to the final good. Now by *self-sufficient* we do not mean a good which is sufficient for a man by himself, for one who lives a solitary life, but also for his parents, children, wife, and in general for his friends and fellow citizens, since man is born for citizenship. But some limit must be set to this; for if we extend our requirement to ancestors and descendants and friends' friends, there is no end to it; let us examine this question, however, on another occasion. For the present we define the self-sufficient to be *that which, by itself, makes life desirable and lacking in nothing*; and such we think *Happiness* to be; and further we think it the most desirable of all things, without being reckoned with any other thing, for if it were so reckoned, it is plain we must then allow it, with the addition of ever so small a good, to be more desirable than it was before: because what is put to it becomes an addition of so much more good, and of goods the greater is ever the more desirable.

Happiness, then, is something final and self-sufficient, and is the end of all action.

Presumably, however, to say that Happiness is the Ultimate Good seems a platitude, and we still need a clearer account of *what it is*. This might perhaps be given, if we could first ascertain the function of man. For just as for a flute-player, a sculptor, or an artist, and, in general, for all things that have a function or activity, their *good* and their *excellence* are thought to reside in their function, so it would seem to be for man, if he has any function.

Are we then to suppose, that while the carpenter and cobbler have certain functions and courses of action, Man as Man has none, but is left by Nature without a function? Or would we not rather hold that as the eye, the hand, the foot, and in general each of the parts evidently has a function, so too the whole Man, apart from all these, has some function of his own?

What then can this be? Not mere life, because that obviously is shared with him even by vegetables, and we want what is peculiar to him. We must separate, then, the life of mere nourishment and growth, and next will come the life of sensation: but this again is common even to the horse, the ox, and every animal. There remains then a kind of life of the *Rational Nature* in action: and of this nature there are two parts denominated Rational, the one as being *obedient to Reason*, and the other as *having and exerting Reason*. Again, as this life is also spoken of in two ways, we must state that *life in the sense of activity* is what we mean, because this seems to be the more proper sense of the term. If, then, *the function of Man is a working of the Soul in accordance with*

Reason, or at least not independently of Reason, and we say that the function of any given subject and the *good* function of the same subject are the same in kind (as, for instance, of a harp-player and a *good* harp-player, and so on in every case, adding to the work eminence in the way of Excellence; I mean, the function of a harp-player is to play the harp, and the function of a *good* harp-player is to play it *well*); if, I say, this is so, and we assume the function of Man to be life of a certain kind, that is to say *an activity or actions of the Soul according to Reason*, and the function of a *good* man to do these things well and nobly, and if in fact everything is performed well in accordance with the Excellence which peculiarly belongs to it: if all this is so, then *the Good of Man comes to be a working of the Soul in the way of Excellence*, or, if Excellence admits of degrees, in the way of the best and most perfect Excellence.

But we must add "in a complete life." For as it is not one swallow or one fine day that makes a spring, so it is not one day or a short time that makes a man blessed and happy.

Let this serve as an outline of the Ultimate Good; for we must presumably first sketch it roughly, and then later fill in the details. But it would seem that anyone is capable of carrying on and articulating what has once been well outlined, and that time is a good discoverer or partner in such a work; to which facts the advances of the arts are due; for anyone can add what is lacking.

And we must also remember what has been said before, and not look for precision in all things alike, but in each class of things such precision as accords with the subject-matter, and so much as is appropriate to the inquiry. For a carpenter and a geometrician, for instance, investigate the right angle in different ways: the former so far as he wants it for his work, while the latter inquires into its nature and properties, because he is concerned with the truth.

We must act in the same way, then, in all other matters as well, that our main task may not be subordinated to minor questions. Nor must we demand the *cause* in all matters alike; it is enough in some cases that the fact be well established, as in the case of the *first principles*; the fact is the primary thing or first principle.

Now of first principles we see some by induction, some by perception, some by a certain habituation, and others too in other ways. But each set of principles we must try to investigate in their own nature, and we must take pains to state them definitely, since they have a great influence on what follows: it is thought, I mean, that the starting-point or principle is more than half the whole matter, and that many of the points of inquiry come simultaneously into view thereby.

VIII

We must now consider Happiness, however, in the light not only of our conclusion and our premises, but also of what is commonly said about it; for with a true view all the data harmonize, but with a false one the facts soon clash.

Now goods have been divided into three classes: some are described as *external*, others as *relating to the body*, and still others as *relating to the Soul*; we call those that relate to the Soul most properly and truly goods. Well, in our definition we assume that *the actions and workings of the Soul constitute Happiness*, and these of course belong to the Soul. And so our account is a good one, at least according to this opinion, which is an old one and agreed on by philosophers. Rightly too are certain actions and workings said to be the End, for thus it falls among goods of the Soul instead and not external goods. Another common belief which harmonizes with our account is that *the happy man lives well and does well*, for we have practically defined Happiness as a sort of good life and good action. All of the characteristics that are looked for in Happiness also seem to belong to what we have defined Happiness as being. For some identify Happiness with Virtue, some with practical wisdom, others with a kind of philosophic wisdom, others with these, or one of these, accompanied by Pleasure, or at least not without Pleasure; while others include also external prosperity.

Some of these views have been held by many men of antiquity, others by a few eminent persons; and it is not probable that any of these men should be entirely mistaken, but rather that they should be right in at least some respect or even in most respects.

Now with those who identify Happiness with Virtue, or some kind of virtue, our account agrees; for to Virtue belongs virtuous activity. But it makes perhaps no small difference whether we place the Ultimate Good in possession or in use, in other words, in *state of mind* or in *activity*. For the state or habit may possibly exist in a subject without effecting any good, as, for instance, in him who is asleep or in any other way inactive; but the activity cannot be so, for it will of necessity act, and act well. And as in the Olympic Games it is not the most beautiful and the strongest who are crowned, but *those who compete* (for it is some of these that are victorious), so too in the life of the honourable and the good, it is *those who act* who rightly win the noble and good things in life.

Their life is also in itself pleasant. For *Pleasure is a state of Soul*; and to each man, that which he is said to be a lover of is pleasant; for instance, as a horse is pleasant to the lover of horses, and a spectacle is pleasant to the lover of sights, so in the same way are just acts pleasant to the lover of justice; and, in general, virtuous acts are pleasant to the lover of virtue. Now for the multitude of men their pleasures are in conflict with one another because these are not pleasant by nature, while the lovers of nobleness find pleasant the things that are truly pleasant by nature; and virtuous actions are of this kind, so that they are pleasant both to such individuals and also in themselves.

Their life, therefore, has no further need of Pleasure as a sort of adventitious charm, but has its Pleasure in itself. For, besides what we have just said, a man is not a good man at all who feels no Pleasure in noble actions; since no one would call a man just who did not enjoy acting justly, nor any man liberal who did not enjoy liberal actions; and similarly in all other cases. If this is so, virtuous actions must be pleasant in themselves. But they are also good and noble, and have each of these attributes in the highest degree, since the good man judges well about these attributes; his judgment is such as we have described. *Happiness then is the best, noblest, and most pleasant thing in the world*, and these attributes are not separated as in the inscription at Delos—

> Most noble is that which is most just, but
>   best is health;
> And naturally most pleasant is obtaining
>   one's desires.

For all these co-exist in the best acts of working: and we say that Happiness is these acts, or one of these—that is, the best of them.

Yet evidently, as we said, Happiness needs the external goods as well; for it is impossible, or not easy, to do noble acts without the proper equipment. For friends, money, and political influence are in a manner instruments whereby many things are done; and there are some things which, when lacking, take the lustre from Happiness, such as good birth, good children, beauty: for he is not at all capable of Happiness who is very ugly, or is ill-born, or solitary and childless; and still less capable perhaps if he has very bad children or friends, or has lost good ones by death. As we have said already, the addition of prosperity of this kind does seem necessary to complete the idea of Happiness; hence some rank Good Fortune, and others Virtue, with Happiness.

IX

And hence too a question is raised, whether Happiness is a thing that can be learned, or acquired by habituation or discipline of some other kind, or whether it comes in the way of divine dispensation, or even in the way of Chance.

Now to be sure, if anything else is a gift of the gods to men, it is probable that Happiness is a gift of theirs too, and especially because of all human goods it is the highest. But this question would perhaps be more appropriate to another inquiry; Happiness seems, however, even if it is not a gift of the gods but comes as a result of Virtue and some process of learning or training, to be among the most godlike things; for that which is the prize and End of Virtue seems to be the best thing in the world, and something godlike and blessed.

It will also on this view be very generally shared; for all who are not maimed as regards their potentiality for Virtue may win it by a certain kind of study and care. But if it is better to be happy thus than by Chance, it is reasonable that the facts should be so, since everything that depends on the action of Nature is by nature as good as it can be, and similarly everything that depends on art or any rational cause, and especially if it depends on the best of all causes. To entrust to Chance what is greatest and most noble would be a very defective arrangement.

The answer to the question we are asking is plain also from the definition of Happiness; for it has been said to be *a virtuous activity of Soul*, of a certain kind. Of the remaining goods, some must necessarily preexist as conditions of Happiness, and others are naturally cooperative and useful as instruments. And this will be found to agree with what we said at the outset; for we stated the End of political science to be the best End, and political science spends most of its pains on making the citizens to be of a certain character, that is, good and capable of noble acts.

It is natural, then, that we call neither ox nor horse nor any other of the animals happy; for none of them is capable of sharing in such activity. And for this same reason a child is not happy either, for he is not yet capable of such acts, owing to his age; and children who are called happy are being congratulated by reason of the hopes we have for them. For there is required, as we said, not only complete Virtue but also a complete life, since many changes occur in life, and all manner of chances, and the most prosperous may fall into great misfortunes in old age, as is told of Priam in the Trojan Cycle; and one who has experienced such chances and has ended wretchedly no one calls happy.

X

Are we then to call no man happy while he lives;[1] must we, as Solon says, look to the end? Even if we are to lay down this doctrine, is a man then happy when he is dead? Or is this not a complete absurdity, especially for us who say that Happiness is an activity? But if we do not call the dead man happy, and if Solon does not mean this, but that one can then safely call a man blessed as being at last beyond evils and misfortunes, this also affords matter for discussion; for both evil and good are thought to exist for a dead man, as much as for one who is alive but not aware of them; e.g. honours and dishonours, and the good or bad fortunes of children and other descendants.

And this also presents a problem; for though a man has lived happily to old age and has had a death worthy of his life, many reverses may befall his descendants—some of them may be good and attain the life they deserve, while with others the opposite may be the case; and clearly too the degrees of relationship between them and their ancestors may vary indefinitely. It would be odd, then, if the dead man were to share in these changes and become at one time happy, at another wretched; while it would also be odd if the fortunes of the descendants did not for some time have some effect on the Happiness of their ancestors.

But we must return to our first difficulty; for perhaps by a consideration of it our present problem might be solved.

Now if we must see the end and only then call a man happy, not as being happy but as having been so before, surely it is absurd that when he *is* happy the truth is not to be asserted of him, because we are unwilling to pronounce the living happy by reason of their liability to changes, and because, whereas we have conceived of Happiness as something stable and no way easily changeable, the fact is that good and bad fortune are constantly circling about the same people: for it

---

[1] Compare with Montaigne's Essay, "That Men Are Not to Judge of Our Happiness Until After Death."

is quite plain that if we are to depend upon the fortunes of men, we shall often have to call the same man happy, and a little while after miserable, thus representing our happy man as chameleon-like and insecurely based.

Or is this keeping pace with his fortunes quite wrong? Success or failure in life does not depend on these, but human life, as we said, needs these as mere additions, while virtuous activities or their opposites are what constitute Happiness or the reverse.

The question we have now discussed confirms our definition of Happiness. For no function of man has so much permanence as virtuous activities (these are thought to be more durable even than knowledge of the sciences), and of these themselves the most valuable are more durable because those who are happy spend their life most readily and most continuously in these; for this seems to be the reason why we do not forget them. The attribute in question, then, will belong to the happy man, and he will be happy throughout his life; for always, or by preference to everything else, he will be engaged in virtuous action and contemplation, and the various chances of life he will bear most nobly, and at all times and in all ways harmoniously, since he is the truly good man, or in the terms of our proverb, "a faultless cube."

Now many events happen by chance, and events differ in importance; small pieces of good or ill fortune clearly do not weigh down the scales of life one way or the other, but a multitude of great events, if they turn out well, will make life happier (for not only do they themselves add beauty to life, but the way a man deals with them may also be noble and good), while if they turn out ill, they crush and maim Happiness; for they bring positive pain to life, and also hinder many activities. Yet even in these nobility shines through, when a man bears with resignation many great misfortunes, not through insensibility to pain but through nobility and greatness of soul.

If activities are, as we said, what give life its character, no happy man can become miserable; for he will never do the acts that are hateful and mean. For the man who is truly good and wise, we presume, bears all fortunes becomingly and always makes the best of circumstances, just as a good general makes the best military use of the army at his command, or a good shoemaker makes the best shoes out of the hides that are given him; and so with all other craftsmen. And if this is the case, the happy man can never become wretched, though he will not be *blessed* if he meets with fortunes like those of Priam.

Nor, again, is he shifting and changeable; for neither will he be moved from his happy state easily or by any ordinary misadventures, but, if at all, by those which are great and numerous; nor, if he has had many great misadventures, will he recover his happiness in a short time, but if at all, only after a long and complete period during which he has made himself master of great and noble things.

Why then should we not call happy the man who works in the way of perfect virtue, and is furnished with external goods sufficient for acting his part in the drama of life: and this during no ordinary period but such as constitutes a complete life as we have been describing it.

Or must we add that not only is he to live so, but his death must be in keeping with such life? Certainly the future is obscure to us, while Happiness, we claim, is an *end* and something in every way final. If so, we shall call happy those among living men in whom these conditions are, or are to be, fulfilled—but they are happy *as Men*.

So much for these questions.

XI

That the fortunes of descendants and of all a man's friends should not affect his happiness at all seems a very unfriendly doctrine, and one opposed to the opinions men hold; but since the events that happen are numerous and admit of all sorts of difference, and some come more near to us and others less so, it seems a long—nay, an infinite—task to discuss each in detail; a general outline will perhaps suffice. If, then, as some of a man's own misadventures have a certain weight and influence on his life while others are, as it were, lighter, so too are there differences among the misadventures of our friends taken as a whole, and it makes a difference whether the various suffering befall the living or the dead (much more even than whether lawless and terrible deeds are presupposed in a tragedy or done on the stage); this difference also must be taken into account; or rather, perhaps, the fact that doubt is felt whether the dead share in any good or evil. For it seems from these considerations that even if anything, whether good or evil, penetrates to them, it must be something weak and negligible, either in itself or for them, or if not, at least it must be such in degree and kind as not to make happy those who are not happy nor to take away the blessedness of those who are blessed. The good or bad fortunes of friends, then, seem to have some effects on the dead, but effects of such a kind and degree as neither to make the happy unhappy nor to produce any other change of the kind.

XII

These questions having been definitely answered, let us consider whether Happiness is among the things that are praised or rather among the things that are prized; for clearly it is not to be placed among the faculties. Everything that is praised seems to be praised because it is of a certain kind and is related somehow to something else; for we praise the just or brave man, and in general both the good man and virtue itself, because of the actions and functions involved, and we praise the strong man, the good runner, and so on, because he is of a certain kind and is related in a certain way to something good and important. This is clear also from the praises of the gods; for it seems absurd that the gods should be referred to our standard, but this is done because praise involves a reference to something else. But if praise is for things such as we have described, clearly what applies to the best things is not praise, but something greater and better, as is indeed obvious; for what we do to the gods and the most godlike of men is to call them blessed and happy. And so too with good things; no one praises Happiness as he does Justice, but rather calls it blessed, as being something more divine and better.

Eudoxus too is thought to have advanced a sound argument in support of the claim that Pleasure is the highest prize: for the fact that, though it is one of the good things, it is not praised, he took as an indication of its superiority to those which are subjects of praise: a superiority he attributed also to God and the Ultimate Good, on the ground that they form the standard to which everything else is referred. For praise applies to virtue, because it makes men apt to do what is noble; but encomia are bestowed to definite works of body or mind.

But perhaps nicety in these matters is more proper to those who have made a study of encomia; to us it is clear from what has been said that Happiness is among the things that are prized and perfect. It seems to be so also from the fact that it is a first principle; for it is for the sake of Happiness that we all do all that we do, and the first principle and cause of good things is, we claim, something prized and divine.

XIII

Since Happiness is an activity of soul in accordance with perfect Virtue, we must consider the nature of Virtue; for perhaps we shall thus see better the nature of Happiness. The true student of political science, too, is thought to have studied Virtue above all things; for he wishes to make his fellow citizens good and obedient to the laws. (As an example of this we have the lawgivers of the Cretans and the Spartans, and any others of the kind that there may have been.) And if this inquiry belongs to political science, clearly the pursuit of it will be in accordance with our original plan.

But clearly the Virtue we must study is human Virtue; for the Good we were seeking was human Good and the Happiness human Happiness. By human Virtue we mean not that of the body but that of the soul; and Happiness also we call an activity of Soul. But if this is so, clearly the student of political science must know somehow the facts about the Soul, as the man who is to heal the eyes or the body as a whole must know about the eyes or the body; and all the more since political science is more prized and better than medicine; but even among doctors the best educated spend much labour on acquiring knowledge of the body. The student of political science, then, must study the Soul, and must study it with these objects in view, and do so just to the extent which is sufficient for the questions we are discussing; for further precision is perhaps something more laborious than our purposes require.

Some things are said about the Soul, adequately enough, even in the discussions outside our school, and we must use these; e.g. that one element in the Soul is Irrational, and one has a Rational principle. Whether these are separated as the parts of the body, or are distinct by definition but by nature inseparable, like convex and concave in the circumference of a circle, does not affect the present question.

Of the Irrational element one division seems to be widely distributed, and vegetative in its nature; I mean that which causes nutrition and growth; for it is this kind of power of the Soul that one must assign to all nurslings and to embryos, and this same power to full-grown creatures; this is more reasonable than to assign some different power to them. Now the Excellence of this seems to be common to all species and not specifically human; for this part or faculty seems to function most in sleep, while goodness and badness are least manifest in sleep (whence comes the saying that the happy are not better off than the wretched for half their lives; and this happens naturally enough, since sleep is an inactivity of the Soul in that respect in which it is called good or bad), unless perhaps to a small extent some of the movements actually penetrate to the Soul, and in this respect the dreams of good men are better than those of ordinary people. Enough of this subject, however; let us leave the nutritive faculty alone, since it has by its nature no share in human Excellence.

There seems to be also another Irrational Nature of the Soul—which yet in a way partakes of Reason. For in the man who controls his appetites, and in him who resolves to do so and fails, we praise the Reason or Rational part of the

Soul, because it exhorts aright and to the best course: but clearly there is in them, beside the Reason, some other natural principle which fights with and strains against Reason. For exactly as paralyzed limbs, when we intend to move them to the right, turn on the contrary to the left, so it is with the Soul; the impulses of men who cannot control their appetites move in contrary directions. But while in the body we see that which moves astray, in the Soul we do not. No doubt, however, we must nonetheless suppose that in the Soul too there is something contrary to the Reason, resisting and opposing it. In what sense it is distinct from the other elements does not concern us.

Now even this seems to have a share in a Reason, as we said; for instance, in the Man of Self-Control it obeys Reason: and perhaps in the man of Perfected Self-Mastery, or the Brave Man, it is yet more obedient; in them it agrees entirely with the Reason.

So then the Irrational is plainly twofold: the one part, the merely vegetative, has no share of Reason, but that of Desire, or appetite generally, does partake of it in a sense, insofar as it is obedient to it and capable of submitting to its rule.

Now, that the Irrational Nature is in some sense persuaded by Reason is indicated also by the giving of advice and by all reproof and exhortation. If then we are to say that this also has Reason, then the Rational, as well as the Irrational, will be twofold, the one supremely and in itself, the other paying it a kind of filial regard.

Virtue too is distinguished into kinds in accordance with this difference, for we say that some of the virtues are *intellectual* and others are *moral*: philosophic wisdom, intelligence, and practical wisdom are *intellectual virtues*, while liberality and perfected self-mastery are *moral virtues*. For in speaking about a man's character we do not say that he is wise or has understanding, but that he is good-tempered or one of perfected self-mastery; yet we praise the wise man with respect to his state of mind; and of states of mind, we call those which merit praise *virtues*.

Book Seven

XI

The study of Pleasure and Pain belongs to the province of the political philosopher; for he is the architect of the End, with a view to which we call one thing evil and another good without qualification. Further, an inquiry into their nature is absolutely necessary; for not only did we say that Moral Virtue and Moral Vice are both concerned with pains and pleasures, but most people say that Happiness involves Pleasure; this is why the blessed man is called by a name derived from a word meaning *enjoyment*.

Now some people think that no pleasure is good, either in itself or incidentally, since the Good and Pleasure are not the same; others think that some pleasures are good but that most are bad; and again there is a third view, that even if all pleasures are good, still the Ultimate Good cannot possibly be Pleasure.

In support of the first opinion (that Pleasure is utterly not good) it is urged that:

1. Every pleasure is a sensible process towards a complete state; but no such process is akin to the end to be attained: e.g. the process of building is not akin to the completed house.

2. The Man of Perfected Self-Mastery avoids pleasures.

3. The Man of Practical Wisdom aims at avoiding Pain, not at attaining Pleasure.

4. Pleasures are an impediment to thought, and the more so the more keenly they are felt, e.g. in sexual pleasure, for no one could think of anything while absorbed in this.

5. There is no Art of Pleasure: and yet every good is the result of some art.

6. Children and brutes pursue pleasures.

In support of the second opinion (that not all pleasures are good), it is argued that there are some pleasures that are actually base and objects of reproach, and there are harmful pleasures: because some things that are pleasant produce disease.

In support of the third opinion (that Pleasure is not the Chief Good), it is argued that Pleasure is not an End but a process towards creating an End.

XII

These are pretty much the things that are said. That it does not follow from these grounds that Pleasure is not a good, or even the Ultimate Good, is plain from the following considerations.

First, since that which is good may be so in either of two senses (one thing good in itself and another good for a particular person), natural constitutions and states of being, and therefore also the corresponding movements and processes, will be correspondingly divisible. Of those which are thought to be bad some will be bad if taken without qualification but not bad for a particular person, but worthy of his choice, and some will not be worthy of choice even for a particular person, but only at a particular time and for a short period, though not without qualification; while others are not even pleasures at all but seem to be so, that is to say, all those which involve pain and whose end is curative, e.g. the processes that go on in sick persons.

Next, one kind of good being activity and another being state, the processes that restore us to our natural state are only *incidentally pleasant*; for that matter the activity at work in the appetites for them is the activity of so much of our state and nature as has remained unimpaired; for there are actually pleasures that involve no pain or appetite, e.g. those of contemplation, in which case there is no deficiency in the nature or state of him who performs the acts.

A proof of this is that men do not enjoy the same pleasant

objects when their nature is in its settled state as they do when it is being replenished; in the former case they enjoy the things that are *pleasant without qualification*, but in the latter case they enjoy also those processes which are only pleasurable when they restore us to our natural state; for at such times they may enjoy even sharp and bitter things, none of which is pleasant either by nature or in itself. The states they produce, therefore, are not pleasures naturally or without qualification; for as pleasant things differ, so do the pleasures arising from them.

Next, it is not necessary that there should be something else better than Pleasure, as some say the End is better than the process; for leisures are not processes, nor do they all involve processes—they are activities and ends; nor do they arise when we are becoming something, but when we are exercising some faculty; and not all pleasures have an end different from themselves, but only the pleasures of persons who are being led to the perfecting of their nature. This is why it is not right to say that Pleasure is a perceptible process, but it should rather be called an activity of the natural state, and instead of "perceptible" we should say "unimpeded." It is thought by some people to be a process just because they think it is in the strict sense good; for they think that any activity is a process, which it is not.

Next, the view that pleasures are bad because some pleasant things are unhealthy is like saying that healthy things are bad because some healthy things are bad for money-making; both are bad in the respect mentioned, but they are not bad for that reason—indeed, thinking itself is sometimes injurious to health. Neither practical wisdom nor any state of being is impeded by the pleasure arising from it; it is foreign pleasures that impede, for the pleasures arising from thinking and learning will make us think and learn all the more.

Next, the fact that no pleasure is the product of any art arises naturally enough; there is no art of any other activity either, but only of the corresponding faculty; though for that matter the arts of the perfumer and the cook are thought to be arts of Pleasure.

Next: "The Man of Perfected Self-Mastery avoids pleasures." "The Man of Practical Wisdom aims at escaping Pain rather than at attaining Pleasure." "Children and brutes pursue pleasures." One answer will do for all. We have pointed out in what sense pleasures are good without qualification and in what sense some are not good: both the brutes and children pursue pleasures of the latter kind, that is, those which are accompanied by desire and pain, i.e. the *bodily pleasures* (for it is these that are of this nature) and the excesses of them, in respect of which the self-indulgent man is self-indulgent. And it is the absence of the pain arising from *these pleasures* that the Man of Practical Wisdom aims at. This is why the Man of Perfected Self-Mastery avoids these pleasures: for obviously he has pleasures peculiarly his own.

XIII

But further it is agreed that Pain is bad and to be avoided; for some pain is bad without qualification, and other pain is bad because it is in some respect an impediment to us. Now the contrary of that which is to be avoided—something to be avoided and bad—is good. Pleasure, then, must be a good. For the answer of Speusippus, that Pleasure is contrary both to Pain and to Good, as the greater is contrary both to the less and to the equal, is not successful; since he would not say that Pleasure is essentially just a species of evil.

And if certain pleasures are bad, that does not prevent the Ultimate Good from being some pleasure, just as the Ultimate Good may be some form of knowledge, though certain kinds of knowledge are bad. Perhaps it is even necessary, if each disposition has unimpeded activities, that, whether the activity (if unimpeded) of one or all of our dispositions is Happiness, this should be the thing most worthy of our choice; and this activity is Pleasure. Thus the Ultimate Good would be *some* pleasure, though *most* pleasures might perhaps be bad without qualification. And for this reason all men think that the happy life is pleasant and weave Pleasure into their ideal of Happiness—and reasonably too; for no activity is perfect when it is impeded, and Happiness is a perfect thing; this is why the happy man needs the goods of the body and external goods, i.e. those of Fortune, in order that he may not be impeded in these ways. Those who say that the victim on the rack or the man who falls into great misfortunes is happy if he is good, are, whether they mean to or not, talking nonsense. Now because we need Fortune as well as other things, some people think Good Fortune is the same thing as Happiness; but it is not that, for even Good Fortune itself, when in excess, is an impediment, and perhaps should then be no longer called Good Fortune; for its limit is fixed by reference to Happiness.

And indeed the fact that all things, both brutes and men, pursue Pleasure is an indication of its being somehow the Ultimate Good:

"There must be some truth in what most people say." But since no one nature or state either is or is thought the best for all, neither do all pursue the same pleasure; yet all pursue Pleasure. And perhaps they actually pursue not the pleasure they think they pursue nor that which they would say they pursue, but the same Pleasure; for all things have by nature something divine in them. But the bodily *pleasures* have appropriated the name of Pleasure both because we most often steer our course for them and because all men share in them; thus, because they alone are familiar, men think there are no others.

It is evident also that if Pleasure, i.e. the activity of our faculties, is not a good, it will not be the case that the happy man lives a pleasant life; for to what end should he need Pleasure if it is not a good, and if the happy man may even live a painful life? For Pain is neither an evil nor a good, if Pleasure is not; why then should he avoid it? Therefore, too, the life of the good man will not be pleasanter than that of anyone else, if his activities are not more pleasant.

XIV

With regard to the bodily pleasures, those who say that some pleasures are very much to be chosen, i.e. the *noble pleasures*, but not the *bodily pleasures*, i.e. those with which the self-indulgent man is concerned, must consider why, then, the contrary pains are bad. For the contrary of bad is good. Are the necessary pleasures good in the sense in which even that which is not bad is good? Or are they good up to a point? Is it that where you have states and processes of which there cannot be too much, there cannot be too much of the corresponding pleasure, and that where there can be too much of the one there can be too much of the other also?

Now, *there can be too much of bodily goods, and the low and evil man is so by virtue of pursuing the excess, not by virtue of pursuing the necessary pleasures* (for all men enjoy in some way or other good foods, wines, and sexual intercourse, but not all men do so in the right manner or degree). But his relation to Pain is exactly the contrary: it is not excessive Pain, but *Pain at all*, that he avoids (which makes him to be in this way too a low and evil man). And this is peculiar to him, for the alternative to excess of Pleasure is not Pain, except to the man who pursues this excess.

Since we should state not only the truth, but also the cause of error—for this contributes towards producing conviction, since when a reasonable explanation is given of why the false view appears true, this tends to produce belief in the true view—then we must state why the bodily pleasures appear to people to be more worthy than others.

Firstly, it is because bodily pleasures expel Pain; owing to the excesses of Pain that men experience, they pursue excessive pleasure, and in general bodily pleasure, as a cure for the Pain. Now curative agencies produce intense feeling—which is the reason why they are pursued—because they show up against the contrary pain.

Indeed, as has been said, pleasure is thought not to be good for these two reasons: that some of them are activities belonging to a bad nature—either congenital, as in the case of a brute, or due to habit, i.e. those of low and evil men; while others are meant to cure a defective nature, and it is better to be in a healthy state in the first place than to see it accrue afterwards; but these arise during the process of being made perfect and are therefore only *incidentally* good.

Further, the bodily pleasures, by the very fact of their being so intense, are pursued by those who cannot enjoy other pleasures. Such men in fact create violent thirsts for themselves (if harmless ones then we find no fault, if harmful then it is low and evil) because they have no other things to take pleasure in, and because the neutral state is distasteful to some people constitutionally; for toil of some kind is inseparable from life, as physiologists testify, telling us that even the acts of seeing and hearing are painful, only that we are used to the pain and do not notice it.

Similarly in youth the constant growth produces a state much like that of vinous intoxication, and youth is pleasant. Again, men of the melancholic temperament constantly need some remedial process (because the body, from its temperament, is constantly being worried), and they are in a chronic state of violent desire. But Pleasure drives out Pain; not only such pleasure as is directly contrary to Pain, but even any pleasure, provided it be strong: and this is how men come to be utterly destitute of Self-Mastery, i.e. low and evil.

But the pleasures that do not involve pains do not admit of excess; and these are among the things pleasant by nature and not incidentally. By things pleasant incidentally I mean those that act as cures (for because as a result people are cured, through some action of the part that remains healthy, the process is thought pleasant); by things naturally pleasant I mean those that stimulate the action of the healthy nature.

The reason why no one thing is always pleasant is that our nature is not simple, but complex, involving something different from itself; so that if one part of this nature does something, this is unnatural to the other part, and when the two natures are evenly balanced, what is done seems neither painful nor pleasant. It is obvious that if there were any being whose nature was simple and not complex, to such a being the same course of acting would always be the most pleasurable. This is why God always enjoys a single and simple pleasure; for there is not only an activity of movement but an activity of immobility, and pleasure is found more in rest than in movement. The reason why the Poet's dictum "change is of all things most pleasant" is true, is due to "a baseness in our blood"; for as it is the vicious man who is easily changeable, so the nature that needs change is vicious, for it is not simple or good.

PRINCIPAL DOCTRINES

by

EPICURUS

1. A happy and eternal being has no trouble himself and brings no trouble upon any other being; and so he is free from anger and partiality, for these imply weakness.

2. Death is nothing to us; for the body, when it has been dissolved into its elements, experiences no sensation, and that which has no sensation is nothing to us.

3. The magnitude of pleasure reaches its limit in the removal of all pain. When pleasure is present, so long as it is uninterrupted, there is no pain either of body or of mind or of both together.

4. Continuous bodily pain does not last long; on the contrary, pain, if extreme, is present only a short time, and even that degree of pain which slightly outweighs bodily pleasure does not last for many days in succession. Illnesses of long duration even allow a surplus of bodily pleasure over pain.

5. It is impossible to live a pleasant life without living wisely, honourably, and justly, and it is impossible to live wisely, honourably, and justly without living pleasantly. Whenever any one of these is lacking—when, for instance, a man is unable to live wisely, though he lives well and justly—it is impossible for him to live a pleasant life.

6. In order to obtain security from other people, any means of achieving this is a natural good.

7. Some people seek fame and status, thinking they would thus make themselves secure against their fellow humans. If such people's lives are really secure, then they have attained a natural good; if, however, their lives are insecure, they have not attained the end which by nature's own prompting they originally sought.

8. No pleasure is in itself evil, but the things which produce certain pleasures entail disturbances many times greater than the pleasures themselves.

9. If all pleasures had been capable of accumulation, not only over time, but also over the whole body, or at least over the principal parts of human nature, then there would be no difference between one pleasure and another, as in fact there is.

10. If the things that produce the pleasures of profligate men really freed them from fears of the mind—the fears, I mean, inspired by natural phenomena, the fear of death, the fear of pain; if, further, these things taught them to limit their desires, we should never have any fault to find with such men, for they would then be filled with pleasures from all sides and would be free from all pain, whether of body or mind—that is, they would be free from all evil.

11. If we had never been troubled by natural phenomena, nor by the fear of how death affects us, nor by our ignorance of the proper limits of pains and desires, we should have had no need to study natural science.

12. It is impossible for someone to banish his fear about the most important matters if he does not know the nature of the whole universe, and lives in dread because of myths and superstitions. Hence without the study of nature there can be no enjoyment of pure pleasure.

13. There is no advantage in obtaining security against our fellow humans so long as we are alarmed by events over our

heads or beneath the earth or in general by whatever happens in the boundless universe.

14. Adequate security against our fellow humans, by means of sufficient power and material prosperity, arises in its most genuine form in a quiet private life withdrawn from the multitude.

15. The wealth required by nature is at once limited and easy to procure; but the wealth demanded by vain fancies extends an infinite distance.

16. Fortune only seldom interferes with the wise man; his greatest and highest interests have been, are, and will be, directed by reason throughout the course of his life.

17. The just man enjoys the greatest peace of mind, while the unjust man is full of the utmost disquietude.

18. Bodily pleasure admits no increase once the pain of want has been removed; after that it only admits of variation. The limit of mental pleasure, however, is reached when we reflect on the things themselves and their related emotions, which no longer disturb the mind as they used to.

19. Unlimited time and limited time afford an equal amount of pleasure, if we measure the limits of that pleasure by reason.

20. The body receives as unlimited the limits of pleasure, and to provide it requires unlimited time. But the mind, grasping in thought what the end and limit of the body is, and banishing the terrors of the future, procures a complete and perfect life, and no longer has any need of unlimited time. Nevertheless the mind does not shun pleasure, and even in the hour of death, when ushered out of existence by circumstances, the mind does not lack enjoyment of the best life.

21. He who understands the limits of life knows how easy it

is to procure enough to remove the pain of want and make the whole of life complete and perfect. Hence he no longer has any need of things that can only be won by struggle and conflict.

22. We must consider all that really exists and all clear evidence of sense to which we refer our opinions; for otherwise everything will be full of uncertainty and confusion.

23. If you fight against all your sensations, you will have no standard to refer to, and thus no means of judging even those judgments which you pronounce false.

24. If you reject absolutely any single sensation without stopping to determine which are matters of opinion awaiting confirmation and which are confirmed to be present, whether in sensation or in feelings or in any immediate perception of the mind, you will throw into confusion even the rest of your sensations by your groundless belief, and so you will be rejecting the standard of truth altogether. If in your ideas based on opinion you hastily affirm as true all that awaits confirmation as well as all that does not, you will not avoid error, as you will be maintaining complete ambiguity whenever it is a case of judging between right and wrong opinion.

25. If you do not on every separate occasion refer each of your actions to the end prescribed by nature, but instead of this in the act of choice or avoidance swerve aside to some other end, your acts will not be consistent with your theories.

26. All desires that lead to no pain when they remain ungratified are unnecessary, and the longing is easily got rid of, when the thing desired is difficult to procure or when the desires seem likely to produce harm.

27. Of all the means employed by wisdom to ensure happiness throughout the whole of life, by far the most important is friendship.

28. The same conviction which inspires confidence that nothing we have to fear is eternal or even of long duration, also enables us to see that even amid the limited dangers of this life nothing enhances our security so much as friendship.

29. Of our desires some are natural and necessary; others are natural, but not necessary; and others are neither natural nor necessary, but are due to illusory opinion.

30. Those natural desires which entail no pain when not gratified, though their objects are vehemently pursued, are also due to illusory opinion; and when they are not gotten rid of, it is not because of their own nature, but because of the person's illusory opinion.

31. Natural justice is a symbol or expression of universal benefit, to prevent one person from harming or being harmed by another.

32. Those animals which are incapable of making binding agreements to neither inflict nor suffer harm are without either justice or injustice. And those tribes which either could not or would not form mutual agreements to the same end are also without justice or injustice.

33. There never was such a thing as absolute justice, but only agreements made in reciprocal associations, in whatever localities now and again from time to time, providing against the infliction or suffering of harm.

34. Injustice is not an evil itself, but only in its consequence, namely the terror caused by the apprehension of being discovered by the authorities.

35. It is impossible for a man who secretly violates any article of the social agreement to feel confident that he will remain undiscovered, even if he has already escaped ten thousand times; for right on to the end of his life he is never sure that

he will not be detected.

36. Taken generally, justice is the same for all, that is to say, something found useful in mutual association; but in its application to particular cases of locality or conditions of whatever kind, it varies under different circumstances.

37. Among the things held to be just by conventional law, whatever in the needs of mutual association is attested to be useful, is thereby stamped as just, whether or not it be the same for all; and if any law is made that does not prove suitable to the usefulness of mutual association, then it is no longer just. And if the usefulness which is expressed by the law varies, and only for a time corresponds with the prior conception, nevertheless for the time being it was just, so long as we do not trouble ourselves about empty words, but look simply at the facts.

38. Where without any change in circumstances the conventional laws, when judged by their consequences, are seen not to correspond with the notion of justice, such laws were never really just; but wherever the laws have ceased to be useful in consequence of a change in circumstances, in that case the laws were for the time being just when they were useful for the mutual association of the citizens, and subsequently ceased to be just when they ceased to be useful.

39. He who best knows how to handle the fear of external foes, makes all the creatures that he can into one family; and those he can not make into one family, he at any rate does not treat as aliens; and where he finds even this impossible, he avoids all association with them, and, so far as is useful, keeps them at a distance.

40. Those who are best able to protect themselves from their neighbours, being thus in possession of the surest guarantee of security, pass the most agreeable life in each other's society; and their enjoyment of the fullest intimacy is such that, if one

of them dies before his time, the survivors do not lament his death as if it called for pity.

THE ENCHIRIDION

by

EPICTETUS

I

There are things that are within our power, and there are things that are beyond our power. Within our power are opinion, aim, desire, aversion, and, in a word, whatever affairs are our own. Beyond our power are body, property, reputation, office, and, in one word, whatever are not properly our own affairs.

Now the things within our power are by nature free, unrestricted, unhindered; but those beyond our power are weak, dependent, restricted, alien. Remember then, that, if you attribute freedom to things by nature dependent, and take what belongs to others for your own, you will be hindered, you will lament, you will be disturbed, you will find fault both with Gods and men. But if you take for your own only that which is your own, and view what belongs to others just as it really is, then no one will ever compel you, no one will restrict you, you will find fault with no one, you will accuse no one, you will do nothing against your will; no one will hurt you, you will not have an enemy, nor will you suffer any harm.

Aiming therefore at such great things, remember that you must not allow yourself any inclination, however slight, towards the attainment of the others; but that you must entirely quit some of them, and for the present postpone the rest. But if you would have these, and possess power and wealth likewise, you may miss the latter in seeking the former; and you will certainly fail of that by which alone happiness and freedom are procured.

Seek at once, therefore, to be able to say to every unpleasing semblance, "You are but a semblance and by no means the real thing." And then examine it by those rules which you have; and first and chiefly, by this: whether it concerns the things which are within our own power, or those which are not; and if it concerns anything beyond our power, be prepared to say that it is nothing to you.

II

Remember that desire demands the attainment of that which you desire; and aversion demands the avoidance of that to which you are averse; that he who fails of the object of his desires, is disappointed; and he who incurs the object of his aversion, is wretched. If, then, you shun only those undesirable things which you can control, you will never incur anything which you shun. But if you shun sickness, or death, or poverty, you will run the risk of wretchedness. Remove aversion, then, from all things that are not within our power, and transfer it to things undesirable which are within our power. But for the present altogether restrain desire; for if you desire any of the things not within our own power, you must necessarily be disappointed; and you are not yet secure of those which are within our power, and so are legitimate objects of desire. Where it is practically necessary for you to pursue or avoid anything, do even this with discretion, and gentleness, and moderation.

III

With regard to whatever objects either delight the mind, or contribute to use, or are tenderly beloved, remind yourself of their nature, beginning with the merest trifles: if you have a favourite cup, that it is an object you are fond of, but if it is broken, you can bear it: if you embrace your child, or your wife, that you embrace a *mortal*, and thus, if either of them dies, you can bear it.

IV

When you set about any action, remind yourself of the nature of the action. If you are going to the public baths, recall to yourself the incidents usual in the bath: some persons pouring out, others pushing in, others scolding, others pilfering. And thus you will more safely go about this action, if you say to yourself, "I will now go to bathe, and keep my own will in harmony with nature." And so with regard to every other action. For thus, if any impediment arises in bathing, you will be able to say, "It was not only to bathe that I desired, but to keep my will in harmony with nature; and I shall not keep it thus, if I am out of humour at things that happen."

V

Men are disturbed not by things, but by the views that they take of things. Thus death is nothing terrible, else it would have appeared so to Socrates. But the terror consists in our notion of death, that it is terrible. When, therefore, we are hindered, or disturbed, or grieved, let us never impute it to others, but to ourselves; that is, to our own views. It is the action of an uninstructed person to reproach others for his own misfortunes; of one entering upon instruction, to reproach himself; and of one perfectly instructed, to reproach neither others nor himself.

VI

Be not elated at any excellence not your own. If a horse should be elated, and say, "I am handsome," it might be endurable. But when you are elated, and say, "I have a handsome horse," know that you are elated only on the merit of the horse. What, then, is your own? The use of the phenomena of existence. So that when you are in harmony with nature in this respect, you will be elated with some reason; for you will be elated at some good of your own.

VII

As in a voyage, when the ship is at anchor, if you go on shore to get water, you may amuse yourself with picking up a shell-fish or a truffle in your way; but your thoughts ought to be bent towards the ship, and perpetually attentive, lest the captain should call; and then you must leave all these things, so that you do not have to be carried on board the vessel, bound like a sheep. Thus likewise in life, if, instead of a truffle or shell-fish, such a thing as a wife or a child be granted you, there is no objection; but if the captain calls, run to the ship, leave all these things, and never look behind. But if you are old, never go far from the ship, lest you should be missing when called for.

VIII

Demand not that events should happen as you wish; but wish them to happen as they do happen, and you will go on well.

IX

Sickness is an impediment to the body, but not to the will, unless the will allows it to be. Lameness is an impediment to the leg, but not to the will; and say this to yourself with regard to everything that happens. For you will find it to be an impediment to something else, but not truly to yourself.

X

Upon every accident, remember to turn towards yourself and inquire what faculty you have for its use. If you encounter a handsome person, you will find self-control the faculty needed; if pain, then fortitude; if reviling, then patience. And when thus habituated, the phenomena of existence will not overwhelm you.

XI

Never say of anything, "I have lost it," but, "It has been restored whence it came." Has your child died? It is restored. Has your wife died? She is restored. Has your estate been taken away? That likewise is restored. "But it was a bad man who took it," you say. What is it to you, by whose hands He who gave it has demanded it back? While He permits you to possess it, hold it as something not your own, as do travellers at an inn.

XII

If you would improve, lay aside such reasonings as these: "If I neglect my affairs, I will not be able to support myself; if I do not punish my servant, he will be good for nothing." For it is better to die of hunger, exempt from grief and fear, than to live in affluence with perturbation; and it is better that your servant should be bad than you unhappy.

Begin therefore with little things. Is a little oil spilt or a little wine stolen? Say to yourself, "This is the price paid for peace and tranquillity; and nothing is to be had for nothing." And when you call your servant, consider that it is possible he may not come at your call; or, if he does, that he may not do what you wish. But it is not at all desirable for him, and very undesirable for you, that it should be in his power to cause you any disturbance.

XIII

If you would improve, be content to be thought foolish and dull with regard to externals. Do not desire to be thought to know anything; and though you should appear to others to be somebody, distrust yourself. For be assured, it is not easy at once to keep your will in harmony with nature, and to secure externals; but while you are absorbed in the one, you must of necessity neglect the other.

XIV

If you wish your children, and your wife, and your friends, to live forever, you are foolish; for you wish things to be in your power which are not so; and what belongs to others, to be your own. So likewise, if you wish your servant to be without fault, you are foolish; for you wish vice not to be vice, but something else. But if you wish not to be disappointed in your desires, that is in your own power. Exercise, therefore, what is in your power. A man's master is he who is able to confer or remove whatever that man seeks or shuns. Whoever then would be free, let him wish nothing, let him decline nothing, which depends on others; else he must necessarily be a slave.

XV

Remember that you must behave as at a banquet. Is anything brought round to you? Put out your hand, and take a moderate share. Does it pass by you? Do not stop it. Is it not yet come? Do not yearn in desire towards it, but wait till it reaches you. So with regard to children, wife, office, riches; and you will some time or other be worthy to feast with the Gods. And if you do not so much as take the things which are set before you, but are able even to forego them, then you will not only be worthy to feast with the Gods, but to rule with them also. For, by thus doing, Diogenes and Heraclitus, and others like them, deservedly became divine, and were so recognized.

XVI

When you see any one weeping for grief, either that his son has gone abroad, or that he has suffered in his affairs; take care not to be overcome by the apparent evil. But discriminate, and be ready to say, "What hurts this man is not this occurrence itself, for another man might not be hurt by it—but the view he chooses to take of it." As far as conversation goes, however, do not disdain to accommodate yourself to him, and if need be, to groan with him. Take heed, however, not to groan inwardly too.

XVII

Remember that you are an actor in a drama of such sort as the author chooses. If it is to be a short drama, then in a short one; if long, then in a long one. If it be his pleasure that you should act a poor man, see that you act it well; or a cripple, or a ruler, or a private citizen. For this is your business, to act well the given part; but to choose it, belongs to another.

XVIII

When a raven happens to croak unluckily, be not overcome by appearances, but discriminate, and say, "Nothing is portended to me, but only to my paltry body, or property, or reputation, or children, or wife. But to me all portents are lucky, if I will. For whatever happens, it belongs to me to derive advantage from it."

XIX

You can be unconquerable, if you enter into no combat in which it is not in your own power to conquer. When, therefore, you see any one eminent in honours or power, or in high esteem on any other account, take heed not to be bewildered by appearances and to pronounce him happy; for if the essence of good consists in things within our own power, there will be no room for envy or emulation. But, for your part, do not desire to be a general, or a senator, or a consul, but to be free; and the only way to do this is to disregard things that do not lie within your own power.

XX

Remember that it is not he who gives abuse or blows who affronts; but the view we take of these things as insulting.

When, therefore, anyone provokes you, be assured that it is your own opinion that provokes you. Try, therefore, in the first place, not to be bewildered by appearances. For if you take a moment to reflect, you will more easily command yourself.

XXI

Let death and exile, and all other things which appear terrible, be daily before your eyes, but death chiefly; and you will never entertain any abject thought, nor too eagerly covet anything.

XXII

If you have an earnest desire towards philosophy, prepare yourself from the very first to have the multitude laugh and sneer, and say, "He is returned to us a philosopher all at once," and "Where does he get this supercilious look?" Now for your part, do not have a supercilious look indeed; but keep steadily to those things which appear best to you, as one appointed by God to this particular station. For remember that, if you are persistent, those very persons who at first ridiculed, will afterwards admire you. But if you are conquered by them, you will incur a double ridicule.

XXIII

If you ever happen to turn your attention to externals, for the pleasure of anyone, be assured that you have ruined your scheme of life. Be contented, then, in everything, with being a philosopher; and, if you wish to seem so likewise to anyone, appear so to yourself, and it will suffice you.

XXIV

Let not such considerations as these distress you: "I shall live in discredit, and be nobody anywhere." For if discredit be an evil, you can no more be involved in evil through another, than in baseness. Is it any business of yours, then, to get power, or to be admitted to an entertainment? By no means. How then, after all, is this discredit? And how is it true that you will be nobody anywhere; when you ought to be somebody in those things only which are within your own power, in which you may be of the greatest consequence? "But my friends will be unassisted," you say. What do you mean by unassisted? They will not have money from you; nor will you make them Roman citizens? Who told you, then, that these are among the things within your own power, and not rather the affairs of others? And who can give to another the things which he himself has not? "Well, but you must get them, then, so that we too may have a share." If I can get them while preserving my own honour, and fidelity, and self-respect, show me the way, and I will get them; but if you require me to lose my own proper good so that you may gain what is no good, consider how unreasonable and foolish you are. Besides, which would you rather have, a sum of money, or a faithful and honourable friend? Rather assist me, then, to gain this character, than require me to do those things by which I may lose it. "Well, but my country," say you, "as far as depends upon me, will be unassisted." Here again, what assistance is this you mean? It will not have porticos nor baths of your providing? And what does that signify? Why, neither does a smith provide the country with shoes, nor does a shoemaker provide it with arms. It is enough if everyone fully performs his own proper business. And were you to supply it with another faithful and honourable citizen, would he not be of use to it? Yes. Therefore neither are you yourself useless to it. "What place then," say you, "shall I hold in the state?" Whatever you can hold with the preservation of your fidelity and honour. But if, by desiring to be useful to the state, you lose your honour, how can you serve your country, when you have become faithless and shameless?

XXV

Is anyone preferred over you at a party, or in courtesies, or in confidential intercourse? If these things are good, you ought to rejoice that he has them; and if they are evil, do not be grieved that you have them not. And remember that you cannot be permitted to rival others in externals, without using the same means to obtain them. For how can he, who will not haunt the door of any man, will not attend him, will not praise him, have an equal share with him who does these things? You are unjust, then, and unreasonable, if you are unwilling to pay the price for which these things are sold, and would have them for nothing. For how much is lettuce sold? A dollar, for instance. If another, then, paying a dollar, takes the lettuce, and you, not paying it, go without lettuce, do not imagine that he has gained any advantage over you? For as he has the lettuces, so you have the dollar that you did not give. So, in the present case, you have not been invited to such a person's entertainment; because you have not paid him the price for which a supper is sold. It is sold for praise; it is sold for attendance. Give him, then, the value, if it be for your advantage. But if you would at the same time not pay the one, and yet receive the other, you are unreasonable and foolish. Have you nothing, then, in place of the supper? Yes, indeed you have; not to praise him whom you do not like to praise; not to bear the insolence of his lackeys.

XXVI

The will of Nature may be learned from things upon which we are all agreed. As, when our neighbour's boy has broken a cup, or the like, we are ready at once to say, "These are casualties that will happen." Be assured, then, that when your own cup is likewise broken, you ought to be affected just as when another's cup was broken. Now apply this to greater things. Is the child or wife of another dead? There is no one who would not say, "This is an accident of mortality." But if anyone's own child happens to die, it is immediately, "Alas! how wretched am I!" We should always remember how we are affected on hearing the same thing concerning others.

XXVII

As a mark[1] is not set up for the sake of missing the aim, so neither does the nature of evil exist in the world.

XXVIII

If a person had delivered up your body to some passerby, you would certainly be angry. And do you feel no shame in delivering up your own mind to some enemy, to be disconcerted and confounded?

XXIX

In every affair consider what precedes and follows, and then undertake it. Otherwise you will begin with spirit; but not having thought of the consequences, when some of them appear you will shamefully desist. "I would conquer at the Olympic games." But consider what precedes and follows, and then, if it is for your advantage, engage in the affair. You must conform to rules, submit to a diet, refrain from dainties; exercise your body, whether you choose it or not, at a stated hour, in heat and cold; you must drink no cold water, nor sometimes even wine. In a word, you must give yourself up to your master, as to a physician. Then, in the combat, you may be thrown into a ditch, dislocate your arm, turn your ankle, swallow dust, be whipped, and, after all, lose the victory. When you have evaluated all this, if your inclination still holds, then go to war. Otherwise, take notice, you will behave like children who sometimes play like wrestlers, sometimes gladiators, sometimes blow a trumpet, and sometimes act a tragedy when they have seen and admired these shows. Thus you too will be at one time a wrestler, at another a gladiator, now a philosopher, then an orator; but with your whole soul, nothing at all. Like an ape, you mimic all you see, and one

---

[1] Translator's Note (Carter): Happiness, the effect of virtue, is the mark which God has set up for us to aim at. Our missing it is no work of His; nor is it anything real, as it is a mere negative and failure of our own.

thing after another is sure to please you, but is out of favour as soon as it becomes familiar. For you have never entered upon anything considerately, nor after having viewed the whole matter on all sides, or made any scrutiny into it, but rashly, and with a cold inclination. Thus some, when they have seen a philosopher and heard a man speaking like Euphrates (though, indeed, who can speak like him?), have a mind to be philosophers too. Consider first what the matter is, and what your own nature is able to bear. If you would be a wrestler, consider your shoulders, your back, your thighs; for different persons are made for different things. Do you think that you can act as you do, and be a philosopher? That you can eat and drink, and be angry and discontented as you are now? You must watch, you must labour, you must get the better of certain appetites, must quit your acquaintance, be despised by your servant, be laughed at by those you meet; come off worse than others in everything, in magistracies, in honours, in courts of judicature. When you have considered all these things round, approach, if you please; if, by parting with them, you have a mind to purchase apathy, freedom, and tranquillity. If not, don't come here; don't, like children, be one moment a philosopher, then a publican, then an orator, and then one of Caesar's officers. These things are not consistent. You must be one man, either good or bad. You must cultivate either your own ruling faculty or externals, and apply yourself either to things within or without you; that is, be either a philosopher, or one of the vulgar.

XXX

Duties are universally measured by relations. Is a certain man your father? In this are implied, taking care of him, submitting to him in all things, patiently receiving his reproaches and his correction. "But he is a bad father," you say. Is your natural tie, then, to a good father? No, it is to a father. Is a brother unjust? Well, preserve your own just relation towards him. Consider not what he does; but what you are to do, to keep your own will in a state conformable to nature. For another cannot hurt you, unless you please. You will then be hurt when you consent to be hurt. In this manner, therefore, if you accustom yourself to contemplate the relations of neighbour, citizen, commander, you can deduce from each the corresponding duties.

XXXI

Be assured that the essence of piety towards the Gods lies in this, to form right opinions concerning them, as existing, and as governing the universe justly and well. And fix yourself in this resolution, to obey them, and yield to them, and willingly follow them amidst all events, as being ruled by the most perfect wisdom. For thus you will never find fault with the Gods, nor accuse them of neglecting you. And it is not possible for this to be effected in any other way, than by withdrawing yourself from things that are not within your own power, and by making good or evil to consist only in those things that are. For if you suppose any other things to be either good or evil, it is inevitable that, when you don't get what you wish, or incur what you wish to avoid, you will reproach and blame their causes. For every creature is naturally formed to flee and abhor things that appear hurtful, and that which causes them; and to pursue and admire those which appear beneficial, and that which causes them. It is impracticable, then, that one who supposes himself to be hurt, should rejoice in the person who, as he thinks, hurts him; just as it is impossible to rejoice in the hurt itself. Hence, also, a father will be reviled by his son when the father does not impart the things that seem to be good; and this made Polynices and Eteocles mutual enemies—that empire seemed good to both, and both desired it. On this account the husbandman reviles the Gods, as does the sailor, the merchant, or he who has lost a wife or child. For where our interest is, there too is piety directed. So that whoever is careful to regulate his desires and aversions as he should, is thus made careful of piety likewise. But it also becomes incumbent on every one to offer libations, and sacrifices, and first-fruits, according to the customs of his country, purely, and not heedlessly nor negligently; not avariciously, nor yet extravagantly.

XXXII

When you have recourse to divination, remember that you know not what the event will be, and you come to learn it of the diviner; but of what nature it is you knew before coming—at least, if you are of philosophic mind. For if it is among the things not within our own power, it can by no means be either good or evil. Do not, therefore, bring with you to the diviner either desire or aversion—else you will approach him trembling—but first clearly understand that every event is indifferent, and nothing to you, of whatever sort it may be; for it will be in your power to make a right use of it, and this no one can hinder. Then come with confidence to the Gods as your counsellors; and afterwards, when any counsel is given you, remember what counsellors you have assumed, and whose advice you will neglect, if you disobey. Come to divination, as Socrates prescribed, in cases of which the whole consideration relates to the event, and in which no opportunities are afforded by reason, or any other art, to discover the matter in view. When, therefore, it is our duty to share the danger of a friend or of our country, we ought not to consult the oracle as to whether we shall share it with them or not. For though the diviner should forewarn you that the auspices are unfavourable, this means no more than that either death or mutilation or exile is portended. But we have reason within us; and it directs us, even with these hazards, to stand by our friend and our country. Attend, therefore, to the greater diviner, the Pythian God, who once cast out of the temple him who neglected to save his friend.[1]

---

[1] Translator's Footnote (Higginson): This refers to an anecdote given in full by Simplicius, in his commentary on this passage, of a man assaulted and killed on his way to consult the oracle, while his companion, deserting him, took refuge in the temple, till cast out by the Deity.

XXXIII

Begin by prescribing to yourself some character and demeanour, such as you may preserve both alone and in company.

Be mostly silent; or speak merely what is needful, and in few words. We may, however, enter sparingly into discourse sometimes, when occasion calls for it; but let it not run on any of the common subjects, as gladiators, or horse-races, or athletic champions, or food, or drink—the vulgar topics of conversation; and especially not on men, so as either to blame, or praise, or make comparisons. If you are able, then, by your own conversation, bring over that of your company to proper subjects; but if you happen to find yourself among strangers, be silent.

Let not your laughter be loud, frequent, or abundant.

Avoid taking oaths, if possible, altogether; at any rate, so far as you are able.

Avoid public and vulgar entertainments; but if ever an occasion calls you to them, keep your attention upon the stretch, that you may not imperceptibly slide into vulgarity. For be assured that if a person be ever so pure himself, yet, if his companion be corrupted, he who converses with him will be corrupted likewise.

Provide things relating to the body no farther than absolute need requires; as meat, drink, clothing, house, retinue. But cut off everything that looks towards show and luxury.

Before marriage, guard yourself with all your ability from unlawful intercourse with women; yet be not uncharitable or severe to those who are led into this, nor frequently boast that you yourself do otherwise.

If any one tells you that such a person speaks ill of you, do not make excuses about what is said of you, but answer: "He was ignorant of my other faults, else he would not have mentioned these alone."

It is not necessary for you to appear often at public spectacles; but if ever there is a proper occasion for you to be there, do not appear more solicitous for any other, than for yourself; that is, wish things to be only just as they are, and only the best man to win; for thus nothing will go against you. But abstain entirely from acclamations, and derision, and violent emotions. And when you come away, do not discourse a great deal on what has passed, and what contributes nothing to your own amendment. For it would appear by such discourse that you were dazzled by the show.

Be not prompt or ready to attend private recitations; but if you do attend, preserve your gravity and dignity, and yet avoid making yourself disagreeable.

When you are going to confer with any one, and especially with one who seems your superior, represent to yourself how Socrates or Zeno would behave in such a case, and you will not be at a loss to meet properly whatever may occur.

When you are going before anyone in power, fancy to yourself that you may not find him at home, that you may be shut out, that the doors may not be opened to you, that he may not notice you. If, with all this, it be your duty to go, bear what happens, and never say to yourself, "It was not worth so much." For this is vulgar, and befitting a man bewildered by externals.

In society, avoid a frequent and excessive mention of your own actions and dangers. For however agreeable it may be to yourself to allude to the risks you have run, it is not equally agreeable to others to hear your adventures. Avoid likewise an endeavour to excite laughter. For this may readily slide you into vulgarity, and, besides, may be apt to lower you in the esteem of your acquaintance. Approaches to indecent discourse are likewise dangerous. Therefore when anything of this sort happens, use the first fit opportunity to rebuke him who makes advances that way; or, at least, by silence, and blushing, and a serious look, show yourself to be displeased by such talk.

XXXIV

If you are dazzled by the semblance of any promised pleasure, guard yourself against being bewildered by it; but let the affair wait your leisure, and procure yourself some delay.

Then bring to your mind both points of time; that in which you shall enjoy the pleasure, and that in which you will repent and reproach yourself, after you have enjoyed it; and set before you, in opposition to these, how you will rejoice and applaud yourself, if you abstain. And even though it should appear to you a seasonable gratification, take heed that its enticements and allurements and seductions do not subdue you; but set in opposition to this, how much better it is to be conscious of having gained so great a victory.

XXXV

When you do anything from a clear judgment that it ought to be done, never shrink from being seen to do it, even though the world should misunderstand it; for if you are not acting rightly, shun the action itself; if you are, why fear those who wrongly censure you?

XXXVI

As the proposition, either it is day, or it is night, has much force in a disjunctive argument, but none at all in a conjunctive one; so, at a feast, to choose the largest share, is very suitable to the bodily appetite, but utterly inconsistent with the social spirit of the entertainment. Remember, then, when you eat with another, not only the value to the body of those things which are set before you, but also the value of proper courtesy towards your host.

XXXVII

If you have assumed any character beyond your strength, you have both demeaned yourself in that character, and abandoned one in which you might have performed well.

XXXVIII

As in walking you take care not to tread upon a nail, or turn your foot, so likewise take care not to hurt the ruling faculty of your mind. And if we were to guard against this in every action, we should enter upon action more safely.

XXXIX

The body is to everyone the proper measure of his possessions, as the foot is of the shoe. If, therefore, you stop at this, you will keep the measure; but if you move beyond it, you must necessarily be carried forward, as down a precipice; as in the case of a shoe, if you go beyond its fitness to the foot, it comes first to be gilded, then made purple, and then studded with jewels. For there is no limit to that which exceeds the proper measure.

XL

Women from fourteen years old are flattered by men with the title of mistresses. Therefore, perceiving that they are regarded only as qualified to give men pleasure, they begin to adorn themselves, and in that to place all their hopes. It is worthwhile, therefore, to try to make it so that they perceive themselves honoured only so far as they appear beautiful in their demeanour, and are modestly virtuous.

XLI

It is a mark of low intellect to spend much time in things relating to the body—to be immoderate in exercises, in eating and drinking, and in the discharge of other animal functions. These things should be done *incidentally*, and our main strength should be applied to our reason.

XLII

When any person does ill by you, or speaks ill of you, remember that he acts or speaks from an impression that it is right for him to do so. Now, it is not possible that he should follow what appears right to you, but only what appears so to himself. Therefore, if he judges from false appearances, he is the person hurt; since he too is the person deceived. For if anyone takes a true proposition to be false, the proposition is not hurt, but only the man is deceived. Setting out, then, from these principles, you will meekly bear with a person who reviles you; for you will say upon every occasion, "It seems so to him."

XLIII

Everything has two handles: one by which it may be borne; another by which it cannot. If your brother acts unjustly, do not lay hold on the affair by the handle of his injustice; for by that it cannot be borne: but rather by the opposite, that he is your brother, that he was brought up with you; and thus you will lay hold on it as it is to be borne.

XLIV

These reasonings have no logical connection: "I am richer than you, therefore I am your superior;" "I am more eloquent than you, therefore I am your superior." The true logical connection is rather this: "I am richer than you, therefore my possessions exceed yours;" "I am more eloquent than you, therefore my style surpasses yours." But you, after all, consist neither in property nor in style.

XLV

Does someone bathe hastily? Do not say that he does it ill, but hastily. Does someone drink much wine? Do not say that he does ill, but that he drinks a great deal. For unless you perfectly understand his motives, how should you know if he acts ill? Thus you will not risk yielding to any appearances but such as you fully comprehend.

XLVI

Never proclaim yourself a philosopher; nor make much talk among the ignorant about your principles, but show them by actions. Thus, at an entertainment, do not talk about how people ought to eat; but eat as you ought. For remember that in this way Socrates too avoided all ostentation. And when persons came to him, and desired to be introduced by him to other philosophers, he took them and introduced them: so well did he bear being overlooked. So if ever there should be among the ignorant any discussion of principles, be for the most part silent. For there is great danger in hastily throwing out what is undigested. And if anyone tells you that you know nothing, and you are not nettled at it, then you may be sure that you have really entered on your work. For sheep do not hastily throw up the grass, to show the shepherds how much they have eaten; but, inwardly digesting their food, they produce it outwardly in wool and milk. In the same way, therefore, do not make an exhibition before the ignorant of your principles, but of the actions to which their digestion gives rise.

XLVII

When you have learned to nourish your body frugally, do not pique yourself upon it; nor, if you drink water, be saying upon every occasion, "I drink water." But first consider how much more frugal are the poor than we, and how much more patient of hardship. But if at any time you want, by practice, to inure yourself to difficulty and privation—for your own sake, do not attempt great feats; but when you are violently thirsty, just rinse your mouth with water, and tell nobody.

XLVIII

The condition and characteristic of a vulgar person is that he never looks for either help or harm from himself, but only from externals. The condition and characteristic of a philosopher is that he looks to himself for all help or harm. The marks of a wise man are that he censures no one, praises no one, blames no one, accuses no one; says nothing concerning himself as being anybody, or knowing anything; when he is in any instance hindered or restrained, he accuses himself; and if he is praised, he smiles to himself at the person who praises him; and if he is censured, he makes no defence. But he goes about with the caution of a convalescent, careful of interference with anything that is doing well, but not yet quite secure. He restrains desire; he transfers his aversion to those things only which thwart the proper use of his own will; he employs his energies moderately in all directions; if he appears stupid or ignorant, he does not care; and, in a word, he keeps watch over himself as over an enemy and one in ambush.

XLIX

When anyone shows himself vain for being able to understand and interpret the works of Chrysippus, say to yourself: "Unless Chrysippus had written obscurely, this person would have had nothing to be vain of. But what do I desire? To understand Nature, and follow her. I ask, then, who interprets her; and hearing that Chrysippus does, I have recourse to him. I do not understand his writings. I seek, therefore, one to interpret them." So far there is nothing to value myself upon. And when I find an interpreter, what remains is, to make use of his instructions. This alone is the valuable thing. But if I admire merely the interpretation, what do I become more than a grammarian, instead of a philosopher? Except, indeed, that instead of Homer I interpret Chrysippus. When anyone, therefore, desires me to read Chrysippus to him, I rather blush, when I cannot exhibit actions that are harmonious and consonant with his discourse.

L

Whatever rules you have adopted, abide by them as laws, and as if you would be impious to transgress them; and do not regard what any one says of you, for this, after all, is no concern of yours. How long, then, will you delay to demand of yourself the noblest improvements, and in no instance to transgress the judgments of reason? You have received the philosophic principles with which you ought to be conversant; and you have been conversant with them. For what other master, then, do you wait as an excuse for this delay in self-reformation? You are no longer a boy, but a grown man. If, therefore, you will be negligent and slothful, and always add procrastination to procrastination, purpose to purpose, and fix day after day in which you will attend to yourself, you will insensibly continue to accomplish nothing, and, living and dying, remain of vulgar mind. This instant, then, think yourself worthy of living as a man grown up and a proficient. Let whatever appears to be the best, be to you an inviolable law. And if any instance of pain or pleasure, glory or disgrace, be set before you, remember that now is the combat, now the Olympiad comes on, nor can it be put off; and that by one failure and defeat honour may be lost—or won. Thus Socrates became perfect, improving himself by everything, following reason alone. And though you are not yet a Socrates, you ought, however, to live as one seeking to be a Socrates.

LI

The first and most necessary topic in philosophy is the practical application of principles, such as, "We ought not to lie." The second topic is that of demonstrations, such as, "Why it is that we ought not to lie?" The third, that which gives strength and logical connection to the other two, for instance, "Why is this a demonstration? For what is demonstration? What is a consequence? What is a contradiction? What is truth? What is falsehood?" The third point is then necessary on account of the second, and the second on account of the first. But the most necessary, and that whereon we ought to rest, is the first. But we do just the contrary. For we spend all our time on the third point, and employ all our diligence about that, and entirely neglect the first. Therefore, at the same time that we lie, we are very ready to show how it is demonstrated that lying is wrong.

LII

Upon all occasions we ought to have these maxims ready at hand:

> Conduct me, Jove, and you, O Destiny,
> Wherever your decrees have fixed my station.
> I follow cheerfully; and, did I not,
> Wicked and wretched, I must follow still.
> —Cleanthes

> Whoe'er yields properly to Fate is deemed
> Wise among men, and knows the laws of Heaven.
> —Euripides

And this third:

> O Crito, if it thus pleases the gods, thus let it be. Anytus and Melitus may kill me indeed, but hurt me they cannot.
> —Plato

from
TUSCULAN DISPUTATIONS

by

CICERO

Book Five

Whether Virtue Alone Be Sufficient for a Happy Life

I

This fifth day, Brutus, shall put an end to our *Tusculan Disputations*—on which day we discussed your favourite subject. For I perceive from that book which you wrote for me with the greatest accuracy, as well as from your frequent conversation, that you are clearly of this opinion, that virtue is of itself sufficient for a happy life: and though it may be difficult to prove this, on account of the many various strokes of fortune, yet it is a truth of such a nature that we should endeavour to facilitate the proof of it. For among all the topics of philosophy, there is not one of more dignity or importance. For as the first philosophers must have had some inducement to neglect everything for the search of the best state of life, surely, the inducement must have been the hope of living happily, which impelled them to devote so much care and pains to that study. Now, if virtue was discovered and carried to perfection by them, and if virtue is a sufficient security for a happy life, who can avoid thinking the work of philosophizing excellently recommended by them, and undertaken by me? But if virtue, as being subject to such various and uncertain accidents, were but the slave of fortune, and were not of sufficient ability to support herself, I am afraid that it would seem desirable rather to offer up prayers, than to rely on our own confidence in virtue as the foundation for our hope of a happy life. And, indeed, when I reflect on those troubles with which I have been so severely exercised by fortune, I begin to distrust this opinion; and sometimes even to dread the weakness and frailty of human nature, for I am afraid lest, when nature had given us infirm bodies, and had joined to them incurable diseases and intolerable pains, she perhaps also gave us minds participating in these bodily pains, and harassed also with troubles and uneasinesses peculiarly their own. But here I correct myself for forming my judgment of the power of virtue more from the weakness of others, or of myself perhaps, than from virtue itself: for she herself (provided there is such a thing as virtue—and your uncle, Brutus, has removed all doubt of it) has everything that can befall mankind in subjection to her; and by disregarding such things, she is far removed from being at all concerned at human accidents; and, being free from every imperfection, she thinks that nothing which is external to herself can concern her. But we, who increase every approaching evil by our fear, and every present one by our grief, choose rather to condemn the nature of things than our own errors.

II

But the amendment of this fault, and of all our other vices and offences, is to be sought for in philosophy: and as my own inclination and desire led me, from my earliest youth upward, to seek her protection, so, under my present misfortunes, I have had recourse to the same port from whence I set out, after having been tossed by a violent tempest. O Philosophy, thou guide of life!—thou discoverer of virtue and expeller of vices!—what had not only I myself, but the whole life of man, been without you? To you it is that we owe the origin of cities; you it was who called together the dispersed race of men into social life; you united them together, first, by placing them near one another, then by marriages, and lastly, by the communication of speech and languages. You have been the inventress of laws; you have been our instructress in morals and discipline; to you we fly for refuge; from you we implore assistance; and as I formerly submitted to you in a great degree, so now I surrender up myself entirely to you. For one day spent well, and agreeably to your precepts, is preferable to an eternity of error. Whose assistance, then, can be of more service to me than yours, when you have bestowed on us tranquillity of life, and removed the fear of death? But Philosophy is so far from being praised as much as she has deserved by mankind, that she is wholly neglected by most men, and is actually spoken evil of by many. Can any person speak ill of the parent of life, and dare to pollute himself thus with parricide, and be so impiously ungrateful as to accuse her whom he ought to reverence, even were he less able to appreciate the advantages which he might derive from her? But this error, I imagine, and this darkness has spread itself over the minds of ignorant men, from their not being able to look so far back, and from their not imagining that those men by whom human life was first improved were philosophers; for though we see philosophy to have been of long standing, yet the name must be acknowledged to be but modern.

III

But, indeed, who can dispute the antiquity of philosophy, either in fact or name? For it acquired this excellent name from the ancients, by the knowledge of the origin and causes of everything, both divine and human. Thus those seven sages, as they were considered and called by the Greeks, have always been esteemed and called wise men by us; and thus Lycurgus many ages before, in whose time, before the building of this city, Homer is said to have lived, as well as Ulysses and Nestor in the heroic ages, are all handed down to us by tradition as having really been what they were called: wise men. Nor would it have been said that Atlas supported the heavens, or that Prometheus was bound to Caucasus, nor would Cepheus, with his wife, his son-in-law, and his daughter have been enrolled among the constellations, but that their more than human knowledge of the heavenly bodies had transferred their names into an erroneous fable. From whence all who occupied themselves in the contemplation of nature were both considered and called wise men; and that name of theirs continued to the age of Pythagoras, who is reported to have gone to Phlius, as we find it stated by Heraclides Ponticus, a very learned man, and a pupil of Plato, and to have discoursed very learnedly and copiously on certain subjects with Leon, prince of the Phliasii; and when Leon, admiring his ingenuity and eloquence, asked him what art he particularly professed, his answer was, that he was acquainted with no art, but that he was a philosopher. Leon, surprised at the novelty of the name, inquired what he meant by the name of philosopher, and in what philosophers differed from other men; to which Pythagoras replied, "That the life of man seemed to him to resemble those games which were celebrated with the greatest possible variety of sports and the general concourse of all Greece. For as in those games there were some persons whose object was glory and the honour of a crown, to be attained by the performance of bodily exercises, so others were led thither by the gain of buying and selling, and mere views of profit; but there was likewise one class of persons, and they were by far the best, whose aim was neither applause nor profit, but who came merely as spectators through curiosity, to observe what was done, and to see in what manner things were carried on there. And thus," said he, "we come from another life and nature unto this one, just as men come out of some other city to some much frequented mart, some being slaves to glory, others to money; and there are some few who, taking no account of anything else, earnestly look into the nature of things; and these men call themselves studious of wisdom, that is, philosophers: and as there it is the most reputable occupation of all to be a looker-on without making any acquisition, so in life, the contemplating things, and acquainting one's self with them, greatly exceeds every other pursuit of life."

IV

Nor was Pythagoras the inventor only of the name, but he enlarged also the thing itself, and, when he came into Italy after this conversation at Phlius, he adorned that Greece, which is called Great Greece, both privately and publicly, with the most excellent institutions and arts; but of his school and system I shall, perhaps, find another opportunity to speak. But numbers and motions, and the beginning and end of all things, were the subjects of the ancient philosophy down to Socrates, who was a pupil of Archelaus, who had been the disciple of Anaxagoras. These made diligent inquiry into the magnitude of the stars, their distances, courses, and all that relates to the heavens. But Socrates was the first who brought down philosophy from the heavens, placed it in cities, introduced it into families, and obliged it to examine into life and morals, and good and evil. And his different methods of discussing questions, together with the variety of his topics, and the greatness of his abilities, being immortalized by the memory and writings of Plato, gave rise to many sects of philosophers of different sentiments, of all which I have principally adhered to that one which, in my opinion, Socrates himself followed; and argue so as to conceal my own opinion, while I deliver others from their errors, and so discover what has the greatest appearance of probability in every question. And the custom Carneades adopted with great copiousness and acuteness, and I myself have often given in to it on many occasions elsewhere, and in this manner, too, I disputed lately, in my Tusculan villa; indeed, I have sent you a book of the four former days' discussions; but the fifth day, when we had seated ourselves as before, what we were to dispute on was proposed thus:

V

A[1]: I do not think virtue can possibly be sufficient for a happy life.

M[2]: But my friend Brutus thinks so, whose judgment, with submission, I greatly prefer to yours.

A: I make no doubt of it; but your regard for him is not the business now: the question is now, what is the real character of that quality of which I have declared my opinion. I wish you to dispute on that.

M: What!—do you deny that virtue can possibly be sufficient for a happy life?

A: It is what I entirely deny.

M: What!—is not virtue sufficient to enable us to live as we ought, honestly, commendably, or, in fine, to live well?

A: Certainly sufficient.

M: Can you, then, help calling anyone miserable who lives ill?—or will you deny that anyone who you admit lives well must inevitably live happily?

A: Why may I not? For a man may be upright in his life, honest, praiseworthy, even in the midst of torments, and therefore live well. Provided you understand what I mean by well; for when I say well, I mean with constancy, and dignity, and wisdom, and courage; for a man may display all these qualities on the rack; but yet the rack is inconsistent with a happy life.

M: What, then? Is your happy life left on the outside of the

---

[1] One of Cicero's students, who proposes the subject for discussion.
[2] Cicero (Marcus Tullius Cicero)

prison, while constancy, dignity, wisdom, and the other virtues, are surrendered up to the executioner, and bear punishment and pain without reluctance?

A: You must look out for something new if you would do any good. These things have very little effect on me, not merely from their being common, but principally because, like certain light wines that will not bear water, these arguments of the Stoics are pleasanter to taste than to swallow. As when that assemblage of virtues is committed to the rack, it raises so reverend a spectacle before our eyes that happiness seems to hasten on towards them, and not to suffer them to be deserted by her. But when you take your attention off from this picture and these images of the virtues to the truth and the reality, what remains without disguise is the question—*can anyone be happy in torment?* Wherefore let us now examine that point, and not be under any apprehensions, lest the virtues should expostulate, and complain that they are forsaken by happiness. For if prudence is connected with every virtue, then prudence itself discovers this, that all good men are not therefore happy; and she recollects many things of Marcus Atilius, Quintus Caepio, Marcus Aquilius; and prudence herself, if these representations are more agreeable to you than the things themselves, restrains happiness when it is endeavouring to throw itself into torments, and denies that it has any connection with pain and torture.

VI

M: I can easily bear with your behaving in this manner, though it is not fair in you to prescribe to me how you would have me carry on this discussion. But I ask you if I have effected anything or nothing in the preceding days?

A: Yes; something was done, some little matter indeed.

M: But if that is the case, this question is settled, and almost put an end to.

A: How so?

M: Because turbulent motions and violent agitations of the mind, when it is raised and elated by a rash impulse, getting the better of reason, leave no room for a happy life. For who that fears either pain or death, the one of which is always present, the other always impending, can be otherwise than miserable? Now, supposing the same person—which is often the case—to be afraid of poverty, ignominy, infamy, or weakness, or blindness, or, lastly, slavery, which does not only befall individual men, but often even the most powerful nations— now can anyone under the apprehension of these evils be happy? What shall we say of him who not only dreads these evils as impending, but actually feels and bears them at present? Let us unite in the same person banishment, mourning, the loss of children—now, how can anyone who is broken down and rendered sick in body and mind by such afflictions be otherwise than very miserable indeed? What reason, again, can there be why a man should not rightly enough be called miserable whom we see inflamed and raging with lust, coveting everything with an insatiable desire, and, in proportion as he derives more pleasure from anything, thirsting the more violently after them? And as to a man vainly elated, exulting with an empty joy, and boasting of himself without reason, is not he so much the more miserable in proportion as he thinks himself happier? Therefore, as these men are miserable, so, on the other hand, those are happy who are alarmed by no fears, wasted by no griefs, provoked by no lusts, melted by no languid pleasures that arise from vain and exulting joys. We look on the sea as calm when not the least breath of air disturbs its waves; and, in like manner, the placid and quiet state of the mind is discovered when unmoved by any perturbation. Now, if there be any one who holds the power of fortune, and everything human, everything that can possibly befall any man, as supportable, so as to be out of the reach of fear or anxiety, and if such a man covets nothing, and is lifted up by no vain joy of mind, what can prevent his being happy? And if these are the effects of virtue, why cannot virtue itself make men happy?

VII

A: But the other of these two propositions is undeniable, that they who are under no apprehensions, who are in no way uneasy, who covet nothing, who are lifted up by no vain joy, are happy: and therefore I grant you that. But as for the other, that is not now in a fit state for discussion; for it has been proved by your former arguments that a wise man is free from every perturbation of mind.

M: Doubtless, then, the dispute is over; for the question appears to have been entirely exhausted.

A: I think, indeed, that that is almost the case.

M: But yet that is more usually the case with the mathematicians than philosophers. For when the geometricians teach anything, if what they have before taught relates to their present subject, they take that for granted which has been already proved, and explain only what they had not written on before. But the philosophers, whatever subject they have in hand, get together everything that relates to it, notwithstanding they may have dilated on it somewhere else. Were not that the case, why should the Stoics say so much on that question—Whether virtue was abundantly sufficient to a happy life?—when it would have been answer enough that they had before taught that nothing was good but what was honourable; for, as this had been proved, the consequence must be that virtue was sufficient to a happy life; and each premise may be made to follow from the admission of the other, so that if it be admitted that virtue is sufficient to secure a happy life, it may also be inferred that nothing is good except what is honourable. They, however, do not proceed in this manner; for they would separate books about what is honourable, and what is the chief good; and when they have demonstrated from the one that virtue has power enough to make life happy, yet they treat this point separately; for everything, and especially a subject of such great consequence, should be supported by arguments and exhortations which belong to that alone. For you should have a care how you imagine philosophy to have uttered anything more noble, or that she has promised anything more fruitful or of greater consequence, for, good Gods!—does she not engage that she will render him who submits to her laws so accomplished as to be always armed against fortune, and to have every assurance within himself of living well and happily—that he shall, in short, be forever happy? But let us see what she will perform? In the meanwhile, I look upon it as a great thing that she has even made such a promise. For Xerxes, who was loaded with all the rewards and gifts of fortune, not satisfied with his armies of horse and foot, nor the multitude of his ships, nor his infinite treasure of gold, offered a reward to anyone who could find out a new pleasure; and yet, when it was discovered, he was not satisfied with it; nor can there ever be an end to lust. I wish we could engage anyone by a reward to produce something the better to establish us in this belief.

VIII

A: I wish that, indeed, myself; but I want a little information. For I allow that in what you have stated the one proposition is the consequence of the other; that as, if what is honourable be the only good, it must follow that a happy life is the effect of virtue: so that if a happy life consists in virtue, nothing can be good but virtue. But your friend Brutus, on the authority of Aristo and Antiochus, does not see this; for he thinks the case would be the same even if there were anything good besides virtue.

M: What, then?—do you imagine that I am going to argue against Brutus?

A: You may do what you please; for it is not for me to prescribe what you shall do.

M: How these things agree together shall be examined somewhere else; for I frequently discussed that point with Antiochus, and lately with Aristo, when, during the period of my command as general, I was lodging with him at Athens. For to me it seemed that no one could possibly be happy under any evil; but a wise man might be afflicted with evil, if there are any things arising from body or fortune deserving the name of evils. These things were said, which Antiochus has inserted in his books in many places—that virtue itself was sufficient to make life happy, but yet not perfectly happy; and that many things derive their names from the predominant portion of them, though they do not include everything, as strength, health, riches, honour, and glory: which qualities are determined by their kind, not their number. Thus a happy life is so called from its being so in a great degree, even though it should fall short in some point. To clear this up is not absolutely necessary at present, though it seems to be said without any great consistency; for I cannot imagine what is wanting to one that is happy to make him happier, for if anything be wanting to him, he cannot be so much as happy; and as to what they say, that everything is named and estimated from its predominant portion, that may be admitted in some things. But when they allow three kinds of evils—when any one is oppressed with every imaginable evil of two kinds, being afflicted with adverse fortune, and having at the same time his body worn out and harassed with all sorts of pains—shall we say that such a one is but little short of a happy life, to say nothing about the happiest possible life?

IX

This is the point which Theophrastus was unable to maintain; for after he had once laid down the position that stripes, torments, tortures, the ruin of one's country, banishment, the loss of children, had great influence on men's living miserably and unhappily, he dared not any longer use any high and lofty expressions when he was so low and abject in his opinion. How right he was is not the question; he certainly was consistent. Therefore, I am not for objecting to consequences where the premises are admitted. But this most elegant and learned of all the philosophers is not taken to task very severely when he asserts his three kinds of good; but he is attacked by everyone for that book which he wrote on a happy life, in which book he has many arguments why one who is tortured and racked cannot be happy. For in that book he is supposed to say that a man who is placed on the wheel (that is a kind of torture in use among the Greeks) cannot attain to a completely happy life. He nowhere, indeed, says so absolutely; but what he says amounts to the same thing. Can I, then, find fault with him, after having allowed that pains of the body are evils, that the ruin of a man's fortunes is an evil, if he should say that every good man is not happy, when all those things which he reckons as evils may befall a good man? The same Theophrastus is found fault with by all the books and schools of the philosophers for commending that sentence in his Callisthenes,

Fortune, not wisdom, rules the life of man.

They say never did philosopher assert anything so languid. They are right, indeed, in that; but I do not apprehend anything could be more consistent, for if there are so many good things that depend on the body, and so many foreign to it that depend on chance and fortune, is it inconsistent to say that fortune, which governs everything, both what is foreign and what belongs to the body, has greater power than counsel? Or would we rather imitate Epicurus, who is often excellent in many things which he speaks, but quite indifferent how consistent he may be, or how much to the purpose he is speaking? He commends spare diet, and in that he speaks as a philosopher; but it is for Socrates or Antisthenes to say so, and not for one who confines all good to pleasure. He denies that anyone can live pleasantly unless he lives honestly, wisely, and justly. Nothing is more dignified than this assertion, nothing more becoming a philosopher, had he not measured this very expression of living honestly, justly, and wisely by pleasure. What could be better than to assert that fortune interferes but little with a wise man? But does he talk thus, who, after he has said that pain is the greatest evil, or the only evil, might himself be afflicted with the sharpest pains all over his body, even at the time he is vaunting himself the most against fortune? And this very thing, too, Metrodorus has said, but in better language: "I have anticipated you, Fortune; I have caught you, and cut off every access, so that you cannot possibly reach me." This would be excellent in the mouth of Aristo the Chian, or Zeno the Stoic, who held nothing to be an evil but what was base; but for you, Metrodorus, to anticipate the approaches of fortune, who confine all that is good to your bowels and marrow—for you to say so, who define the chief good by a strong constitution of body, and well-assured hope of its continuance—for you to cut off every access of fortune! Why, you may instantly be deprived of that good. Yet the simple are taken with these propositions, and a vast crowd is led away by such sentences to become their followers.

X

But it is the duty of one who would argue accurately to consider not what is said, but what is said consistently. As in that very opinion which we have adopted in this discussion, namely, that every good man is always happy, it is clear what I mean by good men: I call those both wise and good men who are provided and adorned with every virtue. Let us see, then, who are to be called happy. I imagine, indeed, that those men are to be called so who are possessed of good without any alloy of evil; nor is there any other notion connected with the word that expresses happiness but an absolute enjoyment of good without any evil. Virtue cannot attain this if there is anything good besides itself. For a crowd of evils would present themselves, if we were to allow poverty, obscurity, humility, solitude, the loss of friends, acute pains of the body, the loss of health, weakness, blindness, the ruin of one's country, banishment, slavery, to be evils; for a wise man may be afflicted by all these evils, numerous and important as they are, and many others also may be added, for they are brought on by chance, which may attack a wise man; but if these things are evils, who can maintain that a wise man is always happy when all these evils may light on him at the same time? I therefore do not easily agree with my friend Brutus, nor with our common masters, nor those ancient ones, Aristotle, Speusippus, Xenocrates, Polemon, who reckon all that I have mentioned above as evils, and yet they say that a wise man is always happy; nor can I allow them, because they are charmed with this beautiful and illustrious title of philosopher, which would very well become Pythagoras, Socrates, and Plato, to persuade my mind that strength, health, beauty, riches, honours, power, with the beauty of which they are ravished, are contemptible, and that all those things which are the opposites of these are not to be regarded. Then might they declare openly, with a loud voice, that neither the attacks of fortune, nor the opinion of the multitude, nor pain, nor poverty, occasions them any apprehensions; and that they have everything within themselves, and that there is nothing whatever which they consider as good but what is within their own power. Nor can I by any means allow the same person who falls into the vulgar opinion of good and evil to make use of these expressions, which can only become a great and exalted man. Struck with which glory, up starts Epicurus, who, with submission to the Gods, thinks a wise man always happy. He is much charmed with the dignity of this opinion, but he never would have owned that, had he attended to himself; for what is there more inconsistent than for one who could say that pain was the greatest or the only evil to think also that a wise man can possibly say in the midst of his torture, "How sweet is this!" We are not, therefore, to form our judgment of philosophers from detached sentences, but from their consistency with themselves, and their ordinary manner of talking.

XI

A: You compel me to be of your opinion; but have a care that you are not inconsistent yourself.

M: In what respect?

A: Because I have lately read your fourth book on Good and Evil: and in that you appeared to me, while disputing against Cato, to be endeavouring to show, which in my opinion means to prove, that Zeno and the Peripatetics differ only about some new words; but if we allow that, what reason can there be, if it follows from the arguments of Zeno that virtue contains all that is necessary to a happy life, that the Peripatetics should not be at liberty to say the same? For, in my opinion, regard should be had to the thing, not to words.

M: What!—you would convict me with my own words, and bring against me what I had said or written elsewhere. You may act in that manner with those who dispute by established rules. We live from hand to mouth, and say anything that strikes our mind with probability, so that we are the only people who are really at liberty. But, since I just now spoke of consistency, I do not think the inquiry in this place is consistent, if the opinion of Zeno and his pupil Aristo be true that nothing is good but what is honourable; but, admitting that, then, whether the whole of a happy life can be rested on virtue alone. Wherefore, if we certainly grant Brutus this, that a wise man is always happy, how consistent he is is his own business; for who, indeed, is more worthy than himself of the glory of that opinion? Still, we may maintain that such a man is more happy than anyone else.

XII

Though Zeno the Cittiaean, a stranger and an inconsiderable coiner of words, appears to have insinuated himself into the old philosophy; still, the prevalence of this opinion is due to the authority of Plato, who often makes use of this expression, "That nothing but virtue can be entitled to the name of good," agreeably to what Socrates says in Plato's Gorgias; for it is there related that when someone asked him if he did not think Archelaus the son of Perdiccas, who was then looked upon as a most fortunate person, a very happy man, "I do not know," replied he, "for I never conversed with him." "What!—is there no other way you can know it by?" "None at all." "You cannot, then, pronounce of the great king of the Persians whether he is happy or not?" "How can I, when I do not know how learned or how good a man he is?" "What!—do you imagine that a happy life depends on that?" "My opinion entirely is, that good men are happy, and the wicked miserable." "Is Archelaus, then, miserable?" "Certainly, if unjust." Now, does it not appear to you that he is here placing the whole of a happy life in virtue alone? But what does the same man say in his funeral oration? "For," says he, "whoever has everything that relates to a happy life so entirely dependent on himself as not to be connected with the good or bad fortune of another, and not to be affected by, or made in any degree uncertain by, what befalls another; and whoever is such a one has acquired the best rule of living; he is that moderate, that brave, that wise man, who submits to the gain and loss of everything, and especially of his children, and obeys that old precept: he will never be too joyful or too sad, because he depends entirely upon himself."

XIII

From Plato, therefore, all my discourse shall be deduced, as if from some sacred and hallowed fountain. Whence can I, then, more properly begin than from Nature, the parent of all? For whatever she produces (I am not speaking only of animals, but even of those things which have sprung from the earth in such a manner as to rest on their own roots) she designed it to be perfect in its respective kind. So that among trees and vines, and those lower plants and trees which cannot advance themselves high above the earth, some are evergreen, others are stripped of their leaves in winter, and, warmed by the spring season, put them out afresh, and there are none of them but what are so quickened by a certain interior motion, and their own seeds enclosed in every one, so as to yield flowers, fruit, or berries, that all may have every perfection that belongs to it—provided no violence prevents it. But the force of Nature itself may be more easily discovered in animals, as she has bestowed sense on them. For some animals she has taught to swim, and designed to be inhabitants of the water; others she has enabled to fly, and has willed that they should enjoy the boundless air; some others she has made to creep, others to walk. Again, of these very animals, some are solitary, some gregarious, some wild, others tame, some hidden and buried beneath the earth, and every one of these maintains the law of nature, confining itself to what was bestowed on it, and unable to change its manner of life. And as every animal has from nature something that distinguishes it, which every one maintains and never quits, so man has something far more excellent, though everything is said to be excellent by comparison. But the human mind, being derived from the divine reason, can be compared with nothing but with the Deity itself, if I may be allowed the expression. This, then, if it is improved, and when its perception is so preserved as not to be blinded by errors, becomes a perfect understanding, that is to say, absolute reason, which is the very same as virtue. And if everything is happy which wants nothing, and is complete and perfect in its kind, and that is the peculiar lot of virtue, certainly all who are possessed of virtue are happy. And in this I agree with Brutus, and also with Aristotle, Xenocrates, Speusippus, Polemon.

XIV

To me such are the only men who appear completely happy; for what can he want to a complete happy life who relies on his own good qualities, or how can he be happy who does not rely on them? But he who makes a threefold division of goods must necessarily be diffident, for how can he depend on having a sound body, or that his fortune shall continue? But no one can be happy without an immovable, fixed, and permanent good. What, then, is this opinion of theirs? So that I think that saying of the Spartan may be applied to them, who, on some merchant's boasting before him that he had despatched ships to every maritime coast, replied that a fortune which depended on ropes was not very desirable. Can there be any doubt that whatever may be lost cannot be properly classed in the number of those things which complete a happy life? For of all that constitutes a happy life, nothing will admit of withering, or growing old, or wearing out, or decaying; for whoever is apprehensive of any loss of these things cannot be happy: the happy man should be safe, well fenced, well fortified, out of the reach of all annoyance, not like a man under trifling apprehensions, but free from all such. As he is not called innocent who but slightly offends, but he who offends not at all, so it is he alone who is to be considered without fear who is free from all fear, not he who is but in little fear. For what else is courage but an affection of mind that is ready to undergo perils, and patient in the endurance of pain and labour without any alloy of fear? Now, this certainly could not be the case if there were anything else good but what depended on honesty alone. But how can anyone be in possession of that desirable and much-coveted security (for I now call a freedom from anxiety a security, on which freedom a happy life depends) who has, or may have, a multitude of evils attending him? How can he be brave and undaunted, and hold everything as trifles which can befall a man?—for so a wise man should do, unless he be one who thinks that everything depends on himself. Could the Lacedaemonians without this, when Philip threatened to prevent all their attempts, have asked him if he could prevent their killing themselves? Is it not easier, then, to find one man of such a spirit as we are inquiring after, than to meet with a whole city of such men? Now, if to this courage I am speaking of we add temperance, that it may govern all our feelings and agitations, what can be wanting to complete his happiness who is secured by his courage from uneasiness and fear, and is prevented from immoderate desires and immoderate insolence of joy by temperance? I could easily show that virtue is able to produce these effects, but that I have explained on the foregoing days.

XV

But as the perturbations of the mind make life miserable, and tranquillity renders it happy; and as these perturbations are of two sorts, grief and fear, proceeding from imagined evils, and as immoderate joy and lust arise from a mistake about what is good, and as all these feelings are in opposition to reason and counsel; when you see a man at ease, quite free and disengaged from such troublesome commotions, which are so much at variance with one another, can you hesitate to pronounce such a one a happy man? Now, the wise man is always in such a disposition; therefore the wise man is always happy. Besides, every good is pleasant; whatever is pleasant may be boasted and talked of; whatever may be boasted of is glorious; but whatever is glorious is certainly laudable, and whatever is laudable doubtless, also, honourable: whatever, then, is good is honourable (but the things which they reckon as goods they themselves do not call honourable); therefore what is honourable alone is good. Hence it follows that a happy life is comprised in honesty alone. Such things, then, are not to be called or considered goods when a man may enjoy an abundance of them and yet be most miserable. Is there any doubt but that a man who enjoys the best health, and who has strength and beauty, and his senses flourishing in their utmost quickness and perfection—suppose him likewise, if you please, nimble and active, nay, give him riches, honours, authority, power, glory—now, I say, should this person, who is in possession of all these, be unjust, intemperate, timid, stupid, or an idiot—could you hesitate to call such a one miserable? What, then, are those goods in the possession of which you may be very miserable? Let us see if a happy life is not made up of parts of the same nature, as a heap implies a quantity of grain of the same kind. And if this be once admitted, happiness must be compounded of different good things, which alone are honourable; if there is any mixture of things of another sort with these, nothing honourable can proceed from such a composition: now, take away honesty, and how can you imagine anything happy? For whatever is good is desirable on that account; whatever is desirable must certainly be approved of; whatever you approve of must be looked on as acceptable and welcome. You must consequently impute dignity to this; and if so, it must necessarily be laudable: therefore, everything that is laudable is good. Hence it follows that what is honourable is the only good. And should we not look upon it in this light, there will be a great many things which we must call good.

XVI

I forbear to mention riches, which, as anyone, let him be ever so unworthy, may have them, I do not reckon among goods; for what is good is not attainable by all. I pass over notoriety and popular fame, raised by the united voice of knaves and fools. Even things which are absolute nothings may be called goods; such as white teeth, handsome eyes, a good complexion, and what was commended by Euryclea, when she was washing Ulysses's feet, the softness of his skin and the mildness of his discourse. If you look on these as goods, what greater encomiums can the gravity of a philosopher be entitled to than the wild opinion of the vulgar and the thoughtless crowd? The Stoics give the name of excellent and choice to what the others call good: they call them so, indeed; but they do not allow them to complete a happy life. But these others think that there is no life happy without them; or, admitting it to be happy, they deny it to be the most happy. But our opinion is that it is the most happy, and we prove it from that conclusion of Socrates. For thus that author of philosophy argued: that as the disposition of a man's mind is, so is the man; such as the man is, such will be his discourse; his actions will correspond with his discourse, and his life with his actions. But the disposition of a good man's mind is laudable; the life, therefore, of a good man is laudable; it is honourable, therefore, because laudable; the unavoidable conclusion from which is that the life of good men is happy.

For, good Gods!—did I not make it appear by my former arguments—or was I only amusing myself and killing time in what I then said?—that the mind of a wise man was always free from every hasty motion which I call a perturbation, and that the most undisturbed peace always reigned in his breast? A man, then, who is temperate and consistent, free from fear or grief, and uninfluenced by any immoderate joy or desire, cannot be otherwise than happy; but a wise man is always so, therefore he is always happy. Moreover, how can a good man avoid referring all his actions and all his feelings to the one standard of whether or not it is laudable? But he does refer everything to the object of living happily: it follows, then, that a happy life is laudable; but nothing is laudable without virtue: a happy life, then, is the consequence of virtue. And this is the unavoidable conclusion to be drawn from these arguments.

XVII

A wicked life has nothing which we ought to speak of or glory in; nor has that life which is neither happy nor miserable. But there is a kind of life that admits of being spoken of, and gloried in, and boasted of, as Epaminondas says,

> The wings of Sparta's pride my counsels
> clipp'd.

And Africanus boasts,

> Who, from beyond Maeotis to the place
> Where the sun rises, deeds like mine can
> trace?

If, then, there is such a thing as a happy life, it is to be gloried in, spoken of, and commended by the person who enjoys it; for there is nothing excepting that which can be spoken of or gloried in; and when that is once admitted, you know what follows. Now, unless an honourable life is a happy life, there must, of course, be something preferable to a happy life; for that which is honourable all men will certainly grant to be preferable to anything else. And thus there will be something better than a happy life: but what can be more absurd than such an assertion? What!—when they grant vice to be effectual to the rendering life miserable, must they not admit that there is a corresponding power in virtue to make life happy? For contraries follow from contraries. And here I ask what weight they think there is in the balance of Critolaus, who having put the goods of the mind into one scale, and the goods of the body and other external advantages into the other, thought the goods of the mind outweighed the others so far that they would require the whole earth and sea to equalize the scale.

XVIII

What hinders Critolaus, then, or that gravest of philosophers, Xenocrates (who raises virtue so high, and who lessens and depreciates everything else), from not only placing a happy life, but the happiest possible life, in virtue? And, indeed, if this were not the case, virtue would be absolutely lost. For whoever is subject to grief must necessarily be subject to fear too, for fear is an uneasy apprehension of future grief; and whoever is subject to fear is liable to dread, timidity, consternation, cowardice. Therefore, such a person may, some time or other, be defeated, and not think himself concerned with that precept of Atreus,

> And let men so conduct themselves in life,
> As to be always strangers to defeat.

But such a man, as I have said, will be defeated; and not only defeated, but made a slave of. But we would have virtue always free, always invincible; and were it not so, there would be an end of virtue. But if virtue has in herself all that is necessary for a good life, she is certainly sufficient for happiness: virtue is certainly sufficient, too, for our living with courage; if with courage, then with a magnanimous spirit, and indeed so as never to be under any fear, and thus to be always invincible. Hence it follows that there can be nothing to be repented of, no wants, no lets or hindrances. Thus all things will be prosperous, perfect, and as you would have them, and, consequently, happy; but virtue is sufficient for living with courage, and therefore virtue is able by herself to make life happy. For as folly, even when possessed of what it desires, never thinks it has acquired enough, so wisdom is always satisfied with the present, and never repents on her own account.

XIX

Look but on the single consulship of Laelius, and that, too, after having been set aside (though when a wise and good man like him is outvoted, the people are disappointed of a good consul, rather than be disappointed by a vain people); but the point is, would you prefer, were it in your power, to be once such a consul as Laelius, or be elected four times, like Cinna? I have no doubt in the world what answer you will make, and it is on that account I put the question to you.

I would not ask everyone this question; for someone perhaps might answer that he would not only prefer four consulates to one, but even one day of Cinna's life to whole ages of many famous men. Laelius would have suffered had he but touched anyone with his finger; but Cinna ordered the head of his colleague consul, Cn. Octavius, to be struck off; and put to death P. Crassus, and L. Caesar, those excellent men, so renowned both at home and abroad; and even M. Antonius, the greatest orator whom I ever heard; and C. Caesar, who seems to me to have been the pattern of humanity, politeness, sweetness of temper, and wit. Could he, then, be happy who occasioned the death of these men? So far from it, that he seems to be miserable, not only for having performed these actions, but also for acting in such a manner that it was lawful for him to do it, though it is unlawful for anyone to do wicked actions; but this proceeds from inaccuracy, of speech, for we call whatever a man is allowed to do lawful. Was not Marius happier, I pray you, when he shared the glory of the victory gained over the Cimbrians with his colleague Catulus (who was almost another Laelius; for I look upon the two men as very like one another), than when, conqueror in the civil war, he in a passion answered the friends of Catulus, who were interceding for him, "Let him die?" And this answer he gave, not once only, but often. But in such a case, he was happier who submitted to that barbarous decree than he who issued it. And it is better to receive an injury than to do one; and so it was better to advance a little to meet that death that was making its approaches, as Catulus did, than, like Marius, to sully the glory of six consulships, and disgrace his latter days, by the death of such a man.

XX

Dionysius exercised his tyranny over the Syracusans for thirty-eight years, being but twenty-five years old when he seized on the government. How beautiful and how wealthy a city did he oppress with slavery! And yet we have it from good authority that he was remarkably temperate in his manner of living, that he was very active and energetic in carrying on business, but naturally mischievous and unjust; from which description every one who diligently inquires into truth must inevitably see that he was very miserable. Neither did he attain what he so greatly desired, even when he was persuaded that he had unlimited power; for, notwithstanding he was of a good family and reputable parents (though that is contested by some authors), and had a very large acquaintance of intimate friends and relations, and also some youths attached to him by ties of love after the fashion of the Greeks, he could not trust any one of them, but committed the guard of his person to slaves, whom he had selected from rich men's families and made free, and to strangers and barbarians. And thus, through an unjust desire of governing, he in a manner shut himself up in a prison. Besides, he would not trust his throat to a barber, but had his daughters taught to shave; so that these royal virgins were forced to descend to the base and slavish employment of shaving the head and beard of their father. Nor would he trust even them, when they were grown up, with a razor; but contrived how they might burn off the hair of his head and beard with red-hot nutshells. And as to his two wives, Aristomache, his countrywoman, and Doris of Locris, he never visited them at night before everything had been well searched and examined. And as he had surrounded the place where his bed was with a broad ditch, and made a way over it with a wooden bridge, he drew that bridge over after shutting his bedchamber door. And as he did not dare to stand on the ordinary pulpits from which they usually harangued the people, he generally addressed them from a high tower. And it is said that when he was disposed to play at ball—for he delighted much in it—and had pulled off his clothes, he used to give his sword into the keeping of a young man whom he was very fond of. On this, one of his intimates said pleasantly, "You certainly trust your life with him;" and as the young man happened to smile at this, he ordered them both to be slain, the one for showing how he might be taken off, the other for approving of what had been said by smiling. But he was so concerned at what he had done that nothing affected him more during his whole life; for he had slain one to whom he was extremely partial. Thus do weak men's desires pull them different ways, and while they indulge one, they act counter to another.

XXI

This tyrant, however, showed himself how happy he really was; for once, when Damocles, one of his flatterers, was dilating in conversation on his forces, his wealth, the greatness of his power, the plenty he enjoyed, the grandeur of his royal palaces, and maintaining that no one was ever happier, Dionysus said, "Have you an inclination, Damocles, as this kind of life pleases you, to have a taste of it yourself, and to make a trial of the good fortune that attends me?" And when he said that he should like it extremely, Dionysius ordered him to be laid on a bed of gold with the most beautiful covering, embroidered and wrought with the most exquisite work, and he dressed out a great many sideboards with silver and embossed gold. He then ordered some youths, distinguished for their handsome persons, to wait at his table, and to observe his nod, in order to serve him with what he wanted. There were ointments and garlands; perfumes were burned; tables provided with the most exquisite meats. Damocles thought himself very happy. In the midst of this apparatus, Dionysius ordered a bright sword to be let down from the ceiling, suspended by a single horse-hair, so as to hang over the head of that happy man. After which he neither cast his eye on those handsome waiters, nor on the well-wrought plate; nor touched any of the provisions: presently the garlands fell to pieces. At last he entreated the tyrant to let him go, for now he had no desire to be happy. Does not Dionysius, then, seem to have declared there can be no happiness for one who is under constant apprehensions? But it was not now in his power to return to justice, and restore his citizens their rights and privileges; for, by the indiscretion of youth, he had engaged in so many wrong steps and committed such extravagances, that, had he attempted to have returned to a right way of thinking, he must have endangered his life.

XXII

Yet, how desirous he was of friendship, though at the same time he dreaded the treachery of friends, appears from the story of those two Pythagoreans: one of these had been security for his friend, who was condemned to die; the other, to release his security, presented himself at the time appointed for his dying: "I wish," said Dionysius, "you would admit me as the third in your friendship." What misery was it for him to be deprived of acquaintance, of company at his table, and of the freedom of conversation!—especially for one who was a man of learning, and from his childhood acquainted with liberal arts, very fond of music, and himself a tragic poet—how good a one is not to the purpose, for I know not how it is, but in this way, more than any other, everyone thinks his own performances excellent. I never as yet knew any poet (and I was very intimate with Aquinius), who did not appear to himself to be very admirable. The case is this: you are pleased with your own works; I like mine. But to return to Dionysius. He debarred himself from all civil and polite conversation, and spent his life among fugitives, bondmen, and barbarians; for he was persuaded that no one could be his friend who was worthy of liberty, or had the least desire of being free.

XXIII

Shall I not, then, prefer the life of Plato and Archytas, manifestly wise and learned men, to his, than which nothing can possibly be more horrid, or miserable, or detestable?

I will present you with an humble and obscure mathematician of the same city, called Archimedes, who lived many years after; whose tomb, overgrown with shrubs and briers, I in my quaestorship discovered, when the Syracusans knew nothing of it, and even denied that there was any such thing remaining; for I remembered some verses, which I had been informed were engraved on his monument, and these set forth that on the top of the tomb there was placed a sphere with a cylinder. When I had carefully examined all the monuments (for there are a great many tombs at the gate Achradinae), I observed a small column standing out a little above the briers, with the figure of a sphere and a cylinder upon it; whereupon I immediately said to the Syracusans—for there were some of their principal men with me there—that I imagined that was what I was inquiring for. Several men, being sent in with scythes, cleared the way, and made an opening for us. When we could get at it, and were come near to the front of the pedestal, I found the inscription, though the latter parts of all the verses were effaced almost half away. Thus one of the noblest cities of Greece, and one which at one time likewise had been very celebrated for learning, had known nothing of the monument of its greatest genius, if it had not been discovered to them by a native of Arpinum. But to return to the subject from which I have been digressing. Who is there in the least degree acquainted with the Muses, that is, with liberal knowledge, or that deals at all in learning, who would not choose to be this mathematician rather than that tyrant? If we look into their methods of living and their employments, we shall find the mind of the one strengthened and improved with tracing the deductions of reason, amused with his own ingenuity, which is the one most delicious food of the mind; the thoughts of the other engaged in continual murders and injuries, in constant fears by night and by day. Now imagine a Democritus, a Pythagoras, and an Anaxagoras; what kingdom, what riches, would you prefer to their studies and amusements? For you must necessarily look for that excellence which we are seeking for in that which is the most perfect part of man; but what is there better in man than a sagacious and good mind? The enjoyment, therefore, of that good which proceeds from that sagacious mind can alone make us happy; but virtue is the good of the mind: it follows, therefore, that a happy life depends on virtue. Hence proceed all things that are beautiful, honourable, and excellent, as I said above (but this point must, I think, be treated of more at large), and they are well stored with joys. For, as it is clear that a happy life consists in perpetual and unexhausted pleasures, it follows, too, that a happy life must arise from honesty.

XXIV

But that what I propose to demonstrate to you may not rest on mere words only, I must set before you the picture of something, as it were, living and moving in the world, that may dispose us more for the improvement of the understanding and real knowledge. Let us, then, pitch upon some man perfectly acquainted with the most excellent arts; let us present him for awhile to our own thoughts, and figure him to our own imaginations. In the first place, he must necessarily be of an extraordinary capacity; for virtue is not easily connected with dull minds. Secondly, he must have a great desire of discovering truth, from whence will arise that threefold production of the mind; one of which depends on knowing things, and explaining nature; the other, in defining what we ought to desire and what to avoid; the third, in judging of consequences and impossibilities, in which consists both subtlety in disputing and also clearness of judgment. Now, with what pleasure must the mind of a wise man be affected which continually dwells in the midst of such cares and occupations as these, when he views the revolutions and motions of the whole world, and sees those innumerable stars in the heavens, which, though fixed in their places, have yet one motion in common with the whole universe, and observes the seven other stars, some higher, some lower, each maintaining their own course, while their motions, though wandering, have certain defined and appointed spaces to run through!—the sight of which doubtless urged and encouraged those ancient philosophers to exercise their investigating spirit on many other things. Hence arose an inquiry after the beginnings, and, as it were, seeds from which all things were produced and composed; what was the origin of every kind of thing, whether animate or inanimate, articulately speaking or mute; what occasioned their beginning and end, and by what alteration and change one thing was converted into another; whence the earth originated, and by what weights it was balanced; by what caverns the seas were supplied; by what gravity all things being carried down tend always to the middle of the world, which in any round body is the lowest place.

XXV

A mind employed on such subjects, and which night and day contemplates them, contains in itself that precept of the Delphic God, so as to "know itself," and to perceive its connection with the divine reason, from whence it is filled with an insatiable joy. For reflections on the power and nature of the Gods raise in us a desire of imitating their eternity. Nor does the mind, that sees the necessary dependences and connections that one cause has with another, think it possible that it should be itself confined to the shortness of this life. Those causes, though they proceed from eternity to eternity, are governed by reason and understanding. And he who beholds them and examines them, or rather he whose view takes in all the parts and boundaries of things, with what tranquillity of mind does he look on all human affairs, and on all that is nearer him! Hence proceeds the knowledge of virtue; hence arise the kinds and species of virtues; hence are discovered those things which nature regards as the bounds and extremities of good and evil; by this it is discovered to what all duties ought to be referred, and which is the most eligible manner of life. And when these and similar points have been investigated, the principal consequence which is deduced from them, and that which is our main object in this discussion, is the establishment of the point, that virtue is of itself sufficient to a happy life.

The third qualification of our wise man is the next to be considered, which goes through and spreads itself over every part of wisdom; it is that whereby we define each particular thing, distinguish the genus from its species, connect consequences, draw just conclusions, and distinguish truth from falsehood, which is the very art and science of disputing; which is not only of the greatest use in the examination of what passes in the world, but is likewise the most rational entertainment, and that which is most becoming to true wisdom. Such are its effects in retirement. Now, let our wise man be considered as protecting the republic; what can be more excellent than such a character? By his prudence he will discover the true interests of his fellow-citizens; by his justice he will be prevented from applying what belongs to the public to his own use; and, in short, he will be ever governed by all the virtues, which are many and various. To these let us add the advantage of his friendships; in which the learned reckon not only a natural harmony and agreement of sentiments throughout the conduct of life, but the utmost pleasure and satisfaction in conversing and passing our time constantly with one another. What can be wanting to such a life as this to make it more happy than it is? Fortune herself must yield to a life stored with such joys. Now, if it be a happiness to rejoice in such goods of the mind, that is to say, in such virtues, and if all wise men enjoy thoroughly these pleasures, it must necessarily be granted that all such are happy.

XXVI

A: What, when in torments and on the rack?

M: Do you imagine I am speaking of him as laid on roses and violets? Is it allowable even for Epicurus (who only puts on the appearance of being a philosopher, and who himself assumed that name for himself) to say (though, as matters stand, I commend him for his saying) that a wise man might at all times cry out, though he be burned, tortured, cut to pieces, "How little I regard it!" Shall this be said by one who defines all evil as pain, and measures every good by pleasure; who could ridicule whatever we call either honourable or base, and could declare of us that we were employed about words, and uttering mere empty sounds; and that nothing is to be regarded by us but as it is perceived to be smooth or rough by the body? What!—shall such a man as this, as I said, whose understanding is little superior to the beasts', be at liberty to forget himself; and not only to despise fortune, when the whole of his good and evil is in the power of fortune, but to say that he is happy in the most racking torture, when he had actually declared pain to be not only the greatest evil, but the only one? Nor did he take any trouble to provide himself with those remedies which might have enabled him to bear pain, such as firmness of mind, a shame of doing anything base, exercise, and the habit of patience, precepts of courage, and a manly hardiness; but he says that he supports himself on the single recollection of past pleasures, as if anyone, when the weather was so hot as that he was scarcely able to bear it, should comfort himself by recollecting that he was once in my country, Arpinum, where he was surrounded on every side by cooling streams. For I do not apprehend how past pleasures can allay present evils. But when he says that a wise man is always happy who would have no right to say so if he were consistent with himself, what may they not do who allow nothing to be desirable, nothing to be looked on as good but what is honourable? Let, then, the Peripatetics and Old Academics follow my example, and at length leave off muttering to themselves; and openly and with a clear voice let them be so bold to say that a happy life may not be inconsistent with the agonies of Phalaris's bull.

XXVII

But to dismiss the subtleties of the Stoics, which I am sensible I have employed more than was necessary, let us admit of three kinds of goods; and let them really be kinds of goods, provided no regard is had to the body and to external circumstances, as entitled to the appellation of good in any other sense than because we are obliged to use them: but let those other divine goods spread themselves far in every direction, and reach the very heavens. Why, then, may I not call him happy, nay, the happiest of men, who has attained them? Shall a wise man be afraid of pain?—which is, indeed, the greatest enemy to our opinion. For I am persuaded that we are prepared and fortified sufficiently, by the disputations of the foregoing days, against our own death or that of our friends, against grief, and the other perturbations of the mind. But pain seems to be the sharpest adversary of virtue; that it is which menaces us with burning torches; that it is which threatens to crush our fortitude, and greatness of mind, and patience. Shall virtue, then, yield to this? Shall the happy life of a wise and consistent man succumb to this? Good Gods!—how base would this be! Spartan boys will bear to have their bodies torn by rods without uttering a groan. I myself have seen at Lacedaemon troops of young men, with incredible earnestness contending together with their hands and feet, with their teeth and nails, nay, even ready to expire, rather than own themselves conquered. Is any country of barbarians more uncivilized or desolate than India? Yet they have among them some that are held for wise men, who never wear any clothes all their life long, and who bear the snow of Caucasus, and the piercing cold of winter, without any pain; and who if they come in contact with fire endure being burned without a groan. The women, too, in India, on the death of their husbands have a regular contest, and apply to the judge to have it determined which of them was best beloved by him; for it is customary there for one man to have many wives. She in whose favour it is determined exults greatly, and being attended by her relations, is laid on the funeral pile with her husband; the others, who are postponed, walk away very much dejected. Custom can never be superior to nature, for nature is never to be got the better of. But our minds are infected by sloth and idleness, and luxury, and languor, and indolence: we have enervated them by opinions and bad customs. Who is there who is unacquainted with the customs of the Egyptians? Their minds being tainted by pernicious opinions, they are ready to bear any torture rather than hurt an ibis, a snake, a cat, a dog, or a crocodile; and should anyone inadvertently have hurt any of these animals, he will submit to any punishment. I am speaking of men only. As to the beasts, do they not bear cold and hunger, running about in woods, and on mountains and deserts? Will they not fight for their young ones till they are wounded? Are they afraid of any attacks or blows? I mention not what the ambitious will suffer for honour's sake, or those who are desirous of praise on account of glory, or lovers to gratify their lust. Life is full of such instances.

XXVIII

But let us not dwell too much on these questions, but rather let us return to our subject. I say, and say again, that happiness will submit even to be tormented; and that in pursuit of justice, and temperance, and still more especially and principally fortitude, and greatness of soul, and patience, it will not stop short at sight of the executioner; and when all other virtues proceed calmly to the torture, that one will never halt, as I said, on the outside and threshold of the prison; for what can be baser, what can carry a worse appearance, than to be left alone, separated from those beautiful attendants? Not, however, that this is by any means possible; for neither can the virtues hold together without happiness, nor happiness without the virtues; so that they will not suffer her to desert them, but will carry her along with them, to whatever torments, to whatever pain they are led. For it is the peculiar quality of a wise man to do nothing that he may repent of, nothing against his inclination, but always to act nobly, with constancy, gravity, and honesty; to depend on nothing as certainty; to wonder at nothing, when it falls out, as if it appeared strange and unexpected to him; to be independent of every one, and abide by his own opinion. For my part, I cannot form an idea of anything happier than this. The conclusion of the Stoics is indeed easy; for since they are persuaded that the end of good is to live agreeably to nature, and to be consistent with that—as a wise man should do so, not only because it is his duty, but because it is in his power—it must, of course, follow that whoever has the chief good in his power has his happiness so too. And thus the life of a wise man is always happy. You have here what I think may be confidently said of a happy life; and as things now stand, very truly also, unless you can advance something better.

XXIX

A: Indeed I cannot; but I should be glad to prevail on you, unless it is troublesome (as you are under no confinement from obligations to any particular sect, but gather from all of them whatever strikes you most as having the appearance of probability), as you just now seemed to advise the Peripatetics and the Old Academy boldly to speak out without reserve, 'that wise men are always the happiest'—I should be glad to hear how you think it consistent for them to say so, when you have said so much against that opinion, and the conclusions of the Stoics.

M: I will make use, then, of that liberty which no one has the privilege of using in philosophy but those of our school, whose discourses determine nothing, but take in everything, leaving them unsupported by the authority of any particular person, to be judged of by others, according to their weight. And you seem desirous of knowing how it is that, notwithstanding the different opinions of philosophers with regard to the ends of goods, virtue has still sufficient security for the effecting of a happy life—which security, as we are informed, Carneades used indeed to dispute against; but he disputed as against the Stoics, whose opinions he combated with great zeal and vehemence. I, however, shall handle the question with more temper; for if the Stoics have rightly settled the ends of goods, the affair is at an end; for a wise man must necessarily be always happy. But let us examine, if we can, the particular opinions of the others, that so this excellent decision, if I may so call it, in favour of a happy life, may be agreeable to the opinions and discipline of all.

XXX

These, then, are the opinions, as I think, that are held and defended—the first four are simple ones: "that nothing is good but what is honest," according to the Stoics; "nothing good but pleasure," as Epicurus maintains; "nothing good but a freedom from pain," as Hieronymus asserts; "nothing good but an enjoyment of the principal, or all, or the greatest goods of nature," as Carneades maintained against the Stoics—these are simple, the others are mixed propositions. Then there are three kinds of goods: the greatest being those of the mind; the next best those of the body; the third are external goods, as the Peripatetics call them, and the Old Academics differ very little from them. Dinomachus and Callipho have coupled pleasure with honesty; but Diodorus the Peripatetic has joined indolence to honesty. These are the opinions that have some footing; for those of Aristo, Pyrrho, Herillus, and of some others, are quite out of date. Now let us see what weight these men have in them, excepting the Stoics, whose opinion I think I have sufficiently defended; and indeed I have explained what the Peripatetics have to say; excepting that Theophrastus, and those who followed him, dread and abhor pain in too weak a manner. The others may go on to exaggerate the gravity and dignity of virtue, as usual; and then, after they have extolled it to the skies, with the usual extravagance of good orators, it is easy to reduce the other topics to nothing by comparison, and to hold them up to contempt. They who think that praise deserves to be sought after, even at the expense of pain, are not at liberty to deny those men to be happy who have obtained it. Though they may be under some evils, yet this name of happy has a very wide application.

XXXI

For even as trading is said to be lucrative, and farming advantageous, not because the one never meets with any loss, nor the other with any damage from the inclemency of the weather, but because they succeed in general; so life may be properly called happy, not from its being entirely made up of good things, but because it abounds with these to a great and considerable degree. By this way of reasoning, then, a happy life may attend virtue even to the moment of execution; nay, may descend with her into Phalaris's bull, according to Aristotle, Xenocrates, Speusippus, Polemon; and will not be gained over by any allurements to forsake her. Of the same opinion will Calliphon and Diodorus be; for they are both of them such friends to virtue as to think that all things should be discarded and far removed that are incompatible with it. The rest seem to be more hampered with these doctrines, but yet they get clear of them—such as Epicurus, Hieronymus, and whoever else thinks it worthwhile to defend the deserted Carneades: for there is not one of them who does not think the mind to be judge of those goods, and able sufficiently to instruct him how to despise what has the appearance only of good or evil. For what seems to you to be the case with Epicurus is the case also with Hieronymus and Carneades, and, indeed, with all the rest of them; for who is there who is not sufficiently prepared against death and pain? I will begin, with your leave, with him whom we call soft and voluptuous. What!—does he seem to you to be afraid of death or pain when he calls the day of his death happy; and who, when he is afflicted by the greatest pains, silences them all by recollecting arguments of his own discovering? And this is not done in such a manner as to give room for imagining that he talks thus wildly from some sudden impulse; but his opinion of death is that on the dissolution of the animal all sense is lost; and what is deprived of sense is, as he thinks, what we have no concern at all with. And as to pain, too, he has certain rules to follow then: if it be great, the comfort is that it must be short; if it be of long continuance, then it must be supportable. What, then? Do those grandiloquent gentlemen state anything better than Epicurus in opposition to these two things which distress us the most? And as to other things, do not Epicurus and the rest of the philosophers seem sufficiently prepared? Who is there who does not dread poverty? And yet no true philosopher ever can dread it.

XXXII

But with how little is this man himself satisfied! No one has said more on frugality. For when a man is far removed from those things which occasion a desire of money, from love, ambition, or other daily extravagance, why should he be fond of money, or concern himself at all about it? Could the Scythian Anacharsis disregard money, and shall not our philosophers be able to do so? We are informed of an epistle of his in these words: "Anacharsis to Hanno, greeting. My clothing is the same as that with which the Scythians cover themselves; the hardness of my feet supplies the want of shoes; the ground is my bed, hunger my sauce, my food milk, cheese, and flesh. So you may come to me as to a man in want of nothing. But as to those presents you take so much pleasure in, you may dispose of them to your own citizens, or to the immortal Gods." And almost all philosophers, of all schools, excepting those who are warped from right reason by a vicious disposition, might have been of this same opinion. Socrates, when on one occasion he saw a great quantity of gold and silver carried in a procession, cried out, "How many things are there which I do not want!" Xenocrates, when some ambassadors from Alexander had brought him fifty talents, which was a very large sum of money in those times, especially at Athens, carried the ambassadors to sup in the Academy, and placed just a sufficiency before them, without any apparatus. When they asked him, the next day, to whom he wished the money which they had for him to be paid: "What!" said he, "did you not perceive by our slight repast of yesterday that I had no occasion for money?" But when he perceived that they were somewhat dejected, he accepted of thirty minas, that he might not seem to treat with disrespect the king's generosity. But Diogenes took a greater liberty, like a Cynic, when Alexander asked him if he wanted anything: "Just at present," said he, "I wish that you would stand a little out of the line between me and the sun," for Alexander was hindering him from sunning himself. And, indeed, this very man used to maintain how much he surpassed the Persian king in his manner of life and fortune; for that he himself was in want of nothing, while the other never had enough; and that he had no inclination for those pleasures of which the other could never get enough to satisfy himself; and that the other could never obtain those pleasures which Alexander enjoyed.

XXXIII

You see, I imagine, how Epicurus has divided his kinds of desires, not very acutely perhaps, yet usefully, saying that "some are natural and necessary; some are natural, but not necessary; and some are neither natural nor necessary." That those which are necessary may be supplied almost for nothing; for that the things which nature requires are easily obtained." As to the second kind of desires, his opinion is that anyone may easily either enjoy or go without them. And with regard to the third, since they are utterly frivolous, being neither allied to necessity nor nature, he thinks that they should be entirely rooted out. On this topic a great many arguments are adduced by the Epicureans; and those pleasures which they do not despise in a body, they disparage one by one, and seem rather for lessening the number of them; for as to wanton pleasures, on which subject they say a great deal, these, say they, are easy, common, and within anyone's reach; and they think that if nature requires them, they are not to be estimated by birth, condition, or rank, but by shape, age, and person: and that it is by no means difficult to refrain from them, should health, duty, or reputation require it; but that pleasures of this kind may be desirable, where they are attended with no inconvenience, but can never be of any use. And the assertions which Epicurus makes with respect to the whole of pleasure are such as show his opinion to be that pleasure is always desirable, and to be pursued merely because it is pleasure; and for the same reason pain is to be avoided, because it is pain. So that a wise man will always adopt such a system of counterbalancing as to do himself the justice to avoid pleasure, should pain ensue from it in too great a proportion; and will submit to pain, provided the effects of it are to produce a greater pleasure: so that all pleasurable things, though the corporeal senses are the judges of them, are still to be referred to the mind, on which account the body rejoices while it perceives a present pleasure; but that the mind not only perceives the present as well as the body, but foresees it while it is coming, and even when it is past will not let it quite slip away. So that a wise man enjoys a continual series of pleasures, uniting the expectation of future pleasure to the recollection of what he has already tasted. The like notions are applied by them to high living; and the magnificence and expensiveness of entertainments are deprecated, because nature is satisfied at a small expense.

XXXIV

For who does not see this, that an appetite is the best sauce? When Darius, in his flight from the enemy, had drunk some water which was muddy and tainted with dead bodies, he declared that he had never drunk anything more pleasant; the fact was, that he had never drunk before when he was thirsty. Nor had Ptolemy ever eaten when he was hungry; for as he was travelling over Egypt, his company not keeping up with him, he had some coarse bread presented him in a cottage, upon which he said, "Nothing ever seemed to him pleasanter than that bread." They relate, too, of Socrates, that, once when he was walking very fast till the evening, on his being asked why he did so, his reply was that he was purchasing an appetite by walking, that he might sup the better. And do we not see what the Lacedaemonians provide in their Phiditia?—where the tyrant Dionysius supped, but told them he did not at all like that black broth, which was their principal dish; on which he who dressed it said, "It was no wonder, for it wanted seasoning." Dionysius asked what that seasoning was; to which it was replied, "Fatigue in hunting, sweating, a race on the banks of Eurotas, hunger and thirst," for these are the seasonings to the Lacedaemonian banquets. And this may not only be conceived from the custom of men, but from the beasts, who are satisfied with anything that is thrown before them, provided it is not unnatural, and they seek no farther. Some entire cities, taught by custom, delight in parsimony, as I said but just now of the Lacedaemonians. Xenophon has given an account of the Persian diet, who never, as he says, use anything but cresses with their bread; not but that, should nature require anything more agreeable, many things might be easily supplied by the ground, and plants in great abundance, and of incomparable sweetness. Add to this strength and health, as the consequence of this abstemious way of living. Now, compare with this those who sweat and belch, being crammed with eating, like fatted oxen; then will you perceive that they who pursue pleasure most attain it least; and that the pleasure of eating lies not in satiety, but appetite.

XXXV

They report of Timotheus, a famous man at Athens, and the head of the city, that having supped with Plato, and being extremely delighted with his entertainment, on seeing him the next day, he said, "Your suppers are not only agreeable while I partake of them, but the next day also." Besides, the understanding is impaired when we are full with overeating and drinking. There is an excellent epistle of Plato to Dion's relations, in which there occurs as nearly as possible these words: "When I came there, that happy life so much talked of, devoted to Italian and Syracusan entertainments, was noways agreeable to me—to be crammed twice a day, and never to have the night to yourself, and the other things which are the accompaniments of this kind of life, by which a man will never be made the wiser, but will be rendered much less temperate—for it must be an extraordinary disposition that can be temperate in such circumstances." How, then, can a life be pleasant without prudence and temperance? Hence you discover the mistake of Sardanapalus, the wealthiest king of the Assyrians, who ordered it to be engraved on his tomb,

> I still have what in food I did exhaust;
> But what I left, though excellent, is lost.

"What less than this," says Aristotle, "could be inscribed on the tomb, not of a king, but an ox?" He said that he possessed those things when dead, which, in his lifetime, he could have no longer than while he was enjoying them. Why, then, are riches desired? And wherein does poverty prevent us from being happy? In the want, I imagine, of statues, pictures, and diversions. But if anyone is delighted with these things, have not the poor people the enjoyment of them more than they who are the owners of them in the greatest abundance? For we have great numbers of them displayed publicly in our city. And whatever store of them private people have, they cannot have a great number, and they but seldom see them, only when they go to their country seats; and some of them must be stung to the heart when they consider how they came by them. The day would fail me, should I be inclined to defend the cause of poverty. The thing is manifest; and nature daily informs us how few things there are, and how trifling they are, of which she really stands in need.

XXXVI

Let us inquire, then, if obscurity, the want of power, or even the being unpopular, can prevent a wise man from being happy. Observe if popular favour, and this glory which they are so fond of, be not attended with more uneasiness than pleasure. Our friend Demosthenes was certainly very weak in declaring himself pleased with the whisper of a woman who was carrying water, as is the custom in Greece, and who whispered to another, "That is he—that is Demosthenes." What could be weaker than this?—and yet what an orator he was! But although he had learned to speak to others, he had conversed but little with himself. We may perceive, therefore, that popular glory is not desirable of itself; nor is obscurity to be dreaded. "I came to Athens," says Democritus, "and there was no one there that knew me:" this was a moderate and grave man who could glory in his obscurity. Shall musicians compose their tunes to their own tastes?—and shall a philosopher, master of a much better art, seek to ascertain, not what is most true, but what will please the people? Can anything be more absurd than to despise the vulgar as mere unpolished mechanics, taken singly, and to think them of consequence when collected into a body? These wise men would contemn our ambitious pursuits and our vanities, and would reject all the honours which the people could voluntarily offer to them; but we know not how to despise them till we begin to repent of having accepted them. There is an anecdote related by Heraclitus, the natural philosopher, of Hermodorus, the chief of the Ephesians, that he said "that all the Ephesians ought to be punished with death for saying, when they had expelled Hermodorus out of their city, that they would have no one among them better than another; but that if there were any such, he might go elsewhere to some other people." Is not this the case with the people everywhere? Do they not hate every virtue that distinguishes itself? What! was not Aristides (I had rather instance in the Greeks than ourselves) banished his country for being eminently just? What troubles, then, are they free from who have no connection whatever with the people? What is more agreeable than a learned retirement? I speak of that learning which makes us acquainted with the boundless extent of nature and the universe, and which even while we remain in this world discovers to us heaven, earth, and sea.

XXXVII

If, then, honour and riches have no value, what is there else to be afraid of? Banishment, I suppose; which is looked on as the greatest evil. Now, if the evil of banishment proceeds not from ourselves, but from the froward disposition of the people, I have just now declared how contemptible it is. But if to leave one's country be miserable, the provinces are full of miserable men, very few of the settlers in which ever return to their country again. But exiles are deprived of their property! What, then!—has there not been enough said on bearing poverty? But with regard to banishment, if we examine the nature of things, not the ignominy of the name, how little does it differ from constant travelling!—in which some of the most famous philosophers have spent their whole life, as Xenocrates, Crantor, Arcesilas, Lacydes, Aristotle, Theophrastus, Zeno, Cleanthes, Chrysippus, Antipater, Carneades, Panaetius, Clitomachus, Philo, Antiochus, Posidonius, and innumerable others, who from their first setting-out never returned home again. Now, what ignominy can a wise man be affected with (for it is of such a one that I am speaking) who can be guilty of nothing which deserves it?—for there is no occasion to comfort one who is banished for his deserts. Lastly, they can easily reconcile themselves to every accident who measure all their objects and pursuits in life by the standard of happiness; so that in whatever place that is supplied, there they may live happily. Thus what Teucer said may be applied to every case:

> Wherever I am happy is my country.

Socrates, indeed, when he was asked where he belonged to, replied, "The world;" for he looked upon himself as a citizen and inhabitant of the whole world. How was it with T. Altibutius? Did he not follow his philosophical studies with the greatest satisfaction at Athens, although he was banished?—which, however, would not have happened to him if he had obeyed the laws of Epicurus and lived peaceably in the republic. In what was Epicurus happier, living in his own country, than Metrodorus, who lived at Athens? Or did Plato's happiness exceed that of Xenocrates, or Polemo, or Arcesilas? Or is that city to be valued much that banishes all her good and wise men? Demaratus, the father of our King Tarquin, not being able to bear the tyrant Cypselus, fled from Corinth to Tarquinii, settled there, and had children. Was it, then, an unwise act in him to prefer the liberty of banishment to slavery at home?

XXXVIII

Besides the emotions of the mind, all griefs and anxieties are assuaged by forgetting them, and turning our thoughts to pleasure. Therefore, it was not without reason that Epicurus presumed to say that a wise man abounds with good things, because he may always have his pleasures; from whence it follows, as he thinks, that that point is gained which is the subject of our present inquiry, that a wise man is always happy. What!—though he should be deprived of the senses of seeing and hearing? Yes; for he holds those things very cheap. For, in the first place, what are the pleasures of which we are deprived by that dreadful thing, blindness? For though they allow other pleasures to be confined to the senses, yet the things which are perceived by the sight do not depend wholly on the pleasure the eyes receive, as is the case when we taste, smell, touch, or hear; for, in respect of all these senses, the organs themselves are the seat of pleasure; but it is not so with the eyes. For it is the mind which is entertained by what we see; but the mind may be entertained in many ways, even though we could not see at all. I am speaking of a learned and a wise man, with whom to think is to live. But thinking in the case of a wise man does not altogether require the use of his eyes in his investigations; for if night does not strip him of his happiness, why should blindness, which resembles night, have that effect? For the reply of Antipater the Cyrenaic to some women who bewailed his being blind, though it is a little too obscene, is not without its significance. "What do you mean?" says he; "do you think the night can furnish no pleasure?" And we find by his magistracies and his actions that old Appius, too, who was blind for many years, was not prevented from doing whatever was required of him with respect either to the republic or his own affairs. It is said that C. Drusus's house was crowded with clients. When they whose business it was could not see how to conduct themselves, they applied to a blind guide.

XXXIX

When I was a boy, Cn. Aufidius, a blind man, who had served the office of praetor, not only gave his opinion in the Senate, and was ready to assist his friends, but wrote a Greek history, and had a considerable acquaintance with literature. Diodorus the Stoic was blind, and lived many years at my house. He, indeed, which is scarcely credible, besides applying himself more than usual to philosophy, and playing on the flute, agreeably to the custom of the Pythagoreans, and having books read to him night and day, in all which he did not want eyes, contrived to teach geometry, which, one would think, could hardly be done without the assistance of eyes, telling his scholars how and where to draw every line. They relate of Asclepiades, a native of Eretria, and no obscure philosopher, when someone asked him what inconvenience he suffered from his blindness, that his reply was, "He was at the expense of another servant." So that, as the most extreme poverty may be borne if you please, as is daily the case with some in Greece, so blindness may easily be borne, provided you have the support of good health in other respects. Democritus was so blind he could not distinguish white from black; but he knew the difference between good and evil, just and unjust, honourable and base, the useful and useless, great and small. Thus one may live happily without distinguishing colours; but without acquainting yourself with things, you cannot; and this man was of opinion that the intense application of the mind was taken off by the objects that presented themselves to the eye; and while others often could not see what was before their feet, he travelled through all infinity. It is reported also that Homer was blind, but we observe his painting as well as his poetry. What country, what coast, what part of Greece, what military attacks, what dispositions of battle, what array, what ship, what motions of men and animals, can be mentioned which he has not described in such a manner as to enable us to see what he could not see himself? What, then!—can we imagine that Homer, or any other learned man, has ever been in want of pleasure and entertainment for his mind? Were it not so, would Anaxagoras, or this very Democritus, have left their estates and patrimonies, and given themselves up to the pursuit of acquiring this divine pleasure? It is thus that the poets who have represented Tiresias the Augur as a wise man and blind never exhibit him as bewailing his blindness. And Homer, too, after he had described Polyphemus as a monster and a wild man, represents him talking with his ram, and speaking of his good fortune, inasmuch as he could go wherever he pleased and touch what he would. And so far he was right, for that Cyclops was a being of not much more understanding than his ram.

XL

Now, as to the evil of being deaf. M. Crassus was a little thick of hearing; but it was more uneasiness to him that he heard himself ill spoken of, though, in my opinion, he did not deserve it. Our Epicureans cannot understand Greek, nor the Greeks Latin: now, they are deaf reciprocally as to each other's language, and we are all truly deaf with regard to those innumerable languages which we do not understand. They do not hear the voice of the harper; but, then, they do not hear the grating of a saw when it is setting, or the grunting of a hog when his throat is being cut, nor the roaring of the sea when they are desirous of rest. And if they should chance to be fond of singing, they ought, in the first place, to consider that many wise men lived happily before music was discovered; besides, they may have more pleasure in reading verses than in hearing them sung. Then, as I before referred the blind to the pleasures of hearing, so I may the deaf to the pleasures of sight: moreover, whoever can converse with himself does not need the conversation of another. But suppose all these misfortunes to meet in one person: suppose him blind and deaf—let him be afflicted with the sharpest pains of body, which, in the first place, generally of themselves make an end of him; still, should they continue so long, and the pain be so exquisite, that we should be unable to assign any reason for our being so afflicted—still, why, good Gods!, should we be under any difficulty? For there is a retreat at hand: death is that retreat—a shelter where we shall forever be insensible. Theodorus said to Lysimachus, who threatened him with death, "It is a great matter, indeed, for you to have acquired the power of a Spanish fly!" When Perses entreated Paulus not to lead him in triumph, "That is a matter which you have in your own power," said Paulus. I said many things about death in our first day's disputation, when death was the subject; and not a little the next day, when I treated of pain; which things if you recollect, there can be no danger of your looking upon death as undesirable, or, at least, it will not be dreadful.

That custom which is common among the Grecians at their banquets should, in my opinion, be observed in life: Drink, say they, or leave the company; and rightly enough; for a guest should either enjoy the pleasure of drinking with others, or else not stay till he meets with affronts from those that are in liquor. Thus, those injuries of fortune which you cannot bear you should flee from.

XLI

This is the very same which is said by Epicurus and Hieronymus. Now, if those philosophers, whose opinion it is that virtue has no power of itself, and who say that the conduct which we denominate honourable and laudable is really nothing, and is only an empty circumstance set off with an unmeaning sound, can nevertheless maintain that a wise man is always happy, what, think you, may be done by the Socratic and Platonic philosophers? Some of these allow such superiority to the goods of the mind as quite to eclipse what concerns the body and all external circumstances. But others do not admit these to be goods; they make everything depend on the mind: whose disputes Carneades, as a sort of honorary arbitrator, used to determine. For, as what seemed goods to the Peripatetics were allowed to be advantages by the Stoics, and as the Peripatetics allowed no more to riches, good health, and other things of that sort than the Stoics, when these things were considered according to their reality, and not by mere names, his opinion was that there was no ground for disagreeing. Therefore, let the philosophers of other schools see how they can establish this point also. It is very agreeable to me that they make some professions worthy of being uttered by the mouth of a philosopher with regard to a wise man's having always the means of living happily.

XLII

But as we are to depart in the morning, let us remember these five days' discussions; though, indeed, I think I shall commit them to writing: for how can I better employ the leisure which I have, of whatever kind it is, and whatever it be owing to? And I will send these five books also to my friend Brutus, by whom I was not only incited to write on philosophy, but, I may say, provoked. And by so doing it is not easy to say what service I may be of to others. At all events, in my own various and acute afflictions, which surround me on all sides, I cannot find any better comfort for myself.

TWO ESSAYS

by

MICHEL DE MONTAIGNE

That Men Are Not to Judge of Our Happiness Until After Death

> Till man's last day is come, we should not dare
> Of happiness to say what was his share;
> Since of no man can it be truly said
> That he is happy till he first be dead.[1]

Children know the story of King Croesus to this purpose, who being taken prisoner by Cyrus and condemned to die, on his way to execution cried out, "O Solon, Solon!" This being reported to Cyrus, and he sending to inquire of him what it meant, Croesus gave him to understand that he now found the teaching Solon had formerly given him true—at his own expense—namely, that "Men, however Fortune may smile upon them, cannot be called happy until they have been seen to pass the last day of their lives," because of the uncertainty and mutability of human things, which, upon very light and trivial occasions, are subject to be totally changed into a quite contrary condition. And so it was that Agesilaus made answer to one who was saying what a happy young man the King of Persia was, to come so young to so mighty a kingdom: "True," said he, "but neither was Priam unhappy at his years."[2]

---

1 Ovid, *Metamorphosis*, III, 135.
2 Plutarch, *Apothegms of the Lacedaemonians*.

In a short time, kings of Macedon, successors to that mighty Alexander, were reduced to clerks and carpenters at Rome; a tyrant of Sicily, reduced to a schoolmaster at Corinth; a conqueror of one-half of the world and general of so many armies, reduced to a miserable suppliant to the rascally officers of a king of Egypt: such was the cost to the great Pompey of having his life prolonged just five or six months; and, in our fathers' days, Ludovico Sforza, the tenth Duke of Milan, under whom all Italy had so long trembled, was seen to die a wretched prisoner at Loches, but not till he had lived ten years in captivity, which was the worst part of his fortune. The fairest of all queens—Mary, Queen of Scots—widow to the greatest king in Europe, did she not come to die by the hand of an executioner? Unworthy and barbarous cruelty! And there are a thousand more examples of the same kind; for it seems that, as storms and tempests have a malice against the proud and overtowering heights of our lofty buildings, there are also spirits above that are envious of the grandeur here below:

> So true it is that some occult power upsets
> human affairs, the glittering fasces and
> the cruel axes spurns under foot, and
> seems to make sport of them.[1]

And it should seem, also, that Fortune sometimes lies in wait to surprise the last hour of our lives, to show the power she has to overthrow, in a moment, what she was so many years in building, making us cry out with Laberius:

> I have lived longer by this one day than I
> should have done.[2]

In this sense, this good advice of Solon may reasonably be taken; but he being a philosopher (men for whom the favours and disgraces of Fortune stand for nothing, either to make

[1] Lucretius, V, 1231.
[2] Macrobius, II, 7.

them happy or unhappy, and with whom grandeurs and powers are accidents of an almost indifferent nature), I am apt to think that he had some further aim, and that his meaning was that the very felicity of life itself, which depends upon the tranquillity and contentment of a well-born spirit and the resolution and assurance of a well-ordered soul, ought never to be attributed to any man until he has first been seen to play the last, and doubtless the hardest, act of his part. There may be disguise and dissimulation in all the rest, where these fine philosophical discourses are only put on, and where accident, not touching us to the quick, gives us leisure to maintain the same gravity of aspect. But, in this last scene of death, there is no more counterfeiting: we must speak plain, and must show what there is of good and clean in the bottom of the pot,

> Then at last truth issues from the heart;
> the visor's gone, the man remains.[1]

That is why all the other actions of our life ought to be tried and tested by this last act: it is the master-day, it is the day that is judge of all the rest, "it is the day," says one of the ancients,[2] "that must be the judge of all my foregoing years." To death do I refer the test of the fruit of all my studies: we shall then see whether my discourses came only from my mouth or from my heart.

I have seen many by their death give a reputation for good or evil to their whole life. Scipio, the father-in-law of Pompey, in dying well, removed the ill opinion that up to then everyone had conceived of him. Epaminondas, being asked which of the three he had in greatest esteem, Chabrias, Iphicrates, or himself: "You must first see us die," said he, "before that question can be resolved."[3] And, in truth, we would infinitely wrong a man if we weighed him without the honour and grandeur of his end.

God has ordered all things as it has best pleased Him; but I

---

1 Lucretius, III, 57.
2 Seneca, *Epistles*, 102.
3 Plutarch.

have, in my time, seen three of the most execrable persons that I ever knew in all manner of abominable living, and the most infamous to boot, who all died a very regular death, and in all circumstances composed, even to perfection. There are brave and fortunate deaths: I have seen death cut the thread of the progress of a prodigious advancement, and in the height and flower of its increase, of a certain person,[1] with so glorious an end that, in my opinion, his ambitious and generous designs had nothing in them so high and great as their interruption. He arrived, without completing his course, at the place to which his ambition aimed, with greater glory than he could either have hoped or desired, anticipating by his fall the name and power to which he aspired in perfecting his course.

In judging the life of another, I always observe how he carried himself at his death; and the principal concern I have for my own life is that I may die well—that is, patiently and tranquilly.

Of Managing the Will

In comparison with most men, few things touch me, or, to put it better, possess me: for it is right that they should concern a man, provided they do not possess him. I take great care to increase by study and by reasoning this privilege of insensibility, which is naturally raised to a high degree in me, so that consequently I espouse and become passionate about very few things. My sight is clear enough, but I fix it upon very few objects; my sense is delicate and tender enough, but my apprehension and application are hard and unreceptive. I am very unwilling to engage myself. As much as I can, I employ myself wholly on myself, and even in this subject should rather choose to restrain my affection from plunging too deeply into it, since it is a subject that I possess at the mercy of others, and over which Fortune has more right than I. So that even with respect to health, which I so much value, it is all the

---

[1] Étienne de la Boétie, or possibly the Duc de Guise.

more necessary for me not to covet it and devote myself to it so passionately as to find diseases therefore insupportable. A man ought to moderate himself between the hatred of pain and the love of pleasure: and Plato sets down a middle path of life between the two.

But the passions that carry me away from myself and fix me elsewhere, those I certainly oppose with all my strength. It is my opinion that a man should lend himself to others, and only give himself to himself. Were my will easy to lend itself out and to be swayed, I would not last: I am too tender both by nature and use:

> Avoiding affairs and born to leisure free
> from care.[1]

Hot and obstinate disputes, wherein my adversary would at last have the advantage, the issue that would render my heat and obstinacy disgraceful would perhaps vex me to the last degree. If I set myself to it at the rate that others do, my soul would never have the strength to bear the emotions and alarms of those who grasp at so much; it would immediately be disordered by this inward agitation. If, sometimes, I have been put upon the management of other men's affairs, I have promised to take them in hand, but not into my lungs and liver; to take them upon me, not to incorporate them; to take pains, yes: to be impassioned about it, by no means; I have a care of them, but I will not sit upon them. I have enough to do to order and govern the domestic throng of those that I have in my own veins and bowels, without introducing a crowd of other men's affairs; and I am sufficiently concerned about my own proper and natural business, without meddling with the concerns of others. Those who know how much they owe to themselves, and for how many duties they are bound to themselves, find that Nature has given them enough work of their own to keep them from being idle. "You have business enough at home: look to that."

---

[1] Ovid, *Tristia*, III, ii, 9.

Men let themselves out to hire; their faculties are not for themselves, but for those to whom they have enslaved themselves; it is their tenants who occupy them, not themselves. This common humour displeases me. We must husband the liberty of our souls, and let it out only on just occasions, which are very few, if we judge rightly. Do but observe those who have accustomed themselves to be at everyone's beck and call: they do it indifferently upon all occasions, little and great—in matters that do not concern them as well as in those that do. They thrust themselves in indiscriminately wherever there is work to do, and are without life when not in tumultuous bustle:

> They are in business for business' sake.[1]

It is not so much that they want to be on the go, as that they cannot keep still, like a rolling stone that cannot stop until it can go no further. Occupation, with a certain sort of men, is a mark of understanding and dignity: their souls seek repose in agitation, as children do by being rocked in a cradle; they may pronounce themselves as serviceable to their friends as they are troublesome to themselves. No one distributes his money to others, but everyone distributes his time and his life: there is nothing of which we are so prodigal as these two things, of which to be thrifty would be both commendable and useful.

I take an altogether different position; I keep myself to myself, and commonly covet with no great ardour what I do desire, and desire little; I employ and busy myself in the same way, rarely and temperately. Other men, whatever they take in hand, they do it with their utmost will and vehemence. There are so many dangerous steps that, for the greatest safety, we must glide a little lightly and superficially over the world, and not rush into it. Pleasure itself is painful in its depth:

> You walk through fires
> 'Neath treacherous ashes set.[2]

[1] Seneca, *Epistles*, XXII.
[2] Horace, *Odes*, II, i, 7.

The Parliament of Bordeaux chose me mayor of their city at a time when I was far from France and still farther from any such thought. I asked to be excused, but I was told by my friends that I had committed an error in doing so, and the greater because the king had, moreover, interposed his command in that affair. It is an office that must seem so much the more honourable as it has no salary or advantage other than the bare honour of its execution. Its term is two years, but may be extended by a second election, which very rarely happens; it was so extended in my case, and this had been done only twice before: some years ago to Monsieur de Lansac, and lately to Monsieur de Biron, Marshal of France, in whose place I succeeded; and, I left mine to Monsieur de Matignon, Marshal of France also. Proud of so noble a fraternity,

> Either one a good minister in peace and war.[1]

Fortune wished to have a hand in my promotion by this particular circumstance which she put in of her own. Not altogether vain: for Alexander disdained the ambassadors of Corinth, who came to offer him a citizenship in their city; but when they went on to tell him that Bacchus and Hercules were also in the register, he graciously thanked them for it.

On my arrival, I faithfully and conscientiously represented myself to them just as I find myself to be—a man without memory, without vigilance, without experience, and without vigour; but also without hatred, without ambition, without avarice, and without violence; that they might be informed of my qualities, and know what they were to expect from my service. And because their knowledge of my late father, and the honour they had for his memory, had alone incited them to confer this favour upon me, I plainly told them that I should be very sorry if anything should make so great an impression upon me as their affairs and the concerns of their city had made upon him, while he held the post to which they

---

[1] Virgil, *Aeneid*, xi, 658.

had called me. I remembered, when a boy, to have seen him in his old age cruelly tormented by these public affairs, neglecting the soft repose of his own house (to which the declension of his age had reduced him for several years before), the management of his own affairs and health, and truly despising his own life, which was in great danger of being lost by being engaged in long and painful journeys on their behalf. Such was he; and this attitude of his proceeded from a marvellous good nature; never was there a more charitable and popular soul. Yet this course which I commend in others, I do not like to follow myself, and am not without excuse.

He had learned that a man must forget himself for his neighbour, and that the individual must not be considered at all in comparison with the general. Most of the rules and precepts of the world run this way, to drive us out of ourselves into the street for the benefit of public society; they thought they were doing us a great service to divert and remove us from ourselves, assuming we were but too much attached to ourselves, and by too natural an inclination; and they have spared no words to that end—for it is no new thing for the sages to preach things as they serve, not as they are. Truth has its drawbacks, inconveniences, and incompatibilities with us; we must often be deceived that we may not deceive ourselves, and shut our eyes, and have our understanding stunned in order to redress and amend them:

> For it is the ignorant who judge, and they
> must frequently be deceived, lest they err.[1]

When they order us to love three, four, or fifty degrees of things above ourselves, they do like archers, who, to hit the white, take their aim a great deal higher than the target; to make a crooked stick straight, we bend it the contrary way.

I believe that in the Temple of Pallas, as we see in all other religions, there were apparent mysteries to be exposed to the people; and others, more secret and high, that were only to

---

[1] Quintilian, *Institutio Oratoria*, XI, 17.

be shown to such as were professed; it is likely that in these the true point of friendship that everyone owes to himself is to be found; not a false friendship, that makes us embrace glory, knowledge, riches, and the like, with a principal and immoderate affection, as members of our being; nor an indiscreet and effeminate friendship, wherein it happens, as with ivy, that it decays and ruins the walls it embraces; but a sound and regular friendship, equally useful and pleasant. He who knows the duties of this friendship and practises them is truly of the cabinet of the Muses, and has attained to the height of human wisdom and happiness; such a one, knowing exactly what he owes to himself, will on his part find that he ought to apply to himself the practices of the world and of other men, and, in order to do this, ought to contribute to public society the duties and offices that pertain to him. He who does not in some way live for others, does not live much for himself:

> He who is his own friend, is a friend to
> everybody else.[1]

The principal charge we have is, to every one his own conduct; and that is what we are here for. As he who should forget to live a virtuous and holy life, and should think he acquitted himself of his duty in instructing and training others to do so, would be a fool, so he who abandons his own particular healthful and pleasant living to serve others thereby takes, in my opinion, a wrong and unnatural course.

I would not want a man to refuse, in the employments he takes on, his attention, pains, eloquence, sweat, and blood if need be:

> For cherished friends
> Or fatherland I do not fear to die.[2]

But it is only borrowed, and accidentally, his mind being always in repose and in health, not without action, but with-

---

[1] Seneca, *Epistles*, VI.
[2] Horace, *Odes*, IV, ix, 51.

out vexation, without passion. To be simply acting costs him so little that he acts even when sleeping; but it must be set in motion with discretion; for the body receives the offices imposed upon it just according to what they are; the mind often extends and makes them heavier at its own expense, giving them what measure it pleases. Men perform like things with different degrees of effort and different exertions of will; the one does well enough without the other;[1] for how many people hazard themselves every day in war without any concern for which way it goes, and thrust themselves into the dangers of battles, the loss of which will not trouble their next night's sleep? Another man is at home, out of the danger which he would not have dared to face, and is more passionately concerned about the outcome of this war—his soul is more anxious than the soldier who stakes his blood and his life. I have been able to engage myself in public employments without quitting my own matters a nail's breadth, and have given myself to others without abandoning myself.

This fierceness and violence of desires hinders more than it serves the execution of what we undertake, fills us with impatience toward slow or contrary events, and with bitterness and suspicion toward those with whom we are dealing. We never conduct well that thing by which we are prepossessed and led:

> For passion handles everything badly.[2]

He who therein employs only his judgment and address proceeds more cheerfully: he counterfeits, he gives way, he defers quite at his ease, according to the necessities of occasions; he fails in his attempt without trouble and affliction, ready and intact for a new enterprise; he always marches with the bridle in his hand. In the man who is drunk with that violent and tyrannical drive, we discover, of necessity, much

---

[1] Action without passion. Compare this with the teaching of *The Bhagavad Gita*: action without attachment to its fruits.
[2] Statius, *Thebaid*, X, 704.

imprudence and injustice; the impetuosity of his desire carries him away. His movements are reckless, and, unless Fortune assists a great deal, of very little fruit.

Philosophy directs that, in the revenge of injuries received, we should strip ourselves of anger; not so that the chastisement should be less, but, on the contrary, so that the revenge may be better and more heavily laid on; it seems to her that impetuosity hinders the purpose. For anger not only disturbs, but by itself it also wearies the arms of those who chastise. This fire benumbs and wastes their strength. As in precipitation, "More haste, less speed,"[1] haste trips on its own heels, gets tangled up, and brings itself to a halt:

> Speed gets entangled in itself.[2]

For example, according to what I commonly see, avarice has no greater impediment than itself; the more strained and vigorous it is, the less it produces, and generally grows rich more readily when disguised in a mask of liberality.

A very excellent gentleman, and a friend of mine, ran a risk of impairing his faculties by a too passionate attention and affection to the affairs of a certain prince, his master. This master portrayed himself to me in this manner: that he foresees the weight of accidents as well as another, but that in those for which there is no remedy, he at once resolves to bear them; in other cases, having taken all the necessary precautions, which he can quickly do because of the vivacity of his mind, he quietly awaits what may follow. And, in truth, I have accordingly seen him maintain a great indifference and liberty of actions and serenity of countenance in very great and difficult affairs: I find him much greater and of greater capacity in adverse than in prosperous fortune; his defeats are to him more glorious than his victories, and his mourning more glorious than his triumph.

Consider that even in vain and frivolous actions, as at chess,

---

[1] Quintus Curtius.
[2] Seneca, *Epistles*, XLIV.

tennis, and the like, this eager and ardent engaging with an impetuous desire immediately throws the mind and members into indiscretion and disorder: a man astounds and hinders himself; he who carries himself more moderately, both towards gain and loss, has always his wits about him; the less peevish and passionate he is at play, he plays much more advantageously and surely.

As to the rest, we hinder the mind's grasp and hold in giving it so many things to seize upon. Some things we should only offer to it, others attach to it, and still others incorporate into it. The mind can feel and discern all things, but ought to feed upon nothing but itself, and should be instructed in what properly concerns itself and what is properly of its own possession and substance. The laws of Nature teach us exactly what we need. After the sages have told us that no one is indigent according to Nature, and that everyone is so according to opinion, they very subtly distinguish between the desires that come from her and those that come from the disorder of our own fancy: those of which we can see the end are hers; those that fly before us, and of which we can see no end, are our own. Poverty of material goods is easily cured; poverty of the soul is irreparable:

> For if what is for man enough, could be
> enough, it were enough; but since it is not
> so, how can I believe that any wealth can
> give my mind content.[1]

Socrates, seeing a great quantity of riches, jewels, and furniture carried in pomp through his city, said, "How many things I do not desire!" Metrodorus lived on twelve ounces a day, Epicurus upon less; Metrocles slept in winter abroad amongst sheep, in summer in the cloisters of churches:

> Nature suffices for what he requires.[2]

---

1 Lucilius, in Nonius Marcellus, V, 98.
2 Seneca, *Epistles*, XC

Cleanthes lived by the labour of his own hands, and boasted that Cleanthes, if he would, could maintain yet another Cleanthes.

If that which Nature exactly and originally requires of us for the conservation of our being is too little (as, in truth, how little this is, and how cheaply our life can be maintained, cannot be better expressed than by this consideration, that it is so little that by its littleness it escapes the grasp and shock of Fortune), let us allow ourselves a little more; let us call every one of our habits and conditions *Nature*; let us rate and treat ourselves by this measure; let us stretch our appurtenances and accounts so far; for so far, I fancy, we have some excuse. Custom is a second Nature, and no less powerful. What is lacking to my customary way of living, I consider to be lacking to me; and I should almost as soon have my life taken away from me as to have it deprived to any great extent of the things with which I have so long lived. I am past the age for any great change, or to put myself into a new and unaccustomed course, even toward improvement. It is past the time for me to become other than what I am. And as I should complain of any great good fortune that might now befall me, because it came too late to be enjoyed,

> For what are Fortune's gifts, if I'm denied
> Their use?[1]

so likewise should I complain of any inward acquisition. It is almost better to never become a wise man, well versed in the art of living, than to become one so late when one has no longer to live. I, who am about to make my exit from the world, would easily resign to any newcomer, who should desire it, all the wisdom I am now acquiring in the world's commerce. Mustard after dinner! I have no use for goods of which I can make no use. For what good is knowledge to one who no longer has a head? It is an insult and unkindness in Fortune to tender us presents that will only inspire us with a

---

[1] Horace, *Epistles*, I, v, 12.

just resentment that we did not have them in their due season. Guide me no more, I can no longer walk. Of the many parts that make up excellence, patience is the most sufficient. Give the capacity of an excellent treble to a singer who has rotten lungs, and eloquence to a hermit exiled to the deserts of Arabia. No art is needed to help a fall; the end finds itself of itself at the conclusion of every affair. My world is at an end, my form expired; I am totally of the past, and am bound to authorise it, and to conform my outgoing to it. I will here declare, by way of example, that the Pope's late ten days' diminution[1] has so taken me aback that I cannot well reconcile myself to it; I belong to the years wherein we kept another kind of account. So ancient and so long a custom calls me to adhere to it, so that I am constrained to be somewhat heretical on this point, incapable of any innovation, even for the better. My imagination, in spite of my teeth, always pushes me ten days forward or backward, and is ever murmuring in my ears: "This rule concerns those who are to come." If health itself, sweet as it is, returns to me by fits, it is rather to give me cause of regret than possession of it; I have no place left to keep it in. Time leaves me, without which nothing can be possessed. Oh, what little account should I make of those great elective dignities I see in the world that are given only to men who are about to leave it; in these offices they do not so much regard how well the man will discharge his trust, as how short his administration will be: from the very entry they look at the exit. In short, I am in the act of finishing this man, and not rebuilding another. By long use, this form of mine has turned into substance, and Fortune into Nature.

I say, therefore, that every one of us feeble creatures is excusable in considering as his own that which is comprised under this measure; but also, beyond these limits, there is nothing but confusion; it is the largest extent we can grant to our own claims. The more we amplify our need and our possession, so much the more do we expose ourselves to the blows of Fortune and adversity. The range of our desires

---

[1] Pope Gregory XIII's calendar reform of 1582.

ought to be circumscribed and restrained to a short limit of the nearest and most contiguous commodities; and their course ought, moreover, to be directed not in a right line that ends elsewhere, but in a circle, of which the two points, by a short wheel, meet and terminate in ourselves. Actions that are carried on without this reflection—a near and essential reflection, I mean—such as those of ambitious men, avaricious men, and so many others who run blindly ahead and whose course always carries them before themselves, such actions, I say, are erroneous and sickly.

Most of our business is farce:

Mundus universus exercet histrioniam.[1]

We must play our part properly, but as a part of a borrowed character; we must not make a real essence of the mask and outward appearance, nor make of something foreign something that is our own; we cannot distinguish the skin from the shirt: it is enough to make up the face without making up the heart. I see some who transform and transubstantiate themselves into as many new shapes and new beings as they undertake new employments; and who strut and fume even to the heart and liver, and carry their state along with them even to the toilet room: I cannot make them distinguish the salutations made to themselves from those made to their office, their retinue, or their mule:

> They so much give themselves up to
> Fortune as even to unlearn their nature.[2]

They swell and puff up their souls and their natural way of speaking according to the height of their magisterial seat. The Mayor of Bordeaux and Montaigne have ever been two, with a very clear separation. Because one is a lawyer or a financier, he must not ignore the knavery there is in such callings; an honest man is not accountable for the vice or absurdity of his

---

[1] "The whole world plays a part."—Petronius.
[2] Quintus Curtius, III, 2.

trade, and ought not on that account refuse to practice it: it is the custom of his country, and there is usefulness in it; a man must live in the world and make his best of it, such as it is. But the judgment of an emperor ought to be above his imperial authority, and he ought to view and consider it as an external circumstance; he ought to know how to enjoy himself apart from it, and to communicate himself as James and Peter, at least to himself.

I cannot engage myself so deeply and so entirely; when my will commits me to anything, it is not with so violent an attachment that my judgment is infected by it. In the present broils of this kingdom, my own interest has not made me blind to the laudable qualities of our adversaries, nor to those that are reproachable in those men of our party. Others adore all of their own side; for my part, I do not so much as excuse most things on my own side: a good work does not lose its grace with me for being made against me. The knot of the controversy excepted, I have always kept myself in equanimity and pure indifference:

> And beyond the necessities of war I bear
> no special hatred.[1]

For which I am pleased with myself, and the more because I see others commonly fail in the contrary direction. *Let him make use of passion who cannot make use of reason.*[2] Those who extend their anger and hatred beyond the dispute in question, as most men do, show that their passion springs from some other source, a personal cause: like one who still has a fever after being cured of an ulcer, it appears it had another more hidden cause. The reason is that they are not concerned with the common cause, because it is wounding to the state and general interest, but are only nettled because it affronts their private interests. This is why they are so especially animated, and to a degree so far beyond justice and

---

1 Livy.
2 Cicero.

public reason:

> Every one was not so much angry against things in general, as against those that particularly concern himself.[1]

I want the advantage to be on our side; but if it is not, I shall not run mad. I adhere heartily to the right party, but I do not want to be taken special notice of as an enemy to others, and beyond the general quarrel. I marvellously challenge this vicious form of opinion: "He is of the League because he admires the graciousness of Monsieur de Guise; he is astonished at the King of Navarre's energy, therefore he is a Huguenot; he finds this to say of the manners of the king, he is therefore seditious in his heart." And I did not grant to the magistrate himself that he did well in condemning a book because it had placed a heretic[2] amongst the best poets of the time. Shall we not dare to say of a thief that he has a handsome leg? If a woman is a strumpet, must it necessarily follow that she has a foul smell? Did they in the wisest ages revoke the proud title of Capitolinus they had before conferred on Marcus Manlius as conservator of religion and the public liberty, and stifle the memory of his liberality, his feats of arms, and military recompenses granted to his valour, because he afterwards aspired to the sovereignty, to the prejudice of the laws of his country? If we take a hatred against an advocate, he will not be allowed the next day to be eloquent. I have elsewhere spoken of the zeal that pushed on worthy men to the like faults. For my part, I can say, "He does this thing ill and another thing well." So in the prognostication or sinister events of affairs they would have everyone in his party blind or a blockhead, and that our persuasion and judgment should serve not truth but the purpose of our desires. I should rather incline towards the other extreme, so much do I fear being suborned by my desire; to which may be added that I am a

---

[1] Livy, XXXIV, 36.
[2] Theodore de Bèze.

little tenderly distrustful of things that I wish.

I have in my time seen wonders in the indiscreet and prodigious facility of men in suffering their hopes and beliefs to be led and governed whichever way best pleased and served their leaders, despite a hundred mistakes one upon another, despite mere dreams and phantasms. I no more wonder at those who have been blinded and seduced by the fooleries of Apollonius and Mahomet. Their sense and understanding are absolutely taken away by their passion; their discretion has no other choice than that which smiles upon them and encourages their cause. I had principally observed this in the beginning of our intestine distempers;[1] that other, which has sprung up since,[2] in imitating, has surpassed it; by which I am satisfied that this is an inseparable characteristic of popular errors; after the first that rolls, opinions drive on one another like waves with the wind: a man is not a member of the body if it is in his power to forsake it and if he does not roll the common way. But, doubtless, they wrong the just side when they go about to assist it with fraud; I have ever been against that practice: it is only fit to work upon weak heads; for the sound, there are surer and more honest ways to keep up their courage and to excuse adverse accidents.

Heaven never saw a greater animosity than that between Caesar and Pompey, nor ever shall; and yet I observe in those brave souls a great moderation towards one another. It was a rivalry of honour and command, which did not transport them to a furious and indiscreet hatred, and it was without malignity and detraction. In their hottest exploits upon one another, I discover some remains of respect and good-will; and I am therefore of opinion that, had it been possible, each of them would rather have liked to attain his ends without the ruin of the other than with it. Take notice how different it was with Marius and Sylla.

We must not precipitate ourselves so headlong after our passions and interests. Just as, when I was young, I used to

[1] Protestants.
[2] The League.

resist the progress of love which I felt advancing too fast upon me, and took pains that it should not become so pleasing as to overpower, captivate, and wholly reduce me to its mercy: so I do the same on all other occasions when my will is running with too warm an appetite. I lean opposite to the side it inclines to, as I find it plunging in and getting drunk on its own wine; I evade nourishing its pleasure so far that I cannot recover it without infinite loss.

Souls that, through their own stupidity, only discern things by halves, have this happiness, that they smart less with hurtful things: it is a spiritual leprosy that has some show of health, and such a health as philosophy does not altogether scorn; but yet it is not right to call it wisdom, as we often do. And in this manner someone in antiquity mocked Diogenes, who, in the depth of winter and quite naked, went embracing a snow figure to test his endurance: the other seeing him in this position, said, "Are you very cold now?" "Not at all," replied Diogenes. "Why, then," pursued the other, "what difficult and exemplary thing do you think you're doing in embracing that snow?" To take a true measure of constancy, one must necessarily know what the suffering is.

But souls that are to meet with adverse events and the injuries of Fortune in their depth and sharpness, that are to weigh and taste them according to their natural weight and bitterness, let them employ their skill in avoiding the causes and diverting the blow. What did King Cotys do? He paid liberally for the rich and beautiful vessel that had been presented to him, but, seeing it was exceedingly brittle, he immediately broke it himself, to prevent so easy an occasion for anger against his servants. In like manner, I have willingly avoided all confusion in my affairs, and never sought to have my estate contiguous to those of my relations and those with whom I coveted a close friendship; for thence proceed grounds for unkindness and falling out.

I formerly loved hazardous games of cards and dice; but have long since left them off, only for this reason, that with whatever good air I carried my losses, I could not help feeling vexed within. A man of honour, who ought to be sharply sensible of a lie or insult, and who is not to take a silly excuse for satisfaction, should avoid occasions of dispute. I shun melancholy and surly men as I would the plague; and I never meddle in matters I cannot discuss without emotion and concern, unless compelled by duty:

> It is better not to begin than to desist.[1]

The surest way, therefore, is to prepare oneself before the occasions.

I know very well that some wise men have taken another way, and have not feared to grapple and engage to the utmost upon several subjects. These men are confident of their own strength, under which they protect themselves in all ill successes, making their patience wrestle and contend with disaster:

> Just as a rock that juts into the far-flung waves
> Athwart the raging winds, exposed to the full sea,
> Bears all the vigour and the threats of sky and deep,
> And stays itself unmoved.[2]

Let us not attempt these examples; we shall never come up to them. They set themselves resolutely, and without agitation, to behold the ruin of their country, which once possessed and commanded all their affection: this is too much, and too hard a task for our commoner souls. Cato gave up to it the noblest life that ever was; we meaner spirits must fly from the storm as far as we can; we must provide for emotions and not for patience, and evade the blows we cannot meet. Zeno, seeing Chremonides, a young man whom he loved, draw near to sit down by him, suddenly started up; and Cleanthes demanding why he did so, Zeno replied, "I hear that physicians especially

---

1 Seneca, *Epistles*, LXXII.
2 Virgil, *Aeneid*, X, 693.

order repose and forbid emotion in all cases of swellings." Socrates does not say, "Do not surrender to the charms of beauty, stand your ground, and do your utmost to oppose it." "Fly from it," says he, "run from the sight and encounter of it as from a powerful poison that darts and wounds at a distance." And his good disciple, feigning or reciting, but, in my opinion, rather reciting than feigning, the rare perfections of the great Cyrus, makes him distrustful of his own strength to resist the charms of the divine beauty of that illustrious Panthea, his captive, and committing the charge of visiting and guarding her to another who could not have as much liberty as himself. And the Holy Ghost in like manner: *Lead us not into temptation.*[1] We do not pray that our reason may not be combated and overcome by concupiscence, but that it may not even be put to the test, that we may not be brought into a state in which we may even have to suffer the approaches, solicitations, and temptations of sin: and we beg of Almighty God to keep our conscience quiet, fully and perfectly delivered from all association with evil.

Those who say that they are justified in their passion for revenge, or in any other troublesome agitation of mind, often speak truly as things now are, but not as they were: they speak to us when the causes of their error have been nourished and advanced by themselves; but look backward—recall these causes to their beginning—and there you will put them to confusion. Do you mean to say their faults are less for being older; and that of an unjust beginning, the sequel can be just?

Whoever desires the good of his country, as I do, without fretting or pining himself, will be troubled, but not dazed, to see it threatened with ruin or a no less ruinous continuance; poor vessel, that the waves, the winds, and the pilot toss and steer to so contrary designs!

> So diversely winds,
> And waves, and pilot pull.[2]

---

[1] Matthew 6:13.
[2] Buchanan, *Franciscanus*.

He who does not gape after the favour of princes, as after a thing he cannot live without, does not much concern himself at the coldness of their reception and countenance, nor at the inconstancy of their wills. He who does not brood over his children or his honours with a slavish fondness does not cease to live commodiously after their loss. He who does good principally for his own satisfaction will not be much troubled at seeing men judge his actions contrary to his merit. A quarter of an ounce of patience will provide sufficiently against such inconveniences. I find ease in this rule, buying my freedom as cheaply as I can from the beginning, and find that by this means I have escaped much trouble and many difficulties. With very little effort I stop the first impulse of my emotions, and leave the subject that begins to be troublesome before it transports me. He who stops not the start will never be able to stop the course; he who cannot keep them out will never get them out once they have got in; and he who cannot arrive at the beginning will never arrive at the end of all. Nor will he bear the fall who cannot sustain the shock:

> For once separated from reason, the
> passions drive forward; and weakness
> yields to itself and is carried out into the
> sea without knowing it, and finds no
> place to come to rest.[1]

I am betimes sensible of the little breezes that begin to sing and whistle within me, forerunners of the storm: *the mind is shaken long before it is overpowered.*[2]

> As when the rising winds, caught in the
>   woods,
> Murmur and roll along with a dull hum,
> Forewarning sailors of the gales to come.[3]

---

1 Cicero, *Tusculans*, IV, 18.
2 Seneca, *Epistles*.
3 Virgil, *Aeneid*, X, 97.

How often have I done myself a manifest injustice to avoid the hazard of having yet a worse one done to me by the judges after an age of vexations, dirty and vile practices, more enemies to my nature than the rack or fire?

> It is right for a man to shrink back from lawsuits as much as is permissible, and, perhaps, even more than is permissible. For it is only generous, but sometimes even advantageous, to give way a little from one's right.[1]

Were we wise, we ought to rejoice and boast, as I one day heard a young gentleman of a good family very innocently do, that his mother had lost her cause, as if it had been a cough, a fever, or something very troublesome to keep. Even the favours that Fortune might have given me through relationship or acquaintance with those who have sovereign authority in those affairs, I have very conscientiously and very carefully avoided employing them to the prejudice of others, and of advancing my pretensions above their true right. In fine, I have so much prevailed by my endeavours (and happily I may say it) that I am to this day a virgin of lawsuits, though I have had very fair offers made me, and with very just title, would I have hearkened to them, and a virgin of quarrels too. I have almost passed over a long life without any offence of moment, either active or passive, or without ever hearing a worse word than my own name: a rare favour of Heaven.

Our greatest agitations have ridiculous springs and causes: what ruin did our last Duke of Burgundy run into over a cartload of sheepskins! And was not the engraving of a seal the first and principal cause of the greatest commotion that this machine of the world ever underwent?—for Pompey and Caesar were but the offsets and continuation of the two others: and I have in my time seen the wisest heads in this kingdom assembled with great ceremony, and at the public expense, about treaties and agreements of which the true de-

---

[1] Cicero, *De Officiis*, II, 18.

cision, in the meantime, absolutely depended upon the ladies' cabinet council and the inclination of some little woman.

The poets very well understood this when they put all Greece and Asia to fire and sword over an apple. See why that man hazards his life and honour on the fortune of his rapier and dagger; let him tell you the cause of the quarrel; he cannot do so without blushing, so idle and frivolous is its cause.

To get a thing started takes only a little effort; but once embarked, all the cords draw; great provisions are then required, more difficult and more important. How much easier it is not to enter than it is to get out! Now we should proceed contrary to the reed, which, at its first springing, produces a long and straight shoot, but afterwards, as if tired and out of breath, runs into thick and frequent joints and knots, like so many pauses, which demonstrate that it no longer has its first vigour and firmness. We must rather begin gently and coolly, and save our breath and vigorous efforts for the height and stress of the task. We guide affairs in their beginnings, and have them in our own power; but afterwards, when they are at work, it is they that guide and govern us, and we have to follow them.

Yet I do not mean to say that this counsel has discharged me of all difficulty, and that I have not often been at pains to curb and restrain my passions; they are not always to be governed according to the importance of the causes, and often even their beginnings are sharp and violent. But still, good fruit and profit may be reaped from it, except for those who in doing good are not satisfied with any benefit if there is no reputation in it; for, in truth, such an act is valued only by each man in himself. You are happier, but not more esteemed, by having reformed yourself before you got into the whirl of the dance and before the matter was in sight. Yet not only in this, but in all other duties of life also, the way of those who aim at honour is very different from that which is followed by those who propose order and reason as their goal.

I find some who rashly and furiously rush into the lists and slow down in the course. Just as Plutarch says that those who, through false shame, are soft and ready to grant whatever is desired of them are afterwards just as ready to break their word and recant; so he who enters lightly into a quarrel is apt to go as lightly out of it. The same difficulty that keeps me from entering into it would incite me to maintain it with great obstinacy and resolution once I have been set in motion and heated. It is the tyranny of custom: once you are in it, you must go through with it, or die. "Undertake coolly," said Bias, "but pursue with ardour." For want of prudence, men fall into want of courage, which is still more intolerable.

Most settlements of the quarrels nowadays are shameful and false; we only seek to save appearances, and at the same time betray and disavow our true intentions; we plaster over the fact. We know very well how we said the thing, and in what sense we spoke it, and the company know it, and our friends whom we have wished to make sensible of our advantage, understand it well enough too: it is at the expense of our frankness and of the honour of our courage that we disown our thoughts, and seek refuge in falsities, to make matters up. We give ourselves the lie, to excuse the lie we have given to another. You are not to consider if your word or action may admit of another interpretation; it is your own true and sincere interpretation, your real meaning in what you said or did, that you must henceforth maintain, whatever it cost you. Men speak to your virtue and conscience, which are not things to be put under a mask; let us leave these pitiful ways and expedients to the jugglers of the law. The excuses and reparations that I see made every day to repair indiscretion, seem to me more scandalous than the indiscretion itself. It would be better to affront your adversary a second time than to offend yourself by giving him so unmanly a satisfaction. You defied him in your heat and anger, and you would flatter and appease him in your cooler and better sense; and by that means you lay yourself lower at the feet of the one who before you pretended to overtop. I do not find anything a gentleman can say so vicious in him as unsaying what he has said is infamous, when to unsay it is authoritatively extracted from him, inasmuch as obstinacy is more excusable in a man of honour than pusillanimity. Passions are as easy for me to evade as they are hard for me to moderate:

> *Exscinduntur facilius ammo, quam temperantur.*[1]

He who cannot attain the noble Stoical impassibility, let him secure himself in the bosom of this popular stolidity of mine; what they performed by virtue, I inure myself to do by temperament. The middle region harbours storms and tempests; the two extremes, of philosophers and peasants, concur in tranquillity and happiness:

> Happy is he who could discover the
> causes of things, and place under his feet
> all fears and inexorable Fate, and the
> sound of rapacious Acheron: he is blest
> who knows the country gods, and Pan,
> and old Sylvanus, and the sister nymphs.[2]

The births of all things are weak and tender; and therefore we should have our eyes intent on beginnings; for as when, in its infancy, the danger is not perceived, so when it is grown up, the remedy is as little to be found. I should have encountered every day a million obstructions more difficult to overcome in the progress of ambition than it has been hard for me to check the natural impulse that inclined me to it:

> I quaked with rightful dread
> Of raising to full view my head.[3]

All public actions are subject to uncertain and various interpretations; for too many heads judge them. Some say of this civic employment of mine (and I am willing to say a word or two about it, not that it is worth so much, but to give an account of my manners in such things), that I have behaved myself in it as a man who is too supine and of a lan-

---

[1] "They are more easily to be eradicated than governed."—Seneca, *Epistles*.
[2] Virgil, *Georgics*, II, 490.
[3] Horace, *Odes*, III, xvi, 18.

guid temperament; and there is some truth in what they say. I endeavoured to keep my mind and my thoughts in repose,

> Always calm by nature and even more so
> now with age.¹

And if they sometimes lash out upon some rude and sensible impression, it is in truth without my intent. Yet from this natural heaviness of mine, men ought not to conclude a total inability in me (for want of care and want of sense are two very different things), and much less any unkindness or ingratitude towards that corporation who employed the utmost means they had in their power to oblige me, both before they knew me and after; and they did much more for me in choosing me anew than in conferring that honour upon me at first. I wish them all imaginable good; and assuredly had occasion been, there is nothing I would have spared for their service; I did for them as I would have done for myself. It is a good, warlike, and generous people, but capable of obedience and discipline, and of whom the best use may be made, if well guided. They say also that my administration passed over without leaving any mark or trace. Good! They moreover accuse my cessation in a time when almost everybody was convicted of doing too much.

My action is lively where my will spurs me on; but this eagerness is an enemy to perseverance. Let him who will make use of me according to my own way employ me in affairs where vigour and liberty are required, where a direct, short, and, moreover, a hazardous conduct are necessary; I may do something; but if it must be long, subtle, laborious, artificial, and intricate, he had better call in somebody else. All important offices are not necessarily difficult: I came prepared to do somewhat rougher work, had there been great occasion; for it is in my power to do something more than I do, or than I love to do. I did not, to my knowledge, omit anything that my duty really required. I easily forgot those offices that ambition

---

1 Cicero, *De Petitione Consulatus*, C, 2.

mixes with duty and palliates with its title; these are the ones that for the most part fill the eyes and ears and give men the most satisfaction; not the thing but the appearance contents them. If they hear no noise, they think we are asleep.

My humour is no friend to tumult; I could appease a commotion without commotion, and chastise a disorder without being myself disorderly; if I stand in need of anger and inflammation, I borrow it, and put it on. My manners are languid, rather faint than sharp. I do not condemn a magistrate who sleeps, provided the people under his charge sleep as well as he: the laws in that case sleep too. For my part, I commend a gliding, staid, and silent life:

> Neither grovelling and abject, nor overbearing.[1]

My fortune will have it so. I am descended from a family that has lived without lustre or tumult, and, time out of mind, particularly ambitious of a character for manliness.

Our people nowadays are so bred up to bustle and ostentation that good nature, moderation, equability, constancy, and such quiet and obscure qualities, are no longer appreciated. Rough bodies make themselves felt; the smooth are imperceptibly handled: sickness is felt, health little or not at all; no more than the oils that soothe us, in comparison to the pains that sting us. It is acting for one's particular reputation and profit, not for the public good, to reserve for the public squares what may be done in the council chamber, and in the full light of noon what might have been done the night before, and to be jealous to do ourselves what our colleagues can do as well as us. So were some surgeons of Greece wont to perform their operations upon scaffolds in the sight of the people, to draw more practice and profit. They think that good rules cannot be understood but by the sound of a trumpet.

Ambition is not a suitable vice for little fellows and for such efforts as ours. Someone said to Alexander: "Your fa-

---

1 Cicero, *De Officiis*, I, 34.

ther will leave you a great dominion, easy and pacific"; this youth was envious of his father's victories and of the justice of his government; he would not have enjoyed the empire of the world in ease and peace. Alcibiades, in Plato, prefers to die young, beautiful, rich, noble, and learned, and all this in full excellence, than to stop short of such condition; this disease is, perhaps, excusable in so strong and so full a soul. When wretched and dwarfish little souls cajole and deceive themselves, and think to spread their fame for having given right judgment in an affair, or maintained the discipline of the guard of a gate of their city, the more they think to exalt their heads the more they show their tails. This little well-doing has neither body nor life; it vanishes in the first mouth, and goes no further than from one street to another. Talk of it by all means to your son or your servant, like that old fellow who, having no other auditor of his praises nor approver of his valour, boasted to his chambermaid, crying, "O Perrete, what a brave, clever man you have for your master!" At the worst, talk of it to yourself, like a councillor of my acquaintance, who, having disgorged a whole cartful of law jargon with great effort and with equal inappropriateness, coming out of the council chamber to the Palace urinal, was heard muttering very complacently between his teeth:

> Not unto us, Oh Lord, not to us, but unto
> Thy name be the glory.[1]

He who gets it of nobody else, let him pay himself out of his own purse.

Fame is not prostituted at so cheap a rate: rare and exemplary actions, to which it is due, would not endure the company of this prodigious crowd of petty daily performances. Marble may exalt your titles, as much as you please, for having repaired a rod of wall or cleansed a public sewer; but men who have any sense will not. Renown does not follow all good deeds, if novelty and difficulty are not conjoined; nay,

---

[1] Psalm 113:1.

so much as mere esteem, according to the Stoics, is not due to every action that proceeds from virtue; nor will they allow the slightest merit to one who, out of temperance, abstains from an old bleary-eyed crone. Those familiar with the admirable qualities of Scipio Africanus deny him the glory that Panaetius attributes to him, of refusing to accept gifts, as a glory not so much his as that of all his age.

We have pleasures suitable to our lot; let us not usurp those of grandeur: our own are more natural, and as much more solid and sure as they are lower. If not for the sake of conscience, then at least for ambition's sake, let us reject ambition; let us disdain that thirst for honour and renown, so low and mendicant, that it makes us beg for it from all sorts of people:

> What praise is that which may be
> obtained in the marketplace,[1]

by abject means and at however low a price? It is dishonour to be so honoured. Let us learn to be no more greedy, than we are capable, of glory. To be puffed up with every useful and harmless action is only for those for whom such things are extraordinary and rare: they will value it as much as it costs them. The more a good effect makes a noise, the more I discount its goodness by my suspicion that it was performed more for the noise than for the good: put on display, it is half sold. Those actions have much more grace and lustre that slip from the hand of him that does them, negligently and without noise, and that some honest man thereafter finds out and raises from the shade, to produce it to the light on its own account,

> All things truly seem more laudable to me
> that are performed without ostentation,
> and without the testimony of the people,[2]

---

[1] Cicero, *De Finibus*, II, 15.
[2] Cicero, *Tusculans*, II, 26.

says the most ostentatious man that ever lived.

I had but to conserve and to continue, which are silent and insensible effects: innovation is of great lustre, but it is interdicted in this age when we are pressed upon and have nothing to defend ourselves from but innovations. To forbear doing is often as generous as to do, but it is less in the light, and the little good I have in me is of this kind.

In short, occasions in my term of office have been in keeping with my humour, and I heartily thank them for it. Is there anyone who desires to be sick so that he may see his physician at work? And would not a physician deserve to be whipped if he wished the plague upon us so that he might put his art in practice? I have never been of that wicked and rather common humour, to desire that troubles and disorders in this city should elevate and honour my government; I have always heartily contributed all I could to their tranquillity and ease.

He who will not thank me for the order, the sweet and silent calm that has accompanied my administration, cannot, however, deprive me of the share that belongs to me by the right of my good fortune. And I am of such a composition that I would as willingly be lucky as wise, and had rather owe my successes purely to the favour of Almighty God than to any operation of my own. I had sufficiently published to the world my unfitness for such public offices, but I have something in me yet worse than incapacity itself, which is that I am not much displeased by it, and that I hardly try to cure it, considering the course of life that I have marked out for myself.

Nor have I satisfied myself in this employment, but I have very near arrived at what I expected from my own performance, and have much surpassed what I promised them with whom I had to deal: for I am apt to promise something less than what I am able to do and what I hope to make good. I assure myself that I have left no offence or hatred behind me. As for leaving amongst them regret or desire for me, I at least know very well that I never much aimed at it:

> Me, in this monster put my trust?

> Me, be deceived by the appearance of the
> placid sea,
> And by the quiet waves?[1]

---

[1] Virgil, *Aeneid*, V, 849.

Sources

Plato. *Republic*. Selection from *The Dialogues of Plato, Translated into English by B. Jowett, M.A., in Five Volumes*, Vol. 3. Oxford: Oxford University Press, 1892. Revised and modernised by Nima Omidi. Copyright 2014.

Schopenhauer, Arthur. *Counsels and Maxims*. Selection from *Counsels and Maxims by Arthur Schopenhauer*, translated by T. Bailey Saunders. London: George Allen & Unwin, 1896. Revised by Nima Omidi.

The Bhagavad Gita. New translation by Nima Omidi, based primarily on *The Bhagavad Gita*, translated by Alladi Mahadeva Sastry. Madras (Chennai), India: Samata Books, 1897. Copyright 2014 by Nima Omidi.

The Holy Bible, King James Version. New York: Oxford Edition, 1769.

Pascal, Blaise. *Pensées*. Selection from *Pascal's Pensées*, translated by W.F. Trotter. New York: P.F. Collier & Son, 1910. Revised and modernised by Nima Omidi. Copyright 2014.

Seneca. *Moral Epistles*. Selection from *Ad Lucilium Epistulae Morales,* translated by Richard M. Gummere. New York: G.P. Putnam's Sons, 1925. Revised by Nima Omidi.

The Dhammapada. New version by Nima Omidi, based on *The Dhammapada*, translated from the Pali by F. Max Muller. Oxford: The Clarendon Press, 1881. Copyright 2014 by Nima Omidi.

Aurelius, Marcus. *Meditations*. New version by Nima Omidi, based on the George Long translation (1862). Copyright 2014 by Nima Omidi.

SOURCES

Aristotle. *Nicomachean Ethics*. New version by Nima Omidi, based on the translations of W.D. Ross (Oxford: Clarendon Press, 1908) and D.P. Chase (Oxford: Henry Hammans, 1861). Copyright 2014 by Nima Omidi.

Epicurus. *Principal Doctrines*. Selection from *Stoic and Epicurean*, by R.D. Hicks. New York: Charles Scribner's Sons, 1910. Revised and modernized by Nima Omidi, copyright 2014.

Epictetus. *The Enchiridion*. Selection from *The Works of Epictetus. Consisting of His Discourses, in Four Books, The Enchiridion, and Fragments*. A Translation from the Greek based on that of Elizabeth Carter, by Thomas Wentworth Higginson. Boston: Little, Brown, and Co., 1865.

Cicero. *Tusculan Disputations*. Selection from *Cicero's Tusculan Disputations; Also, Treatises on the Nature of the Gods, and on the Commonwealth*. Translated by C.D. Yonge. New York: Harper & Brothers, 1877.

Montaigne, Michel de. *That Men Are Not to Judge of Our Happiness Until After Death*. Selection from *Essays of Montaigne*, Translated by Charles Cotton. London: Reeves and Turner, 1877. Revised and modernized by Nima Omidi. Copyright 2014.

Montaigne, Michel de. *Of Managing the Will*. Selection from *Essays of Montaigne*, Translated by Charles Cotton. London: Reeves and Turner, 1877. Revised and modernized by Nima Omidi. Copyright 2014.

www.ingramcontent.com/pod-product-compliance
Lightning Source LLC
Chambersburg PA
CBHW070310180426
43195CB00055B/1335